Health and socio-economic status over the life course

Health and socio-economic status over the life course

First results from SHARE Waves 6 and 7

Edited by
Axel Börsch-Supan
Johanna Bristle
Karen Andersen-Ranberg
Agar Brugiavini
Florence Jusot
Howard Litwin
Guglielmo Weber

DE GRUYTER

ISBN 978-3-11-061723-8
e-ISBN [PDF] 978-3-11-061724-5
e-ISBN [EPUB] 978-3-11-061745-0

Library of Congress Control Number: 2019935653

Bibliographic information published by the Deutsche Nationalbibliothek
The Deutsche Nationalbibliothek lists this publication in the Deutsche Nationalbibliografie; detailed bibliographic data are available on the Internet at http://dnb.dnb.de.

Cover image: skynesher / E+ / gettyimages.de
Typesetting: Integra Software Services Pvt. Ltd.
Printing and Binding: CPI books GmbH, Leck

www.degruyter.com

Contents

Editors

Prof. Karen Andersen-Ranberg, Ph.D. is Professor at the Department of Clinical Research and affiliated with the Department of Public Health, both at the University of Southern Denmark, from where she also holds her Ph.D. In addition, she is a clinically working Consultant Geriatrician at Odense University Hospital. Within SHARE, Andersen-Ranberg is the SHARE area coordinator for health. Furthermore, she is an active member of the board of the European Academy for Medicine in Ageing.

Prof. Axel Börsch-Supan, Ph.D. is Director of the Max Planck Institute for Social Law and Social Policy in Munich, Director of the Munich Center for the Economics of Aging, Professor at the Technical University of Munich, Research Associate at the National Bureau of Economic Research, Cambridge, USA, and Principal Investigator of SHARE. He holds a Diploma in Mathematics from Bonn University and a Ph.D. in Economics from M.I.T. Börsch-Supan is member of the Council of Advisors to the German Economics Ministry and is member of the German, the Berlin-Brandenburg and the Austrian Academy of Sciences.

Prof. Agar Brugiavini, Ph.D. is Professor of Economics at the Ca‘ Foscari University of Venice, Director of the Ca'Foscari International College and the SHARE area coordinator for work and retirement. She holds a MSc in Econometrics and Mathematics from the London School of Economics and a Ph.D. in Economics from the London School of Economics. She is an international research fellow of the Institute for Fiscal Studies.

Dr. Johanna Bristle is Senior Researcher at the Munich Center for the Economics of Aging, Max Planck Institute for Social Law and Social Policy in Munich and is a member of the SHARE central coordination team. She holds a MA in Sociology from Mannheim University and a doctoral degree in Sociology from Friedrich-Alexander University Erlangen-Nürnberg.

Prof. Florence Jusot is Professor of Economics at Paris-Dauphine University, member of the Laboratory for the Economics and Management of Health Organizations, Country Team Leader of SHARE France and SHARE area coordinator for healthcare. Jusot holds a Ph.D. in Economics from the School for Advanced Studies in the Social Sciences and a habilitation in Economics from Paris-Dauphine University. She is a research associate at The Institute for Research and

https://doi.org/10.1515/9783110617245-201

Information in Health Economics and member of the boards of the French, European and International Health Economics Associations.

Prof. Howard Litwin, Ph.D. is Professor (emeritus) at the Paul Baerwald School of Social Work and Social Welfare and the founding head of the Israel Gerontological Data Center (IGDC), both at the Hebrew University of Jerusalem. He holds a doctoral degree from Columbia University in New York. Litwin is also the SHARE area coordinator for social networks and Country Team Leader of SHARE Israel. He is a fellow of the Gerontological Society of America (GSA).

Prof. Guglielmo Weber, Ph.D. is Professor of Econometrics at the University of Padua, Italian Country Team Leader, Vice Coordinator of SHARE and SHARE area coordinator for income and wealth. He holds a MSc in Econometrics and a Ph.D. in Economics from the London School of Economics. He is an international research affiliate of the Department of Economics and Management and Centre for Economic Policy Research fellow.

Contributors

Liili Abuladze
Estonian Institute for Population Studies, Tallinn University, Estonia
liili@tlu.ee

Linda Juel Ahrenfeldt
Unit of Epidemiology, Biostatistics and Biodemography, Department of Public Health, University of Southern Denmark, Denmark
lahrenfeldt@health.sdu.dk

Karen Andersen-Ranberg
Danish Aging Research Center, Department of Public Health, Uni versity of Southern Denmark, Denmark
karanberg@health.sdu.dk

Alin Marius Andrieş
Faculty of Economics and Business Administration, Alexandru Ioan Cuza University of Iasi, Romania
alin.andries@uaic.ro

Louis Arnault
Department of Economics and Management of Health Organizations (EMOS), Bordeaux Population Health Research Center, France
louis.arnault@u-bordeaux.fr

Fátima Barbosa
Communication and Society Research Centre University of Minho, Portugal
fatimabarbosa@ics.uminho.pt

Michele Belloni
Department of Economics, Ca' Foscari University of Venice, Italy
michele.belloni@unito.it

Michael Bergmann
Munich Center for the Economics of Aging, Max Planck Institute for Social Law and Social Policy, Technical University of Munich, Germany
bergmann@mea.mpisoc.mpg.de

Marco Bertoni
Department of Economics and Management, University of Padua, Italy
marco.bertoni@unipd.it

Anikó Bíró
Health and Population Momentum Research Group, Institute of Economics, Centre for Economic and Regional Studies of the Hungarian Academy of Sciences, Hungary
biro.aniko@krtk.mta.hu

Andrea Bonfatti
Department of Economics and Management, University of Padua, Italy
andrea.bonfatti@unipd.it

Nis Borbye-Lorenzen
Danish Center for Neonatal Screening, Department of Congenital Disorders, Statens Serum Institut, Denmark
nbop@ssi.dk

Axel Börsch-Supan
Munich Center for the Economics of Aging, Max Planck Institute for Social Law and Social Policy, Technical University of Munich, Germany, and National Bureau of Economic Research, USA
boersch-supan@mea.mpisoc.mpg.de

Martina Börsch-Supan
SHARE-ERIC Biomarker Project, Munich, Germany
m.boersch-supan@mea.mpisoc.mpg.de

https://doi.org/10.1515/9783110617245-202

Réka Branyiczki
Central European University and TÁRKI, Hungary
reka.branyiczki@tarki.hu

Marie-Anne Brieu
International Longevity Centre-France, France
brieu@ilcfrance.org

Johanna Bristle
Munich Center for the Economics of Aging, Max Planck Institute for Social Law and Social Policy, Germany
bristle@mea.mpisoc.mpg.de

Agar Brugiavini
Department of Economics, Ca' Foscari University of Venice, Italy
brugiavi@unive.it

Raluca Elena Buia
Department of Economics, Ca' Foscari University of Venice, Italy
elenabui@unive.it

Danilo Cavapozzi
Department of Economics, Ca' Foscari University of Venice, Italy
danilo.cavapozzi@unive.it

Martina Celidoni
Department of Economics and Management, University of Padua, Italy
martina.celidoni@unipd.it

Agnieszka Chłoń-Domińczak
Institute of Statistics and Demography, SGH Warsaw School of Economics, Poland
agnieszka.chlon@sgh.waw.pl

Terkel Christiansen
Department of Business & Economics, University of Southern Denmark, Denmark
tch@sam.sdu.dk

Ivan Čipin
Faculty of Economics & Business, University of Zagreb, Croatia
icipin@efzg.hr

Angela Crema
Department of Economics and Management, University of Padua, Italy
angela.crema@unipd.it

Cláudia Cunha
Communication and Society Research Centre University of Minho, Portugal
claudiacunha@ics.uminho.pt

Chiara Dal Bianco
Department of Economics and Management, University of Padua, Italy
chiara.dalbianco@unipd.it

Noam Damri
Israel Gerontological Data Center, The Hebrew University of Jerusalem, Israel
noam.damri@mail.huji.ac.il

Alice Delerue Matos
Department of Sociology University of Minho, Portugal
adelerue@ics.uminho.pt

David Dias Neto
ISPA Instituto Universitário, Portugal
dneto@ispa.pt

Loretti Isabella Dobrescu
School of Economics, UNSW Business School University of New South Wales, Australia
dobrescu@unsw.edu.au

Bracha Erlich
Israel Gerontological Data Center, The Hebrew University of Jerusalem, Israel
bracha.erlich@mail.huji.ac.il

Yarine Fawaz
Center for Monetary and Financial Studies (CEMFI), Spain
fawaz@cemfi.es

Simona Fiore
Department of Economics, University of Bologna, Italy
s.fiore@unibo.it

Françoise Forette
International Longevity Centre-France, France
forette@ilcfrance.org

Thomas Georgiadis
Department of Economic & Regional Development, Panteion University, Greece
thomas.georgiadis@panteion.gr

Didier Halimi
International Longevity Centre-France, France
halimi@ilcfrance.org

Ina Holdik
Munich Center for the Economics of Aging, Max Planck Institute for Social Law and Social Policy, Germany
holdik@mea.mpisoc.mpg.de

Hendrik Jürges
Schumpeter School of Business and Economics,
University of Wuppertal, Germany
juerges@uni-wuppertal.de

Florence Jusot
Laboratory for the Economics and Management of Health Organizations (LEDa-LEGOS), University Paris Dauphine, France
florence.jusot@dauphine.psl.eu

Thorsten Kneip
Munich Center for the Economics of Aging, Max Planck Institute for Social Law and Social Policy, Germany
kneip@mea.mpisoc.mpg.de

Matija Kovacic
Department of Economics, Ca' Foscari University of Venice, Italy
matija.kovacic@unive.it

Fabian Kratz
Department of Sociology,
University of Munich (LMU), Germany
fabian.kratz@soziologie.uni-muenchen.de

Judith Kronschnabl
Munich Center for the Economics of Aging, Max Planck Institute for Social Law and Social Policy, Germany
kronschnabl@mea.mpisoc.mpg.de

Anne Laferrère
Laboratory for the Economics and Management of Health Organizations (LEDa-LEGOS), University Paris Dauphine, France
anne.laferrere@dauphine.psl.eu

Jørgen T. Lauridsen
Department of Business and Economics, University of Southern Denmark, Denmark
jtl@sam.sdu.dk

Adèle Lemoine
Laboratory for the Economics and Management of Health Organizations (LEDa-LEGOS), University Paris Dauphine, France
adele.lemoine@dauphine.fr

Rune Lindahl-Jacobsen
Department of Public Health, University of Southern Denmark, Denmark
rjacobsen@health.sdu.dk

Howard Litwin
Israel Gerontological Data Center, The Hebrew University of Jerusalem, Israel
howie.litwin@mail.huji.ac.il

Antigone Lyberaki
Department of Economic & Regional Development, Panteion University, Greece
alymber@panteion.gr

Iga Magda
SGH Warsaw School of Economics, Insitute for Structural Research (IBS), Poland
iga.magda@sgh.waw.pl

Ekaterina Markova
Institute for the Study of the Societies and Knowledge, Bulgarian Academy of Sciences, Bulgaria
emarkova@bas.bg

Elena Meschi
Department of Economics, Ca' Foscari University of Venice, Italy
elena.meschi@unive.it

Pedro Mira
Center for Monetary and Financial Studies (CEMFI), Spain
mira@cemfi.es

Stipica Mudražija
Urban Institute, Washington, D.C., McCourt School of Public Policy, Georgetown University, USA
smudrazija@urban.org

Michal Myck
Centre for Economic Analysis (CenEA), Poland
mmyck@cenea.org.pl

Katarzyna Nocoń
Institute of Environmental Engineering, Polish Academy of Sciences, Poland
knocon@ibmed.pl

Monika Oczkowska
Centre for Economic Analysis (CenEA), Poland
moczkowska@cenea.org.pl

Cristina Orso
Department of Economics, Ca' Foscari University of Venice, Italy
cristina.orso@unive.it

Ela Ostrovsky-Berman
Israel Gerontological Data Center, The Hebrew University of Jerusalem, Israel
ela.ostrovsky@mail.huji.ac.il

Yao Pan
Economics School, Zhongnan University of Economics and Law, China
yaopan@zuel.edu.cn

George Papadoudis
National Centre for Social Research, Institute of Social Research, Greece,
gpapadoudis@ekke.gr

Giacomo Pasini
Department of Economics, Ca' Foscari University of Venice, Italy
giacomo.pasini@unive.it

Yuri Pettinicchi
Munich Center for the Economics of Aging, Max Planck Institute for Social Law and Social Policy, Germany
pettinicchi@mea.mpisoc.mpg.de

Fernando M. Pimentel-Santos
Nova Medical School, Universidade Nova de Lisboa, Portugal
pimentel.santos@nms.unl.pt

Pedro Pita Barros
Nova School of Business and Economics, Universidade Nova de Lisboa, Portugal,
ppbarros@novasbe.pt

Valentina Prevolnik Rupel
Institute for Economic Research, Slovenia
rupelv@ier.si

Jens Emelund Rise
Department of Public Health, University of Southern Denmark, Denmark
jerise@health.sdu.dk

Luule Sakkeus
Estonian Institute for Population Studies, Tallinn University, Estonia
luule.sakkeus@tlu.ee

Ella Schwartz
Israel Gerontological Data Center, The Hebrew University of Jerusalem, Israel
ella.schwartz1@mail.huji.ac.il

Jonathan Shemesh
Israel Gerontological Data Center, The Hebrew University of Jerusalem.
jonathan.shemesh@mail.huji.ac.il

Nicolas Sirven
Health Economics Research Center, University Paris-Descartes, France
nicolas.sirven@parisdescartes.fr

Šime Smolić
Faculty of Economics & Business, University of Zagreb, Croatia
ssmolic@efzg.hr

Andrej Srakar
Institute for Economic Research, and Faculty of Economics, University of Ljubljana, Slovenia
andrej.srakar@ier.si

Luca Stella
Department of Social and Political Sciences, Bocconi University, Italy
luca.stella@unibocconi.it

Paweł A. Strzelecki
Institute of Statistics and Demography, SGH Warsaw School of Economics, Poland
pawel.strzelecki@sgh.waw.pl

Platon Tinios
Department of Statistics and Insurance Science, University of Piraeus, Greece
ptinios@unipi.gr

Roman Topór-Mądry
Department of Epidemiology and Population Research, Jagiellonian University, Poland
mxtopor@cyf-kr.edu.pl

Serena Trucchi
Department of Economics, Ca' Foscari University of Venice, Italy
serena.trucchi@unive.it

Astrid Roll Vitved
Department of Business and Economics, University of Southern Denmark, Denmark
vitved@sam.sdu.dk

Gina Voss
Communication and Society Research Centre University of Minho, Portugal
ginavoss@ics.uminho.pt

Melanie Wagner
Munich Center for the Economics of Aging, Max Planck Institute for Social Law and Social Policy, Germany wagner@mea.mpisoc.mpg.de

Guglielmo Weber
Department of Economics and Management, University of Padua, Italy
guglielmo.weber@unipd.it

Luzia M. Weiss
Munich Center for the Economics of Aging, Max Planck Institute for Social Law and Social Policy, Germany
l.weiss@mea.mpisoc.mpg.de

Gabriela Yordanova
Institute for the Study of the Societies and Knowledge, Bulgarian Academy of Sciences, Bulgaria
gyordanova@bas.bg

Axel Börsch-Supan, Johanna Bristle, Karen Andersen-Ranberg, Agar Brugiavini, Florence Jusot, Howard Litwin and Guglielmo Weber

1 A spotlight on health and life courses in Europe using SHARE Waves 6 and 7

1.1 Health and socio-economic status over the life course

The Survey of Health, Ageing and Retirement in Europe (SHARE) puts special emphasis on the interplay among the triangular connections of health, social embeddedness and the socio-economic status of older individuals. Waves 6 and 7 add three important innovations to this triangle and make SHARE a highly powerful tool for investigating ageing societies in Europe First, Wave 6 deepens the objective measurement of health via biomarkers obtained from dried blood spot samples (DBSS). Second, Wave 7 finally achieves the cross-nationality that was demanded in the SHARE-ERIC statutes and covers all 26 continental EU member states plus Switzerland and Israel. Third, Wave 7 strengthens longitudinality reaching far back into childhood by collecting life-history data in all 28 countries.

These three innovations substantially enrich the multidisciplinary SHARE data and belong together because health, economic and social status in later life emerge from complex interactions over the entire life course (see Figure 1.1).

Departing from a person's biological make-up, parental conditions and early education (indicated by the left box in Figure 1.1), the trajectories of health, economic status and social embeddedness are not determined in isolation but through mutual interactions over the entire life course (as indicated by the many two-sided arrows between the three trajectories). Health, for instance, influences economic status because healthier bodies are likely to support higher learning capacities at younger ages and higher workloads at older ages (e.g. Deaton 2002). In turn, income inequalities are likely also to cause inequalities in health because richer individuals can afford higher out-of-pocket healthcare costs and may have easier access to healthcare, especially in certain healthcare systems (e.g., Smith 2003). Health behaviours, lifestyle and environmental and occupational conditions add to these mutual interactions between health and economic status and simultaneously introduce interactions with the

https://doi.org/10.1515/9783110617245-001

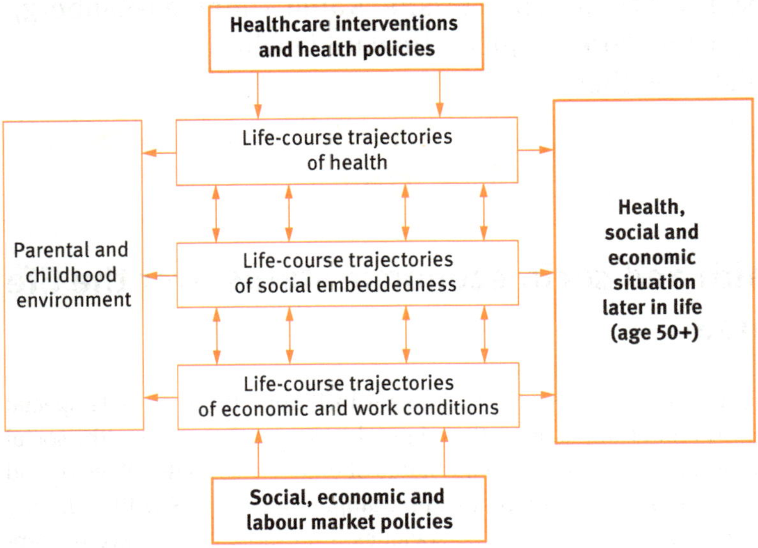

Figure 1.1: Conceptual background.
Source: Own illustration.

social environment in which individuals live. For example, ample evidence exists that embeddedness in a good family background is beneficial for the health of the family members (Fagundes et al. 2011). An important insight of recent research is that these interactions manifest their effects starting very early in life and then accumulate during positive and negative feedback cycles over the entire life course (Heckman and Conti 2013) before they determine later-life health, economic and social outcomes at older ages (right box in Figure 1.1).

Many of these interactions can be modified by policies, such as education, workplace regulations, poverty prevention or healthcare (indicated by the boxes at the top and bottom of 1. 1). Some welfare state interventions directly affect health and employment. Early retirement, for example, is directly and often immediately influenced by the rules of the pension, disability and unemployment systems (Börsch-Supan and Coile 2018). Health is directly affected by healthcare systems (Sirven and Or 2011). In addition, long-run interventions of the welfare state exist, such as education, preventive healthcare and workplace regulations, which have complex indirect and interrelated effects over the life course on both health and employment. Preventive healthcare, for instance, not only increases health but also makes meaningful occupation feasible at older ages (Jusot et al. 2012). High workplace standards not only improve employment at older ages by reducing early retirement but also tend to improve physical and mental health (Reinhardt et al. 2013).

This volume presents 38 short studies that summarize SHARE-based research on these interactions over the lifecycle. These studies are showcases of the interdisciplinary and cross-nationally comparative research results obtained from Waves 6 and 7 of SHARE. Almost all contributions have a special focus on health. Collecting objective health data in Wave 6 was important because the health of the general population and, in particular, of the older aged population is very different across countries. Comparisons between SHARE, the English Longitudinal Study of Ageing (ELSA) and the US Health and Retirement Study (HRS) have documented that older people in continental Europe have better health than those in England. In turn, English people have better health than their American counterparts. For example, the percentages of individuals aged 50–74 years with at least one limitation in activities of daily living (ADL) is 12 per cent in the United States, 10 per cent in the United Kingdom and only 7 per cent in the European Union (Avendano et al. 2009).

Many reasons exist for these cross-national health differences. Healthcare systems are very different between the United States and Europe because almost all European countries have mandatory universal health insurance and the United States does not. Coverage, ease of access, co-payments, administrative rules and quality also differ across EU countries, as do historical life circumstances, income and wealth distributions, lifestyles and health behaviours. In addition, cross-Europe differences exist in the interactions between healthcare systems and lifestyles, such as when healthcare systems attempt to influence health behaviours, and in social policies and programmes potentially affecting health across the life course. The latter includes differences in early education and childcare programmes, employment protection and support programmes during middle age and social security and pension systems affecting older individuals. Although the impact of many of these policies on social outcomes is well documented, the extent to which they influence health and contribute to differences in longevity among high-income countries has yet to be established.

Understanding the reasons for cross-national health differences requires that studies use comparable health measurements. The findings by Avendano et al. (2009) were based on comparable measures, but these were self-reports and may have suffered from reporting biases. Few studies use more objective measurements of health-related biomarkers. SHARE Wave 6 was designed to fill this gap: We collected dried blood spot samples (DBSS) from approximately 27,000 respondents in 13 countries, which is among the largest collection of DBSS from a representative adult population. The DBSS include a small calibration sample from Poland in which both DBSS and venous blood were collected. SHARE has also collected retrospective histories of participants' life courses and health events. Although we are still awaiting the laboratory results, preliminary analyses and validations are described in Part 8 of this book.

The central innovation in SHARE Wave 7 was the collection of highly structured retrospect life histories that are fully harmonized in all continental EU countries, Switzerland and Israel. This collection was achieved by using electronic displays that show the timeline of events and risk factors in several dimensions, such as health, work, family and housing. This display permits the respondent to see related events in one domain (family) with events in another domain (health), which significantly facilitates recall and improves the accuracy of the retrospective data.

Although we are aware that the hindsight perspective may create reporting biases, Smith (2003) shows the power and usefulness of retrospective data in detecting associations between health and socio-economic variables. More specifically, Korbmacher (2014) demonstrated the accuracy of retrospectively collected employment histories in a large-scale validation study comparing SHARE with linked administrative data. Life-course data on the timing of the major social, health and economic events over long segments of the lifecycle have been shown to be extremely helpful in identifying the causal mechanisms in the dynamic and cumulative relationship among health, lifestyles and socio-economic resources. Such data capture biological and socio-economic risk factors in early and mid-life, including health shocks, working conditions and behaviour during childhood and adulthood. Thus, these data allow us to not only quantify the long-lasting effects of early-life events (including interventions by health and social policies) on later-life health status but also to study potential behavioural channels causing associations between risk factors and health outcomes.

Many contributions in this book use the life-history data from Wave 7; some also use the earlier life histories collected in Wave 3. Therefore, this book is organized along the course of life. Part 1, edited by Agar Brugiavini and Guglielmo Weber, begins with the development of personality in early childhood and its influence until late in life. This part of the book features the inclusion of the widely used Big Five dimensions of personality in SHARE. Part 2, edited by Guglielmo Weber, describes how health inequalities are generated during the life course by inequalities in education and income. Part 3 is edited by Agar Brugiavini and uses another innovation of the SHARE data, namely, the 'job-coder', to describe labour market careers, occupation and retirement. Part 4, edited by Axel Börsch-Supan, celebrates the inclusion of eight new countries in SHARE. Based on the life-history data, this part showcases social transitions in the new accession countries and the effects of the economic crisis. Part 5, edited by Howard Litwin, exploits the longitudinal social network data obtained in Wave 6, another innovation of the SHARE panel. Such data permit studies on the interactions between health and its social context. Healthcare and health behaviours are the subject of Part 6, which is edited by Florence Jusot. In Part 7, we focus on how objective health measures contribute to our understanding of the ageing process, which was edited by Karen Andersen-Ranberg. This topic is taken up in Part 8, edited by Axel Börsch-Supan, with a first glance at the dried blood spot analyses.

1.2 Personality and childhood

In the seventh wave of SHARE, respondents were for the first time asked a set of questions aimed at eliciting their five most important personality traits (John and Srivastava, 1999). These traits, or factors, known as the Big Five are Openness to experience, Conscientiousness, Extraversion, Agreeableness, and Neuroticism. For each of them, the respondents answered two – in one case, three – questions representing the high and the low poles (Rammstedt and John, 2007). Most respondents who participated in Wave 7 also answered a large number of questions on their life histories going back to their childhoods (with a special focus on their situation at age 10), and including the relationship they remember having with their parents.

In this part, edited by Agar Brugiavini and Guglielmo Weber, we present three chapters that analyse personality traits and their relationships with well-being, physical health and financial investment decisions late in life. We also present two chapters that relate the abuse respondents suffered from in their childhood with their current well-being and mental health.

A word of caution is necessary here. As Bertoni et al. note in Chapter 4, "estimating a model with adult-life outcomes as the dependent variable and personality traits as the explanatory variable is not without problems. First, personality cannot be measured directly: the measures used in our empirical analysis might be imperfect proxies of true non-cognitive abilities, introducing measurement error. Second, personality traits may themselves be the result of a dynamic process of investment in cognitive and non-cognitive skills." We urge the reader to keep in mind these caveats when interpreting the evidence presented in this part.

The first chapter by Bracha Erlich and Howard Litwin describes in detail the Big Five personality traits and the manner in which they are elicited in

SHARE. The chapter examines the way in which these traits vary with age – and finds that Agreeableness shows a moderate rise across age groups and Openness to experience and Extraversion show small declines. The authors are careful to point out that their evidence could alternatively be interpreted as cohort effects (younger respondents belong to cohorts born in more recent years) or might even reflect selective mortality (if more agreeable individuals live longer, for instance). Perhaps the most important take-home message is that some traits – Neuroticism and Conscientiousness – are age-invariant. This age-invariance is important because the authors also study how the personality attributes relate to life satisfaction and find that a major negative role is played by Neuroticism and positive roles are played by Extraversion and Conscientiousness.

The second chapter, written by Jonathan Shemesh, Ella Schwartz and Howard Litwin, concentrates on personality and physical health. The authors point out that the determinants of health include genetics and lifestyle, such as physical activity and diet. However, they cite recent evidence suggesting that personality also exerts significant effects on health throughout the lifespan (Murray and Booth 2015). The authors investigate the manner in which personality traits are associated with a number of health indicators in older European adults, controlling for age, gender, marital status, financial capacity, years of education and country of residence. The strongest and most consistent personality-level correlates of good health are shown to be high Conscientiousness and low Neuroticism. To the extent that these personality traits are stable over time, as we observed in the previous chapter, and are not themselves affected by health, one might be tempted to interpret this finding as indicating a possible cause of good health in old age. However, even if this is not the case, an interesting policy implication is that personality testing can be used to assess the health risks of older people.

The role of personality traits is also investigated in further research areas in addition to health. It is well known from the behavioural finance literature that an investor's personality traits are significantly associated with his or her financial behaviour, even conditioning on his or her partner's cognition and other observable characteristics. In the chapter 'Personality traits and financial behaviour', Marco Bertoni, Andrea Bonfatti, Martina Celidoni, Angela Crema and Chiara Dal Bianco show that the personalities of both partners matter in determining household financial decision making, although to different extents and through different traits. The authors find that some personality traits of the financial household head (that is, the person who volunteered to answer questions on assets and debts), namely, Consciousness and Neuroticism, are significantly associated with stock market participation. Also reported was that risk aversion plays a role, but its role is much less strong when the likelihood of having financial liabilities is considered. In this case, whenever the financial household head is a female, her degrees of Agreeableness and Neuroticism are positively associated with proneness to indebtedness, and the Openness and Consciousness of her (male) partner also attract significant coefficients.

The following chapter by Noam Damri and Howard Litwin, titled 'Relationships with Parents in Childhood and Well-Being in Later Life', shows that the familial environment that older Europeans experienced during childhood is associated with their well-being in later life. The chapter contributes to the vast socio-economic literature on the long-term effects of early childhood events by focusing on the broad quality of the parent–child relationship and more specifically on physical abuse by either parent. The authors show that the six survey questions can be combined into two factors: one for the quality of the relationship with the parents, and the other for the frequency of parental abuse. They then take two different measures of (current) well-being and relate them to the two indices of the childhood interpersonal environment in the home, controlling for a host of confounders that are generally associated with these same measures, such as age, gender, education, number of children, marital status, health status, financial status and social activity.

Their key finding is that people who had good relationships with their parents show higher well-being scores at older ages, whereas those who grew up in an abusive familial environment show a lower quality of life scores in old age. This result can partly be attributed to a form of recall or justification bias whereby unhappy people tend to blame others for the low quality of their lives, whereas happy people put to rest their memories of past negative events. Even if this is the case, the implication of these findings for policy and practice are that the childhood interpersonal environment of older people needs to be addressed when dealing with ways to maintain or promote well-being in late life.

The last chapter of this part is written by Raluca E. Buia, Matija Kovacic and Cristina E. Orso. Similar to the preceding chapter, the motivation of this chapter is the concern that adverse childhood experiences may exert a negative influence on emotional well-being later in life. However, and unlike the preceding chapter, this contribution puts a specific focus on mental health problems. The authors investigate the extent to which exposure to adverse early life experiences favours the onset of emotional disorders. The chapter addresses the potential relationship between emotional neglect and physical harm in childhood and adolescence, and the onset of emotional disorders later in life. The authors recognize a potential recall bias: if depressed individuals tend to remember negative episodes more than otherwise identical individuals, this situation may lead to an overestimate of the effect. However, to the extent that such bias is invariant across individuals, the reader may want to focus on some very interesting differences in the effects of adverse childhood circumstances by cohort and gender.

First, the authors find that the intensity of the effects of adverse childhood experiences on mental well-being displays important differences between the pre- and post-war cohorts. A poor relationship with parents has a stronger and more significant impact on the post-war cohort, whereas having experienced physical harm from parents is not significantly different from having experienced zero harm for the pre-war cohort. However, physical abuse from persons outside the family has a more important effect for the older respondents. Interestingly, most adverse childhood experiences have a stronger and more significant impact on women. In particular, the analysis shows that physical harm from parents is not significant for men but is for women.

1.3 Health inequalities—Education and income

Income and wealth inequality have attracted much attention in both the public debate and academia – going back to the work by Tony Atkinson and collaborators and leading to the highly influential (and controversial) volume by Piketty. The link between economic resources (such as income and wealth) and health has also been recognized as empirically relevant. For instance, Shorrocks (1975) pointed out that the strong relationship between wealth and mortality should lead to great caution in the analysis of cross-sectional age effects because richer individuals live longer; therefore, older individuals are on average richer. More recently, health inequality has attracted renewed attention, as testified by the media coverage of the recent work by Deaton and Case on the rise of mid-life mortality and morbidity in the United States.

SHARE data are ideal not only to document patterns of health inequalities across elderly Europeans and to focus on specific aspects of health (such as frailty) but also to investigate the roots behind health inequality in old age and its long-term determinants. For instance, thanks to the rich life history information collected in the seventh wave, one can trace health inequality back to early life conditions and check the extent to which poorer health in old age can be attributed to the effects that a bad start in life has on education, income and wealth. This part on health inequality is edited by Guglielmo Weber.

The first chapter of this part, with the title 'Dynamic Changes in Determinants of Inequalities in Health in Europe with a Focus on Retirement' by Terkel Christiansen, Jørgen T. Lauridsen and Astrid Roll Vitved, computes a concentration index for health in eleven SHARE countries and investigates the extent to which current income, education, age and other observable characteristics explain the index. The authors are particularly interested in the role of retirement from work on health inequality and allow the role to vary not only by country but also by age group (50–64; 65–74; 75+). The authors are also interested in changes over time and, thus, carry out their analysis on the first and seventh waves of SHARE.

The authors find that retirement status contributes to a varying extent to income-related inequality in health across European countries and that the differences can be associated with income inequality as well as health differences depending on the country considered. The intuition behind some of the results is not obvious because disentangling the effect of retirement from the effect of age is difficult. However, the approach taken in this chapter is promising, and future research along these lines may be able to develop more solid and more policy-relevant conclusions.

The following chapter by Louis Arnault, Florence Jusot, Nicolas Sirven, Marie-Anne Brieu, Didier Halimi and Françoise Forette focuses on a specific health indicator – frailty – that is particularly important at older ages. This indicator provides an analysis of the trends of inequalities in frailty in nine European countries. The key findings are that large and significant social inequalities exist in the prevalence of frailty between high and low education groups: frailty prevalence is on average 4.5 percentage points higher for less educated men than for more educated men; this figure increases to 6.7 percentage points for women. These social inequalities tend to increase with age, reaching 6.6 percentage points for men and 10.9 percentage points for women in the 75+ age class. These results are stable over time, indicating that new generations face a similar risk of frailty as previous generations. The authors point out that two counteracting effects may be at play here: medical progress reduces the risk of frailty for any given age but also increases the pool of survivors such that the prevalence of frailty is stable over time.

Michele Belloni, Danilo Cavapozzi, Chiara Dal Bianco, Yao Pan and Serena Trucchi investigate in their contribution how health dynamics late in life vary with early-life conditions. They document that better early-life conditions are associated with better health outcomes and find that education as well as current income and wealth are important mediating factors of this relationship. They first establish that socioeconomic status in childhood is positively correlated with health in late life. This association holds for both physical and mental health and is stronger for females than for males. In most cases, this association remains stable over the entire age range considered (50–80 years). They also find evidence that this effect is mostly indirect, that is, mediated by socioeconomic status in adulthood. This evidence suggests that an individual who grew up in adverse conditions is penalized in terms of education, income and wealth over the lifecycle, leading to worse health in old age. However, a small direct effect remains, suggesting that childhood circumstances partly act as an indelible imprint on individuals' health.

This part concludes with the chapter 'Tracking and educational inequality in health in later life' by Fabian Kratz and Johanna Bristle. This chapter focuses on the role that certain features of education systems play in explaining health inequality late in life by classifying countries according to the amount of tracking, which is the extent of 'separation of students into specialized schools and ability groups'. The authors show that countries with more tracking (that is, stronger separation) display larger educational disparities in subjective and objective health.

The authors identify three possible pathways. First, in countries with higher levels of tracking, parental background might have a stronger influence on educational attainment. Second, the higher the level of tracking, the stronger the impact that education may have on adult socioeconomic status. Third, a higher level of tracking may exacerbate the negative effects of low educational achievement on health. A limitation of the analysis lies in the authors' assumption that tracking does not change over time, such that the effects of tracking are necessarily captured at the country, and not the individual, level. Previous work on tracking (Brunello and Checchi, 2007) suggests that tracking has changed over the years, albeit slowly and not in all countries. Future research should use historical changes in tracking that reflect the education system at the time that the respondents were in school to produce cohort-level evidence on the importance of this feature of the educational system on health inequality in old age.

1.4 Labour market, occupation and retirement

A salient innovation of the seventh wave of SHARE is represented by the 'life histories', which investigate the major events, the different experiences and the choices made by individuals over their life course. The SHARELIFE data allow the researcher to construct a retrospective panel, that is, the entire sequence of events taking place, year-by-year, back to when the respondent was age ten or even younger, and to pinpoint the relevant changes in their lives such as leaving school, starting a job, getting married and having children. Because the same data collection mode was implemented in the third wave, the SHARELIFE component of SHARE provides an impressive mapping of the life of Europeans over almost a century. An important dimension of the life events is labour market participation and respondents' labour supply, which is relevant *per se* but is also central to the relationship to a variety of benefits that the respondent may have access to in the different welfare systems. Thanks to the richness of SHARELIFE, researchers can investigate respondents' careers under different circumstances and different labour market arrangements. Early-life events can be related to patterns of work and inactivity with a specific focus, such as the gender differences in wages and pension benefits for older individuals, controlling for the many other determinants of economic outcomes, such as education levels or parental effect on occupational choices.

An important innovation of SHARE (in Waves 6 and 7) is the use of the 'job-coder', that is, a feature built in the questionnaire that elicits 'ex ante' the respondent's occupation by matching open-ended answers on job type with a list of existing occupations and related ISCO codes. This feature allows the researcher to associate a very detailed definition of the job to the self-reported occupation. This part on labour market, occupation and retirement is edited by Agar Brugiavini.

The chapter 'Long-term effects of different labour careers' by Yuri Pettinicchi and Axel Börsch-Supan addresses the challenging question of the consequences of different types of labour market participation. The general view is that multiple jobs, labour inactivity and non-standard working patterns are associated with lower employability and lower social protection, leading to poor financial conditions in old age. However, job mobility is not necessarily a negative event and could represent a rational decision of the worker in the expectation of obtaining a better contract and/or higher wages, a conclusion that can be reached only by taking advantage of empirical evidence. The authors identify different career modes and relate them to the actual *ex post* outcomes observed in the data in terms of access to resources. They find that 15 per cent of men and 52 per cent of women in the SHARE sample experience some inactivity in their life and that older women have more variability in their working patterns. A substantial history of inactivity is related to a higher risk of falling into poverty, whereas a higher number of job spells has a mitigating effect on this outcome.

In a second chapter, Pettinicchi and Börsch-Supan analyse a very relevant labour market condition that is neglected in much of the literature, that is, the late-in-life consequences of being a self-employed worker. Self-employment is typically associated with precarious working conditions given the reduced welfare coverage and the prevalence of more volatile earnings. The evidence from SHARELIFE shows that self-employed workers are in fact a heterogeneous group: some workers make an explicit choice to gain control over their working conditions, whereas for others self-employment is a transitory stage leading to (or coming from) dependent employment. In all cases, public pension provisions are limited and self-employed workers are more likely to be at risk of poverty in old age. However, the first group offsets the higher costs involved with the job transitions with higher earnings growth, which may in turn provide higher private wealth in old age. The second group, which end up in self-employment because of exogenous factors, is not in a condition to accumulate sufficient financial assets to protect their retirement.

The contribution 'Patterns of labour market participation and their impact on the well-being of older women' by Agnieszka Chłoń-Domińczak, Iga Magda and Paweł A. Strzelecki is motivated by the observation that women have shorter and more interrupted careers if compared with men and that career patterns differ among countries. The authors maintain that the patterns of female life-course working careers depend on the institutional organization of the labour market, including the regulation of part-time work. Using SHARELIFE, in 13 countries, they distinguish women who have had full labour market careers and women with interrupted careers and relate these patterns to current outcomes at older age, including health, income and life satisfaction. The chapter uses sequence analysis to describe in a parsimonious manner the patterns of work and out-of-work during the life of the respondents. Pronounced differences emerge in labour market participation within and between countries: in southern Europe, women normally withdrew from the labour market for good, whereas in Scandinavian and some continental countries (i.e., Germany, France, Switzerland), women were more likely to continue part-time labour market careers. Predominant patterns of interrupted careers affect the current health assessment, life satisfaction and financial situation: women who worked either full- or part-time currently have a better overall financial situation. The level of life satisfaction is also higher among those women who were economically active during their working lives.

The fourth chapter of this part by Marco Bertoni, Andrea Bonfatti, Martina Celidoni, Angela Crema and Chiara Dal Bianco investigates the unexplained part (termed the 'gender discrimination' component) of gender differences in occupation and earnings once one has considered other determinants, such as education or job experience. One explanation of gender discrimination is a (supposedly) lower attachment of women to work, but this explanation does not consider several factors over the life course of women. In particular, differences in individual characteristics may lead women to prefer jobs that pay on average lower wages and/or might prevent them from entering certain top-paid jobs. In these dimensions, parental education, non-cognitive skills and health shocks occurring over one's life may play a role over and above the standard characteristics. One important modelling aspect is to control for the endogeneity of occupational choices. Indeed, the authors find that the end-of-working life wage gap is approximately 28 per cent, and about one fifth can be explained by standard personal and job characteristics. Accounting for the endogeneity of job selection raises the explained part of the total wage gap to about 50 per cent, whereas adding parental education, health shocks and non-cognitive skills increases the explained part of the gap only marginally. The authors conclude that the wage penalty for women is mostly explained by a within-occupation differential.

The chapter by Danilo Cavapozzi, Simona Fiore, and Giacomo Pasini analyses the association between family dissolution and labour supply decisions during the life course of Europeans aged 50 and over. Family dissolution episodes, that is, a household split or divorce, can force individuals – especially women – to enter the labour market to make ends meet and may induce others to leave the labour market because of stress and related psychosocial effects. Family dissolution typically takes place in two steps. First, the household splits and an agreement is made about income support of the former partner (the most vulnerable) and children, which is then formally specified in the case of divorce. The employment consequences of family dissolution are analysed by considering household split and divorce separately also to exploit the timeframe necessary to adjust the labour supply. After a divorce, alimonies mitigate the adverse effects of family dissolution on the dependent partner, thus inducing former partners with a low labour market attachment to exit the labour force. At the other extreme, the need to pay alimony is expected to increase the employment participation of the former household breadwinner. The authors find that employment choices are affected by the occurrence of family dissolution episodes and, as expected, the effect is stronger for women. The magnitude of this effect increases with the presence of children.

The concluding contribution of this part by Michele Belloni, Raluca Elena Buia, Matija Kovacic and Elena Meschi observes the relationship between job characteristics and health of older workers by using the detailed coding of occupations in SHARE Waves 6 and 7 obtained from the SHARE jobcoder. Some occupations are more physically or mentally demanding than others or have higher exposure to risk, which may affect health. The authors characterize each job category in terms of a set of job quality dimensions measured using data from recent waves of the European Working Conditions Survey (EWCS, Eurofound). The measures of job quality are drawn from an external source to reduce the subjective bias that would exist if workers were self-reporting their jobs' working conditions. Thanks to the presence of a detailed ISCO code, associating a set of job characteristics to each respondent is possible. The authors then use some standard measures of general (physical) health and mental health. The chapter finds that general health correlates with the physical environment, the work intensity, the skills and discretion associated with the job. Low job security and uncertain career prospects are associated with mental and behavioural disorders late in life. These findings have policy implications because an increase in the legal retirement age can have adverse effects on workers' health and should be accompanied by policies aimed at protecting the most vulnerable workers and jobs.

1.5 Social transitions and economic crises

Wave 7 was also the first time that SHARE and its sister surveys in the British Isles – ELSA in England and TILDA in Ireland – covered the entire European Union. The expansion of SHARE to all 26 continental EU member states was an important landmark for SHARE. This part, edited by Axel Börsch-Supan, includes three chapters that focus on EU accession countries and their transition challenges.

Large social transitions were also sparked by the economic crisis and affected the original EU member countries in an unprecedented way. These transitions are the focus of two chapters that analyse how the economic crisis has changed patterns of care giving and intergenerational exchange. All contributions in this part are showcases of the complex and sometimes unpredictable interactions between historical changes of the political landscape and responses at the family and the social levels.

The health of the population in post-socialist CEE countries lags considerably behind the European Union average. For example, life expectancy at birth and at age 65 is approximately 3–6 years lower than the EU-average. The authors of the opening chapter, Anikó Bíró and Réka Branyiczki, do not focus on mortality but on health status and its evolution before and after the transition from a socialist to a capitalist system, conditional on having survived at least 20 years after the transition and based on individual life history data. This transition implied a dramatic restructuring of the CEE economies and their social security systems. Such major events could have affected not only the healthcare system but also the health status of the population in CEE. The authors attempt to disentangle these two effects: the 'shock effect' through the transition and the effect of changing healthcare systems. The authors document that health disparities existed even before the transition. They also showed that the era of post-socialist transition was more often associated with the start of stressful periods and financial difficulties in post-socialist CEE countries than in the West. Finally, they found evidence that stressful periods, financial difficulties and job loss around the period of transition are all associated with worse health at older ages, even after netting out the effect of childhood health and demographic factors. Overall, the results by Anikó Bíró and Réka Branyiczki suggest that the post-socialist transition itself increased the health disadvantage of the post-socialist CEE countries.

The contribution by Ekaterina Markova and Gabriela Yordanova has a special focus on ageing Bulgarians. Bulgaria is the country with the deepest demographic change not only throughout Europe but also among the oldest populations worldwide. The authors' aim is to employ the new data on Bulgaria to describe what is hidden behind the unprecedented ageing in the country. They frame together three domains relevant for an ageing society – general physical health in Bulgaria, attitudes towards early retirement and elderly care within family networks – and take a comparative perspective with Germany, Belgium, Croatia and Romania as comparison countries. Regarding health, Ekaterina Markova and Gabriela Yordanova detect the problematic health status of older Bulgarians, which contrasts starkly with their relatively positive self-assessment of general health. This contrast is in line with the underutilization of the healthcare system. The authors also find that a comparatively large share of currently employed Bulgarians seeks early retirement, especially women and individuals with a primary or lower education. Finally, the authors point out the importance of family networks in developing integrated long-term care policies but also of overcoming the negative public attitudes towards institutionalized elderly care in times of rapid population ageing.

Numerous adult outcomes can be influenced by childhood health and cognition, as suggested in the chapter by Loretti I. Dobrescu and Alin Marius Andrieș. Their contribution, 'The link to the past and the post-communist welfare state', focuses on the prevalence of adverse health and financial circumstances among older Romanians. The authors investigate how these relations are affected by the generosity (or stinginess) of the welfare state. Thus, their analysis is particularly relevant in light of the current social and political debate in Romania that has seen the public affected by extreme polarization around two main camps defined by their support for or against the welfare state. Loretti Dobrescu and Alin Marius Andrieș find that childhood health and cognition have long-lasting effects on the prevalence of dire health and financial circumstances later in life. Such bad health effects appear mitigated across various dimensions by the generosity of the welfare state, mostly related to extreme but reversible circumstances (serious – but not long-term or chronic – illnesses, financial hardship or hunger). Superior cognitive skills are associated with better chances of making ends meet or avoiding hunger, whereas having experienced financial hardship seems unavoidable given the last 30–40 years of turmoil.

Long-term care (LTC) is an example of a family need that is met by a mix of public, private professional and family care. Given that most formal care is provided by public bodies, LTC is likely to be on the receiving end of austerity policies. If access to public LTC is affected, the family will be called to make up any deficit using its own resources, which is the topic of the fourth contribution in this part by Antigone Lyberaki, Platon Tinios, George Papadoudis and Thomas Georgiadis. This chapter aims to identify how and whether needs for LTC were met. The authors do so by focusing on three southern countries that participated in both Wave 2 and Wave 6 (Greece, Italy and Spain) and that share a familial model of LTC. Their results are very surprising at first glance: the proportion of needy people without any care shrank between 2007 and 2016. Despite austerity, professional care and not family-based solidarity expanded. Taking a second glance, Lyberaki, Tinios, Papadoudis and Georgiadis provide a convincing explanation for this apparent paradox. One part of the explanation is that formal systems were maturing; in addition, in the open market, the incomes of beneficiaries fell less than the wages of carers.

The contribution 'Financial and time transfers from parents to adult children after the economic crisis' by Ela Ostrovsky-Berman and Howard Litwin nicely complements the preceding one. Its central question is: do financial shocks have long-term consequences for the intra-familial exchange of resources and for intergenerational solidarity? The great financial crisis that struck Europe in 2008 provides a unique opportunity to address this important research question. Towards this aim, this contribution presents analyses using data from SHARE to consider the effects of the economic crisis on the parental provision of financial and non-financial assistance to adult children. The longitudinal SHARE data, which span some six waves of data collection from 2004 to 2015, make it possible to examine the trends in private familial transfers before and after the crisis. The main aim of the enquiry is to clarify whether macroeconomic shocks indeed have long-term effects on the provision of private transfers from older parents to their adult children. An additional aim is to shed light on the inter-relationship between financial and non-financial transfers following an economic crisis. Ela Ostrovsky-Berman and Howard Litwin shed light on the question of whether these two types of transfers re-enforce themselves or whether one substitutes for the other in times of deep financial distress. The results are clear. Indeed, the economic crisis has had a long-term effect on financial and time transfers from older Europeans to their adult children: large financial transfers from parents aged 65 and older to their adult children increased dramatically during the crisis and remain higher than they were before the crisis. In turn, the frequency of looking after grandchildren has decreased since the crisis and continues to be lower than it was before the crisis.

1.6 Social context and health

The fifth part, edited by Howard Litwin, looks at the intersection of the social environment and health in later life. The social environment, or the interpersonal relations that one variously maintains during one's lifetime, can impact one's health in a variety of ways, and its effects are not absent in older age. Moreover, the cumulative role of the social environment seems to increase as one moves across the life course, such that 'who you're with' strongly shapes 'how you feel' in your older years. The social network, or the convoy of close social ties that accompanies one through life, is an especially important component of the quality of late life as well as a key predictor of health outcomes.

The first set of chapters in this part examines selected aspects of the social network in relation to late-life health. SHARE is a pioneer in the study of social networks because it is the first major European survey to systematically examine the changing landscape of meaningful interpersonal relations among those in the third age and beyond. The SHARE questionnaire employs a name-generating social network inventory that captures the key aspects of one's closest social ties. The inventory was first applied in Wave 4 of SHARE in 2011 and then again in Wave 6 in 2015. Because SHARE is a panel study that returns in each wave of data collection to the same survey participants, the SHARE data allow an unprecedented look at the dynamics of personal social networks and, in particular, how they change.

The chapter by Ella Schwartz and Howard Litwin examines the changes in the personal social networks of older adults and their effects on cognitive health. The chapter considers the four most prevalent social ties, namely, spouse, children, relatives and friends, as well as the stability of these types of ties in relation to cognitive function. Their analysis reveals that the loss of social ties is, indeed, a risk factor for cognitive decline even in the short term. However, on a more positive note, they find that the addition of new ties can be helpful towards maintaining one's cognitive capabilities.

Liili Abuladze and Luule Sakkeus consider the effect of social networks on survival, particularly among those who have some degree of disability in later life. They find that more extensive social networks protect from dying earlier, which is the case for everyone – those with disabilities and those without. Moreover, among people with disabilities, having no friends in their social network is a mortality risk factor. In contrast, having children in the network among those in this same group does not increase their survival prospects.

In their chapter, Melanie Wagner and Ina Holdik look at the social networks of an important subset of older adults – those who provide long-term care to a dependent spouse, usually because of poor health. Also considered are the corresponding networks of the spouses who receive care from their partners. The authors find that both the care recipients and their spousal caregivers actually have more extensive networks than their non-care-providing counterparts. Interestingly, the uptake of care decreases the quality of the partner relationship for the spouse who provides the care but does not have the same effect for the care-receiving spouse.

The second set of chapters in this part of the volume examines the absence of social networks and health effects. That is, the authors look at how social isolation and loneliness impact a range of health states. This area of inquiry is particularly important insofar as loneliness among older people is increasingly being recognized as a significant problem in modern society. The SHARE data enable us to systematically scrutinize the concomitants and outcomes of the loneliness/health nexus.

In their analysis, Fátima Barbosa, Cláudia Cunha, Gina Voss and Alice Delerue Matos consider the impact of living alone on physical and mental health among older persons. Their findings show that, although solo living is currently on the rise, the negative effect of living alone on health is explained primarily by how lonely one feels. That is, when the effect of loneliness is taken into account, the fact of living alone is not a risk factor in itself for poor late-life health.

Stipica Mudražija, Šime Smolić and Ivan Čipin extend the study of living alone to the domain of health behaviours, particularly those that enhance or restrain good health. They demonstrate that older adults living alone tend to smoke more and eat less healthy food than those living with others. In contrast, solo dwellers are less likely to drink excessively. The authors also note that both residential arrangements and health behaviours vary substantially across countries, suggesting that health policy in this area should be formulated in response to the unique characteristics of each country.

Finally, Yarine Fawaz and Pedro Mira study both social networks and loneliness in relation to the health of those who lost a spouse or another close confidant. Their analysis reveals that, when a spouse or close confidant dies, loneliness and depressive symptoms increase. In addition, the death of a confidant reduces one's satisfaction with one's social network. The findings from their innovative study underscore the concept that bereavement is an important factor in the association between social connectedness and health and should receive more attention from health policy analysts.

1.7 Healthcare and health behaviour

The sixth part of this volume, edited by Florence Jusot, concentrates on health in old age with regard to individual health investments and health behaviours. Additionally, the issue of access to care plays an important role in this part. Healthcare depicts inequalities in different ways. If healthcare use is an individual decision that may depend on individual preferences, incentives and expectations, healthcare access can also be highly dependent on education and origin and migration status. As this part shows, the interaction of barriers to healthcare access and individual health behaviours as well as out-of-pocket expenses are also important to look at, not the least because it is telling with regard to public health and insurance systems.

In the first chapter of this part, the authors Hendrik Jürges and Luca Stella look into social inequality in access to healthcare. They examine how access to healthcare varies across European countries as well as over time by analysing three relevant dimensions: unmet need, catastrophic healthcare expenses and satisfaction with health insurance coverage. The authors use data from three waves of SHARE, including the retrospective data of Wave 7. These data allow them to document healthcare access over time and to investigate the dynamics of access barriers by exploring whether those barriers are only temporary or persistent. Jürges and Stella find that a remarkable cross-national heterogeneity exists in terms of healthcare access, with Greece, Italy and Poland being the countries with the most serious deficiencies in Waves 6 and 7. Over the life-cycle, however, unmet healthcare needs are most prevalent among eastern European countries, although in those countries educational inequalities in healthcare access are not as high as in southern Europe. Regarding the persistence of access barriers, the analyses reveal that low-educated, sick, disabled or divorced individuals face a greater risk of suffering from constant difficulties with access to care.

In the subsequent chapter, Simona Fiore, Matija Kovacic and Cristina Orso approach the issue of health by comparing the situation of immigrants and natives in different European countries. More precisely, they investigate the extent to which immigrants and natives utilize health services and examine their health-related expenditures to assess the differences in health-related behaviours between the two demographic groups. Because Fiore, Kovacic and Orso use data from SHARE Waves 6 and 7, they are able to exploit information on healthcare utilization, out-of-pocket expenditures and polypharmacy. The authors also control for socio-demographic variables and healthcare needs. For instance, they take into account that immigrants' self-perceived health status is better but that they have greater limitations in daily activities and have more chronic diseases. The results suggest that immigrants and locals have different healthcare behaviours. For example, the authors find that the immigrant population is more likely than the local population to postpone a doctor's visit due to financial difficulties. Additionally, immigrants' out-of-pocket expenditures for medical aids and appliances are lower than those of natives, suggesting that immigrants face more important barriers to healthcare use.

Marco Bertoni, Andrea Bonfatti, Martina Celidoni, Angela Crema and Chiara Dal Bianco analyse in their chapter the association between life expectancy and health investments. They argue that, in light of increasing lifespans of Europeans, health investments need to be a focus because they have important implications for the sustainability of public health systems. The authors state that the theoretical predictions for the association between life expectancy and health investments are ambiguous, suggesting, on the one hand, that a longer lifespan may generate an incentive to invest more in health, but, on the other hand, that it might also provide a disincentive because of the lower marginal value of additional years of life. Bertoni and colleagues analyse data from SHARE Waves 4, 5 and 6 for 16 European countries and consider health behaviours such as body weight, nutrition, physical activity and smoking. They find that life expectancy has a causal positive effect on most of the considered health behaviours and conclude that a longer life increases the incentive to invest in health to improve quality of life in old age. Therefore, longer lives do not necessarily imply a more extensive time spent in poor health, which in turn is beneficial for the sustainability of public health systems.

The last chapter of this part more deeply investigates health issues. Andrej Srakar and Valentina Prevolnik Rupel propose a network analysis approach to analyse the prevalence of multiple chronic conditions in older people in European countries and to explore whether some health systems are more exposed to comorbidities than some others. The data from SHARE Wave 6 allow them to show that European countries differ in their distribution of comorbidities of older people and that those differences largely follow Esping Andersen's welfare regime typology. In particular, strong connections among diseases are found in eastern European countries. Systems that already suffer from healthcare problems, including eastern European countries, are likely to suffer even more in the future given the prevalence of comorbidities. Because the question of comorbidities brings worse health outcomes, more complex clinical management and increased healthcare costs, this issue should receive additional attention in the future from policymakers.

1.8 Objective health

This part, edited by Karen Andersen-Ranberg, addresses the domain of health. The four contributions are examples of the broadness of the SHARE data and, except for one chapter, the value of including objective tests to self-reported information. One contribution also shows the benefits of adding new countries mainly from eastern Europe in the SHARE survey.

The first chapter by Luzia M. Weiss, Judith Kronschnabl, Thorsten Kneip and Michael Bergmann dives into the obesity paradox. Obesity is mainly associated with adverse health outcomes, such as diabetes, hypertension and poorer cognitive performance. However, in recent years, the term obesity paradox has emerged, where obesity counterintuitively is protective and associated with greater survival in people suffering from, for example, cognitive impairment. The critics have put forward many arguments against the paradox, one being that normal weight could be obtained through weight loss as a result of a disease process. Given the panel structure of SHARE, the authors were able to use changes in both BMI and cognitive performance over time, as well as grip strength – a proxy for muscle mass – and show in their chapter that being underweight is associated with poorer cognitive performance relative to normal weight, whereas being overweight is neither better nor worse. In their analyses of weight changes, the authors found no benefits of a weight increase on cognitive performance, whereas weight loss was associated with cognitive decline.

Good cognitive functioning is a prerequisite for being able to live an independent life at older ages; good physical functioning is another. Being physically active is well-known to be important to maintain good health and independent living. However, with advancing age, the tendency is to adapt to a more sedentary lifestyle that causes loss of muscle strength and eventually loss of independence in activities of daily living. The chapter by Jens Elmelund Rise, Linda Juel Ahrenfeldt, Rune Lindahl-Jacobsen and Karen Andersen Ranberg explores the association between self-reported physical activity and higher physical performance in relation to age. The authors use SHARE Waves 1 to 6 and demonstrate that older people who engage in moderate or vigorous physical activities have more muscle strength than their physically inactive peers. In addition, the benefits of physical activity are larger with advancing age and seem to be highest in the oldest age groups – 80+ years. The results underline the importance of supporting initiatives to increase physical activity among older people and to promote healthy ageing.

Recently, a new definition of sarcopenia uses grip strength measurements to identify people at risk of probable sarcopenia, that is, the probable state of low muscle strength, quality and quantity that leads to functional loss and dependency in activities in daily living. Using data from SHARE Wave 2, a north to south gradient in grip strength has previously been shown to exist, with the highest levels in the more northern and the lowest in the most southern countries. In their contribution, Pedro Pita Barros, Fernando M. Pimentel-Santos and David Dias Neto use data from SHARE Wave 7. They not only confirm this earlier finding but also show that a western to eastern gradient exists. Eastern European countries have the lowest levels of grip strength relative to the rest of the SHARE regions and thus seem to have a higher probability of sarcopenia than their more western, northern and even southern peers (except for Spain). Although SHARE cannot disentangle the degree to which these gradients are explained by inherent or socio-cultural factors, the results from the aforementioned chapter by Rise and colleagues indicate that physical activity may reduce the risk of probable sarcopenia.

Hendrik Jürges, Anne Laferrère and Adèle Lemoine conclude this part with their chapter on palliative care and address the end of life of Europeans. The authors describe the care and need for care at the end of life and address the quality of care delivery. The authors show that room for improvement exists in the care provided at the end of life, but with large variations across countries. Although the need for relief from pain, dyspnea or anxiety before dying was similar across the countries, the need for palliative care and the quality of palliative care both differ, as does the provision of relief of pain, dyspnea or anxiety. Moreover, low income and low educational levels increase the risk of receiving inadequate palliative care. How we provide good care at the end of life deserves greater attention in society.

1.9 Dried blood spot samples

Health, as important as it becomes when individuals age, is not straightforward to measure, as the preceding part has shown. This difficulty is partially the result of the multidimensionality of health and partially the result of the subjectivity by which individuals classify themselves as healthy or ill. Wave 6 has added a key element to the health measurement: blood. Although venous blood is the gold standard of medicine in hospitals and clinical studies, obtain venous blood samples in a population survey such as SHARE has been financially prohibitive. Therefore, SHARE has resorted to taking dried blood spot samples (DBSS) from its respondents. This part of the volume, edited by Axel Börsch-Supan, describes the first results from the laboratory analyses generated by the Danish Staten Serum Institute (SSI) in Copenhagen and the University of Washington (UW) in Seattle in the United States.

Laboratory results from DBSS assays cannot be directly compared with the results that would be obtained from assays of venous plasma samples using standard laboratory methods. Although the 'gold standard' values from venous blood also have considerable measurement variations, DBS values of total cholesterol, for example, have both a larger mean and a larger variance, influenced by many laboratory and fieldwork-related factors. The first chapter of this part, 'Dried blood spot samples and their validation', by Axel Börsch-Supan, Martina Börsch-Supan and Luzia M. Weiss summarizes an important innovation of SHARE, namely, a set of structured validation studies of the DBSS results. They establish an equation that computes a 'gold standard' value from the DBS value obtained from the respondents, the applicable field and laboratory conditions (e.g., temperature, humidity protection, drying time, shipment time, spot size) and donor characteristics (e.g., health, age, sex) with a degree of accuracy comparable with the measurement variation of the gold standard values obtained from plasma or wet blood.

The second chapter of this part by Luzia M. Weiss and Axel Börsch-Supan describes one element of our structured validation studies. This part explores the systematic associations of raw DBS values with a set of fieldwork conditions and quality measures. Our main result is that some of these associations are statistically significant and substantially large. Moreover, they cannot be measured in isolation but interact with each other, such as short drying time and the lack of humidity protection. The main result of this contribution is that understanding DBS results requires understanding the fieldwork process.

The Polish test study to be introduced in the third chapter of this part addresses the validation challenge head-on. This study was twofold. The first aim was to collect venous blood samples in addition to DBS samples in the sometimes-difficult circumstances of fieldwork using a population survey and to compare the analyses' results from both types of blood samples. The second aim was to serve as the basis for a potential full-scale roll-out of the collection of biomaterials from a large and representative population. Luzia M. Weiss, Martina Börsch-Supan, Michal Myck, Kataryna Nocoń, Monika Oczkowska, Roman Topór-Mądry and Axel Börsch-Supan outline the concept and implementation of the blood sample collection in the field through this small-scale experiment. The collected samples allowed for a meaningful comparison of the DBS and venous blood results, and the exercise has provided a number of useful lessons for the conduct of similar studies in the future.

Nis Borbye-Lorenzen and Martina Börsch-Supan conclude with the chapter 'Identification of cytokine and lipoprotein markers for analyses in SHARE wave 6 dried blood spots'. Cytokines are small blood-based proteins prominently involved in the inflammatory process. They are signalling molecules between cells, crucial for fighting off infections, and are important in other immune responses. Cytokines are not routinely analysed in a blood count but offer innovative opportunities to better understand low-level chronic inflammation, such as in atherosclerosis and the onset of CVD. They biologically back up the results of objective cognitive testing in the survey questionnaire. This contribution describes the selection of ten protein markers to be determined from the SHARE Wave 6 DBS and their potential for studying ageing and cognitive decline.

1.10 Special thanks go to . . .

As in previous waves, our greatest thanks belong first and foremost to the participants of this study. None of the work presented here and in the future would have been possible without their support, time, and patience. It is their answers which allow us to sketch solutions to some of the most daunting problems of ageing societies. The editors and researchers of this book are aware that the trust given by our respondents entails the responsibility to use the data with the utmost care and scrutiny.

The editors also thank the authors in this collection for their impressive work. We owe many thanks to Manuel Kronenberg for supporting Johanna Bristle in format editing and Thorsten Kneip and Stephanie Lasson for sharing their experiences with prior FRB publications. We are also thankful for the fruitful collaboration with American Journal Experts, who professionally proof-read all chapters. The resulting book is the third open access project in a SHARE-De Gruyter-collaboration, and we are grateful to Stefan Giesen and Andreas Brandmair for making this possible.

The country teams are the backbone of SHARE and provided invaluable support: Rudolf Winter-Ebmer, Nicole Halmdienst and Michael Radhuber (Austria); Tim Goedemé, Koen Decancq and Daniela Skugor (Belgium-NL), Sergio Perelman and Xavier Flawinne (Belgium-FR); Ekaterina Markova, Gabriela Yordanova, Diana Nenkova, Eugenia Markova and Vassil Kirov (Bulgaria); Šime Smolić and Ivan Čipin (Croatia); Nikolaos Theodoropoulos and Alexandros

Polycarpou (Cyprus); Radim Bohacek, Jan Kroupa, Filip Pertold, Jiri Satava and Jaroslava Pospisilova (Czech Republic); Karen Andersen-Ranberg and Jørgen T. Lauridsen (since Wave 7), Mette Lindholm Eriksen, Nanna Flink Knudsen and Astrid Roll Vitved (Denmark); Luule Sakkeus, Kaia Laidra, Tiina Tambaum, Liili Abuladze, Orsolya Soosaar, Kati Karelson, Ardo Matsi, Maali Käbin, Lauri Leppik, Anne Tihaste, Lena Rõbakova and Kai Saks, Marju Medar (since Wave 7) and the whole team of Statistics Estonia, who carried out the fieldwork (Estonia); Anna Rotkirch and Miika Mäki (Finland); Marie-Eve Joël and Florence Jusot (since Wave 7), Anne Laferrère, Nicolas Briant, Romain Sibille, Ludivine Gendre and Emily Bourgeat and Benjamin Levy (both since Wave 7) (France); Annette Scherpenzeel, Felizia Hanemann, Michael Bergmann and Imke Herold (Germany); Antigone Lyberaki, Platon Tinios, Tassos Philalithis, Clive Richardson, George Papadoudis, Thomas Georgiadis (Greece); Anikó Bíró, Gábor Kézdi, Réka Branyiczki (Hungary); Howard Litwin, Lahav Karady, Noam Damri, Ella Schwartz and Maayan Levinson (Israel); Guglielmo Weber, Elisabetta Trevisan, Martina Celidoni, Andrea Bonfatti, Marco Bertoni, Angela Crema (Italy-Padua) and Agar Brugiavini, Giacomo Pasini, Michele Belloni, Elena Raluca Buia (Italy-Venice); Andrejs Ivanovs, Diana Baltmane and Signe Tomsone (Latvia); Antanas Kairys and Olga Zamalijeva (Lithuania); Maria Noel Pi Alperin, Gaetan de Lanchy, Jordane Segura (LISER) and Wim van Oorschot (KU Leuven) (Luxembourg); Marvin Formosa and Katia Mifsud (Malta); Adriaan Kalwij and Marika de Bruijne (the Netherlands); Michał Myck, Monika Oczkowska, Mateusz Najsztub, Dominika Duda, Wojciech Pauksztelo and Michał Kundera (Poland); Alice Delerue Matos, Pedro Pita Barros, Katiusce Perufo, Fátima Barbosa, Patrícia Silva, Mara Silva, Cláudia Cunha and Gina Voss (Portugal); Alin Marius Andrieș, Mircea Asandului, Bogdan Căpraru, Iulian Ihnatov and Daniela Viorică (Romania); Ján Košta, Gabriela Dovaľová, Dana Vokounová, Ľubica Knošková (Slovakia); Pedro Mira, Laura Crespo and Yarine Fawaz (Spain); Josep Garre-Olmo, Laia Calvò-Perxas, Secundí López-Pousa and Joan Vilalta-Franch (Spain, Girona); Gunnar Malmberg, Mikael Stattin, Filip Fors Connolly and Jenny Olofsson (Sweden); Carmen Borrat-Besson (FORS), Sarah Vilpert (IUMSP), Jürgen Maurer (HEC), Alberto Holly (HEC), Peter Farago (FORS), Nora Dasoki (FORS) and Georg Lutz (both since Wave 7) (Switzerland); Boris Majcen, Vladimir Lavrač, Saša Mašič, Andrej Srakar and Sonja Uršič (since Wave 7) (Slovenia).

The innovations of SHARE rest on many shoulders. The combination of an interdisciplinary focus and a longitudinal approach has made the English Longitudinal Survey on Ageing (ELSA) and the US Health and Retirement Study (HRS) our main role models. We are grateful to James Banks, Carli Lessof, Michael Marmot, James Nazroo and Andrew Steptoe from ELSA; to Michael Hurd, Mary Beth Ofstedal, Jim Smith, David Weir and Bob Willis from HRS; and to the members of the SHARE scientific monitoring board (Arie Kapteyn, chair, Orazio

Attanasio, Lisa Berkman, Nicholas Christakis, Mick Couper, Finn Diedrichsen, Michael Hurd, Annamaria Lusardi, Daniel McFadden, Pierre Pestieau, Norbert Schwarz, Andrew Steptoe, Arthur Stone and Robert Willis) for their intellectual and practical advice, and their continuing encouragement and support.

We are very grateful to the contributions of the five area coordination teams involved in the design process. Agar Brugiavini (Ca' Foscari University of Venice) led the work and retirement area with Giacomo Pasini and Elena Raluca Buia. Guglielmo Weber (University of Padua) led the income and wealth area with Anne Laferrère, Andrea Bonfatti and Chiara Dal Bianco. The health area was led by Karen Andersen-Ranberg and assisted by Camilla Riis Nielsen and Jens Elmelund Rise (University of Southern Denmark). healthcare and health services utilization fell into the realm of Hendrik Jürges (University of Wuppertal) in Wave 6 and Florence Jusot (University of Paris-Dauphine) (since Wave 7). The fifth area, family and social networks, was led by Howard Litwin from Hebrew University with assistance from Ella Schwartz, Noam Damri and Maayan Levinson.

The coordination of SHARE entails a large amount of day-to-day work which is easily understated. We would like to thank Kathrin Axt, Corina Lica, Karl Riedemann, and Andrea Oepen for managing SHARE ERIC and SHARE finances; Philipp Beck, Verena Coscia, Veronika Máté and Tobias Roeckl for their efforts in public relations; and Renate Eggenreich, and Hannelore Henning and Stephanie Lasson at MEA in Munich for their administrative support throughout various phases of the project. Thorsten Kneip and Frederic Malter acted as assistant coordinators and were first accompanied, later followed by Annette Scherpenzeel as international coordinator. They carried most of the burden of coordinating, developing, and organizing Waves 6 and 7 of SHARE. Preparing the data files for the fieldwork, monitoring the survey agencies, testing the data for errors and consistency are all tasks which are essential to this project. The authors and editors are grateful to Michael Bergmann, Arne Bethmann, Tim Birkenbach, Johanna Bristle, Theresa Fabel, Fabio Franzese, Sabine Friedel, Stefan Gruber, Felizia Hanemann, Imke Herold, Markus Kotte, Julie Korbmacher, Judith Kronschnabl, Yuri Pettinicchi, Gregor Sand, Daniel Schmidutz, Karin Schuller, Elena Sommer, Stephanie Stuck, Senta-Melissa Pflüger, Jeny Tony Philip, Melanie Wagner, Luzia Weiss, and Sabrina Zuber for questionnaire development, dried blood spot logistics, data cleaning and monitoring services at MEA in Munich. We owe thanks to Giuseppe de Luca and Claudio Rosetti for weight calculations and imputations in Palermo and Rome.

Programming and software development for the SHARE survey was done by CentERdata in Tilburg. We want to thank Eric Balster, Marcel Das, Maurice

Martens, Lennard Kuijten, Marije Oudejans, Iggy van der Wielen, Arnaud Wijnant, Edwin de Vet, Bart van Nieuwburg and Sebastiaan Pennings for their support, patience and dedication to the project.

The fieldwork of SHARE relied in most countries on professional survey agencies: IFES (Austria), CELLO and Université de Liège (Belgium), GfK Bulgaria (Bulgaria), GfK (Croatia), RAI Consultants Ltd (Cyprus), SC&C (Czech Republic), DST Survey (Denmark), Statistics Estonia (Estonia), Taloustutkimus (Finland), GfK-ISL (Wave 6), Kantar Public-Sofres (Wave 7) (France), Kantar Public (formerly known as TNS Infratest) (Germany), Kapa research (Greece), TARKI Social Research Institute (Hungary), The B. I. and Lucille Cohen Institute for Public Opinion Research (Israel), Ipsos (Italy), Institute of Sociological research, Ltd. (Latvia), Kantar TNS (Lithuania), LISER – Luxembourg Institute of Socio-Economic Research (Luxembourg), EMCS Group (Malta), Kantar TNS (formerly known as TNS Polska) (Poland), DOMP – Desenvolvimento Organizacional, Marketing e Publicidade, SA and QMetrics (Wave 7) (Portugal), GfK Romania (Romania), GfK Slovakia (Slovakia), Ipsos (Slovenia), TNS Demoscopia (Spain and sub-study in the Region of Girona), Ipsos Observer (Sweden), and Link (Switzerland). We thank their representatives for a productive and successful cooperation. We especially appreciate their constant feedback, the many suggestions, their patience in spite of a sometimes arduous road to funding, and their enthusiasm to embark innovative survey methods and contents. Much gratitude is owed to the nearly 2000 interviewers across all countries whose cooperation and dedication was, is and will be crucial to the success of SHARE.

Collecting these data has been possible through a sequence of contracts by the European Commission and the U.S. National Institute on Aging, and the support by the member states.

The EU Commission's contribution to SHARE through the 7th and 8th framework program (SHARE-M4, No.261982) and H2020 (SHAREDEV3, No. 676536) is gratefully acknowledged. The SHARE-M4 and DEV 3 project financed the international coordination outside of Germany. We thank, in alphabetical order Peter Droell, Ales Fiala, Philippe Froissard, Jean-David Malo, Robert-Jan Smits, Dominik Sobczak, Maria Theofilatou, and Harry Tuinder in DG Research for their continuing support of SHARE. We are also grateful for the support by DG Employment, Social Affairs, and Equal Opportunities through Georg Fischer, Ralf Jacob, Ettore Marchetti and Fritz von Nordheim.

Substantial co-funding for add-ons such as the physical performance measures, the train-the-trainer program for the SHARE interviewers, and the respondent incentives, among others, came from the US National Institute on Ageing (P30 AG12815, R03 AG041397, R21 AG025169, R21 AG32578, R21 AG040387,

Y1 AG4553-01, IAG BSR06-11, OGHA 04-064, R01 AG052527, R01 AG052527, R01 AG056329, and HHSN271201300071C). We thank John Haaga, Georgeanne Patmios and John Phillips their enduring support and intellectual input. We are especially grateful to the late Richard Suzman who is sorely missed and who was instrumental for SHARE from its very beginning.

The German Ministry of Science and Education (BMBF) and the Max-Planck-Society (MPG) financed all coordination activities at MEA, the coordinating institution. Regarding the BMBF and its associated project administration we owe special thanks to Angelika Willms-Herget and Klaus Schindel who served as chairs of the SHARE-ERIC Council, and, in alphabetical order, Gisela Helbig, Hans Nerlich, Ranyana Sarkar, Brunhild Spannhake, Monika van Ooyen, Beatrix Vierkorn-Rudolph and Monika Wächter who helped us with determination and patience to set up SHARE as a research infrastructure in Germany. Representative for all those who contributed to the SHARE project within the MPG, we are grateful to Presidents Peter Gruß and Martin Stratmann, Vice President Angela Friederici, Secretary-Generals, Ludwig Kronthaler and Rüdiger Willems, as well as Corinna Heel, Sabine Mellinghoff and Maximilian Prugger.

The bulk of funding of Waves 6 and 7 came from national sources of the member states. We are grateful for the efforts it took to fund SHARE in each SHARE country, the perseverance of our ERIC delegates and ministry appointees in times in which funding social sciences and public health is all but trivial. Austria received funding from the Bundesministerium für Bildung, Wissenschaft und Forschung (BMBWF) and acknowledges gratefully the support from the Bundesministerium für Arbeit, Soziales, Gesundheit und Konsumentenschutz (BMASGK). Belgium was funded by the Belgian Federal Science Policy Administration (BELSPO), as well as the Hercules foundation in Wave 6, the Fonds Wetenschappelijk onderzoek (FWO) in Wave 7, the Wallonia-Brussels Federation and the Institut Wallon de la Prospective et de la Statistique (IWEPS). Croatia got funding from the European Union Programme for Employment and Social Innovation 'EaSI' (2014–2020), grant agreement VS/2015/0193, the Faculty of Economics and Business at the University of Zagreb, grant agreement 2013-ZUID-09, the Ministry of Labour and Pension Systems and the Ministry of Science and Education. Wave 7 fieldwork operations in Croatia have been funded from the European Programme Horizon 2020 – Infrastructures, project 'SHARE-DEV3 Achieving world-class standards in all SHARE countries'. The Czech Republic received funding from the Ministry of Education, Youth and Sports. Denmark was funded by the National Committee for Research Infrastructure (NUFI) and a consortium of research institutions. In Estonia SHARE Wave 6 was funded through European Structural funds via the program

„Internationalization of research“ at the Ministry of Education and Research and co-funded by the Ministry of Social Affairs and grants by Tallinn University nos. TF2514, TF4216. Wave 7 was co-funded by Tallinn University grant nos. TF1615, TF2316 and the Estonian Institute for Population Studies. France was financed by Ministère de l‘enseignement supérieur et de la recherche (MESR), Caisse nationale de solidarité pour l‘autonomie (CNSA), Caisse nationale d‘assurance vieillesse (CNAV), Conseil d‘orientation des retraites (COR), Centre National de la Recherche Scientifique (CNRS), Ecole des hautes études en sciences sociales (EHESS) and Institut National de la Santé de la Recherche Médicale (INSERM) (Wave 6 only). Greece gratefully acknowledges the support from DG Employment, VS/2013/0095, and the General Secretariat of Research and Technology (GSRT), MIS/441832. Germany received funding from the Bundesministerium für Bildung und Forschung (BMBF), the Deutsche Forschungsgemeinschaft (DFG) and the Forschungsnetzwerk Alterssicherung (FNA) of the Deutsche Rentenversicherung (DRV). The Israeli team received funding from the National Institute on Aging (U.S.), the Israeli Ministry for Social Equality and the Israeli Ministry of Science, Technology & Space. In Italy, funding for the sixth and seventh wave of SHARE was provided by the Ministry of University and Research (MIUR), in conjunction with the National Research Council (Consiglio Nazionale delle Ricerche – CNR), and by the following foundations: Fondazione Cassa di Risparmio di Padova e Rovigo and Fondazione Cariplo. Luxembourg received funding from the Ministère de l’Enseignement Supérieur et de la Recherche du Luxembourg. Support of realization of the Polish panel surveys of individuals aged 50+ in the international project Survey of Health, Ageing and Retirement in Europe (SHARE) was co-financed from the European Social Fund and conducted in cooperation with the Polish Ministry of Family, Labour and Social Policy. Portugal acknowledges the support of FCT/MCTES – Fundação para a Ciência e a Tecnologia and Fundação Calouste Gulbenkian. Slovenia received funding from the Ministry of education, science and sport. Spain acknowledges gratefully the financial support from DG Employment and the Bank of Spain and the support and collaboration of MINECO (Ministerio de Economía y Competitividad, Subdirección de Relaciones Internacionales) and Instituto Nacional de Estadística (INE). The Region of Girona in Catalonia (Spain) acknowledges gratefully the support from the Organisme de Salut Pública de la Diputació de Girona (DIPSALUT) and especially thanks the Girona Biomedical Research Institute (IDIBGI), the Institut d’Assistència Sanitària de Girona (IAS) and the Institut d’Estadística de Catalunya (IDESCAT) for their collaboration. Sweden was supported by the Swedish Research Council. Switzerland received funding from the Swiss national science foundation (SNSF), grant number 10FI14_150997/1 (Wave 6) and 10FII14_170403/1 (Wave 7).

The eight new countries (Bulgaria, Cyprus, Finland, Latvia, Lithuania, Malta, Romania and Slovakia) that joined SHARE in Wave 7, received funding from the European Commission, DG Employment, Social Affairs and Inclusion, Grant Agreement Number VS/2016/0135. Thanks go to Ettore Marchetti, Ana Carla Pereira and Valdis Zagorskis to make this support possible.

SHARE is a great example how much power a research infrastructure can generate if funders and researchers develop a common vision to improve the well-being of Europe's citizens.

References

Avendano, Mauricio, Glymour, M. Maria, Banks, James, and Mackenbach, Johan P. (2009). Health disadvantage in US adults aged 50 to 74 years: A comparison of the health of rich and poor Americans with that of Europeans. *American Journal of Public Health*, 99: 540–548.

Brunello, Giorgio, and Checchi, Daniele (2007). Does school tracking affect equality of opportunity? New international evidence. *Economic Policy*, 22: 781–861.

Börsch-Supan, Axel, and Coile, Courtney (2019) forthcoming. Reforms and Retirement Incentives: Introduction and Summary. In Axel Börsch-Supan and Courtney Coile (eds.): *Social Security Programs and Retirement around the World: Reforms and Retirement Incentives*. Chicago: University of Chicago Press.

Deaton, Angus (2002). Policy Implications of the Gradient of Health and Wealth. *Health Affairs*, 21(2): 13–30.

Fagundes, Cristopher P., Bennett, Jeanette M., Derry, Heather M., and Kiecolt-Glaser, Janice K. (2011). Relationships and Inflammation across the Lifespan: Social developmental pathways to disease. *Social and Personality Psychology Compass*, 5(11): 891–903.

Heckman, James J., and Conti, Gabriella (2013). The Developmental Approach to Child and Adult Health. *Pediatrics*, 131(2): 133–141.

John, Oliver P., and Srivastava, Sanjay (1999). The Big Five trait taxonomy: History, measurement, and theoretical perspectives. In Lawrence A. Pervin & Oliver P. John (eds.): *Handbook of personality theory and research* (2nd ed., pp. 102–138). New York: Guilford Press.

Jusot, Florence, Or, Zeynep, and Sirven, Nicolas (2012). Variations in preventive care utilisation in Europe. *European Journal of Ageing*, 9(1): 15–25.

Korbmacher, Julie M. (2014). Interviewer Effects on the Willingness to Provide Blood Samples in SHARE. In Julie Korbmacher (ed.): *New Challenges for Interviewers when Innovating Social Surveys: Linking Survey and Objective Data, Ph.D. Dissertation*. Munich: Ludwig Maximilian University.

Murray, Aja Louise, and Booth, Tom (2015). Personality and physical health. *Current Opinion in Psychology*, 5: 50–55.

Rammstedt, Beatrice, and John, Oliver P. (2007). Measuring personality in one minute or less: A 10-item short version of the Big Five Inventory in English and German. *Journal of research in Personality*, 41(1): 203–212.

Reinhardt, Jan D., Wahrendorf, Morten, and Siegrist, Johannes (2013). Socioeconomic position, psychosocial work environment and disability in an ageing workforce: A longitudinal analysis of SHARE data from 11 European countries. *Occupational and Environmental Medicine*, 70(3): 156–163.
Shorrocks, Anthony (1975). The Age-Wealth Relationship: A Cross-Section and Cohort Analysis. *Review of Economics and Statistics*, 57: 155–163.
Sirven, Nicolas, and Or, Zeynep (2011). Disparities in regular health care utilisation in Europe. In Axel Börsch-Supan, Martina Brandt, Karsten Hank, and Mathis Schröder (eds.): *The Individual and the Welfare State – Life Histories in Europe* (pp. 241–254). Berlin/ Heidelberg: Springer-Verlag.
Smith, James P. (2003). Unraveling the SES-Health Connection, working paper, 10063, RAND.

Part I Personality and childhood

Edited by Agar Brugiavini and Guglielmo Weber

Bracha Erlich and Howard Litwin

2 Personality, age and the well-being of older Europeans

- SHARE Wave 7 collected, for the first time, a measure of personality traits.
- Agreeableness shows a moderate increase across age groups.
- Openness to experience and extraversion showed small declines.
- The personality attributes are variously related to life satisfaction.

2.1 Introduction

Personality traits and, specifically, age related differences in personality attributes have been the focus of research attention for quite some time. Numerous variable sets and several taxonomies of personality structure have been suggested to reflect the complexity of personality, that is, the most characteristic patterns of thinking, feeling and behaving among people. In the late 1980s, a five-factor structure of personality that reflected five broad dimensions was introduced. This framework stands, until today, as the prevailing conceptual construct for the identification and understanding of individual personality differences (John and Srivastava, 1999). The five factors, known simply as 'the Big Five', are *openness to experience* (vs. closedness), *conscientiousness* (vs. lack of direction), *extraversion* (vs. introversion), *agreeableness* (vs. antagonism) and *neuroticism* (vs. emotional stability). They are often referred to by the acronym OCEAN. Using the OCEAN data that were collected for the first time in SHARE Wave 7, we present in this chapter an initial description of the personalities of the age 50+ population in Europe. We also examine whether different personality traits are differentially associated with well-being in late life.

2.2 Measuring personality in SHARE

Based on the 10-item version of the Big Five Inventory from Rammstedt and John (2007), the SHARE Wave 7 questionnaire included a similar brief means to measure personality traits. For each of the Big Five dimensions, two prototypical

https://doi.org/10.1515/9783110617245-002

traits that represent the high and the low pole of each factor, respectively, were queried. Each such item was rated on a 5-point Likert scale (ranging from strongly disagree to strongly agree). SHARE utilized an 11-item version of the inventory because the trait of agreeableness sometimes varies in this measure. For the analyses in this chapter, we employed the version of the brief Big Five inventory using the two agreeableness items that were the most fitting. More information on the Big Five Inventory in SHARE may be found in the methodology volume (in preparation).

The domain that reflects *openness to experience* includes both 'open' characteristics (e.g., artistic, curious, original, imaginative and with broad interests) and 'intellectual' attributes (e.g., intelligent, insightful and sophisticated) (John and Srivastava, 1999). To measure the high pole of this particular personality trait, respondents are asked about the extent to which they agree or disagree with the statement, 'I see myself as someone who has an active imagination'. In contrast, the assertion, 'I see myself as someone who has few artistic interests' measures its opposite, that is, the low pole of the trait.

Conscientiousness refers to individual differences in the propensity to be self-controlled and to delay gratification, to be task and goal directed, organized, efficient, precise and deliberate (John and Srivastava, 1999). The factor is measured positively by the declaration, 'I see myself as someone who does a thorough job' and negatively by the sentence 'I see myself as someone who tends to be lazy'.

Extraversion implies an energetic approach to the social world and includes characteristics such as sociability, activity, assertiveness and positive emotions (John and Srivastava, 1999). The statements, 'I see myself as someone who is outgoing, sociable' and 'I see myself as someone who is reserved', measure the positive and negative ends of this dimension, respectively.

The trait *agreeableness* covers themes such as tender-mindedness (sensitive, kind, soft-hearted, sympathetic), altruism (generous, helping, praising) and trust (trusting, forgiving), in contrast to hostility and quarrelsomeness (John and Srivastava, 1999). The high pole of this trait is reflected in the assertion, 'I see myself as someone who is generally trusting'. The second statement relating to this domain, 'I see myself as someone who tends to find fault with others', measures the low pole of the trait.

Finally, *neuroticism* is characterized by tension, anxiety and the tendency to be temperamental. Emotional stability, in contrast, is characterized by calmness and contentedness. Hence, the high pole of neuroticism is reflected in the comment, 'I see myself as someone who gets nervous easily'. Conversely, the remark, 'I see myself as someone who is relaxed, handles stress well', reflects the low pole of this same personality trait.

2.3 Personality differences over the life course

The first analysis in this chapter examines the association between age and personality attributes among older Europeans. Until recently, theories of personality development generally offered a static depiction of the developmental process in adulthood, suggesting that around age 30, once adulthood is reached, no subsequent change in personality traits occurs (Roberts, Walton, and Viechtbauer, 2006). Since then, however, both cross-sectional and longitudinal studies have revealed age-related differences in the Big Five personality traits (Donnellan and Lucas, 2008; Roberts, Walton, and Viechtbauer, 2006). In addition, recent literature contradicts the perception that, at a specific age, personality traits stop changing. In contrast, the literature suggests that personality traits show patterns of change across the life course and even into later life. For example, older people tend to demonstrate a decrease in the traits of openness to experience and extraversion, whereas the attribute of agreeableness shows the reverse pattern; that is, it tends to increase with increasing age. Empirical results are less conclusive, however, with respect to the traits of conscientiousness and neuroticism. Some studies suggest that these two traits increase with age, whereas others indicate that they trend downward with older age. Moreover, of the two, the attribute of neuroticism showed the least consistent age-related differences (Donnellan and Lucas, 2008; Roberts, Walton, and Viechtbauer, 2006).

In the current analysis, we regressed the respective personality trait variables on age group (60–69, 70–79, 80+; reference category: 50–59), controlling for the effects of the potentially confounding variables of gender, years of education and country of residence. The scores on the personality probes were reverse-coded where necessary, such that the summed trait scores represented the presence of each of the respective personality traits. The sample for the analysis consisted of all respondents for whom data existed on all relevant variables – 46,708 individuals representing all of the SHARE countries in Wave 7. Figure 2.1 presents a graph of the results. The bars in the graph (representing the beta coefficients) show that two personality attributes – conscientiousness and neuroticism – hardly varied across age. This result supports prior evidence that suggests that these two characteristics are, indeed, largely age-invariant traits within the personality structure. However, age-related differences emerged in the other three personality attributes, in line with the trends reported in the literature. The trait of agreeableness revealed a moderate rise as age increases [beta = 0.02; $p < 0.05$ for those in the 70–79 age group, and beta = 0.041; $p < 0.01$ for those aged 80+ (relative to respondents aged 50–59)]. The traits of extraversion and openness, in contrast, showed a decline across the age groups (extraversion: beta = –0.03; $p < 0.01$ for individuals aged 70–79

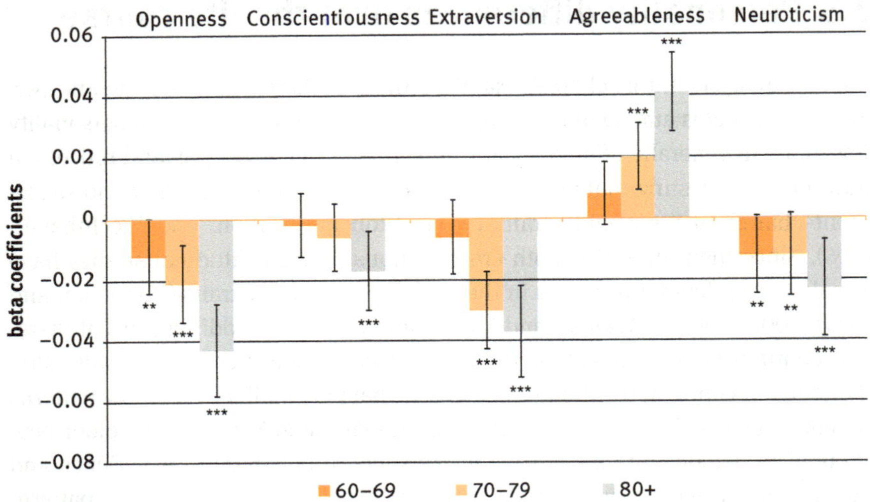

Figure 2.1: Trends in personality attributes by age group (beta coefficients and S.E.).
Note: *** p < 0.01, ** p < 0.05, * p < 0.1
Adjusted for gender, years of education and country of residence. Reference category: ages 50–59.
Source: SHARE Wave 6 release 6.1.0, Wave 7 release 0.

and beta = −0.037; p < 0.01 for individuals aged 80+, and openness: beta = −0.012; p < 0.05 for individuals aged 60–69, beta = −0.021; p < 0.01 for individuals aged 70–79 , beta = −0.043; p < 0.01 for individuals aged 80+).

Two caveats are in order:

1) In a cross-section, older individuals are born earlier. Thus, in fact, age differences could be cohort differences;
2) Age differences may also reflect differences in survival.

2.4 Personality traits and well-being

The current analysis also looks at the association between the five personality attributes and well-being in later life. A growing body of research supports the existence of a strong relationship between personality and subjective well-being. Moreover, a reported systematic examination of the multivariate impact of all major personality traits simultaneously reveals that individuals who are more open to experience, conscientious, extraverted, agreeable and emotionally stable tend to experience greater satisfaction with life (Steel et al., 2008).

To confirm the posited association between personality and subjective well-being among older Europeans as well, we examine the respective key personality traits in relation to a global measure of life satisfaction. This particular outcome measure is a widely accepted indicator of well-being. The analysis regresses the life satisfaction score, which ranges from 0 to 10 on the personality trait variables, controlling again for age group, gender, years of education and country of residence. The results, presented in Figure 2.2, show that the personality attributes are related to life satisfaction after controlling for the potential confounders. Among the respective traits, neuroticism emerges as the most powerful of the personality predictors and its association is negative (beta = −0.191; $p < 0.01$). That is, the more neurotic people are in later life, the less satisfied they are with their lives. The remaining four personality attributes also show a meaningful association (all $p < 0.01$) with life satisfaction as well, in this case positive. The trait of extraversion is the most positively related of the four attributes, relatively (beta = 0.100), whereas agreeableness is the least related (beta = 0.034).

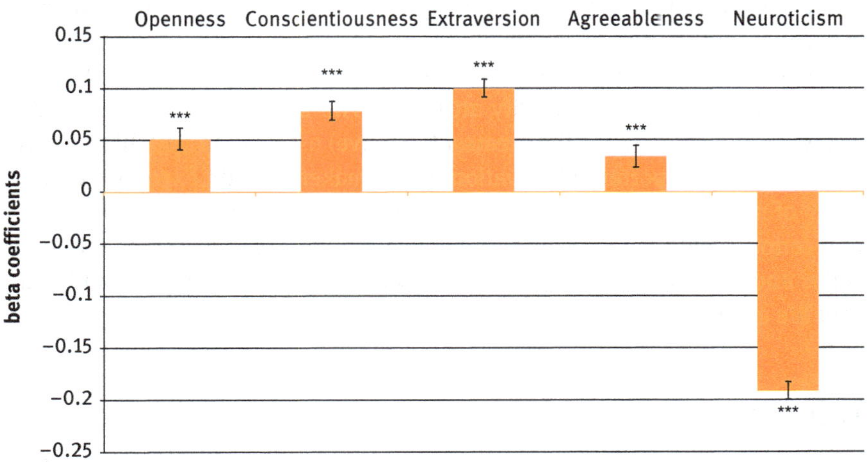

Figure 2.2: Personality and life satisfaction (beta coefficients).
Note: *** $p < 0.01$, ** $p < 0.05$, * $p < 0.1$
Adjusted for age, gender, years of education and country of residence.
Source: SHARE Wave 6 release 6.1.0, Wave 7 release 0.

2.5 Personality, age and well-being among older Europeans

The current findings, albeit preliminary, suggest that efforts to guarantee life satisfaction in later life cannot ignore the effect of personality. The results of this analysis, which are consistent with those reported in the contemporary literature, indicate that the traits of extraversion, openness and agreeableness are potentially age-related and are related in varying degrees to the well-being outcome considered in this study. This indication raises the possibility that appropriate intervention programmes might modify the respective trajectories of these attributes across the latter part of the life course. Specifically, diminishing the downward trend in extraversion and openness might be possible. As the current analysis showed, these two particular personality attributes are associated with better well-being.

Regarding the trait of conscientiousness, our analysis tentatively suggests that it undergoes only minor changes in the latter half of life. Therefore, given the relative stability of this particular personality attribute and its positive association with life satisfaction, efforts should be made to allow older adults to continue to control their lives as much as possible. Public services and facilities sometimes undermine the independence of older people in the name of efficiency and, thus, may compromise their conscientiousness as well, along with its positive contribution to quality of life.

Finally, this study shows that the trait of neuroticism is, perhaps, the most challenging of the five personality attributes. The trait lessens only to a small degree later in life and has the greatest (negative) association with life satisfaction. Given this important observation, policymakers should expand the availability of mental health services, which will help those older people who suffer from serious neurotic tendencies to more easily address their personality difficulties and prevent an unnecessary downward spiral in their morale and quality of life as they age.

References

Donnellan, M. B., and Lucas, R. E. (2008). Age differences in the Big Five across the life span: evidence from two national samples. *Psychology and aging*, *23*(3), 558.

John, O. P., and Srivastava, S. (1999). The Big Five trait taxonomy: History, measurement, and theoretical perspectives. In L. A. Pervin and O. P. John (Eds.), Handbook of personality theory and research (Vol. 2, pp. 102–138). New York: Guilford Press.

Rammstedt, B., and John, O. P. (2007). Measuring personality in one minute or less: A 10-item short version of the Big Five Inventory in English and German. *Journal of research in Personality*, *41*(1), 203–212.
Roberts, B. W., Walton, K. E., and Viechtbauer, W. (2006). Patterns of mean-level change in personality traits across the life course: a meta-analysis of longitudinal studies. *Psychological bulletin*, *132*(1), 1.
Steel, P., Schmidt, J., and Shultz, J. (2008). Refining the relationship between personality and subjective well-being. Psychological bulletin, 134(1),138–161.

Jonathan Shemesh, Ella Schwartz and Howard Litwin

3 Personality and physical health among older Europeans

- Personality is associated with an array of health indicators in older European adults.
- The strongest and most consistent personality-level correlates of good health are high conscientiousness and low neuroticism.
- Personality testing can be used to assess the health risks of older people.

3.1 Introduction

When considering the determinants of health, we tend to think first about genetics and lifestyle, especially long-term behavioural patterns such as physical activity and diet. However, current evidence suggests that personality – an individual's habitual way of viewing and interacting with the world – also exerts significant effects on health throughout the lifespan (Murray and Booth 2015). Personality is partly heritable, fairly stable throughout adult life and strongly predictive of health and risk behaviours (Murray and Booth 2015; Strickhouser et al. 2017). Using new data from SHARE, this chapter examines the relationship between personality and health among older Europeans.

3.2 The Big Five Personality Factors

As noted in the previous chapter by Erlich and Litwin, the prevailing framework for understanding individual differences in personality is the Five Factor Model of Personality (McCrae and Costa 1987). This framework defines personality along five distinct dimensions, dubbed the Big Five: *openness to experience, conscientiousness, extraversion, agreeableness* and *neuroticism* (acronymised as OCEAN; McCrae and Costa 1987).

Of the five factors, the ones most strongly and consistently associated with health are *conscientiousness* (Bogg and Roberts 2012) and *neuroticism* (Lahey 2009). *Conscientiousness* refers to an individual's tendency to be self-controlled, disciplined, responsible, organised and purposeful (McCrae and Costa 1987).

https://doi.org/10.1515/9783110617245-003

People with low conscientiousness have been shown to have increased risk for health problems, including diabetes, high blood-pressure, stroke and a higher risk of mortality (Bogg and Roberts 2012).

Neuroticism denotes an individual's propensity for frequently and intensely feeling negative emotions, such as anxiety, depression, anger and guilt (McCrae and Costa 1987). Depression and anxiety – both mood disorders highly correlated with neuroticism – have been found to be associated with compromised immune function, abnormal cardiac function and increased risk of mortality (Lahey 2009). Even after controlling for these mood disorders, high levels of neuroticism are linked to numerous health problems, including cardiovascular disease, atopic eczema, asthma and irritable bowel syndrome (Lahey 2009).

The other three personality factors – extraversion, agreeableness and openness to experience – have been found to affect health less consistently and to a lesser degree. They also have been less studied (Strickhouser et al. 2017).

Despite the importance of personality for late-life health, large-scale data allowing for the examination of the links between personality and health among older Europeans are largely lacking. However, the SHARE survey introduced a personality inventory for the first time through the implementation of Wave 7 in 2017. Consequently, personality data can now be paired with a broad range of indicators in SHARE concerning the health of people aged 50 and older in some 27 European countries and Israel.

3.3 Personality and health among older Europeans

Using the new SHARE data, this chapter presents the results of a preliminary examination of the association between personality and physical health among older Europeans. Personality was measured using a 10-item abbreviated version of the Big Five Inventory, which includes two items per personality factor rated on a scale from one (low) to five (high). A person's score on each personality trait consists of the average of the pair of items (one of them reverse coded) by which it is measured (for more details, see the previous chapter by Erlich and Litwin). To assess physical health, we observed five different measures available in SHARE: (1) number of physician-diagnosed diseases; (2) mobility limitations (ML); (3) difficulties in activities of daily living (ADL); (4) instrumental activities of daily living (IADL); and (5) self-rated health (SRH).

The first four measures were computed by summing the total number of diseases/limitations reported by the respondents. To analyse these outcomes, we applied Poisson regressions for the count variables. The last measure (self-assessment of health) was rated by participants on a scale from one to five, where higher scores represent better health. This outcome was analysed using an OLS regression. All analyses controlled for the possible effects of other key variables known to affect health, namely, age, gender, marital status, financial capacity, years of education and country of residence. We simultaneously entered all five personality factors into all regression models to account for any inter-correlations among the traits.

The sample consisted of individuals from all SHARE countries who had complete data on the variables of interest. We pooled those who were married or in a civil partnership into one group (*partnered*) and those who were divorced, widowed or never married into another group (*single*). To assess financial capacity, we used a single item probing respondents' ease in 'making ends meet' with their monthly household income. The final sample consisted of N = 57,982.

The Poisson regressions showed high conscientiousness to be associated with fewer physician-diagnosed diseases (IRR = 0.96), less mobility limitations (IRR = 0.90), and fewer difficulties with activities of daily living (ADL; IRR = 0.80) and instrumental activities of daily living (IADL; IRR = 0.79; all $p < 0.01$), after taking account of all control variables. The OLS regression showed that high conscientiousness is also related to better overall self-assessments of health (Beta = 0.05; $p < 0.01$). Neuroticism was characterised by the converse pattern, with higher levels of neuroticism being associated with more physician-diagnosed diseases (IRR = 1.14), more mobility limitations (IRR = 1.20) and greater difficulty with activities of daily living (IRR = 1.33) and instrumental activities of daily living (IRR = 1.30; all $p < 0.01$). In addition, high neuroticism was associated with poorer self-assessments of health (Beta = –0.17; $p < 0.01$) The results of the Poisson regressions are plotted in Figure 3.1.

We also found extraversion, agreeableness and openness to experience as being associated with health, although to a lesser degree and not as consistently as conscientiousness and neuroticism. Extraversion was related to fewer mobility limitations, fewer difficulties with instrumental activities of daily living and better self-rated health (ML: IRR = 0.99; IADL: IRR = 0.96; SRH: Beta = 0.03; all $p < 0.01$). Openness to experience was linked to fewer mobility limitations, fewer difficulties with (instrumental) activities of daily living and better self-rated health (ML: IRR = 0.97; ADL: IRR = 0.97; IADL: IRR = 0.92; SRH: Beta = 0.03; all $p < 0.01$). In contrast, agreeableness was related to greater mobility limitations and greater difficulty with (instrumental) activities of daily living (ML: IRR = 1.03; ADL: IRR = 1.02; IADL: IRR = 1.08; all $p < 0.01$, see Figure 3.1).

What explains these results? Conscientious people are thought to stay healthier by maintaining certain health-enhancing habits and avoiding harmful

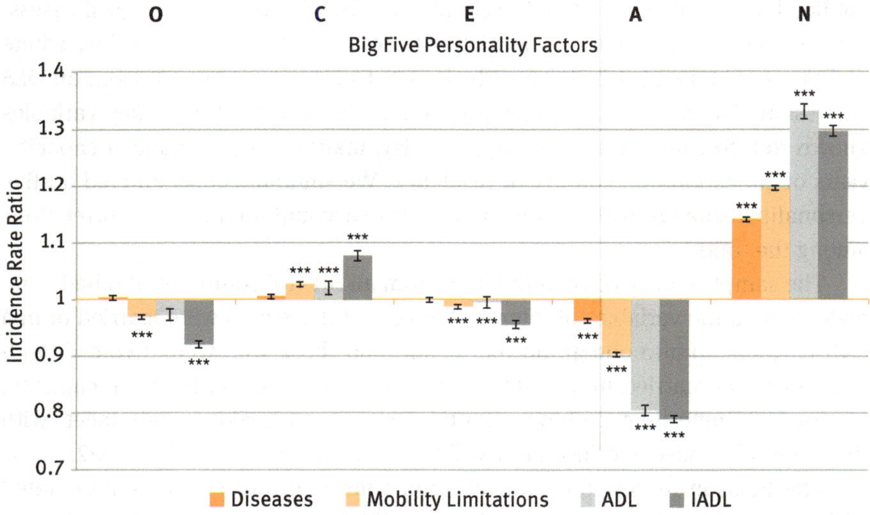

Figure 3.1: Association between Big Five personality traits and physical health
O = Open to experience; C = Conscientiousness; E = Extraversion; A = Agreeableness; N = Neuroticism
Note: *** $p < 0.01$, ** $p < 0.05$, * $p < 0.1$.
Adjusted for age, gender, marital status, years of education, financial capacity and country; error bars denote standard error
Source: SHARE Wave 6 release 6.1.0, Wave 7 release 0.

ones. They tend to exercise, maintain a healthy diet and undergo routine health screening. They also tend to minimise their exposure to stress and avoid excessive drinking and smoking (Murray and Booth 2015; Bogg and Roberts 2012). As such, conscientious people are active participants in their own health promotion throughout the life course.

Individuals who are high in neuroticism presumably experience higher levels of stress for more prolonged periods. Stress has been hypothesised to play a role in the development of chronic diseases (Lahey 2009). Consequently, the stress experienced by those who are more highly neurotic may be the reason for their poorer physical health in later life.

What about the last three traits? As previously stated, extraversion, agreeableness and openness to experience have not been consistently found to affect health and, thus, have also not been the focus of much study. Explaining these associations should be the subject of future research. For now, we offer several possibilities worth exploring.

In personality research, extraverts score high on items measuring descriptions such as 'sociable, fun-loving, affectionate, friendly, and talkative' (McCrae and Costa 1987, p. 87). These individuals likely inhabit broad and highly developed social networks and enjoy the full gamut of their benefits. Thus, their better health may be the result of the abundant emotional and material support at their disposal, which buffers the effects of stress and provides the necessary resources to maintain a healthy lifestyle and cope with disease.

How might openness to experience lead to better health? Openness may play a role in shaping attitudes to behavioural change. Health issues often present people with the challenge to adapt. The cognitive and motivational flexibility associated with high openness could be a helpful resource for older adults in adapting their lifestyles to health issues and other challenges that they might face. Such adaptations may include changing one's lifelong patterns of diet and exercise, taking up new hobbies or learning new ways to do old things.

Finally, our finding that agreeableness is associated with slightly poorer health is slightly more difficult to explain (although not unprecedented; see Strickhouser et al. 2017). Agreeable people are described as sympathetic, generous, lenient and courteous. The opposite pole on this dimension ('antagonism') is occupied by people best described as irritable, mistrustful, callous, unsympathetic, uncooperative and rude (McCrae and Costa 1987). Could it be that antagonistic people, with their hostile interpersonal style, enjoy better health? McCrae and Costa point out that 'unappealing as antagonism may be, it is necessary to recognise that extreme scores on the agreeable pole may also be maladaptive' (McCrae and Costa, 1987, p. 88). Too-high agreeableness can manifest as being dependent, submissive and self-sacrificing. High agreeableness may take its long-term toll in the form of burnout, possibly explaining why agreeableness in our sample was associated with slightly poorer health.

A last point to keep in mind when interpreting these results is that health status is one of the most important factors that affects changes in personality (Murray and Booth 2015). In a pooled analysis encompassing several longitudinal samples, the onset of chronic diseases was found to be accompanied by a decline in extraversion, conscientiousness and openness to experience, and an increase in neuroticism (reported in Murray and Booth, 2015).

3.4 Concluding remarks

Our study provides evidence from an unprecedented large-scale survey of older Europeans that personality is, indeed, related to physical health in late life. The policy implication of this important finding is that personality testing may be a cost-effective strategy for assessing health risk in older adults. That is, knowing an individual's personality can give us an idea of his or her health behaviours and stress levels and, by extension, an indication of their vulnerability to disease and disability. The inclusion of short personality tests, such as the one utilised in this study, may help identify and address these vulnerabilities in advance. Future research should work to establish the benefits of such an approach.

Our findings also suggest several fruitful avenues for research using the SHARE dataset. For instance, does personality relate to health differently across countries? Can different health policies in different countries compensate for vulnerabilities created by low conscientiousness and high neuroticism? To what extent are personality-related differences in health attributable to healthcare utilization? On another level, we could ask how one's perceived level of social support interacts with the effects of personality on health and whether social support (emotional or material) buffers against the effects of low conscientiousness and high neuroticism. These topics represent areas worthy of further inquiry.

References

Bogg, T. and Roberts, B.W. (2012). The case for conscientiousness: Evidence and implications for a personality trait marker of health and longevity. *Annals of Behavioral Medicine, 45*(3), pp. 278–288.

Lahey, B.B. (2009). Public health significance of neuroticism. *American Psychologist, 64*(4), pp. 241–256.

McCrae, R.R. and Costa, P.T. (1987). Validation of the five-factor model of personality across instruments and observers. *Journal of personality and social psychology, 52*(1), pp. 81–90.

Murray, A.L. and Booth, T. (2015). Personality and physical health. *Current Opinion in Psychology, 5*, pp. 50–55.

Strickhouser, J.E., Zell, E. and Krizan, Z. (2017). Does personality predict health and well-being? A metasynthesis. *Health Psychology, 36*(8), pp. 797–810.

Marco Bertoni, Andrea Bonfatti, Martina Celidoni,
Angela Crema and Chiara Dal Bianco

4 Personality traits and financial behaviour

- Personality traits are significantly associated with household financial behaviour, even when conditioning on partners' cognition and other observable characteristics
- The personality of both partners matters when determining household financial decision making, although to different extents and through different traits

4.1 Introduction

The recent financial crisis has exacerbated the potential negative consequences of the lack of portfolio diversification and of the presence of financial indebtedness for households. Although the traditional economic literature has analysed individuals' financial behaviour through the lens of cognitive abilities and socio-demographic characteristics, light has been recently cast on the role played by non-cognitive skills and personality traits in determining risk-taking behaviours (Almlund et al., 2011). This stream of research is clearly relevant to help better address policy interventions that aim to increase the level of citizens' financial knowledge through incentives for education and financial literacy.

Our chapter aims to estimate the association between individual personality traits and financial behaviours among European couples with a financial head aged 50 or older. In doing this, we add to the existing literature (Bucciol and Zarri, 2017; Parise and Peijnenburg, 2017) by explicitly accounting for both partners' personality traits. Compared with the exercise proposed by Brown and Taylor (2014), who are inspired by a similar intent and use a couple's average personality as an explanatory variable, we explicitly distinguish between household financial head and non-financial head, as well as by the gender of the financial head.

Estimating a model with adult-life outcomes as a dependent variable and personality traits as an explanatory variable is not without problems. First, personality cannot be measured directly and must instead be inferred from questionnaires. Therefore, the measures used in our empirical analysis might be

https://doi.org/10.1515/9783110617245-004

imperfect proxies of true non-cognitive abilities, introducing measurement error. Second, personality traits may themselves be the result of a dynamic process of investment in cognitive and non-cognitive skills, such that there might be omitted variables that jointly determine both personality and the outcome. Together with measurement error, their presence would bias estimates of the effects of personality traits. The literature has deeply investigated these issues. For instance, Heckman, Stixrud, and Urzua (2006) proposed a dynamic factor model in which cognitive and non-cognitive skills influence a large set of behaviours. Their approach allows for the presence of measurement errors and permits latent skills to determine measured skills and schooling, as well as schooling to determine measured skills. Such a setup is beyond the purposes of this descriptive paper; however, bearing in mind these considerations when interpreting our results is important.

We find that some personality traits of the financial household head, namely, consciousness, risk aversion and neuroticism, are significantly associated with stock market participation. The role played by risk aversion shrinks or is even absent when the likelihood of having financial liabilities is considered. In this case, whenever the financial household head is female, her degree of agreeableness and neuroticism are positively associated with proneness to indebtedness. The openness and consciousness of the (male) partner also attract significant coefficients.

The next section describes the data used in the empirical analysis. The following section illustrates the empirical specification and the main results, and the last section concludes.

4.2 Data

We use data on individuals who were interviewed in both Wave 6 and Wave 7. We retain only financial respondents – individuals who answered questions on financial investments on behalf of the entire household – aged between 50 and 80 years who are in a couple and whose partner has been interviewed. We consider such financial respondents to be the financial heads for their households. We end up with a reference sample of 11,976 observations from 17 European countries and Israel. The 50.12 per cent of the financial respondents are males and the average age of the household head (financial respondent) is 64.93. Approximately 94 per cent of the couples are married.

We draw most of our data on personality traits from Wave 7, which asked questions on the so-called Big Five (extraversion, agreeableness, consciousness, neuroticism and openness) for the first time. Our set of personality traits includes also a measure of risk aversion that is available for SHARE interviewees – although only at the entry wave – who were asked to state the amount of risk that they are willing to take when they save or make investments.

Table 4.1 shows the correlation between partners' personality traits: all correlation coefficients are positive and statistically significant at the 1 per cent level, with values ranging from 0.11 for neuroticism to 0.44 for risk aversion. See, for instance, Bacon et al. (2014) on assortative mating and risk attitude.

Table 4.1: Correlation coefficients among partners' personality traits.

Personality traits	Correlation between spouses' personality traits
Extraversion	0.12
Agreeableness	0.23
Consciousness	0.25
Neuroticism	0.11
Openness	0.28
Risk aversion	0.44

Note: N = 11,976.
Source: SHARE Wave 7 release 0 (for risk aversion also Wave 4, Wave 5, Wave 6 release 6.1.1)

We obtain our outcomes from Wave 6. We investigate two main financial behaviours: participating in the stock market and having or not having financial liabilities. Stock market participation is interesting because it is considered a suitable measure of the individual propensity to take financial risks. We define stock market participation as investing in stocks, mutual funds and/or individual retirement accounts (see Bucciol and Zarri, 2017). Differently, the presence of financial liabilities can be considered a risk factor for financial distress. A better understanding of the individual traits that increase the likelihood of going through financial distress in old age may well be relevant from a policy perspective.

Figures 4.1 and 4.2 show the fractions of households that participate in the stock market and have financial liabilities across countries and distinguishes between couples with a male or female financial respondent. The percentage of couples that invest in stocks, mutual funds or individual retirement

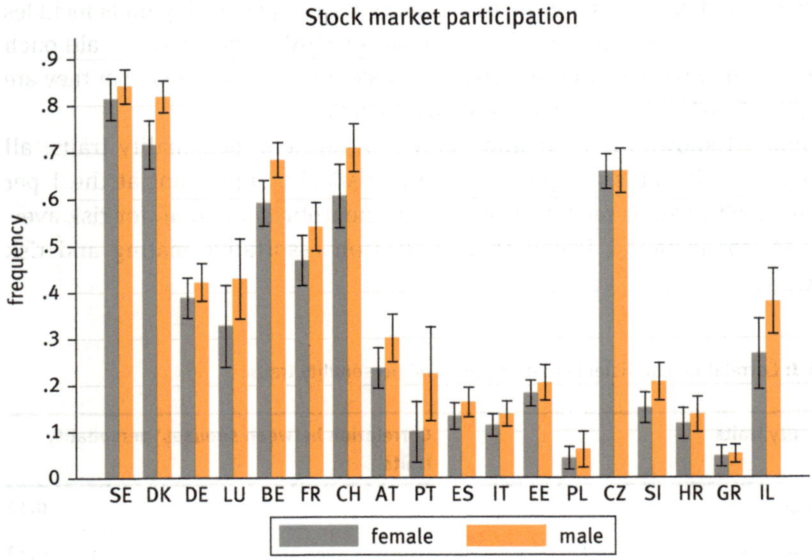

Figure 4.1: Stock market participation across SHARE countries. N = 11,976.
Source: Wave 6 release 6.1.1.

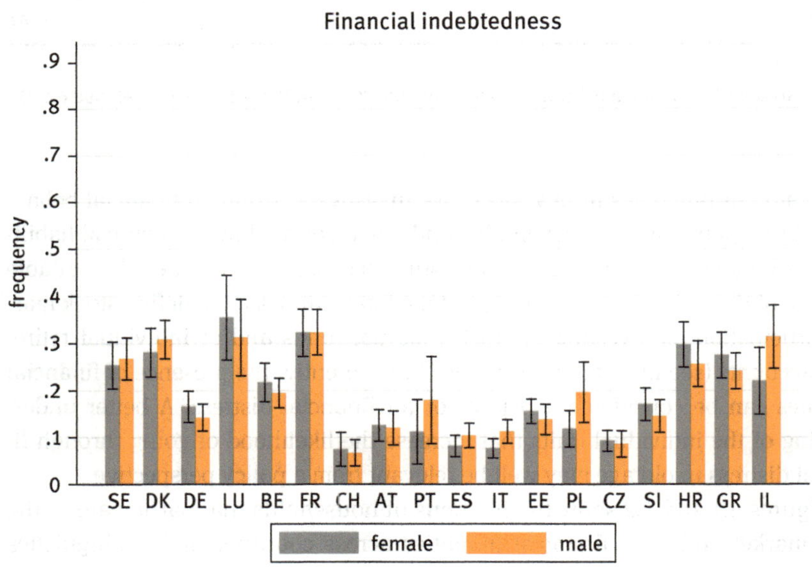

Figure 4.2: Frequency of financial indebtedness across SHARE countries. N=11,976.
Source: Wave 6 release 6.1.1.

accounts varies significantly across countries, with Sweden and Denmark being countries in which stocks market participation is most common, with Greece and Poland the least. Additionally, in all countries, stock market participation turns out to be higher among couples with a male financial head relative to households with a female financial respondent. Noticeably, a lower variation can be observed for the frequency of financial indebtedness. In that case, no systematic difference between households with a male or a female financial respondent can be observed.

4.3 Empirical specification and results

We use a linear probability model to estimate the association between stock market participation/financial indebtedness and partners' personality traits. In doing so, we distinguish between the personality traits of the financial respondent and those of the non-financial respondent. Our list of control variables for both financial and non-financial respondents includes gender, age, age squared, education, employment status, self-reported health and numeracy. Additional household controls are household size, total net wealth and total net yearly income.

Figure 4.3 shows the results obtained from this exercise when the outcome is a dummy that takes the value of 1 if the couple has invested in stocks, mutual funds and/or individual retirement accounts and 0 otherwise. The top-left panel shows the estimates obtained from a specification that controls only for the financial respondent's characteristics. The top-right panel adds the personality traits and other individual controls of the non-financial respondents. The bottom panel of Figure 4.3 restricts the sample to male (left panel) and female (right panel) financial respondents, respectively. A focus on the financial respondent (Figure 4.3 top-left and top-right) shows that the personality traits that matter for stock market participation are consciousness and risk aversion, and both are negatively correlated with the outcome. Switching from a consciousness level of 1 (minimum) to a level of 5 (maximum) decreases, *ceteris paribus*, the probability of investing in stocks, mutual funds or individual retirement accounts by approximately 4.8 percentage points (Figure 4.3 top-right). The change associated with a switch from willingness to unwillingness to take any financial risk is larger in magnitude (12 %). Additionally, consciousness seems to matter only (and risk aversion matters more) for male financial respondents (Figure 4.3 bottom panels). Interestingly, a positive significant association between neuroticism and stock market participation is observed for

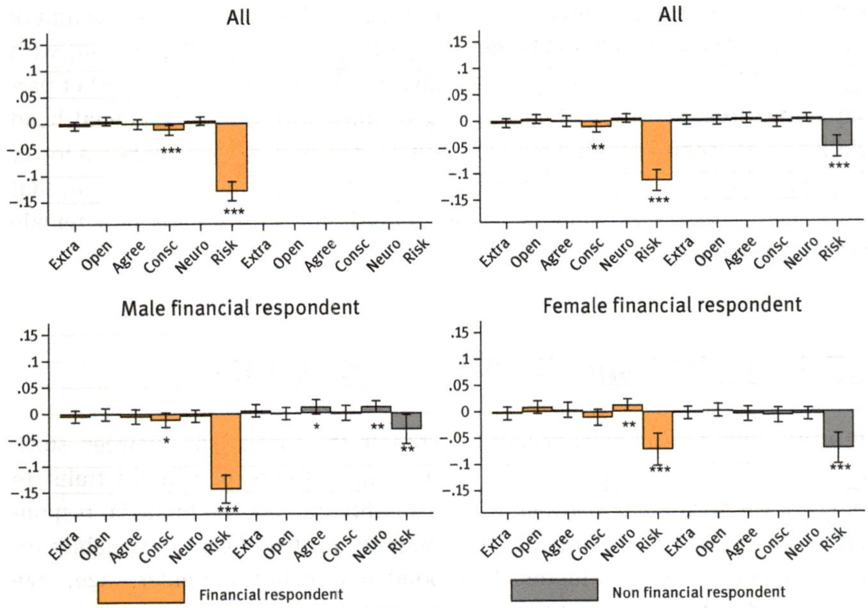

Figure 4.3: Linear probability model estimates. Outcome: respondent and partner have invested in stocks, individual retirement accounts and/or mutual funds (AS section, items AS063, AS064 and AS065).

Note: N = 11,976 in the top-left panel; N = 11,059 in the top-right panel; N = 5,691 in the bottom-left panel; N = 5,368 in the bottom-right panel. Individual controls for financial and non-financial respondents include gender, age, age squared, education, employment status, self-reported health and numeracy. Household controls include household size, total net wealth and total net yearly income. Robust standard errors in parentheses. *** $p < 0.01$, ** $p < 0.05$, * $p < 0.1$

Source: SHARE Wave 6 release 6.1.1, Wave 7 release 0.

female financial respondents. Regarding the non-financial respondent, risk aversion again matters, although to a lesser extent, and agreeableness and neuroticism are positively and significantly (though at the margin) associated with the outcome for female non-financial respondents. Financial respondent's education is positively and significantly correlated with the outcome across all specifications, except for the one that restricts the sample to female financial respondents: in this case, the partner's numeracy attracts a positive and significant coefficient.

Figure 4.4 shows the results obtained for the likelihood of financial indebtedness. Focusing on the financial respondent, our results suggest that a couple

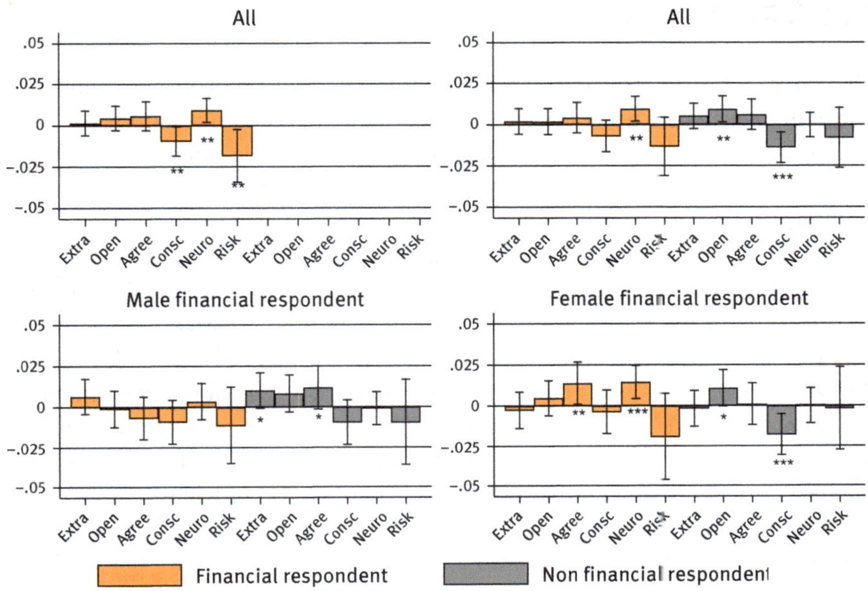

Figure 4.4: Linear probability model estimates. Outcome: respondent and partner have financial liabilities (AS section, item AS054).
Note: N = 11,976 in the top-left panel; N = 11,059 in the top-right panel; N = 5,691 in the bottom-left panel; N = 5,368 in the bottom-right panel. Individual controls for financial and non-financial respondents include gender, age, age squared, education, employment status, self-reported health and numeracy. Household controls include household size, total net wealth and total net yearly income. Robust standard errors in parentheses. *** $p < 0.01$, ** $p < 0.05$, * $p < 0.1$.
Source: SHARE Wave 6 release 6.1.1, Wave 7 release 0.

is more likely to incur financial liabilities if, holding other factors fixed, the household head is a female with a relatively high degree of agreeableness and/or neuroticism. Regarding the non-financial respondent, openness and consciousness attract significant coefficients (one positive, the other one negative) for males, whereas extraversion and agreeableness are positively and significantly associated – although marginally – with the outcome when the non-financial respondent is a woman. Financial indebtedness is more likely among (non-female) financial respondents with a high education or low numeracy skills. A partner's numeracy skills contribute to decreasing the likelihood of financial indebtedness because they are negatively associated with the outcome.

4.4 Conclusions

This chapter has investigated the association between financial decisions and partners' personality traits in late adulthood. The research question is relevant in light of the urgency of better addressing households' financial investments via public policy interventions and incentives to invest in education and financial literacy.

Our results suggest that some personality traits of the financial household head, namely, consciousness, risk aversion and neuroticism, are significantly associated with the proneness to participate in the stock market. The effect of risk aversion is reduced or even absent when the outcome of interest is the likelihood of having financial liabilities. In that case, whenever the financial household head is a female, her degree of agreeableness and neuroticism are positively associated with indebtedness proneness, and openness and consciousness of the (male) partner also attract significant coefficients.

Overall, our results suggest that considering non-cognitive skills is important in studying individual attitudes towards financial risk. Additionally, finding evidence that both partners' personality matters on top of education and numeracy is of potential policy relevance from the perspective of better addressing policy interventions that aim to increase financial literacy, especially among the adult and elderly population.

References

Almlund, M., Duckworth, A. L., Heckman, J., and Kautz, T. (2011). Personality psychology and economics. In Handbook of the Economics of Education (Vol. 4, Ch. 1, pp. 1–181). Editors: Eric A. Hanushek, Stephen Machin, Ludger Woessmann. Publisher: Elsevier, Amsterdam: North Holland.

Bacon P. M., Conte A. and Moffatt P. G. (2014) Assortative mating on risk attitude. Theory and Decision, 77(3),389–401.

Brown, S., and Taylor, K. (2014). Household finances and the 'Big Five' personality traits. Journal of Economic Psychology, 45, 197–212.

Bucciol, A., and Zarri, L. (2017). Do personality traits influence investors' portfolios? Journal of behavioural and experimental economics, 68, 1–12.

Heckman, J. J., Stixrud, J., and Urzua, S. (2006). The effects of cognitive and noncognitive abilities on labor market outcomes and social behavior. Journal of Labor economics, 24 (3),411–482.

Parise, G., and Peijnenburg, K. (2017). Noncognitive Abilities and Financial Distress: Evidence from a Representative Household Panel. 7th Miami Behavioural Finance Conference 2016; HEC Paris Research Paper No. FIN-2017–1193. Available at SSRN: https://ssrn.com/abstract=2924527

Noam Damri and Howard Litwin

5 Relationships with parents in childhood and well-being in later life

- The familial environment that older Europeans experienced during childhood is associated with their well-being in later life.
- People who had good relationships with their parents show higher well-being scores at older ages.
- Those who grew up in an abusive familial environment show lower quality of life scores in old age.
- Social and healthcare professionals should address the lingering effects of interpersonal deficits during the childhoods of their older clients.

5.1 Introduction

Early life experiences impact late life outcomes in many domains, such as employment and socio-economic status. Studies also document how early-life socio-economic conditions influence psychological outcomes in later life. The results from such studies suggest that early-life circumstances have a lasting effect on the well-being of older adults. Although the effect of early-life conditions can be mitigated or modified by subsequent life course events, such as protracted disadvantages in the labour market, research shows that early-life conditions have a lasting effect on the psychological attributes of individuals, even in old age (vast literature exists on this subject; see, e.g. Wahrendorf and Blane, 2015).

The psychological literature underscores the important role of the relationship with parents during childhood in shaping one's personality and traits. This relationship serves as the context in which future relationships and psychological developments take place (Bowlby, 1988). Studies that consider early-life relationships in relation to well-being indicate that a positive and supportive familial environment during one's childhood is associated with better health and personal well-being in adulthood. Conversely, a harmful or abusive early life familial environment is associated with poorer health and/or well-being (Shaw et al., 2004).

To verify whether the social relations that reigned in the home in early life are indeed related to the well-being of older Europeans today, we consider in

https://doi.org/10.1515/9783110617245-005

this chapter the association between relations with parents and two measures of current well-being: the CASP scale and a global measure of life satisfaction. Consideration of the interpersonal environment in the childhood home was addressed for the first time in SHARE Wave 7. The analysis reported in this chapter focuses on respondents aged 65 and older (n = 27,347).

5.2 Emotional support from parents – scores and measures

The Wave 7 questionnaire introduced new questions on the relations with parents and friends during childhood. Relationships with parents were captured through six questions. The first four questions inquired about the quality of the relationship with parents (or the woman/man that raised the respondent), with two questions for each parent: (a) 'How much did your mother/father… understand your problems and worries?' (answers were on a 4-point scale ranging from 'a lot' to 'not at all') and (b) 'How would you rate the relationship with your mother/father?' (answers were on a 4-point scale ranging from 'excellent' to 'poor'). Two additional questions measured harmful relations with parents, asking 'How often did your mother/father push, grab, shove, throw something at you, slap or hit you?' (answers were on a 4-point scale ranging from 'Often' to 'Never'). This question was asked in relation to each parent or caregiver.

In the first stage of the analysis, a principal component factor analysis was carried out to map the domains of the relationship with parents during childhood. The analysis confirmed that the six questions measured two constructs and could be combined into two factors: one for the quality of relations with parents and the other for the frequency of parental abuse. The first factor was based on the first four questions and accounted for almost 45 per cent of the variance, whereas the second was based on the last two questions and accounted for approximately 20 per cent of the variance. The internal reliability of the four items in the first factor displayed a good fit ($\alpha = 0.80$). Thus, a measure for the quality of relations with parents was constructed using these four items, with all items being standardized and an overall mean calculated. The harmful relations measure, in turn, was calculated as the mean of the last two items from the set of variables.

By design, SHARE respondents who participated in the previous retrospective wave of SHARE (SHARELIFE Wave 3) were not asked the retrospective questions again. Thus, approximately 12,800 respondents age 65 and older were excluded from the current analytical sample. Among them were almost all respondents from Hungary, which led to the exclusion of that country from the analysis. Portugal was also not included in the analysis because of a small sample size.

5.3 Emotional support in childhood – demographic characteristics

Figures 5.1 and 5.2 shows the respective means of relationship quality and parental abuse by age, gender and education. As seen, the younger respondents tend to rate their childhood relationship with their parents as better and report, on average, marginally less physical harm relative to the other respondents in the current sample. Although men rated their relationship with parents as slightly better than did women, they also reported experiencing more frequent physical harm. Respondents with a secondary education and higher rated the relationship as better, and those with a high education experienced on average less physical harm than the less educated.

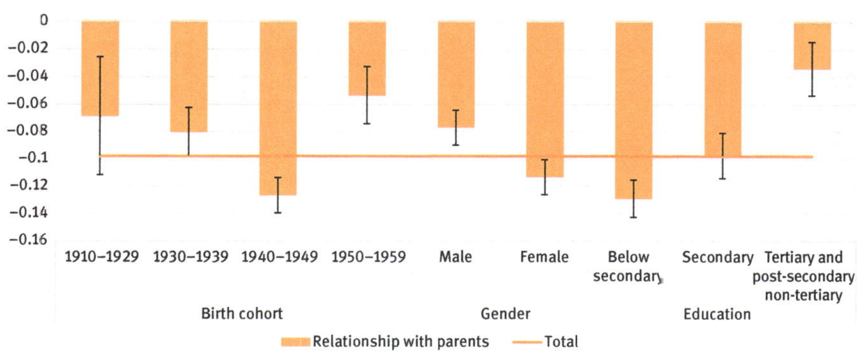

Figure 5.1: Quality of relationship with parents by demographic attributes.
Note: N = 26,703, weighted data.
Source: Wave 7 release 0.

The distribution of these same measures across the 26 countries in the current sample may be viewed in Figures 5.3 and 5.4. Different patterns can be detected. For example, the German and Italian respondents reported low quality relationships with parents and a high frequency of physical harm relative to the other countries. In France and Sweden, low scores for the quality of parental

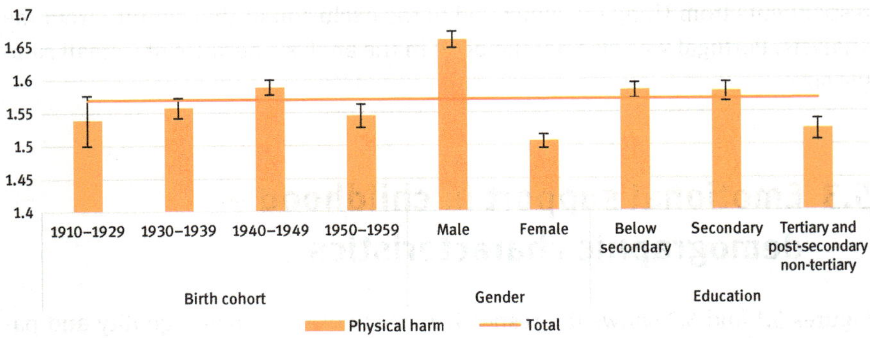

Figure 5.2: Physical harm from parents by demographic attributes.
Note: N = 26,703, weighted data.
Source: Wave 7 release 0.

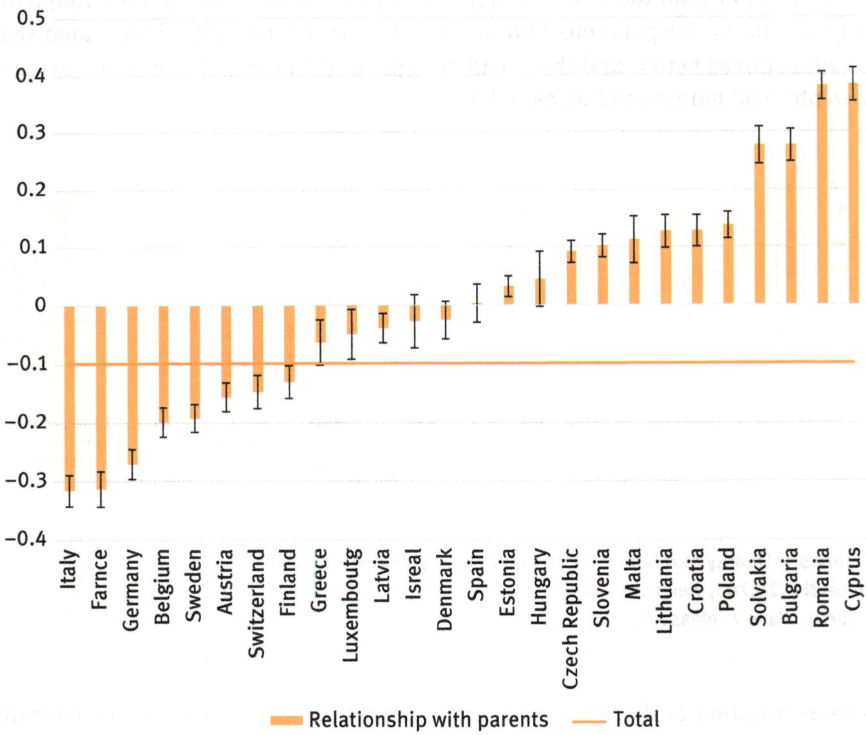

Figure 5.3: Quality of relationship with parents by country.
Note: N = 26,703, weighted data.
Source: Wave 7 release 0.

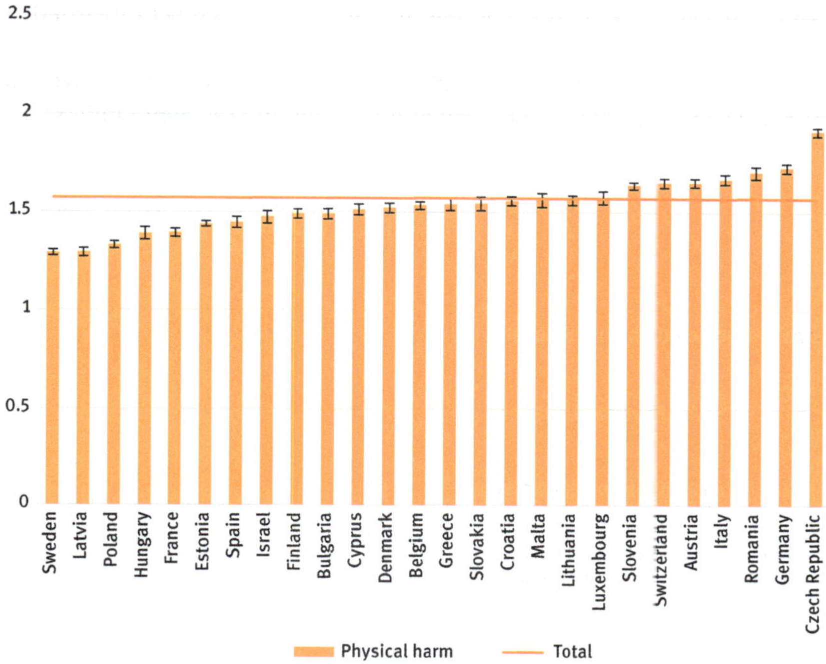

Figure 5.4: Physical harm from parents by country.
Note: N = 26,703, weighted data.
Source: Wave 7 release 0.

relationships are observed, along with a low frequency of physical harm. Thus, different patterns of parenthood and parent–child relationships may be found in different countries.

5.4 Subjective well-being and emotional support in childhood – regression analysis

In the next stage of the inquiry, we regressed the respective well-being outcomes on the two indices of childhood interpersonal environment in the home in two separate regression analyses, controlling for a host of confounders that are generally associated with these same measures (George, 2010), specifically: age, gender, education, number of children, marital status, health status, financial status and social activity. We added two additional indicators to control for cases in which respondents reported that they never lived with their father or mother.

The results of the multivariate OLS regression analysis is summarized in Figure 5.5. The results show that, even after considering the confounders, the

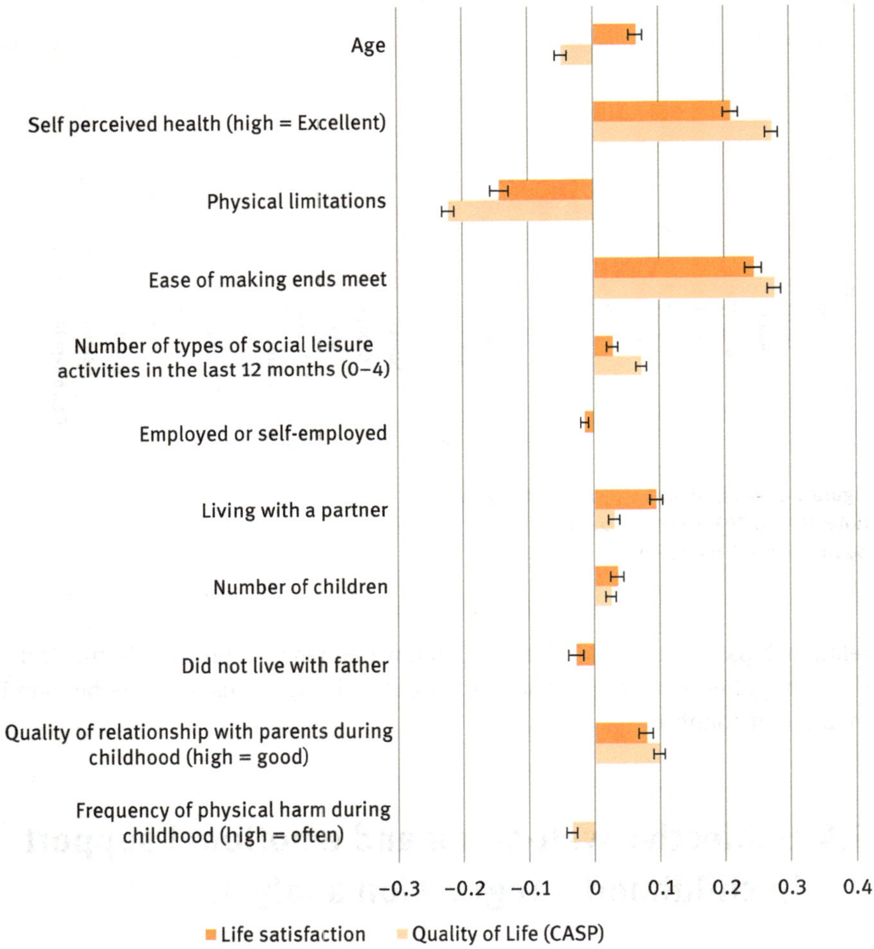

Figure 5.5: Multivariate OLS regressions results for well-being, beta coefficients.
Note: N = 26,703; only significant results ($p < 0.05$) are displayed. Gender, education level and not living with mother during childhood had no significant association with the outcome measures. All models account also for country; R2 for CASP = 0.514, R2 for life satisfaction = 0.279. Weighted data.
Source: Wave 7 release 0.

parental relation quality summary measure is correlated with the two well-being outcome measures. A better relationship quality in the home was positively associated with CASP ($\beta = 0.098$, $p < 0.001$) and with satisfaction with life ($\beta = 0.079$, $p < 0.001$). In other words, even after controlling for different confounding variables, the better the relationship quality in the home, the better one's well-being in older age.

Considering the effect of physical harm during childhood, the reverse effect could be seen. Namely, abusive parental relations during one's childhood is associated with poorer well-being in late life, all else considered. The association is statistically significant for CASP ($\beta = -0.035$, $p < 0.001$) but not for life satisfaction ($\beta = -0.013$, $p > 0.05$).

In the last part of the present analysis, we took a first look at a potential path by which parental support and abuse during childhood respectively influence well-being in late life. Previous studies have shown complex associations between the relations of children with parents and their educational achievements (Davis-Kean, 2005), as well as the associations between socio-economic status and well-being in middle and old ages (George, 2010). Thus, we looked specifically at the role of educational achievement (measured as completing tertiary or post-secondary non-tertiary education) as a proxy for socio-economic status. To consider this potential pathway, a path analysis was applied using the structural equation modelling (SEM) framework. As Figure 5.6 indicates, a significant association exists between the two aspects of one's relationship with one's parents during childhood and both years of education reported and measures of well-being in late life. However, no statistically significant association emerged between years of education and well-being outcomes. These results suggest that the effect of the interpersonal environment in the childhood home on well-being in late life does not necessarily work through socio-economic mechanisms. Rather, other explanations need to be sought. These preliminary results emphasize that further study is, thus, warranted to disentangle the complex mechanism by which the interpersonal environment during childhood affects one's well-being in older age.

5.5 Summary and conclusions

Previous studies have highlighted the role that early life circumstances have on different outcomes in later stages of life and that the relationship with parents during childhood has a significant effect on subsequent well-being.

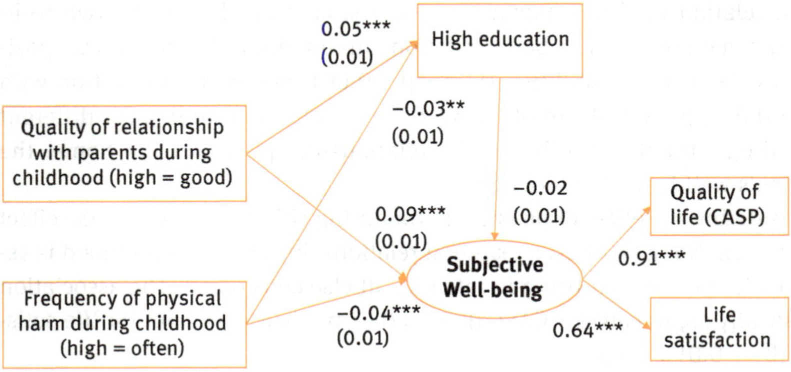

Figure 5.6: Well-being, relationship with parents and years of education.
Note: Weighted data.
Standard coefficients (std. error in parenthesis).
Fit statistics: χ^2 (36)= 30837.6***, df = 36, comparative fit index (CFI) = 0.976; root mean squared error of approximation (RMSEA) = 0.051; standardized root mean squared residual (SRMR) = 0.011.
Model also controls for age, gender, self-perceived health, physical limitations, ease of making ends meet, years of education, social activity, employment status, living with a partner and number of children.
*** p < 0.001. ** p < 0.01.
Source: Wave 7 release 0.

The current study affirms this notion and demonstrates the importance of the familial environment during childhood. Our study results suggest that, among older Europeans today, those who were raised in a supportive environment, had a good relationship with their parents and felt that their parents understood them during their childhood show higher scores in current well-being measures. in contrast, those who were subject to physical abuse from their parents present lower scores in the quality of life measure, on average.

The implication of our findings for policy and practice are that the childhood interpersonal environment of older people needs to be addressed when dealing with ways to maintain or promote well-being in late life. Although past events, whether positive or negative, cannot be undone, they certainly can be processed and used as a means to reflect upon one's past. Such an intervention can potentially aid social and healthcare professionals in addressing the lingering effects of interpersonal deficits during the childhoods of their older clients.

References

Bowlby, J. (1988). *A secure base : parent-child attachment and healthy human development.* New York, NY: Basic Books.

Davis-Kean, P. E. (2005). 'The influence of parent education and family income on child achievement: The indirect role of parental expectations and the home environment', *Journal of Family Psychology*, 19(2), pp. 294–304. doi: 10.1037/0893-3200.19.2.294.

George, L. K. (2010). 'Still happy after all these years: research frontiers on subjective well-being in later life.', *Journals of Gerontology – Series B Psychological Sciences and Social Sciences*, 65B(3), pp. 331–339. doi: 10.1093/geronb/gbq006.Advance.

Shaw, B. A., Krause, N., Chatters, L.M., Connell, C. M. and Ingersoll-Dayton B. (2004). 'Emotional support from parents early in life, aging, and health', *Psychology and Aging*, 19(1), pp. 4–12. doi: 10.1037/0882-7974.19.1.4.

Wahrendorf, M. and Blane, D. (2015). 'Does labour market disadvantage help to explain why childhood circumstances are related to quality of life at older ages? Results from SHARE', *Aging and Mental Health*. Taylor & Francis, 19(7), pp. 584–594. doi: 10.1080/13607863.2014.938604.

Raluca E. Buia, Matija Kovacic and Cristina E. Orso

6 Effects of adverse childhood experiences on mental well-being later in life

- Adverse childhood experiences may influence mental health status and emotional well-being later in life.
- Exposure to adverse early life experiences may favour the onset of emotional disorders.
- Early recognition of adverse childhood experiences and appropriate interventions may play an important role in the prevention of emotional disorders in adulthood.

6.1 Introduction

The medical literature documents the existence of a relationship between adverse childhood experiences (ACEs) and the occurrence/onset of emotional disorders (e.g. Pirkola et al., 2005, Hughes et al., 2016) and/or of risky behaviours later in life. ACEs include a set of events such as physical, sexual and emotional abuse, physical and emotional neglect, household substance abuse, household mental illness and parental separation or divorce (Finkelhora et al., 2015). Anda et al. (2002) found that experiencing adversities in early life is positively correlated with the insurgency of depression and alcoholism in adulthood. In the same vein, Chapman et al., 2004, documented a strong relationship between the number of adverse childhood experiences and the probability of lifetime and recent depressive disorders. Although the medical literature has deeply investigated this correlation, most studies are based on rather restricted samples, generally at national or even regional levels. SHARE allows us to fill in this gap and consider country-specific heterogeneity when investigating the long-run effects of exposure to early-life adverse experiences on mental health.

In this chapter, we explore the effects that ACEs may have on mental well-being in old age. More specifically, we focus on the potential relationship between emotional neglect and physical harm in childhood and adolescence and the onset of emotional disorders later in life. We analyse the probability that some emotional disorder episodes arise, and we attempt to establish whether a relationship exists with early-life negative emotional experiences.

To perform our analysis, we employ data from Waves 4 to 7 of the SHARE survey. We keep all respondents that participated in a regular SHARE wave and

https://doi.org/10.1515/9783110617245-006

participated in the SHARELIFE interview of Wave 7. The regular waves provide information with respect to the current health conditions and mental health as well as the personal characteristics of the individuals (gender, education, behavioural risks, marital status, number of children alive and others). From SHARELIFE, we need information on the retrospective childhood conditions and the respondent's household situation and new records on the quality of a parent-child relationship and early-life emotional experiences.

6.2 Adverse childhood experiences in SHARELIFE Wave 7

The key explanatory variables in the regression analysis that we illustrate in the sequel are several events that may be considered adverse early-life experiences. SHARELIFE asks respondents to report information on exposure to child neglect and childhood physical abuse separately for the mother and the father.

With respect to physical abuse in the family, the questionnaire addresses one item:

1. *How often did your mother/your father push, grab, shove, throw something at you, slap or hit you? 1. Often 2. Sometimes 3. Rarely 4. Never*

In addition, the survey also collects data on child physical abuse by persons outside the family:

2. *How often did anybody else physically harm you in any way? 1. Often 2. Sometimes 3. Rarely 4. Never*

Although different with respect to the items used in the epidemiological research, we consider that a good indicator for child neglect could be derived from the following question:

3. *How much did your mother/your father (or the woman/man that raised you) understand your problems and worries? 1. A lot 2. Some 3. A little 4. Not at all*

Finally, we also include among the explanatory variables the self-reported quality of the relationship with each of the parents:

4. *How would you rate the relationship with our mother/your father (or the woman/man that raised you)? 1. Excellent 2. Very good 3. Good 4. Fair 5. Poor*

Our sample consists of 18,068 men and 23,915 women, and the mean age of the respondents is 65.83 years.

Approximately 17.12% of the respondents in our sample (6,931 individuals) reported having been exposed often or sometimes to physical harm from the mother, 14.35% from the father and 6.76% from others. In the sample, 8,164 individuals (20.32% of the total) responded that the mother understood their problems 'a little' or 'not at all', whereas 12,037 (approximately 31.1%) responded that fathers had little or no understanding.

Table 6.1 presents descriptive statistics for the previous questions, separately by region in Europe.

Table 6.1: Descriptive statistics.

Region	Understanding			Relationship			Harm		
				Mother					
	Obs	**median**	**mean**	**Obs**	**median**	**mean**	**Obs**	**median**	**mean**
North	8,453	2	1.77	8,644	2	2.14	8,631	4	3.56
Center	13,143	2	1.92	13,254	2	2.36	13,242	4	3.38
South	12,218	2	1.77	12,245	2	2.10	12,201	4	3.37
East	4,760	1	1.63	4,783	2	2.02	4,776	4	3.20
Israel	1,621	2	1.98	1,670	2	2.07	1,656	4	3.45
				Father					
	Obs	**median**	**mean**	**Obs**	**median**	**mean**	**Obs**	**median**	**mean**
North	7,871	2	2.10	7,994	2	2.37	8,101	4	3.58
Center	12,661	2	2.22	12,756	3	2.61	12,803	4	3.39
South	11,947	2	2.04	11,967	2	2.36	11,985	4	3.49
East	4,676	2	1.93	4,689	2	2.29	4,694	4	3.32
Israel	1,562	2	2.14	1,603	2	2.22	1,609	4	3.39
				Other					
	Obs	**median**	**mean**	**Obs**	**median**	**mean**	**Obs**	**median**	**mean**
North							8,703	4	3.71
Center							13,377	4	3.71
South							12,324	4	3.81
East							4,799	4	3.75
Israel							1,676	4	3.55

Source: SHARELIFE Wave 7 release 0

Following the existing research in the field, we recoded the answers into dichotomous variables, where a value of 1 indicates that the individual was exposed to a negative experience in early life. We consider that an individual experienced physical abuse in the family if he/she answers '1. Often' or '2. Sometimes' for question 1, for either the mother or the father. We treated question 2 in the same manner to capture physical harm from other persons. A situation of 'child neglect' corresponds to answers '3. A little' or '4. Not at all' for question 3. The relationship with the mother/father in childhood is rated 1, that is, 'problematic'/negative, if the respondent answers '4. Fair' or '5. Poor' to the last query.

6.3 Determinants of emotional disorders and the role of adverse early-life experiences

To investigate the impact of early adversities on the insurgency of emotional disorders, we estimate a set of logistic regressions. The dependent variable is an indicator that takes the value of 1 if the respondent has ever experienced an emotional disorder and 0 otherwise.

In addition to adverse childhood experience variables, we control for gender, marital status, level of education, number of children and a dummy indicator, assigning the value of 1 if respondents were born after World War II. Marital status is included through four dummy variables: single (never married), currently married (reference category), widowed and divorced or separated. Finally, we also control for the importance of religion in childhood. To account for unobserved country-specific effects, we include country dummies.

Our empirical exercise consists of five separated specifications. We first consider the entire sample and control for gender and cohort using two dummy variables. In addition, we run separate regressions for pre- and post-war cohorts and for men and women.

Figures 6.1 and 6.2 report the results from our regressions for the probability of occurrence of emotional disorders. We report the estimated coefficients as odds ratios.

The results indicate a significant relationship between adverse childhood conditions and mental health problems later in life. Having parents that do not understand their children's concerns leads to an increase by a factor of 1.23 in the probability of experiencing an emotional disorder, whereas a poor relationship with at least one of the parents increases it by a factor of 1.49. Rather interesting is the result for the relationship between exposure to physical harm and mental well-being. Having experienced physical harm from persons outside the family has a stronger impact on the probability of mental disorders than physical harm from parents.

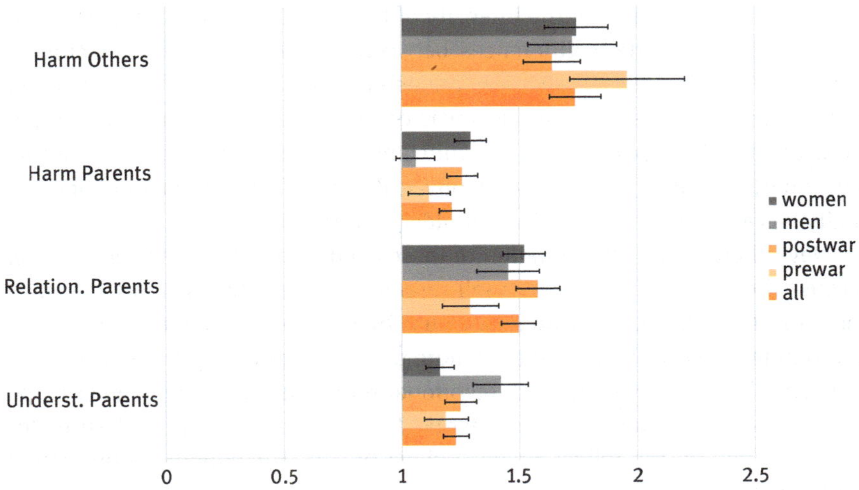

Figure 6.1: Odds ratios for adverse childhood experiences variables.
Note: Logit is used as the estimation method. All regressions include country dummies.
Source: SHARE Waves 4–6 release 6.1.1, Wave 7 release 0.

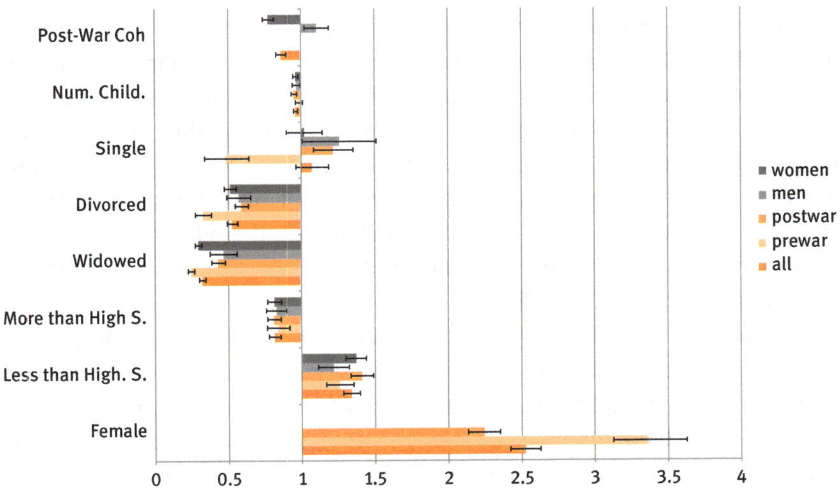

Figure 6.2: Odds ratios for other control variables.
Note: Logit is used as the estimation method. All regressions include country dummies.
Source: SHARE Waves 4–6 release 6.1.1, Wave 7 release 0.

Worth observing is that the intensity of the effects of ACEs on mental well-being displays important differences between the pre- and post-war cohorts (bars 2 and 3 in Figure 6.1). A poor relationship with parents has a stronger and more significant impact on the post-war cohort, whereas having experienced physical harm from parents is not significantly different from zero for the pre-war cohort. However, we note that physical abuse from persons outside the family has a more important effect for older respondents.

Nevertheless, the interpretation of these coefficients requires some caution because the dependent variable is self-reported and selective memory bias may arise. In other words, individuals affected by emotional disorder may have a distorted memory of the past and be more prone to report negative experiences from early life. If individuals with emotional problems tend to remember negative episodes more than otherwise identical individuals, the reported estimates are biased and do not reflect a causal effect of early-life conditions on mental health later in life.

Moreover, our results show important gender differences: being a woman increases by a factor of 2.5 the probability that an emotional disorder will be reported in adulthood (by 3.37 for the pre-war cohort and by 2.24 for the post-war cohort) (see Figure 6.2). This sizeable difference by gender may be driven by differences in survival and health but may also be attributable to different reporting styles if men are less likely to tell their doctor about their mental health problems. Running separate regressions for men and women allows us to obtain more insights into these gender effects (bars 4 and 5 in Figure 6.1): except for the variable that indicates little or no understanding of children's concerns, all other adverse childhood experiences have a stronger and more significant impact for women. Importantly, note that physical harm from parents is not significant for men but is for women, and the odds ratio indicates that, for the last ones, it increases by a factor of 1.29 the probability of experiencing emotional disorders later in life.

Figure 6.2 describes the estimation results for other control variables.

We observe that, in all specifications, education has a significant impact on mental well-being in adulthood. Keeping in mind that the reference category is represented by individuals with a high school degree, being less educated increases the probability of reporting mental distress, whereas more education is associated with a significantly lower probability of experiencing emotional disorders. These effects are stronger and more important for women and for post-war cohorts.

Divorced/separated and widowed respondents have lower odds of being diagnosed with an emotional disorder. Interestingly, individuals born after World War II are less prone to report an emotional disorder. However, this phenomenon may be the result of the fact that the post-war cohort includes respondents in a broad range of younger ages.

Moreover, respondents with more children are less likely to report negative mental health conditions.

6.4 Conclusion

In this chapter, we analyse the relationship between early-life adverse experiences and mental well-being later in life. The study uses data on mental health from the regular waves of the SHARE survey and exploits the new retrospective information on childhood emotional experiences from SHARELIFE Wave 7. The results reveal that adverse early life conditions have a negative impact on individuals' mental health because they increase the probability of an insurgence of emotional disorders.

The importance of recognizing and preventing early adversities represents a prominent public health concern because it may play an important role in the prevention of emotional disorders in adulthood. One of the potential interventions relates to primary care routine screening because most youth make annual visits to their primary care physician – visits during which these adversities and disorders are often first detected.

References

Anda R.F., Whitfield, C.L., Felitti, V.J., Chapman D., Edwards V.J., Dube S.R. and Williamson D.F. (2002). Adverse childhood experiences, alcoholic parents, and later risk of alcoholism and depression. *Psychiatric Services*, 53(8), pp. 1001–1009.

Chapman D. P., Whitfield C. L., Felitti V. J., Dube S. R., Edwards V. J. and Anda R. F. (2004). Adverse childhood experiences and the risk of depressive disorders in adulthood. *Journal of Affective Disorders*, 82(2), pp. 217–225

Finkelhor D., A. Shattuck, H. Turner, S. Hamby (2015). A revised inventory of Adverse Childhood Experiences. *Child Abuse & Neglect*, 48, pp. 13–21.

Hughes K., Lowey H., Quigg Z., and Bellis M. A. (2016). Relationship between adverse childhood experiences and adult mental well-being: results from an English national household survey. *BMC Public Health*. 16:222, pp.1–11.

Pirkola S., E. Isometsä, H. Aro, L. Kestilä, J. Hämäläinen, J. Veijola, O Kiviruusu, J. Lönnqvist, (2005). Childhood adversities as risk factors for adult mental disorders. *Social Psychiatry and Psychiatric Epidemiology*" 40(10), pp. 769–777.

Part II Health inequalities – Education and income

Edited by Guglielmo Weber

Jørgen T. Lauridsen, Terkel Christiansen and Astrid R. Vitved

7 Dynamic changes in determinants of inequalities in health in Europe with a focus on retirement

- Equity in health at older ages is an important policy objective in Europe.
- Inequality in health among the elderly in Europe increased from 2004 to 2017.
- Retirement is substantially associated with inequality in health.

7.1 Introduction

Equity in health and healthcare is an important health policy objective in most European countries (OECD, 2017), but a number of empirical studies have shown the existence of inequities. Access to international comparative data from European countries allows a comparative study of the determinants of income-related inequalities in a population's health. Of particular interest are the contributions to socioeconomic inequality in health from being retired because retirees most often have lower income and lower health status relative to their working peers. Demographic changes in an ageing society add further to the importance of investigating inequalities in health among the retired. The present study contributes to the literature on the association between retirement and income-related health inequality by using SHARE data from the 11 countries that participated in Waves 1 and 7. Our focus is on a comparison of contributions from three age groups of retired individuals (younger than 65 years; 65–74 years; 75 years and older).

7.2 Methods and data

Similar to the standard Lorenz curve, which shows how income is concentrated across income classes, the concentration curve (Figure 7.1) shows how health is concentrated across income classes. The x-axis shows the percentage of households ranked by income, and the y-axis represents the corresponding share of cumulated health. Hence, the concentration curve shows the joint distribution of two variables in contrast to the Lorenz curve.

https://doi.org/10.1515/9783110617245-007

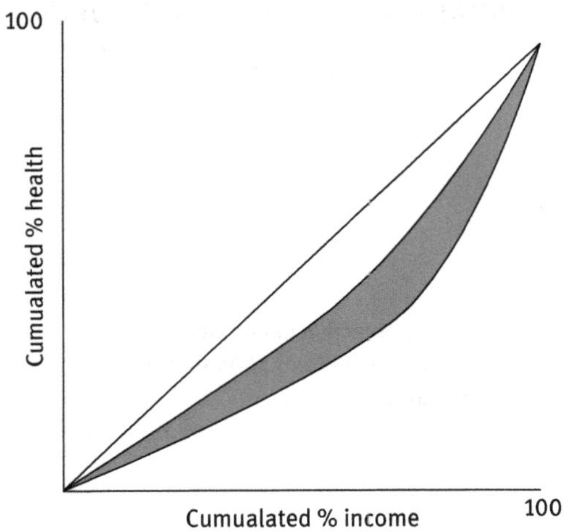

Figure 7.1: Concentration curve and its decomposition into explained and non-explained inequality.

If health is concentrated among the ‘wealthy’ (i.e. those with relatively high income), then the curve is located below the equity line (diagonal). The concentration index (C) is calculated as twice the area between the curve and the equity line. Typically, part of the inequality can be explained by socioeconomic and demographic determinants (the shaded area), whereas another part remains unexplained (the white area). A simple linear relationship applies, and C can be written as:

$$C = \sum_{(k=1)}^{K} \frac{\beta_k \bar{x}_k C_k}{\mu} + C_\varepsilon = \hat{C} + C_\varepsilon. \tag{7.1}$$

This equation shows how C can be expressed as a sum of an explained $(\hat{C})$ and an unexplained part. (C_ε) The explained part, $\hat{C}$ is the sum of K contributions: is β_k the regression coefficient of the k-th determinant in a linear regression explaining health, $\bar{x}_k$ is the mean of the determinant, C_k its concentration index for the determinant and μ is the mean of health.

Given that health is measured by self-assessed health on a cardinal 5-point scale, we use interval regression as suggested by Kakwani et al. (1997) and van Doorslaer and Koolman (2004). The determinants of health considered include gender-specific age dummies (50–59, 60–69, 70+), employment dummies (employed or self-employed, unemployed, homemaker, disabled), three retirement dummies by age (younger than 65, 65–74, 75 and older), current income, educational attainment dummies (basic, secondary and higher education), civil status (single or married / cohabitated) and a dummy for being born in a different country. Intuitively, one may be tempted to interpret the division of retired into three age groups as an interaction between retirement status and age. However, the intention of the paper is not to provide such an interpretation, which would only be consistent if a full interaction between age and employment status were included. Specifically, the aim of the division is to quantify the degree to which each retired age group contributes to inequality.

Data included were respondents from the 11 countries that participated in both Wave 1 and Wave 7. All results were estimated based on individual-level data. We only excluded respondents with missing values on the variables needed for the study. Finally, to ensure representative and comparative results, sampling weights were applied.

7.3 Results

We report only a subset of the calculated results that relate to the role of retirement in explaining health inequality; the full set of calculations are reported in Lauridsen et al. (2018).

Table 7.1 shows calculations from Wave 1 of the mean and the concentration index for the outcome variable. Given that health is an unobserved latent variable, these figures are reported for health as predicted from the interval regression. Furthermore, regression coefficients, means, concentration indices and contributions are reported for the three indicators: Retired, 64 years or younger; Retired, 65–74 years; and Retired, 75 years and older. The reference group for retirement is defined as those not retired and, thus, is heterogenous because it is made up of different groups. This definition implies that we can interpret the contribution from retirement because it compares only with the non-retired and not with any specific group.

From Table 7.1, the positive concentration indices for predicted health ($\hat{C}$) show that health is better for the economically wealthier. These measures vary across countries: they are overall highest in Israel, Germany, Denmark and Greece, and lowest in Austria, Switzerland and Belgium. For the three groups of retired individuals, the means show the proportions of the populations being retired in the age group considered. Thus, the proportion of retired aged 64 or younger is highest in Austria (23.1%) and lowest in Switzerland (4.8%), whereas the proportion of retired aged 65 to 74 is highest in Germany (25.5%) and lowest in Israel (16.6%), and the proportion of retired aged 75 or older is

Table 7.1: Selected results for Wave 1.

	SE	DK	DE	BE	FR	CH	AT	ES	IT	GR	IL
Mean of predicted health	0.858	0.847	0.790	0.833	0.804	0.878	0.819	0.775	0.782	0.826	0.776
$\hat{C}$ for predicted health	0.020*	0.024*	0.029*	0.010*	0.019*	0.009*	0.005*	0.016*	0.020*	0.022*	0.032*
Means:											
RETIRED –64	0.075	0.131	0.100	0.112	0.119	0.048	0.231	0.068	0.178	0.111	0.084
RETIRED 65–74	0.231	0.200	0.255	0.224	0.232	0.207	0.225	0.161	0.226	0.221	0.166
RETIRED 75+	0.236	0.198	0.188	0.198	0.206	0.215	0.198	0.132	0.162	0.146	0.161
Regression coefficients:											
RETIRED –64	−0.118*	−0.093*	−0.041*	−0.022*	−0.019*	−0.022*	−0.056*	−0.073*	−0.032*	−0.027*	−0.022*
RETIRED 65–74	−0.021*	−0.062*	−0.039*	−0.033*	−0.013*	−0.029*	−0.055*	−0.039*	−0.046*	−0.036*	−0.035*
RETIRED 75+	−0.041*	−0.096*	−0.099*	−0.045*	−0.065*	−0.030*	−0.081*	−0.073*	−0.059*	−0.070*	−0.058*
Concentration indices:											
RETIRED –64	−0.070*	0.010	0.001	0.088*	0.067*	−0.031	0.111*	0.182*	0.162*	0.173*	0.221*
RETIRED 65–74	−0.092*	−0.263*	−0.109*	−0.013*	−0.029*	−0.055*	0.085*	0.007*	−0.042*	−0.078*	−0.009
RETIRED 75+	−0.398*	−0.474*	−0.248*	−0.088*	−0.127*	−0.225*	0.001	−0.138*	−0.149*	−0.283*	−0.063*
Contributions (%):											
RETIRED –64	3.60*	−0.59	−0.02	−2.63*	−1.01*	0.41	−36.50*	−7.20*	−5.78*	−2.77*	−1.71*
RETIRED 65–74	2.57*	16.30*	4.67*	1.15*	0.59*	4.22*	−26.55*	−0.36*	2.68*	3.35*	0.21
RETIRED 75+	22.01*	45.09*	19.73*	9.64*	11.04*	18.10*	0.05	10.68*	8.90*	15.71*	2.41*

Note: Significance at the 5%-level is indicated by a star (*).

highest in Sweden (23.6%) and lowest in Spain (13.2%). The mean of a binary indicator should be noted as equal to the proportion of the sample assuming the value of 1 on the indicator and, thus, an estimate of the population proportion assuming the value of 1. Thus, the mean of the indicator 'Retired 75 and older' is the proportion of the full population (not the proportion of the population 75 years and older) who is retired. This figure is the mean needed to provide an estimate of the contribution from this group of retired to the overall societal inequality in health.

Turning to the contributions to health inequality from the three retirement groups, it should be kept in mind (cf. Formula 7.1) that a positive figure indicates that the determinant increases inequality, whereas a negative figure indicates the opposite. Thus, for most countries, early retirement (younger than 65 years of age) reduces health inequality. A possible explanation could be that retired individuals who are younger than 65 years are economically better off than the employed population (as indicated by the positive concentration indices) but are at the same time in worse health (as indicated by the negative regression coefficients for health). An exception is Sweden, where a significantly positive contribution occurs because both the regression effect and the concentration index are negative.

Similarly, the contributions for normal retirement age (65–74 years) are positive for most countries, thus indicating that this age group increases the health inequality. For these countries, the positive contribution occurs from a combination of a negative regression coefficient and a negative concentration index, indicating that low income and ill-health are concentrated in this group. An exception is represented by Austria, where a negative contribution occurs due to a positive concentration index (i.e., the group is economically better off than the employed).

Finally, for the older retirees (75 years and older), the significant contributions are uniformly positive, caused by negative regression coefficients and negative concentration indices; that is, ill-health and low income are concentrated in this group. The magnitude of the contributions for this group is considerably larger than for the group aged 65–74 years, thus indicating that the major contribution to inequality from retirement stems predominantly from the elder (aged 75 and older) group and less from the younger (aged 65–74) group.

Table 7.2 provides similar results for Wave 7, together with the changes in the per cent contribution since Wave 1.

Table 7.2 shows that health is still distributed in favour of the economically better off. The concentration indices vary across countries in a pattern much similar to that found for Wave 1. However, for most countries, the concentration indices have increased from Wave 1 to Wave 7, thus confirming that socioeconomic inequality in health has increased over time.

Table 7.2: Selected results for Wave 7.

	SE	DK	DE	BE	FR	CH	AT	ES	IT	GR	IL
Mean of predicted health	0.802	0.817	0.712	0.773	0.747	0.829	0.760	0.704	0.737	0.772	0.756
$\hat{C}$ for predicted health	0.034*	0.026*	0.050*	0.022*	0.027*	0.015*	0.028*	0.029*	0.029*	0.027*	0.052*
Means:											
RETIRED –64	0.027	0.048	0.047	0.077	0.111	0.024	0.186	0.038	0.053	0.061	0.035
RETIRED 65–74	0.273	0.253	0.224	0.260	0.258	0.216	0.231	0.182	0.190	0.155	0.165
RETIRED 75+	0.246	0.221	0.279	0.209	0.232	0.208	0.242	0.174	0.251	0.257	0.139
Regression coefficients:											
RETIRED –64	−0.117*	−0.137*	−0.058*	−0.019*	−0.018*	0.026*	−0.064*	−0.020*	−0.018*	−0.018*	−0.028*
RETIRED 65–74	−0.054*	−0.040*	−0.024*	−0.015*	−0.059*	−0.019*	−0.060*	−0.044*	−0.032*	−0.032*	−0.027*
RETIRED 75+	−0.097*	−0.085*	−0.032*	−0.036*	−0.092*	−0.043*	−0.094*	−0.106*	−0.085*	−0.115*	−0.075*
Concentration indices:											
RETIRED –64	−0.077	0.075*	−0.068*	0.082*	0.153*	0.005	−0.017*	0.144*	0.168*	0.282*	0.282*
RETIRED 65–74	−0.107	−0.194*	−0.035*	−0.062*	0.075*	−0.069*	−0.012*	0.119*	0.103*	0.141*	0.006
RETIRED 75+	−0.418	−0.439*	−0.130*	−0.233*	−0.099*	−0.170*	−0.100*	−0.117*	−0.138*	−0.160*	−0.086*
Contributions (%):											
RETIRED –64	0.90*	−2.29*	0.53*	−0.70*	−1.50*	0.03	0.98*	−0.53*	−0.75*	−1.55*	−0.71*
RETIRED 65–74	5.87*	9.20*	0.54*	1.44*	−5.66*	2.41*	0.81*	−4.63*	−2.88*	−3.39*	−0.07
RETIRED 75+	37.08*	38.64*	3.26*	10.35*	10.56*	12.54*	10.73*	10.47*	13.59*	23.22*	2.28*
Change in % of contribution Wave 1 to 7:											
RETIRED –64	−2.70*	−1.69*	0.55*	1.92*	−0.49*	−0.38	37.48*	6.67*	5.03*	1.22*	1.00*
RETIRED 65–74	3.30*	−7.11*	−4.13*	0.30	−6.25*	−1.81*	27.36*	−4.28*	−5.56*	−6.74*	−0.27
RETIRED 75+	15.08*	−6.45	−16.47*	0.72	−0.49	−5.57*	10.68*	−0.21	4.69*	7.52*	−0.13

Note: Significance at the 5%-level is indicated by a star (*).

Turning to the contributions to the inequality in health from the determinants, the retired in the two older age groups were generally confirmed (although with exceptions) as contributing to increased inequality in health, whereas the pattern is more mixed for the younger group under age 65. Thus, for Spain, Italy, France, Denmark, Greece, Belgium and Israel, the retired younger than 65 years reduces health inequality through a negative contribution. As in Wave 1, the reason for this phenomenon appears to be that the retired younger than 65 years are economically better off than the employed population (as indicated by the positive concentration indices, cf. Formula 7.1) but are simultaneously in worse health (as indicated by the negative regression coefficients for health, cf. Formula 7.1). For Austria, Germany and Sweden, a significantly positive contribution occurs because the regression effect and the concentration index are both negative.

Similarly, for the retired (65–74 years), the contributions are seen as positive for several countries, thus indicating that this age group increases inequality in health. For these countries, the positive contribution occurs from a combination of a negative regression coefficient and a negative concentration index, indicating that low income and ill-health are concentrated in this group. For other countries, negative contributions occur due to the combination of a positive concentration index and a negative coefficient for health (i.e., the group is economically better off but in less good health than the employed).

Next, for the elder retired (75 and older), the pattern from Wave 1 is confirmed; that is, the age group contributes to increased inequality in health given a combination of negative regression coefficients and negative concentration indices. Again, the magnitude of the contributions for this group is considerably larger than for the group aged 65–74 years.

Finally, considering development from Waves 1 to 7, a quite mixed pattern with increases and decreases is seen. For Austria and to some extent Belgium, all three age groups have increased their contributions to health inequality. The increase for Austria is caused by a shift in the sign of the concentration indices for retirement for all three groups from positive to negative, indicating increased inequality over time. For Denmark and to some extent France and Belgium, all three age groups have decreased their contributions. The decrease for Denmark is caused by improved concentration indices for all three groups because the index for the group younger than 65 years shifted from zero to significantly positive, whereas the magnitude of the negative indices for the two elder groups declined. For Germany and to some extent Spain and Israel, a mixed pattern is found because the contribution to inequality has risen for the group younger than 65 years and has fallen for the two older groups. In Germany, the increase for the group younger than 65 years is especially connected to an increase in the concentration index for this group from zero to significantly negative, whereas the reductions for the elder groups are related to reductions in the magnitude of their negative indices. An opposite pattern, with reduced contribution for the group younger than 65 years and increased contribution for the two elder groups, is found for Sweden. Turning next to Italy and Greece, both the younger than 65 and older than 75 groups increased their contributions to inequality, whereas the intermediate group reduced its contribution.

7.4 Conclusion

The present study confirms that health is distributed in favour of the wealthy across European countries and adds evidence that this inequality is increasing over time. Retirement is shown to be a significant contributor to income-related health inequality, especially regarding the 75 and older age group. The development over time is mixed because the contributions increased for some countries and reduced for others. This mix is important because it calls for different policy initiatives in different countries. See Lauridsen et al. (2019) for a discussion of the shortcomings of a joint specification implying a joint European policy.

References

Kakwani N, Wagstaff A, van Doorslaer E. 1997. Socioeconomic inequalities in health: Measurement, computation, and statistical inference. *Journal of Econometrics* 77(1): 87–103.

Lauridsen J, Christiansen T, Vitved AR. 2019. Dynamic Changes in Determinants of Inequalities in Health in Europe with Focus on Retirement. *SHARE Working Paper Series* (forthcoming)

OECD. 2017. *Inequalities in health.* Paris: OECD. http://www.oecd.org/health/inequalities-in-health.htm.

van Doorslaer E, Koolman X. 2004. Explaining the differences in income-related health inequalities across European countries. *Health Economics* 13(7): 609–628.

Louis Arnault, Florence Jusot, Nicolas Sirven,
Marie-Anne Brieu, Didier Halimi and Françoise Forette

8 Persistence in inequalities of frailty at older age: A comparison of nine EU countries

- Women are more at risk of frailty than men.
- Strong inequalities exist among men and women according to their levels of education.
- These social inequalities persisted during 2004–2014.

8.1 Aim of the study

Reducing inequalities in health and mortality among socioeconomic groups has become a major goal of health policy in many European countries (Marmot et al., 2008). Although remarkable declines in amenable mortality among groups of both low and highly educated individuals have been achieved, social inequalities in mortality remain large and persistent in Europe and seem to increase among men but remain quite stable among women (Mackenbach et al., 2017).

One way to reduce this gap is to monitor populations that are at risk of over-mortality, with a focus on gender issues, to implement targeted preventive interventions for tackling health inequalities. As such, frailty has become an important indicator to be measured in clinical settings and in the general population (Santos-Eggiman and Sirven, 2016).

Frailty is defined as increased vulnerability to stressors resulting from a decrease in the physiological reserves of multiple systems. Frailty has been operationalized as a phenotype, determined by the presence of a critical number of impairments in physical strength, physical activity, nutrition, mobility and energy (Fried et al., 2001). Studies have shown that frailty is associated with a higher use of healthcare resources and predicts health outcomes, such as occurrence or aggravation of functional limitations, falls, hospitalizations and mortality.

Despite the ever-increasing interest in frailty, little attention has been given to the analysis of social inequality in frailty over time. Analysis of change in the prevalence of frailty over time is particularly relevant because one of the key aspects of the prevention concept is that frailty is reversible. Monitoring changes in

https://doi.org/10.1515/9783110617245-008

social inequalities in frailty may be important for designing relevant preventive policies. In addition, although gender issues have always been at the heart of social inequalities analysis, to the best of our knowledge, no study has yet proposed to measure inequalities in frailty by gender from a dynamic perspective. The aim of this paper is to compare the prevalence of frailty by age groups, gender and socioeconomic groups across Europe.

8.2 Methodology

We use data from Waves 1, 2, 4, 5 and 6 of SHARE. We consider respondents aged 50+ who answered questions related to frailty, live in the community and reside in countries that participated in the first five standard waves of SHARE (i.e., all but Wave 3, which is retrospective), namely, Austria, France, Germany, Sweden, Denmark, Switzerland, Belgium, Italy and Spain.

Following Santos-Eggimann et al. (2009), who first proposed an operational measures of Fried's frailty phenotype based on SHARE data, we measure frailty as a clinical syndrome in which three or more of the following criteria are observed: shrinking, self-reported exhaustion, weakness as measured by a grip strength lower than several thresholds as defined by gender and BMI groups and slowness as measured by having difficulties walking 100 metres or climbing one flight of stairs without resting and low physical activity. All of these measures were collected from each respondent starting with Wave 1; grip strength is the only non-declarative health measure.

Education is the indicator of the current socioeconomic status that we used to assess social inequality in frailty and more generally to assess social health inequalities. We first develop a binary variable of education based on the International Standard Classification of Education scale (ISCED-97) and consider individuals with a scale equal to 0, 1 or 2 as less educated and others as highly educated. Based on this information, we propose assessing the prevalence of frailty by age groups, gender, education groups and waves in Europe. Inequalities in frailty will be analysed by computing the difference in frailty prevalence between less and highly educated groups.

We develop a pseudo-panel approach through which clusters of individuals rather than individuals are the units of analysis. The clusters are groups defined by sex (female, male), age class (50–64, 65–74 and 75+), education levels (low, high), countries (nine European countries) and Waves (1, 2, 4, 5 and 6). These 540 clusters are socio-demographic groups for which the prevalence of frailty is computed at every wave using sampling weights to provide an estimate representative of the population. This method allows a comparison over time through which age and year effects can be decomposed: the age effect is given by a comparison of frailty prevalence among age classes at each wave, whereas the year effect is given by the comparison of frailty prevalence among waves for each age class.

Our results depict education-related inequality in frailty prevalence by gender and age group based on a comparison of frailty prevalence (graphs) and time trend (first-difference models with cluster fixed effects). In detail, we provide statistics for:

- Education-related inequalities in frailty prevalence by gender and by age group on the average for all periods (Figure 8.1); and
- Difference-in-difference education-related inequalities in frailty prevalence by gender and age group for all periods (Table 8.1).

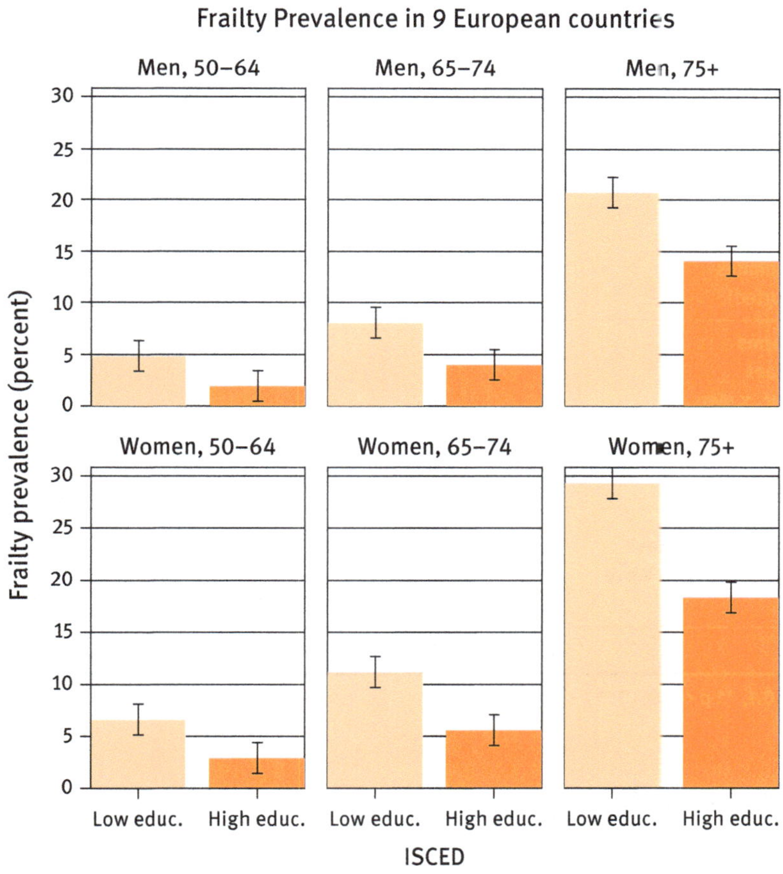

Figure 8.1: Frailty Prevalence in 9 European countries.
Source: SHARE Wave 1,2,4,5,6 release 6.1.1.

Table 8.1: Difference-in-difference of frailty prevalence by education over time in nine European countries.

Dep. Var.	OLS			Panel FE	
Prevalence of frailty	**M1**	**M2**	**M3**	**M4**	**M5**
Main variables					
Wave (1, 2, 4, 5, 6)	0.01	0.01	0.01	0.01	0.01
Education (ISCED)					
Low	ref.	ref.	ref.	–	–
High	−0.05***	−0.05***	−0.05***	–	–
Interaction term					
Wave x Low educ.	ref.	ref.	ref.	ref.	ref.
Wave x High educ.	−0.01	−0.01	0.01	−0.01	0.00
Controls					
Sex					
Men		ref.	ref.	–	–
Women		0.03***	0.04***	–	–
Age class					
50–64		ref.	ref.	–	–
65–74		0.03***	0.03***	–	–
75+		0.16***	0.16***	–	–
Country dummies (not reported)				–	–
Crossed–terms					
Time invariant					
High educ. x Men			ref.	–	–
High educ. x Women			−0.01	–	–
Time variant					
Men x Wave			ref.		ref.
Women x Wave			0.01		0.01
High educ. x Men x Wave			ref.		ref.
High educ. x Women x Wave			−0.01		−0.01
Intercept	0.13***	0.05***	0.05***	0.10***	0.10***
N	540	540	540	540	540

Note: * $p < 0.1$, ** $p < 0.05$, *** $p < 0.01$.

8.3 First results

Our first descriptive results show inequalities in frailty prevalence according to age and gender on average for all periods (Figure 8.1). On average for different periods, the prevalence of frailty is approximately 9 per cent among men and 12 per cent among women. In addition, regardless of the period considered, we note a strong increase in the risk of frailty with age, at approximately 4 per cent of the population aged 50 to 65, 7 per cent of the population aged 65 to 74 and 20 per cent of the population aged 75 and older.

The results of the pseudo panel displayed in Table 8.1 (M1–M3) show that women are always more at risk of frailty than men, and strong social inequalities exist among men and women: the risk of frailty is lower among highly educated individuals. In addition, the risk of frailty increases with age (M2–M3).

Regarding the trends during 2004–2015 (Table 8.1, crossed-terms in M3 and M5), the prevalence of frailty remains quite stable for both women and men. The patterns appear to be similar among education groups, suggesting a persistence of social inequalities in frailty during the period. The time trend is nil (Table 8.1, variable "Wave" in M1–M5), indicating that the prevalence of frailty remained constant over the pseudo-panel. Decomposition of the trend, that is, time-fixed effects crossed with cluster fixed-effects (sex, and education level) one after the other, did not reveal any specific trends between men and women, and similar results occur for education levels. In any case, we find no compensation effect – for instance, when the increase in one cluster is compensated by a decrease in the other cluster such that the average is nil.

8.4 Conclusion

This analysis of the trends in inequalities in frailty in Europe from a pseudo-panel perspective suggests two main results. First, we account for large and significant social inequalities in the prevalence of frailty between less and highly educated groups: frailty prevalence for less educated men is on average higher by 4.5 percentage points relative to more educated men; this figure increases to 6.7 percentage points for women. These social inequalities tend to increase with age, reaching 6.6 percentage points for men and 10.9 percentage points for women in the 75+ age class. Second, these results are stable over time, meaning that the new generations face a similar risk of frailty as did the previous generation. In a nutshell, social inequalities in frailty are strong and persistent.

Despite many efforts made to date with the aim of reducing social inequalities in health, these inequalities remain large, at least in the case of frailty. Two sets of reasons could be advocated here to explain this result. First, the mechanisms at play may need to be assessed in the long run, such that the period of observation is relatively short. Second, two counteracting effects may be at play: medical progress reduces the risk of frailty for any given age but also increases the pool of survivors such that we did not observe any change in the prevalence of frailty over time.

References

Fried, L. P., Tangen, C. M., Walston, J., Newman, A. B., Hirsch, C., Gottdiener, J., Seeman, T., Willem, R. T., Burke, G., & McBurnie, M. A. (2001). Frailty in older adults: evidence for a phenotype. *The Journals of Gerontology Series A: Biological Sciences and Medical Sciences*, *56*(3), M146–M157.

Mackenbach J. P. et al., (2017), Determinants of the magnitude of socioeconomic inequalities in mortality: A study of 17 European countries, *Health and Place*, 47; 44–53.

Marmot, M., Friel, S., Bell, R., Houweling, T., Taylor, S., & the Commission on Social Determinants of Health (2008). Closing the gap in a generation: health equity through action on the social determinants of health. *The Lancet*, 372, 1661–1669.

Santos-Eggimann, B., Cuénoud, P., Spagnoli, J., & Junod, J. (2009). Prevalence of frailty in middle-aged and older community-dwelling Europeans living in 10 countries. *The Journals of Gerontology: Series A*, 64(6), 675–681.

Santos-Eggimann, B., & Sirven, N. (2016). Screening for frailty: older populations and older individuals. Public health reviews, 37(1), 7.

Michele Belloni, Danilo Cavapozzi, Chiara Dal Bianco,
Yao Pan and Serena Trucchi

9 How do early-life conditions shape health age profiles late in life?

- We investigate how health dynamics late in life vary with early-life conditions
- Better early-life conditions are associated with better health outcomes
- Education as well as current income and wealth are important mediating factors of this relationship

9.1 Health profiles and early-life conditions

The change in the demographic structure of the population poses concerns over the sustainability of public healthcare programmes because the increase in the number of older people is likely to increase the demand for care services. Understanding how health patterns evolve with age and whether their trends differ by the socioeconomic conditions experienced during the lifecycle might help predict how demand for care services will evolve.

A growing body of economic literature has focused on the long-run consequences of the early stage of the lifecycle and investigated the effect of the socioeconomic status of individuals during their childhoods on several adult outcomes, such as earnings (Brunello et al., 2017), cognitive and non-cognitive skills (Cunha et al., 2010) and health conditions (Mazzonna, 2014). These studies point out the significant role played by socioeconomic conditions during childhood on human capital accumulation for children and, thus, on adult socioeconomic outcomes. This chapter contributes to the literature by examining the impact of early-life conditions on not only the health *status* but also its *dynamics* in later stages of the lifecycle.

We describe early-life conditions using a multidimensional index based on a battery of indicators designed to describe the socioeconomic context in which respondents grew up. Building on the SHARE and SHARELIFE questionnaires, we focus on the socioeconomic background of respondents at age 10. Our multidimensional indicator for early-life conditions considers whether parents were alive, their education, the number of books at home, the number of rooms per capita and other relevant accommodation characteristics. For respondents'

https://doi.org/10.1515/9783110617245-009

current health status, we use alternative measures. We focus on overall health self-assessment, an objective indicator of physical health, as well as on the EURO-D scale score for mental health.

Further, we investigate the extent to which the long-run influence of early-life conditions on the health of older individuals is indirect, in other words, the extent to which it is mediated by the current individual and household characteristics (see, e.g. Bengtsson and Broström, 2009). Empirically, we assess whether the characteristics of socioeconomic status during childhood remain significantly associated with health later in life once we condition on education and current socioeconomic status indicators (e.g., household composition, household income and wealth measures). Analysing these patterns provides evidence of the channels according to which childhood conditions can shape health later in life and can inform policymakers about the intergenerational consequences of public policies designed to improve the social and economic inclusion of individuals.

We find that socioeconomic status in childhood is positively correlated with health in later life. This association holds for both physical and mental health and is stronger for females than for males. In most cases, it remains stable over the age range we consider. We find evidence that this effect is mostly indirect; that is, it is mediated by socioeconomic status in adulthood. This evidence suggests that an individual who grows up in bad conditions is penalized in the areas of education, income and wealth over their lifecycle, which leads to worse health in old age. However, a small direct effect remains, suggesting that childhood circumstances partly act as an indelible imprint on individuals' health.

9.2 Data and variables

The sample includes respondents aged between 50 and 80 years, living in countries that participated in all SHARE waves, namely, Austria, Belgium, Denmark, Germany, France, Italy, Spain, Sweden and Switzerland. After excluding respondents with missing information on relevant variables, we end up with 85,519 observations referring to 15,502 women and 12,643 men.

As anticipated in the previous section, we focus on three different outcome variables that measure current physical and mental health. We draw current health indicators from Waves 1, 2, 4, 5 and 6. The first health indicator considered is the self-assessed overall health status, which takes the values 1 (poor) to 5 (excellent). To provide an objective assessment of an individual's physical health status, we construct an indicator combining information on Activities of Daily Living (ADLs), Instrumental Activities of Daily Living (IADLs), mobility limitations and chronic diseases (we consider only the chronic condition items included in all waves). Our objective physical health indicator is the weighted sum of individual outcomes with respect to these health indicators. Weights are defined by running a principal component analysis. We assigned to each indicator a weight derived from the corresponding item in the first principal component. The objective physical health indicator is standardized to lie between 0 (worst physical health) and 1 (best physical health). We also consider mental health status, which is measured by the EURO-D indicator. The EURO-D indicator counts the number of mental diseases suffered by individuals. For comparability with the other health measures considered, we reversed its scale and standardized its range to between 0 and 1, where 0 indicates worst mental health and 1 indicates best mental health.

To investigate the impact of early-life conditions on health dynamics later in life, we exploit a unique characteristic of the SHARE dataset. In SHARELIFE (Wave 3 and Wave 7) and SHARE (Wave 5 and Wave 6) information is collected on family background during childhood, along with several well-established measures.

We specifically exploit the following information: the number of books at home at age 10 (we create a variable equal to 1 for those with more than 10 books and 0 otherwise), the number of rooms per-capita (we create a variable equal to 1 if the number equals or is higher than the country median and 0 otherwise), plus some features of the family home at age 10 (whether equipped with central heating, an inside toilet, a fixed bath, cold running water and hot running water, each treated as a separate dummy variable). We also use information on whether both parents were alive at age 10 and their education attainment (a dummy equal to 1 if at least one parent was highly educated, that is, an education level classified with an ISCED code equal to 3 or higher).

Our early-life conditions index is defined as the weighted sum of individual outcomes with respect to this battery of binary indicators, where the weights are defined by a principal component analysis. The early-life condition indicator takes values between 0 (worst conditions) and 1 (best conditions). The country median of the index is lowest in southern Europe (0.3 in Italy and Spain) and highest in Sweden, where the median is approximately 0.9. This evidence parallels the evidence by Mazzonna (2014) that shows cross-country heterogeneity in rooms per capita, accommodation facilities and books at home based on SHARELIFE.

9.3 Methods and results

To examine the health dynamics of individuals later in life, we estimate the age profile of our three health indicators. Each current health measure is regressed on our early-life condition indicator, a second-order polynomial of age and its interactions with the early-life condition indicator. Interaction terms play a crucial role in our identification strategy because they allow the role of early-life conditions to vary with age. We consider two alternative sets of control variables. The first set of controls ('basic set of controls') includes a full set of country dummies and birth-cohort dummies. In the second set of controls ('full set of controls'), the set of covariates is augmented to reflect respondents' socioeconomic status in adulthood. More specifically, we add educational attainment dummies (ISCED levels 0–2, 3–4 and 5–6), country-specific quartile dummies for household income and wealth and family current characteristics (household size, number of children and grandchildren). Each regression is run separately by gender. Standard errors are clustered at the individual level to account for the longitudinal dimension of the dataset. Different degrees of the age polynomial lead to unchanged findings.

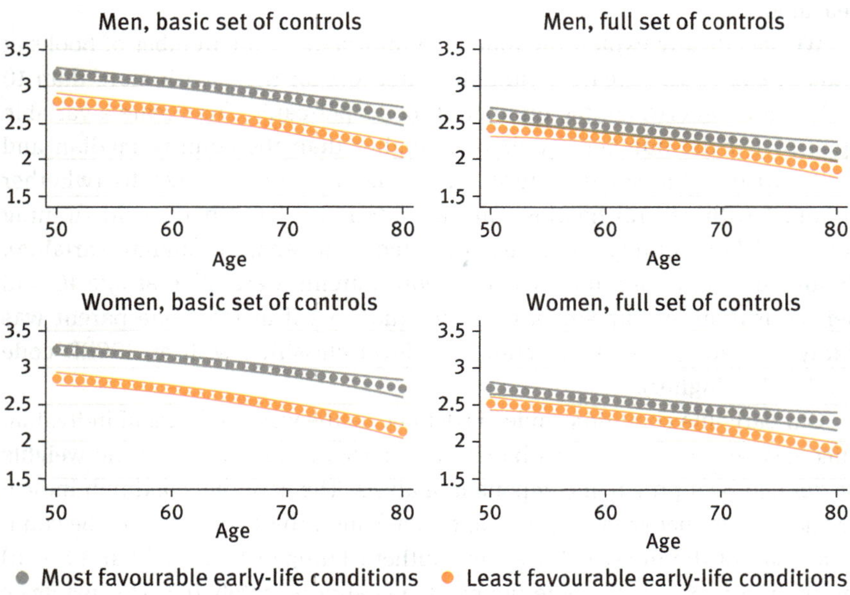

Figure 9.1: Health age profiles: Self-assessed overall health indicator.
Note: Solid lines indicate 95 per cent confidence intervals.
Source: SHARE Wave 1–6 release 6.1.0, Wave 7 release 0.

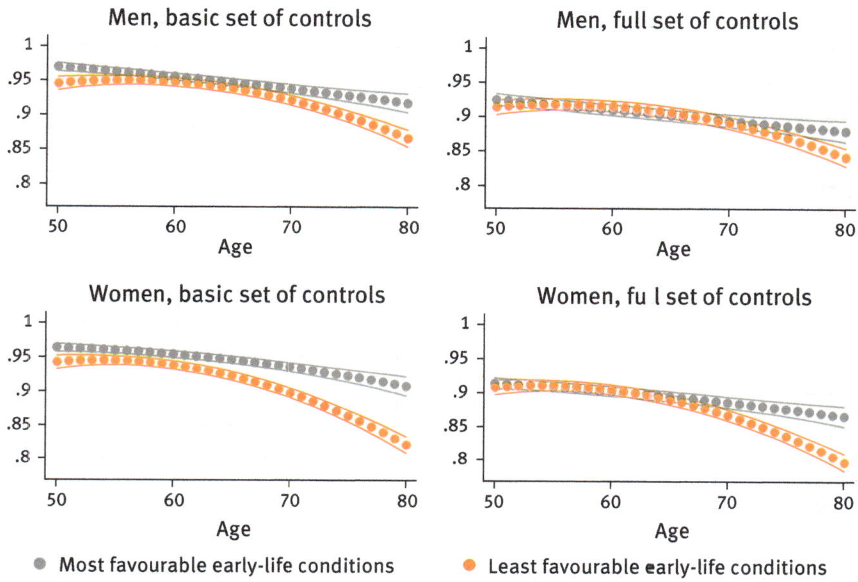

Figure 9.2: Health age profiles: Physical health indicator.
Note: Solid lines indicate 95 per cent confidence intervals.
Source: SHARE Wave 1–6 release 6.1.0, Wave 7 release 0.

Based on the results from these regressions and holding the control variables fixed, we computed the age profile of each health outcome for individuals with the least and the most favourable early-life conditions (which implies setting our early-life condition indicator alternatively equal to 0 and 1). The predictions are plotted in Figures 9.1–9.3, which show the predicted (mean and 95% confidence interval) health-age profiles for respondents with the most (grey dots and lines) or least favourable (orange dots and lines) early-life conditions. Each figure reports results for a specific health outcome by gender and by set of control variables used.

Figure 9.1 illustrates the dynamics of self-assessed overall health. As expected, health declines after the age of 50 for both men (upper panels) and women (lower panels). Observing the most parsimonious specification (left graphs in Figures 9.1), the health status of individuals who experienced the worst early-life conditions is on average significantly lower with respect to respondents who grew up in the best socioeconomic environments. This pattern is confirmed throughout the age range considered. However, the distance between the groups shrinks when we allow for the full set of controls, which includes the level of education and the position in the country-specific income

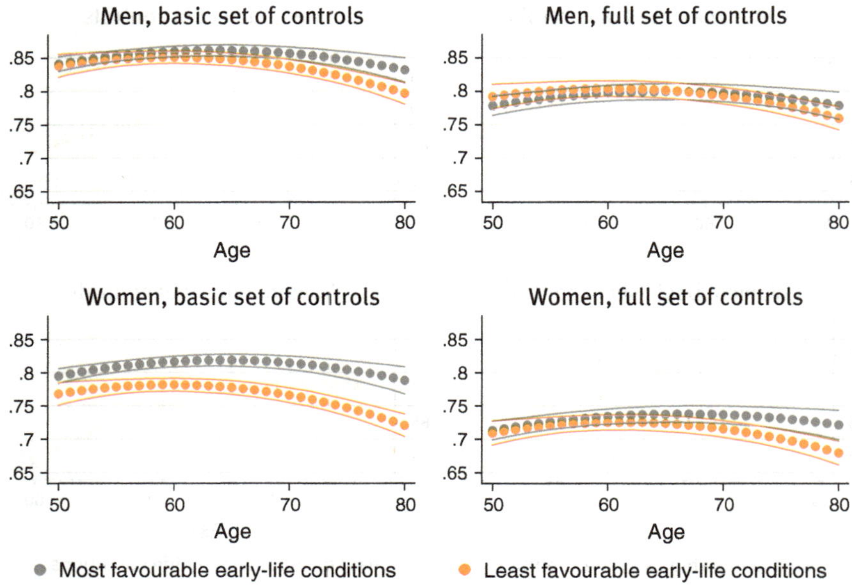

Figure 9.3: Health age profiles: Mental health indicator.
Note: Solid lines indicate 95 per cent confidence intervals.
Source: SHARE Wave 1–6 release 6.1.0, Wave 7 release 0.

and wealth distribution (right graphs in Figures 9.1). This evidence supports the hypothesis of a relevant role played by these variables in explaining heterogeneity in health over the lifecycle, where adult socioeconomic status partially mediates the impact of early-life socioeconomic background.

The results in Figure 9.2 replicate the analysis considering the objective physical health indicator as an outcome variable. The differences in the predicted health outcomes for men are narrower than in Figure 9.1 but still statistically significant. Individuals who experienced better early-life conditions enjoy better physical health outcomes later in life. For both genders, the difference between the two profiles increases after a certain age, approximately 70 for men and 60 for women. After controlling for the richest set of covariates (right graphs in the figure), we find that the divergence between the two age profiles shrinks, and the age when it starts increasing is slightly postponed (to age 70 for men and 65 for women). Attrition related to mortality can affect the composition of our sample and our findings, inasmuch as life expectancy depends on gender, education and, potentially, early-life conditions.

Along with physical health, we also analyse the dynamics of mental health later in life. As emerges from Figure 9.3, gender differences are more pronounced with respect to physical health. In line with the previous literature (Riecher-Rössler, 2016), we find that women are more likely to experience the worst mental health at each age. In addition, the divergence in the age profile of mental health between individuals who were exposed to good or bad early-life conditions is more pronounced in the female sample. Regarding overall and physical health indicators, after controlling for adult socioeconomic conditions, the differences in the age profiles related to early-life conditions are significantly reduced.

9.4 Conclusions

The evidence in this chapter supports the hypothesis that early-life conditions are powerful predictors of health dynamics later in life. Individuals who grew up in a more favourable socioeconomic context are characterized by better physical and mental conditions later in life. This pattern appears to be largely explained by the positive effect played by a more inclusive parental background in improving the educational attainment, income and wealth outcomes of individuals over the lifecycle. These results highlight the long-run effects of public policies: promoting the social and economic inclusion of current generations improves their own lifetime well-being and that of their offspring.

References

Bengtsson, T. and Broström, G. (2009). Do conditions in early life affect old-age mortality directly and indirectly? Evidence from 19th-century rural Sweden. *Social Science & Medicine*, 68, pp. 1583–1590.

Brunello, G., Weber, G. and Weiss, C. T. (2017). "Books are forever: Early life conditions, education and lifetime earnings in Europe". *Economic Journal*, 127, pp. 271–296.

Cunha, F., Heckman, J. J. and Schennach, S. M. (2010). "Estimating the technology of cognitive and noncognitive skill formation". *Econometrica*, 78, pp. 883–931.

Mazzonna, F. (2014). The long-lasting effects of family background: A European cross-country comparison. *Economics of Education Review*, 40, pp. 25–42.

Riecher-Rössler, A. (2016). Sex and gender differences in mental disorders. *The Lancet Psychiatry*, 4(1), pp. 8–9.

Fabian Kratz and Johanna Bristle

10 Tracking and educational inequality in health in later life

- The role of educational systems in shaping health inequalities has received little attention
- Tracking, as one important property of educational systems, is associated with larger educational disparities in subjective and objective health
- The currently built policy databank SPLASH provides information and indicators on educational systems across European countries and policy changes over time

10.1 Educational tracking and health inequalities

Social conditions that shape processes of cumulative disadvantage over the life course heavily depend on the structure of the welfare state and vary cross-nationally. Although the role of the healthcare system gains significant attention in the literature on socio-economic disparities in health, the educational system is rarely considered. The initial empirical evidence on the importance of the educational system in shaping health inequalities comes from Mazzonna (2014), who showed that country-average years of education are related to health inequality. Carstensen and Jungbauer-Gans (2016) went one step further and theorized in detail how properties of the educational system, such as standardization and stratification, affect health levels and health inequality. We build on these considerations by arguing that one specific property of educational systems – tracking – reinforces the relation between education and health.

Following Kerckhoff (1995, 323), we define tracking as the extent of 'separation of students into specialized schools and ability groups'. Drawing on recent studies, we assume that the extent of tracking of an educational system is higher when the age at first selection into higher or lower educational tracks is lower, the relative length of the tracked curriculum is longer and the number of different school types that exist at age fifteen is higher (Bol and Van de Werfhorst, 2013).

Theoretical arguments and empirical findings provide a rational as to why educational systems with higher levels of tracking may generate a stronger link between education and health. We term them the stronger selection, the intermediate goods and the deprivation explanation.

https://doi.org/10.1515/9783110617245-010

First, the stronger selection explanation: In countries with higher levels of tracking, parental privilege might have a stronger influence on educational attainment (Brunello and Checchi, 2007). The younger the children are when decisions for school tracks need to be made, the higher the parental influence. Higher educated parents then pave the way into a higher education. Such a stronger positive selection of the highly educated may also relate to a stronger health advantage and, thus, a stronger link between education and health.

Second, the intermediate goods explanation: The higher the level of tracking, the stronger is the impact of education on adult socioeconomic status (i.e. employment probability, income, prestige or wealth; Bol and Van de Werfhorst, 2013). Such a stronger link between education and the intermediate goods that affect health may reinforce the link between education and health.

Third, the deprivation explanation: A higher level of tracking may exacerbate the negative effects of low educational achievement on health. Higher levels of tracking and, thus, a high selectivity in the educational system may exacerbate relative deprivation experiences, stigmatization processes and, thus, the psychological stress and burden from failure of those with low education. Higher psychological stress and the burden of having a lower education may reduce health and, thus, broaden the health gap between the lower and the higher educated (Carstensen and Jungbauer-Gans, 2016). As a result of these partly intertwined social processes, we expect that educational systems with higher levels of tracking generate stronger education-specific health inequality.

10.2 Data and method

This study uses data from SHARE Waves 1 to 6 from 15 countries (Sweden, Denmark, Germany, Luxembourg, the Netherlands, Belgium, France, Switzerland, Austria, Spain, Italy, Estonia, the Czech Republic, Slovenia and Israel). Furthermore, we concentrate on non-institutionalized individuals aged 50 to 85 years. Our analytical sample consists of 43,645 individuals with an average participation in 3 waves, resulting in 130,987 person-years; see Table 10.1 for descriptive statistics by country. We ran wave and country pooled regressions with country fixed-effects (Table 10.2).

We use two health measures as outcome variables. Self-perceived health, measured on a five-point scale ranging from 1 (poor) to 5 (excellent), provides a comprehensive and subjective health measure. In addition, physical impairment is used as an objective health measure and consists of self-reports on needing assistance with six activities of daily living (ADL).

Table 10.1: Descriptive Statistics by Country.

Country	Health (mean)		Education			Tracking	$N_{persons}$
	Sphus	noADL	Primary	Secondary	Tertiary		
SE	3.40	0.90	0.21	0.48	0.31	−1.06	3,023
DK	3.57	0.90	0.08	0.48	0.44	−.93	3,133
DE	2.85	0.84	0.01	0.68	0.31	1.79	3,441
LU	3.08	0.86	0.25	0.56	0.19	0.76	648
NL	3.17	0.92	0.09	0.62	0.29	0.97	1,926
BE	3.07	0.80	0.15	0.52	0.33	1.04	3,993
FR	2.89	0.84	0.32	0.47	0.22	−0.48	3,254
CH	3.40	0.94	0.09	0.77	0.15	−0.24	2,194
AT	3.08	0.85	0.12	0.64	0.25	1.75	3,392
ES	2.74	0.80	0.54	0.35	0.11	−0.80	4,070
IT	2.79	0.82	0.46	0.46	0.08	0.18	3,524
EE	2.21	0.74	0.04	0.74	0.22	n.a.	3,773
CZ	2.67	0.82	0.12	0.75	0.13	1.67	4,394
SI	2.71	0.80	0.08	0.75	0.17	0.76	2,163
IL	3.32	0.86	0.26	0.40	0.35	−0.13	717
Total	2.95	0.91	0.20	0.57	0.23	0.39	43,645

Note: All descriptives are clustered at the person level.
Source: SHARE Wave 1–6 release 6.1.0, Tracking indicator by Bol and Van de Werfhorst (2013).

Table 10.2: Pooled LPM Regression with Education-Country Interactions.

	Self-perceived health	No physical impairment
Education (ref: primary)		
secondary	0.340***	0.046**
	(0.038)	(0.014)
tertiary	0.544***	0.073***
	(0.044)	(0.014)
Country dummies	x	x
Country*Education interactions	x	x
Observations	130,987	130,987
R^2	0.211	0.053

Note: Beta coefficients reported. Standard errors are clustered at the person level and are reported in parentheses; * $p < 0.05$, ** $p < 0.01$, *** $p < 0.001$. Unweighted sample. Controlled for gender, birth cohort, parental status during childhood, health conditions during childhood, period effects, panel conditioning and panel attrition.
Source: SHARE Wave 1–6 release 6.1.0.

Educational attainment is measured by ISCED-97 and is divided into three categories (ISCED level 0–1 refers to primary, 2–4 to secondary and 5–6 to tertiary).

As a measure of the extent of tracking of the educational system, we use a relative tracking index developed by Bol and Van de Werfhorst (2013). The authors combine OECD indicators from 2002 and 2005 and a measure by Brunello and Checchi (2007) and derive the index using a factor analysis. This latent concept of tracking comprises three variables: age at first selection into higher or lower educational tracks, relative length of the tracked curriculum and the number of different school types that exist at age fifteen. The tracking index is available for all countries in our sample, besides Estonia. We prefer tracking during the historical time when our respondents attended school (1940–1970) but do not have this information available. However, the educational expansion and significant educational reforms, such as the extension of compulsory schooling in the last century, do not necessarily imply changes in educational tracking. Bol and Van de Werfhorst (2013) showed that, over time, this tracking index varies significantly between countries but little within countries.

In all models, we control for gender, birth cohort before, during or after World War II, parental socio-economic status during childhood, self-perceived health, having two or more diseases and illnesses during childhood and school performance at age 10 in mathematics and language. Parental socio-economic status during childhood is constructed as an index based on principal component analysis following Mazzonna (2014) and includes parental education, the financial situation of the household at age 10 and the rooms-per-person ratio of the household at age 10. We expect period effects of the financial crisis in 2009 and control whether the interview was conducted before 2009. We also control for ageing as age deciles and its squared term. We account for panel conditioning in all models using an indicator for the first participation and for panel attrition by including a dummy if the respondent dropped out of the sample (alive or unknown) or died during the observation period (reference is stayed in the panel). In all models, we include country-fixed effects for the entire sample.

10.3 Results

In a first step, we ran pooled linear probability models (LPM) with binary outcomes on '*very good/excellent health*' (versus *poor, fair* and *good* on the self-perceived health scale) and '*not reporting any physical impairment*' (out of the six potential limitations) with country fixed effects. This approach allows for a comparison of the magnitude of the coefficients. Although the coefficients of objective health were smaller than for subjective health, especially for tertiary education, they showed significant disparities between low and high education. Therefore, qualitatively, the objective and subjective measures revealed the same conclusions on health inequality, and our results were in line with the general tendency that subjective measures showed larger inequalities than objective measures.

In a second step, we graphically explore the association of our baseline results from the pooled sample with a tracking indicator to descriptively investigate one precise institutional measure. In Figure 10.1 and Figure 10.2, the country-specific education effect on health (more specifically, the average marginal effect of tertiary education with reference to primary education for each country) is contrasted with the degree of educational tracking in each country. The results show that the educational health gap indeed relates to the level of tracking of the national educational system. The association appears regardless of whether we use subjective or objective health measures.

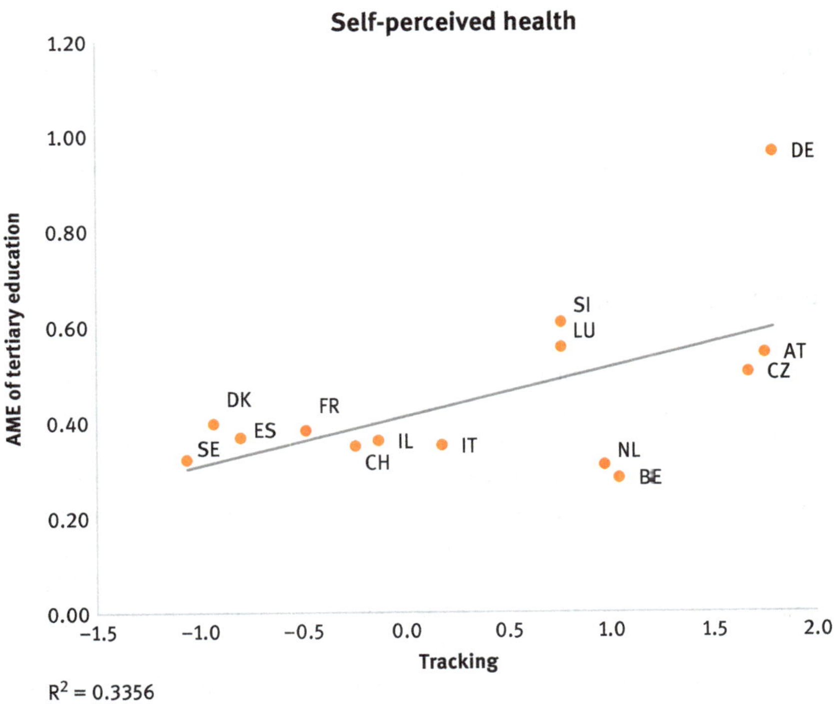

Figure 10.1: Education-health gap and tracking for subjective health (self-rated health).
Source: SHARE Wave 1–6 release 6.1.0.

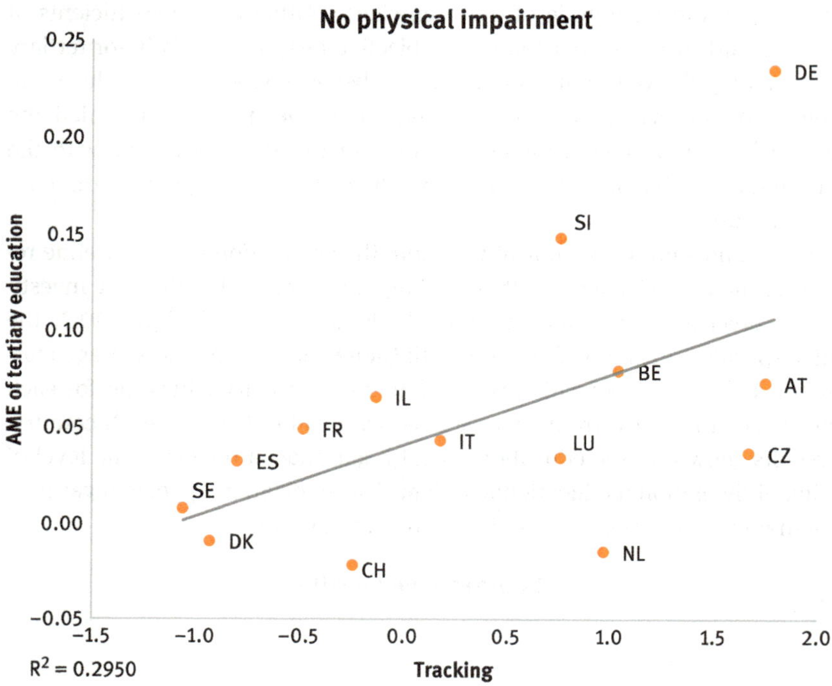

Figure 10.2: Education-health gap and tracking for objective health (no physical impairment).
Source: SHARE Wave 1–6 release 6.1.0.

10.4 Conclusion

This paper provides theoretical considerations and the first empirical evidence on the relation between educational tracking and educational inequalities in health. The descriptive analysis clearly has methodological drawbacks.

One limitation relates to (unobserved) heterogeneity. Our descriptive approach does not preclude the possibility that country characteristics relate to tracking and brings about stronger education health gaps at older ages. For example, countries with higher degrees of tracking may also be those with higher proportions of private healthcare, and inequalities in access to healthcare may generate a stronger link between education and health.

To tackle this issue, future research could employ a multilevel analysis with cross-level interactions between tracking at the country level and educational attainment at the individual level. When the number of countries is sufficiently large, such an empirical strategy allows for controlling of country-specific characteristics, thereby accounting for time-constant, country-specific observed heterogeneity. Starting Wave 7, the number of countries participating in SHARE increased to 28, which enables the analysis of a broad range of countries in the upcoming waves. A further, perhaps even more promising, approach could use historical changes in tracking that reflect the education system when the respondents were of schooling age. Such inter-cohort variations within countries allow for within-country analyses that allow accounting for observed time-variant and unobserved time-constant heterogeneity.

New data collection projects give reason to hope that the basis for such analyses will soon be available. The promising new research project SPLASH (Social Policy and Law Shared Database) is currently establishing a large policy databank on European countries that dates back in time and will incorporate information on educational systems. Further research could use the SPLASH indicators to employ the empirical strategies previously sketched out.

Furthermore, future research should attempt to disentangle different explanations for the reported association between tracking and education-specific health inequality at older ages. To examine the importance of the selection explanation, scholars could investigate how much of the larger education health gap in countries with higher levels of tracking relates to greater selectivity of those with higher education than those with lower education. To scrutinize the intermediate goods explanation, scholars could include a variety of adult socio-economic status measures in the analysis to investigate how much of the larger education health gap in countries with higher levels of tracking relates to stronger education-specific differences in intermediate goods that affect health. To investigate the importance of the deprivation explanation, scholars could examine the role of education-specific differences in relative deprivation experiences, stigmatization processes and psychological stress in explaining tracking variations in the educational health gap.

Having said this, this contribution also has important strengths. This study outlines the theoretical mechanisms for why higher levels of tracking may exacerbate the link between education and old age health. Furthermore, this study sketches empirical strategies and their respective assumptions. Finally, this study is the first to show descriptive evidence that allows for the cautious conclusion that such a relation could exist for both objective and subjective health. If future research shows that this relation is robust, our findings imply that higher levels of tracking generate inequalities that go a long way and may even increase health inequalities in old age.

References

Bol, T., and Van de Werfhorst, H. (2013). The measurement of tracking, vocational orientation, and standardization of educational systems: a comparative approach. *Gini Discussion Paper*, 81 AIAS, Amsterdam Institute for Advanced Labour Studies.

Brunello, G., and Checchi, D. (2007). Does school tracking affect equality of opportunity? New international evidence. *Economic Policy*, 22, 781–861.

Carstensen, J., and Jungbauer-Gans, M. (2016). Health returns on education and educational systems. In A. Hadjar, and C. Gross (Eds.), *Education Systems and Inequalities: International Comparisons* pp. (301–320). Bristol: Policy Press.

Kerckhoff, A.C. (1995). Institutional arrangements and stratification processes in industrial societies. *Annual Review of Sociology*, 21, 323–347.

Mazzonna, F. (2014). The long-lasting effects of family background: A European cross-country comparison. *Economics of Education Review*, 40, 25–42.

Part III Labour market, occupation and retirement

Edited by Agar Brugiavini

Yuri Pettinicchi and Axel Börsch-Supan

11 Long-term effects of different labour careers

- Many individuals experience some inactivity during their working lives: 15 per cent of men and 52 per cent of women
- Female working careers are also characterized by a broader dispersion, especially among older women. The reverse is true for males: younger males show a broader dispersion, probably attributable to the unemployment effects of the great recession following the financial crisis
- At-risk-of-poverty rates are higher for individuals with a large share of inactiveness but decrease with the number of job spells

11.1 Introduction

Multiple jobs and labour inactivity are usually associated with lower employability and lower social protection. Therefore, the long-term effect of such careers may be monetary poverty in old age. This topic is important because non-standard labour careers, that is, careers in which individuals have not always been working between the end of their full-time education and the beginning of their retirement, have recently become more prevalent. Career breaks often affect the ability to accumulate tenure-specific rights that provide social security. Specifically, individuals with longer spells of labour inactivity have reduced access to pension rights and, therefore, lower pension income. Career breaks occur because of unemployment, care for children and other dependent family members or homemaking.

This chapter computes the share of active labour market participation during an individual's life course. We also count the number of job spells to distinguish workers with dynamic careers, that is, workers who changed several jobs over a lifetime. On the one hand, jobs changes may imply income improvements attributable to promotion or better matching. On the other hand, a large number of job changes may also be attributable to many exits from and re-entries into the labour market that are likely to reduce income growth over the life cycle.

We identify four categories of labour careers: always active individuals with one job spell, always active individuals with several job spells, seldom active individuals with one job spell and seldom active individuals with several job spells.

https://doi.org/10.1515/9783110617245-011

11.2 Working careers

The richness of the information available in the SHARE Wave 7 data allows us to identify the working careers of older workers and retirees in Europe. SHARE Wave 7 asked respondents about each working spell longer than 6 months during their lifetimes. A similar set of retrospective questions was asked in Wave 3 ('SHARELIFE'). We use the information available in both the retrospective waves (Waves 3 and 7) and the interim waves (4, 5 and 6) to bridge the information gap for the respondents whose working histories were collected in Wave 3.

To each year of life, we assign an employment state beginning at age 6 and ending at the age at the time of the interview. Employment states can take one of the following values: full-time education, active, inactive, retired and other. 'Active' refers to any paid job, that is, employee, self-employed, civil servant and military services, whereas 'inactive' refers to unemployment (whether or not actively searching for a job), homemaking and caring for dependent family members.

Approximately 70,000 individuals participated in the Wave 7 survey in 2017. Table 11.1 reports the number of observed spells and the average length of the different employment states. The average length of the sequences is approximately 63.5 years. For men, 60 per cent of this time is spent in the active state (38 years), while only 44 per cent (28 years) is spent in the active state for women. The subgroup of individuals who experienced some inactivity during their working life is large: 15 per cent of the male sample and 52 per cent for the female sample. Among them, years of inactivity amount to 7 years for men and 20 years for women.

Figure 11.1 also splits the sample into three age classes: 50–64, 65–80 and 80+. Figure 11.1 also shows that the average length of inactivity is shorter for men than for women in all age groups and is becoming longer for older cohorts.

We also want to account for differences in the institutional framework that regulates the labour market and social security across European countries. Figure 11.2 reports the average length of employment states by country and by gender. The set of countries includes Austria, Belgium, Bulgaria, Croatia, Cyprus, Czech Republic, Denmark, Estonia, Finland, France, Germany, Greece, Hungary, Israel, Italy, Latvia, Lithuania, Luxembourg, Malta, Poland, Portugal, Romania, Slovakia, Slovenia, Spain, Sweden and Switzerland.

Differences between countries reflect differences in the institutional framework. Richer countries have a longer average duration of full-time education and shorter average duration of inactivity.

Table 11.1: Employment spells

	Number of spells Men/ Women	Average Length Men	Average Length Women	Conditional Average Length Men	Conditional Average Length Women
Whole sequence	29,929 / 39,678	63.7	63.6	--	--
Potential Working Life	29,515 / 38,529	39.7	39.2	40.3	39.8
Employment states					
Full time education	29,233 / 38,384	12.7	12.1	13.1	12.5
Active	29,424 / 35,271	38.7	28.4	39.3	32.0
Inactive	4,400 / 20,477	1.0	10.8	7.2	20.8
• Unemployed	3,645 / 5,509	0.8	1.3	6.6	9.9
• Family	8,43 / 16,645	0.3	9.4	9.3	22.3
Retired	20,632 / 26,994	9.0	8.8	13.3	14.4
Do not know – other	8,364 / 10,340	2.2	3.4	7.7	13.3

Note: The table reports the averaged length in years by employment state of the individual careers. Row "Whole sequence" refers to the full sequence from 6 to the age of the interview. Row "Potential Working life" refers to the subsequence from the end of the full time education up to retirement (or up the age of interview if still working). Column "Number of spells" reports the number of sequence with at least one year with the related state for men and women. Column "Average Length" is the average duration of the related state in the whole sample. Column "Conditional Average Length" refers to the average of the sample with sequences having at least one year with the related states.
Source: SHARE wave 7 release 7.0.0.

11.3 Labour inactivity as a share of working life

A closer look at respondents who experienced at least one year of inactivity helps clarify whether career interruptions have a temporary nature or are a

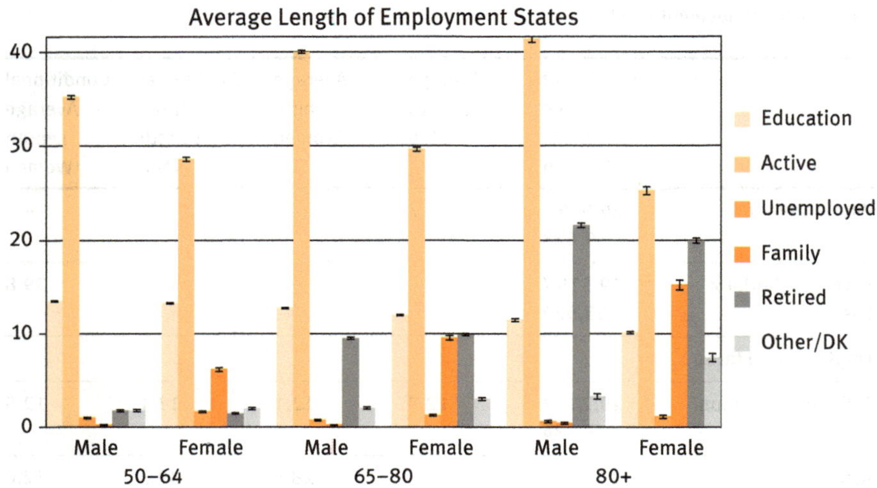

Figure 11.1: Average length (in years) of the employment states of SHARE Wave 7 respondents by gender and class of age.

Note: Sample size for age group 50–64 is 9,685/13,892 (M/F), for 65–80 is 15,208/18,492 and for 80+ is 5,036/7,294.

Source: SHARE Wave 7 release 0.

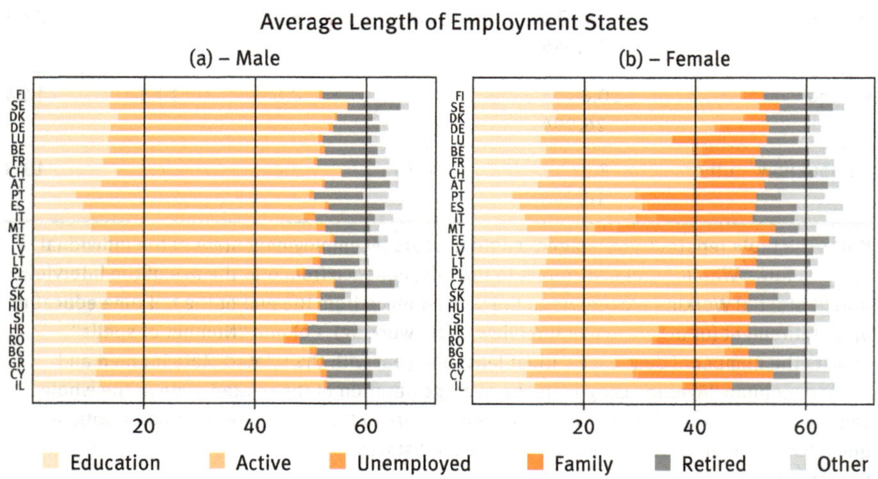

Figure 11.2: Average length (in years) of employment states of SHARE Wave 7 respondents by country.

Note: Sample sizes of the countries range between 390 (PT) to 4,620 (EE), mean 2,578, std. dev. 1,198.

Source: SHARE Wave 7 release 0.

signal of permanent exit from the labour market. Moreover, we assess the impact on the sustainability of the pension system by studying the distribution of the inactivity shares.

Figure 11.3 displays the conditional distribution of the inactivity share by year of birth. Conditional means that the sample is restricted to those with at least one year of inactivity and more than 50 per cent of their life before retirement (interview) as a potential worker. Figure 11.3 displays the median (p50) and four percentiles (10%, 25%, 75% and 90%). The dispersion is expressed as the difference between p10 and p75 or p90. Older women have higher median values of inactiveness and are characterized by a broader dispersion. Thus, in future years, a smaller fraction of women is likely to need access to minimum social security benefits because they will probably acquire more often adequate own contribution records. For men, the picture is reversed. Younger males show a larger dispersion probably as a result of the unemployment effects of the great recession following the financial crisis.

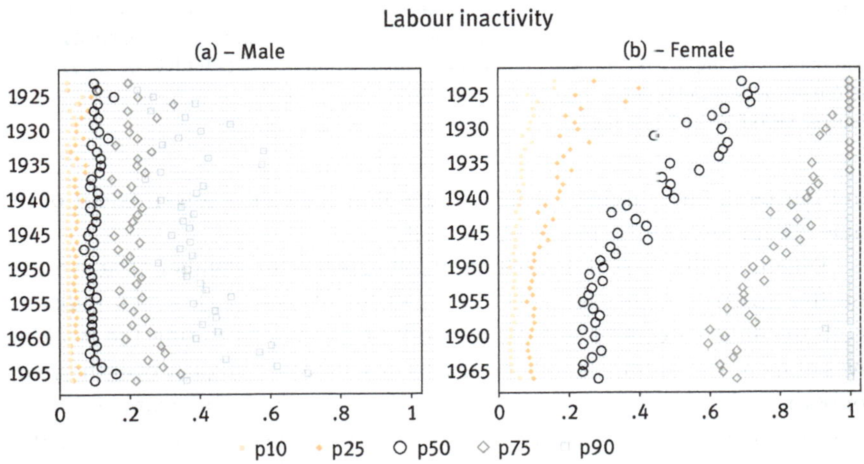

Figure 11.3: Conditional distribution of share of inactivity by year of birth
Note: Share of inactivity is the percentage of potential working life in unemployment and family caring. The sample is restricted to respondents with at least one year of inactivity, with year of birth during 1923–1966 and a potential working life that accounts for half of the years before retirement (interview).
Source: SHARE Wave 7 release 0.

Considerable differences also exist across countries, which may be the result of welfare state policies, social norms or cultural factors. Figure 11.4 displays the conditional distribution of the share of inactiveness by country. Countries that are more 'family centred', such as Austria, Belgium, Greece, Italy, Spain

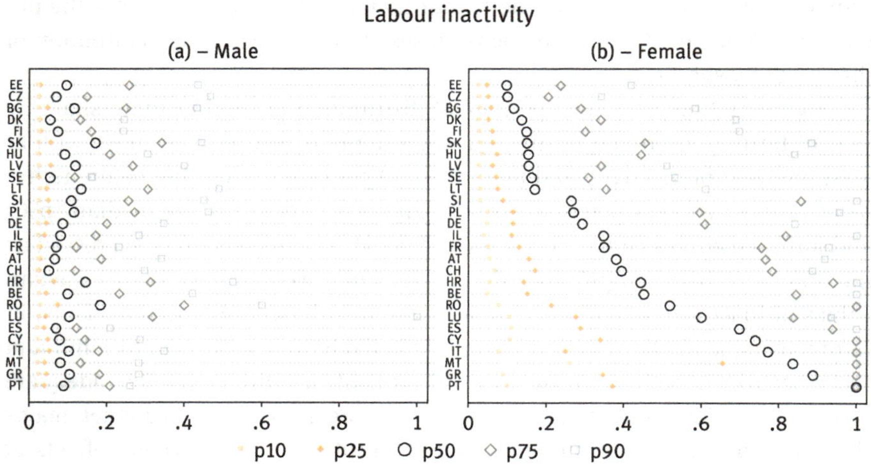

Figure 11.4: Conditional distribution of share of inactivity per country.
Note: Share of inactivity is the percentage of potential working life in unemployment and family caring. The sample is restricted to respondents with at least one year of inactivity, with year of birth during 1923–1966 and potential working life that accounts for half of the years before retirement (interview).
Source: SHARE Wave 7 release 0.

and Portugal, have higher median values that indicate a lower extent of female labour force participation in the past.

Regarding the second dimension of job careers, the number of active and inactive spells is higher for men (2.6) than for women (2.2), which indicates more dynamic careers or less stable working conditions during the working lives of men. The average number of spells has increased slightly over the years for both men and women: younger cohorts have more often interrupted careers. This phenomenon, which deserves further analysis, might be the result of structural changes in the economy, macroeconomic conditions in the wake of the financial crisis or other reasons.

11.4 Impact on current household income and old-age poverty

To analyse monetary poverty, we use the concept of household equivalized disposable income, which is defined as a household's total income after taxes and other deductions that is available for spending or saving, divided by the weighted number of household members. Household members are weighted according to their age using the so-called modified OECD equivalence scale.

Figure 11.5 reports median household equivalized income by number of active spells and share of inactiveness. The number of active spells is grouped into 6 categories from zero to 5 or more. The inactivity share is reported in 3 categories from 100 per cent active, 50–99 per cent active to less than 50 per cent active. As expected, active workers always have higher current incomes. Income is also increasing in the number of job spells. Median incomes for always-active men are higher than for always-active women but lower in the case of career interruptions. This finding is interesting and requires a deeper analysis of multiple spell careers observed in the appropriate household context.

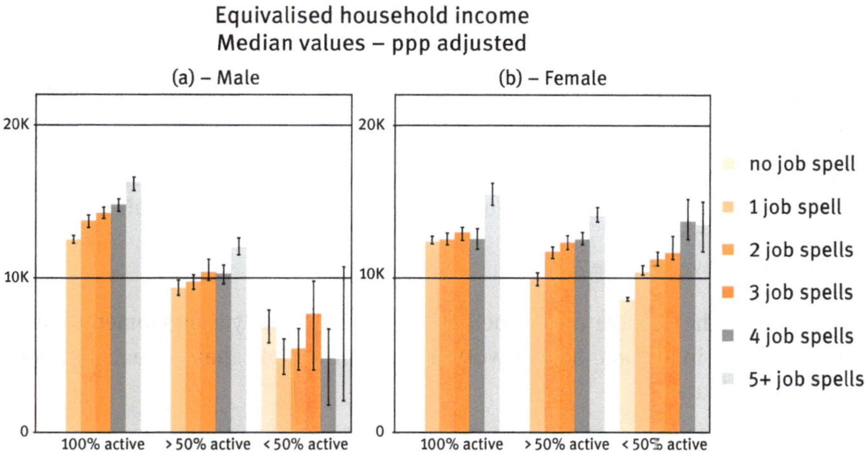

Figure 11.5: Equivalized household income per share of inactivity and number of job spells, median values.

Note: Sample size per share of activity class: Male – 100% (0/6,402/5,717/3,673/2,279/2,923), > 50% (0/829/853/693/461/714), > 50% (83/63/55/26/18/14); Female – 100% (0/5,787/3,958/2,402/1,333/1,646), > 50% (0/1,980/2,685/2,126/1,512/1,958), > 50% (2,604/2,248/1,033/499/201/118).

Source: SHARE Wave 7 release 0.

We define an individual as 'at risk of poverty' if it has an equivalized disposable income (after social transfers) lower than 60 per cent of the national median equivalized disposable income (after social transfers). The share of individuals at-risk-of-poverty, the AROP rate, measures not absolute poverty but low income in comparison to other residents in that country.

Figure 11.6 reports the AROP rates by number of active spells and share of inactiveness. AROP rates increase as the share of inactiveness increases but

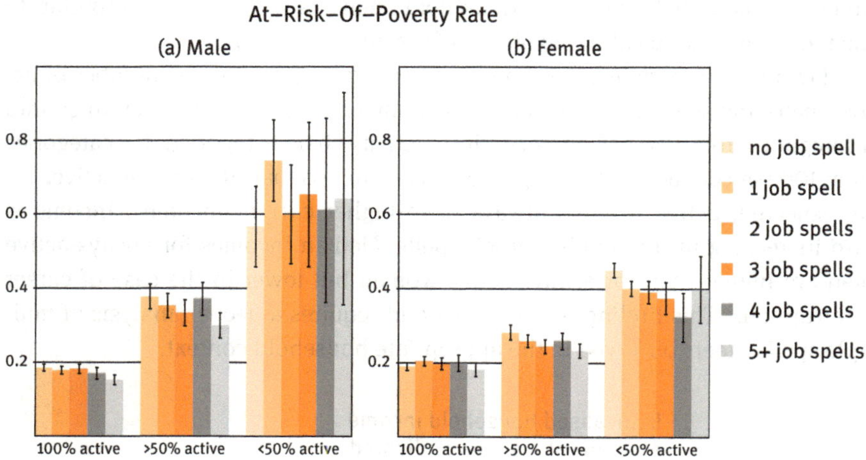

Figure 11.6: At-Risk-Of-Poverty (AROP) rates per share of inactivity and number of job spells, values in percentages.

Note: Sample size per share of activity class: Male – 100% (0/6,402/5,717/3,673/2,279/2,923), >50% (0/829/853/693/461/714), <50% (83/63/55/26/18/14); Female – 100% (0/5,787/3,958/2,402/1,333/1,646), >50% (0/1,980/2,685/2,126/1,512/1,958), <50% (2,604/2,248/1,033/499/201/118).

Source: SHARE Wave 7 release 7.0.0.

decrease with the number of job spells. Men are more likely than women to be at risk of poverty in old age after a working life with a low share of active labour market participation.

11.5 Conclusions

This paper uses approximately 70,000 life histories from Wave 7 to measure the share of active labour market participation during the life course and counted the number of job spells. On average, our data cover approximately 63.5 years. For men, 60 per cent of this time is spent in the active state (38 years), but this figure is only 44 per cent (28 years) for women. Many individuals experience some inactivity during their working lives: 15 per cent of the male sample and 52 per cent for female. For them, years of inactivity amount to 7 (men) and 20 (women).

Female working careers are also characterized by a broader dispersion. Thus, in future years, a smaller fraction of women will likely need to access minimum social security benefits because they will probably acquire more often adequate own contribution records. For men, the picture is reversed. Younger males show a larger dispersion, probably the result of the unemployment effects of the great recession following the financial crisis.

Differences across countries may be the result of welfare state policies. Countries that are more 'family-centred', such as Austria, Belgium, Greece, Italy, Spain and Portugal, have higher median values of inactivity, indicating a lower extent of female labour force participation in the past.

Always active workers have higher current incomes. Income is also increasing with the number of job spells. Median incomes for always-active men are higher than for always-active women during their life course. Interestingly, this situation is reversed in the case of career interruptions.

At-risk-of-poverty rates are higher for individuals with a large share of inactiveness but decrease with the number of job spells. Men are more likely than women to be at risk of poverty in old age after a working life with a low share of active labour market participation.

Yuri Pettinicchi and Axel Börsch-Supan

12 The economic situation of formerly self-employed workers

- Formerly self-employed workers earn lower pension incomes than formerly traditionally-employed workers
- Formerly self-employed workers are more at risk of poverty during retirement
- Formerly self-employed workers rely more on financial assets outside the public pension systems

12.1 Introduction

Many self-employed workers deal with more precarious working conditions than their traditionally-employed counterparts and lack the safety net provided by job-related agreements between workers and employers. During their working life, many earn less and bear more risk than employees (Hamilton 2000, Maskowitz and Vissing-Jørgensen 2002). In many countries, self-employed workers also have reduced access to public pension rights and often need to manage on an individual basis their risky financial decisions, such as pension plan participation and contributions (Möhring 2014). Thus, their pension adequacy is of significant concern (EU Pension Adequacy Report 2018).

The aim of this chapter is to use the SHARE life histories collected in Wave 7 to compare the economic situation in old age of formerly self-employed and formerly traditionally-employed workers.

A closer look at self-employed workers shows different groups of these workers. One group chooses self-employment to have a greater degree of control over their working conditions. For the other group, self-employment is a transitory stage in the struggle to access a traditionally-employed job.

The first group offsets the higher costs involved in the risky income profile with higher income growth. The jobs taken by the first group can be viewed as experiments of innovative ideas that continue in the case of success or that revert to employed jobs in the case of failure (Kerr *et al.* 2014). These workers can rely on market solutions to insure themselves against negative shocks (income, health, others) that could lead to poverty.

https://doi.org/10.1515/9783110617245-012

The second group is self-employed for exogenous factors specific to the labour market. Their self-employment could be the result of sector characteristics, such as seasonality in agriculture and fishery. Self-employment could also be the result of legal innovations aimed at increasing the flexibility of the labour market, which is in turn exploited by employers to externalize labour costs, creating *bogus* self-employment figures (self-employed with a one-to-one work relationship). Self-employment could be the result of technological innovation that fosters the so-called gig-economy and on-demand jobs. These workers are constrained by lower labour income when they rely on personal savings to insure themselves.

12.2 Prevalence of former self-employment

The comparison between current retirees who were formerly self-employed versus those who were formerly employees in dependent employment is made possible by the availability of the retrospective information of respondents in Wave 7. SHARE asked each respondent about each working spell longer than 6 months. A similar set of retrospective questions was asked in Wave 3 (named 'SHARELIFE'). We use the information available in the interim Waves (4, 5 and 6) to bridge the information gap for respondents who were interviewed in Wave 3.

We distinguish two subsamples: retirees and workers. In both subsamples, individuals are older than 50 years according to the SHARE eligibility age. We call a respondent 'formerly self-employed' if she has worked for at least 50 per cent of her working life to date. More information about the sample selection criteria is available in Pettinicchi and Börsch-Supan (2018). The average duration of working lives accounts for 38 (41) years for workers (retirees).

Figure 12.1 reports the prevalence of former self-employment in the two subsamples.

Differences between countries reflect differences in labour markets. South European countries display a higher prevalence of self-employed, whereas the lower prevalence in eastern European countries is the result of the non-market economy in place during the pre-1990 period.

12.3 Old-age poverty measures

We follow two different approaches to measure monetary poverty: self-reported financial distress and an income-based poverty measure.

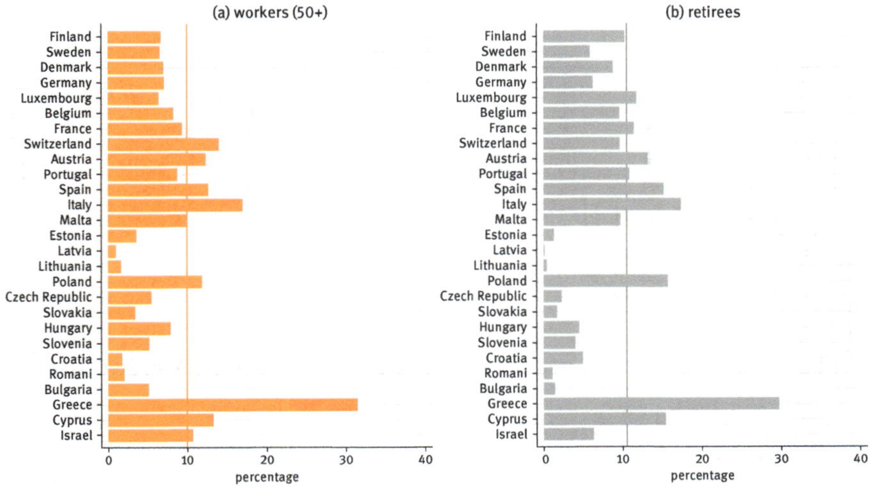

Figure 12.1: Prevalence of formerly self-employed workers by country.
Note: Vertical lines show the weighted average. Panel (a) refers to workers. Panel (b) refers to retirees.
Source: SHARE Wave 7 release 0.

Self-reported financial hardship is captured by the SHARE question '*Thinking of your household's total monthly income, would you say that your household is able to make ends meet… 1. With great difficulty 2. With some difficulty 3. Fairly easily 4. Easily*'. This computation is based on recoded answers (1 to 'easily' and 4 to 'with great difficult'). Higher values mean a greater inability to make ends meet. Figure 12.2 displays the weighted average values by country. Formerly self-employed workers (retirees) report higher financial distress with respect to formerly traditionally-employed workers.

The income-based poverty measure is computed using equivalized disposable income, which is the total income of a household after taxes and other deductions that is available for spending or saving, divided by the equivalized number of household members. Household members are equivalized by weighting each member according to their age using the so-called modified OECD equivalence scale.

Figure 12.3 displays country-specific median values of the equivalized disposable income. The values are adjusted for international differences in purchasing power.

Although we find mixed evidence for current workers, we find a statistically significant income gap between the formerly self-employed and the formerly traditionally-employed in the subsample of retirees.

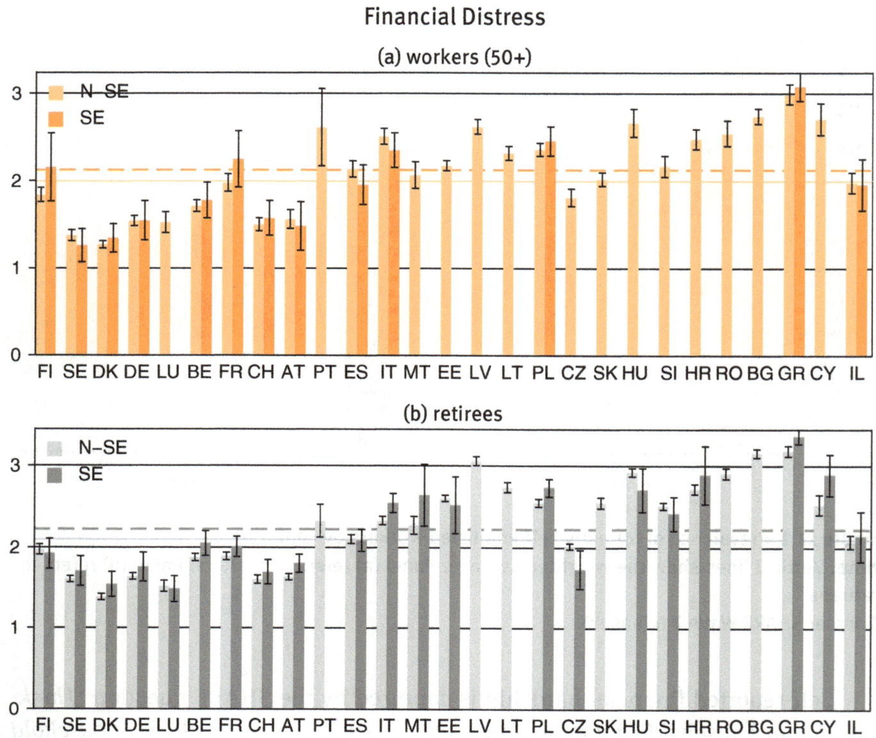

Figure 12.2: Average financial distress by country.
Note: A high score indicates lower quality of life. Min: 1, Max: 4. Panel (a) refers to workers. Panel (b) refers to retirees. N-SE refers to formerly traditionally-employed. SE refers to formerly self-employed. Horizontal lines are weighted averages over the SHARE countries. The value is not reported if the sample size is smaller than 25 observations.
Source: SHARE Wave 7 release 0.

The income-based poverty measure is computed as the share of people with equivalized disposable income (after social transfer) below the at-risk-of-poverty threshold, which is set at 60 per cent of the national median equivalized disposable income (after social transfers). This indicator, the at-risk-of-poverty (AROP) rate, does not measure wealth or poverty but rather income relative to other residents in that country, which does not necessarily imply a low standard of living.

Figure 12.4 reports the AROP rates by country. The formerly self-employed receive a lower income than the formerly traditionally-employed, perhaps explained by missing opportunities in income growth. The gap becomes more severe during retirement and is almost twice as large as that of current workers.

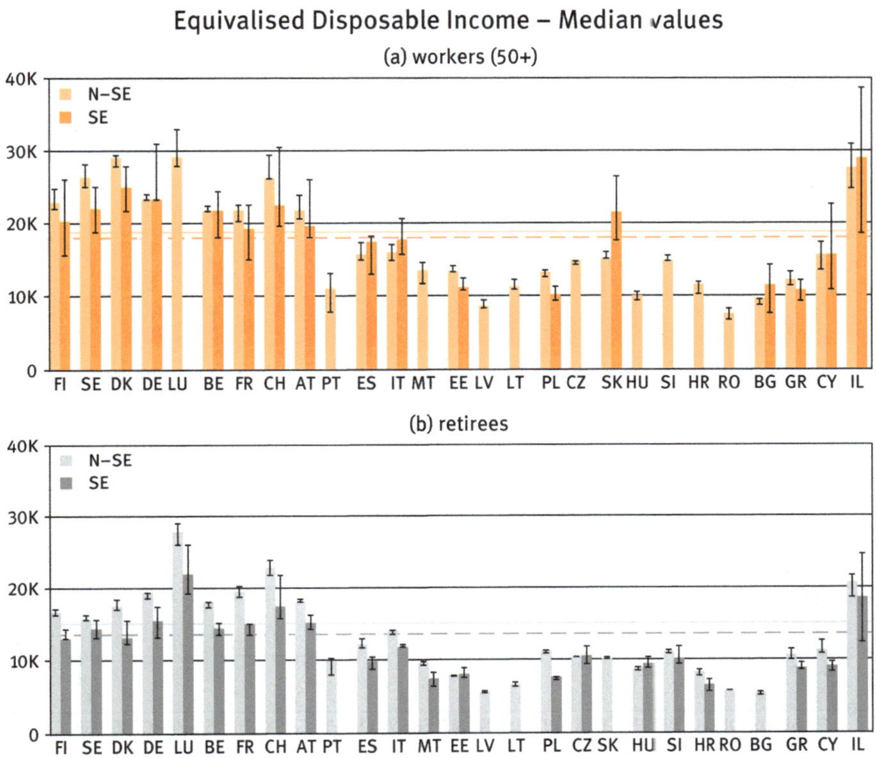

Figure 12.3: Equivalized disposable income by country (median values).
Note: Panel (a) refers to workers. Panel (b) refers to retirees. N-SE refers to formerly traditionally-employed. SE refers to formerly self-employed. Horizontal lines are weighted averages over the SHARE countries. The value is not reported if the sample size is smaller than 25 observations.
Source: SHARE Wave 7 release 0.

12.4 Income distributions and inequality

To shed light on the composition of the formerly self-employed group, we look at country-specific income distributions. For several countries, the mode of income distribution of the formerly self-employed is just before the AROP threshold. This finding implies that a lump-sum transfer in addition to their pension income would considerably reduce the AROP rates.

The income distribution of the formerly self-employed has a fatter right tail than that of the formerly traditionally-employed. This distribution reflects the presence of highly successful self-employed. For more details, see

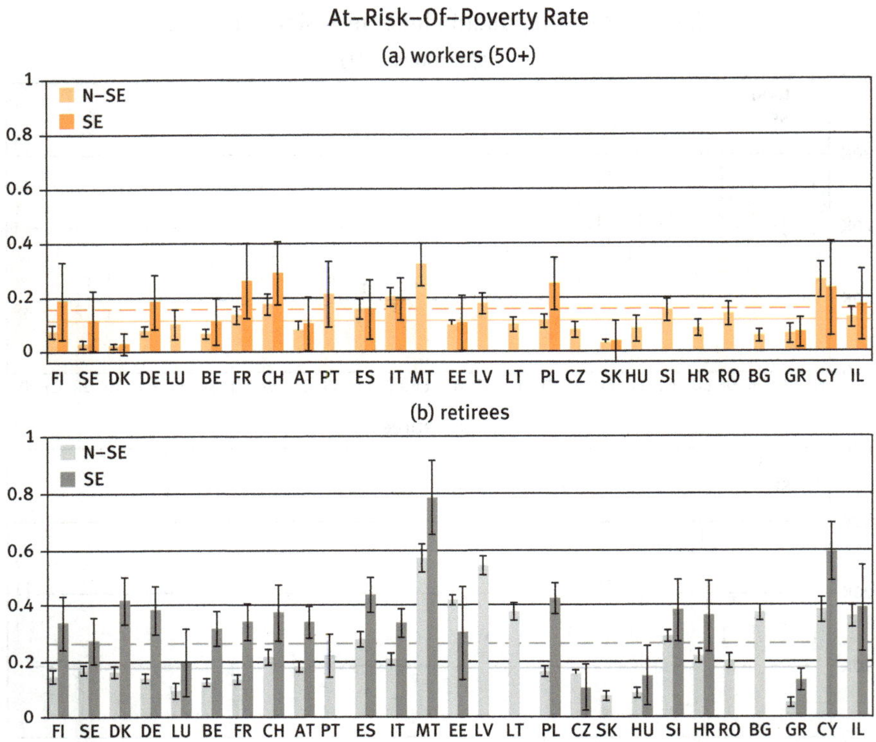

Figure 12.4: At-risk-of-poverty (AROP) rates by country.
Note: Panel (a) refers to workers. Panel (b) refers to retirees. N-SE refers to formerly traditionally-employed. SE refers to formerly self-employed. Horizontal lines are weighted averages over the SHARE countries. The value is not reported if the sample size is smaller than 25 observations.
Source: SHARE Wave 7 release 0.

Pettinicchi and Börsch-Supan (2018). We can describe income inequality with a single number using the income quintile share ratio (also called the S80/S20 ratio). This ratio is calculated as the ratio of total income received by the 20 per cent of the population with the highest income (the top quintile) to that received by the 20 per cent of the population with the lowest income (the bottom quintile). Figure 12.5 displays the income quintile share ratio by country.

Formerly self-employed workers displayed higher income inequality than formerly traditionally-employed workers. This difference is smaller for the subsample of retired workers.

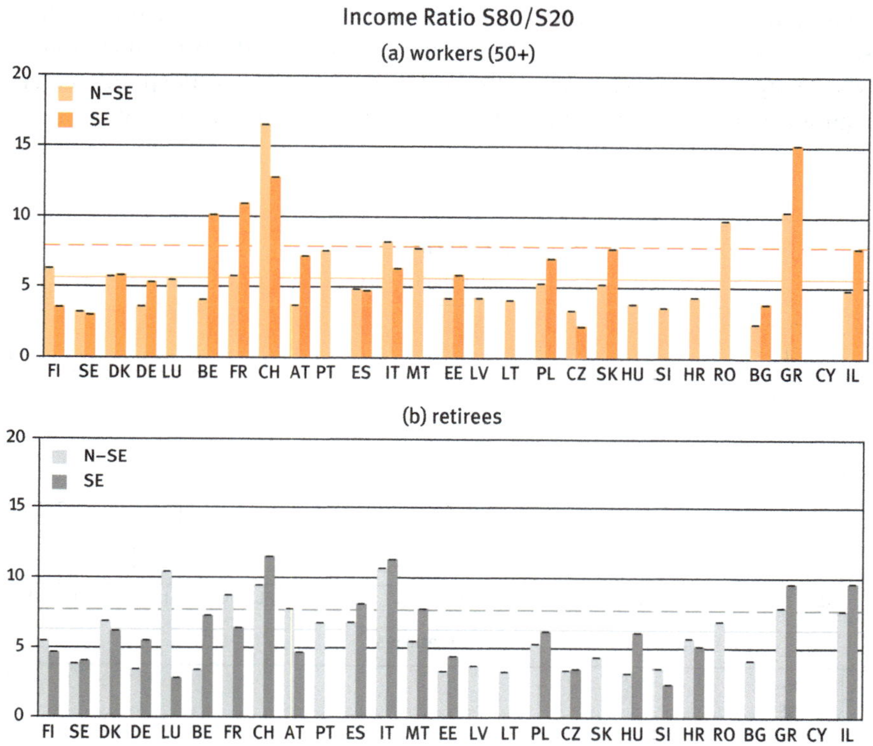

Figure 12.5: Income quintile share ratio by country, which is the ratio of the sum of the average equivalized household size of the top quintile to that of the bottom quintile of the income distribution.
Note: Panel (a) refers to workers. Panel (b) refers to retirees. N-SE refers to formerly traditionally-employed. SE refers to formerly self-employed. Horizontal lines are weighted averages over the SHARE countries. The value is not reported if the sample size is smaller than 25 observations.
Source: SHARE Wave 7 release 0.

12.5 Financial assets as self-insurance

SHARE also provides information about the accumulated financial assets of the formerly self-employed out of the public pension system. We compute the net liquid assets–income ratio, that is, the ratio of liquid assets minus debts to household annual income. This ratio conveys the notion of how many years a household can live on only its liquid assets. We use SHARE Wave 6 data.

Relative to their income, formerly self-employed workers accumulate more financial assets outside the public pension system than formerly traditionally-employed workers. This situation holds for both workers and retirees and is stronger for richer countries. Moreover, the gap between the two groups widens when they retire, which may be the result of cashing in work-specific assets. Figure 12.6 displays the net financial asset to income ratio by country.

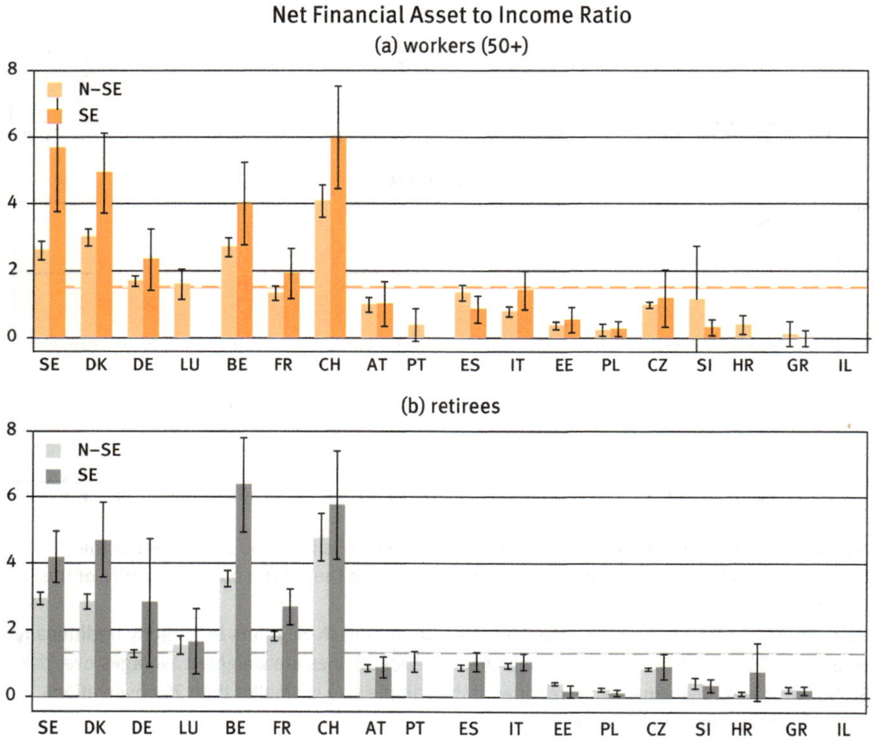

Figure 12.6: Net financial asset to income ratio by country.

Note: Net financial assets are calculated as the sum of the value of deposits, mutual funds, bonds, non-self-employment business wealth, (publicly traded) shares and managed accounts, net of credit line/overdraft debt, credit card debt and other non-mortgage debt. Income is the total household income. Both measures use imputed values. Panel (a) refers to workers. Panel (b) refers to retirees. N-SE refers to formerly traditionally-employed. SE refers to formerly self-employed. Horizontal lines are weighted averages over the SHARE countries. The value is not reported if the sample size is smaller than 25 observations.

Source: SHARE Wave 6 release 6.1.0.

12.6 Conclusions

Formerly self-employed retirees report a higher degree of financial distress and have lower incomes. They rely more on financial assets outside the public pension systems to cope with income and health shocks during their retirement. Their empirical income distribution represents them as a highly diverse group with a high degree of income inequality. Although some are rich in retirement, the formerly self-employed are more often at risk of poverty than their formerly traditionally-employed counterparts.

References

Hamilton, B H. (2000) Does Entrepreneurship Pay? An Empirical Analysis of the Returns to Self-Employment. *Journal of Political Economy*, 108 (3) pp. 604–631, DOI: 10.1086/262131

Kerr, W R., Nanda, R., and Rhodes-Kropf, M. (2014) Entrepreneurship as Experimentation. *Journal of Economic Perspectives*, 28 (3) pp. 25–48, DOI: 10.1257/jep.28.3.25

Möhring, M. (2014) Employment Histories and Pension Incomes in Europe. *European Societies*, 17 (1) pp. 3–26, DOI: 10.1080/14616696.2014.934874

Moskowitz, T. J., Vissing-Jørgensen, A. (2002) The Returns to Entrepreneurial Investment: A Private Equity Premium Puzzle? *American Economic Review*, 92 (4) pp. 745–778. DOI: 10.1257/00028280260344452

Pension adequacy report 2018 – Current and future income adequacy in old age in the EU (Volume 1). Catalog N.: KE-01-18-457-EN-N

Pettinicchi, Y., Börsch-Supan, A. (2018) Using SHARE data to measure pension and other income among old workers and retired self-employed people. *Internal Working Document*, Munich Center for the Economics of Aging (MEA) at the Max Planck Institute for Social Law and Social Policy.

Agnieszka Chłoń-Domińczak, Iga Magda
and Paweł A. Strzelecki

13 Patterns of labour market participation and their impact on the well-being of older women

- There are pronounced differences in women's lifetime employment patterns across the EU
- Women who worked either full- or part-time currently have better financial situation and life satisfaction than women who had very short or interrupted labour market careers
- Policy developments related to the reconciliation of work and family life are not only important for current situation of women on the labour market but may also affect future outcomes after retirement

13.1 Introduction

The levels of income and well-being and the socio-economic situation of older people depend on their life choices. Patterns of employment and earnings differ significantly within and between countries, in particular from a gender perspective. Women have shorter and more interrupted careers than men. Our hypothesis is that the patterns of the working careers of the female life course depend on the institutional organization, including regulations of part-time work, which translates into its varying incidences across countries.

We focus on identifying the patterns of the full and interrupted careers of women in 13 European countries that participated in the third and subsequent waves of SHARE, in particular the retrospective SHARELIFE survey. Using the survey results, we distinguish women who have had full or interrupted labour market careers. We also analyse differences in the patterns of women's interrupted careers among countries. We then assess whether a link exists between the pattern of labour market career and the current socio-economic situation of older women, including their health, income and life satisfaction levels. Thus, we contribute to studies on various dimensions of life at later stages.

https://doi.org/10.1515/9783110617245-013

13.2 Family and child leave policies and labour market activity are strongly intertwined

There are many explanations for the different patterns of women's work careers among various countries. First, the presence of children at home will have an impact on a woman's decision to work and the number of hours worked. Thus, mothers can have little or no work experience or decide to reconcile work and family lives with more frequent career breaks or by working part-time. The heterogeneity of these decisions can be explained by individual factors that lead to more childcare-oriented behaviour (Hakim, 2003). Second, such choices also frequently reflect the limitations of institutional childcare and the necessity to provide care at home. Third, policies on parental leave, child care and school schedules affect mothers' employment patterns. Fourth, the heterogeneity of health and disabilities also translates into various working career patterns. Fifth, the process of building human capital during the life course can also lead to heterogeneity in patterns depending on educational status. Workers with a tertiary education usually enter the labour market later but are also more attached to employment in subsequent ages. Finally, a significant share of unstable work careers can also be an indicator of a dual labour market with relatively better opportunities for persons without interrupted careers.

The cross-country variation in policies may affect not only the labour market participation of women during the first years of children's lives but also their entire life course, thus affecting the lifetime length of career and wages. The decision to take maternity leave can influence well-being later in life. Maternity leave and the protected period around the birth of a child (particularly the first child) has important long-run mental health benefits for mothers, including reducing the risk of depression at an older age (Avendano *et al.*, 2015). Differences in labour market choices of individuals with respect to childcare affect individual pension levels (Kotowska, Stachura, and Strzelecki, 2008).

There is also a large diversity of gender norms and perceptions of men's and women's family roles. Women spend more time than men on housework and caring activities, particularly in southern European countries. EU countries also differ in the level of acceptance of men taking parental leave and/or doing an equal share of household activities. Whereas the labour market participation and presented perceptions are based on today's outcomes, they reflect the policies and societal norms that are frequently path-dependent, which may affect an individual's situation in later life.

13.3 Labour market careers of women follow a few typical patterns from a life course perspective

Interruptions in working careers are usually not randomly distributed in the population but are cumulated for specific individuals. To identify the existing differences, we compare the individual working careers from the retrospective SHARE database to find typical patterns of the full and interrupted careers characteristics for the countries analysed. In particular, this paper uses data from the generated Job Episodes Panel (see Brugiavini et al., 2013; Antonova et al., 2014) for methodological details. The aim of the analysis is to cluster the individual life course developments of women to define average patterns of interrupted and uninterrupted careers and to find a share of women with careers described as interrupted.

We use data on the episodes of work in each year of a career for all countries discussed in the paper based on the answers of persons aged 50 and older. Therefore, this sample describes the careers of generations that experienced their prime age in the labour market at least 20 years ago. Nevertheless, the country differences illustrate divergent labour market developments that are still likely to affect different pension and life outcomes for people by country.

To analyse the typical work career patterns based on the retrospective data, we applied a sequence analysis technique (Brzinsky-Fay, Kohler, and Luniak 2006) that allows for the definition of a measure of similarity between the different life paths of individuals. Three possible states are distinguished in each year of observation: full-time employment, part-time employment and inactivity/unemployment. The technical assumption that enables a calculation of the matrix of distances (similarities) between individuals in the sequence analysis is that part-time employment is the state exactly halfway between full-time employment and the lack of work (unemployment and inactivity).

Then, a cluster analysis with the Ward metric is used to identify no more than three most distinct groups of careers for the sample of all countries. As a result, each person in the SHARE survey was assigned to one of the three groups (Figure 13.1). The first cluster includes women with very short spells of employment at a younger age and who spend the majority of their lives outside the labour market. The second cluster includes careers dominated by part-time employment, sometimes also with short episodes of full-time employment and inactivity at the beginning of the working career. The most numerous is the third cluster, which can be described by a relatively high share of full-time employment in the working careers. However, the latter also covers women whose careers combined full-time work with relatively long periods of part-time employment.

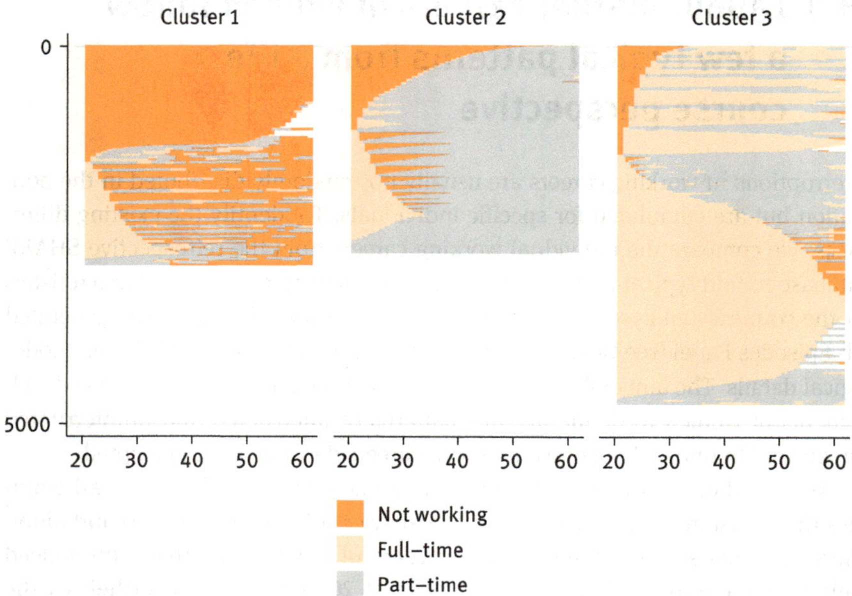

Figure 13.1: Results of the cluster analysis on the full sample of countries.
Source: SHARE Wave 3 (SHARELIFE) release 6.1.0.

Figure 13.2 shows the shares of women in the selected countries who are attached to one of the three types of careers. The highest share of uninterrupted careers can be found in the Czech Republic and Poland. More than half of the women have full-time careers in Denmark, France and Sweden. In contrast, the dominant type of career in southern European countries is outside work (Italy, Spain and Greece). In western European countries (the Netherlands, Switzerland and Germany) and Scandinavian (Denmark, Sweden) countries, careers with long periods of part-time employment are also relatively frequent.

13.4 Institutional factors at country level are important determinants of types of work careers

There are different factors that determine the type of work careers in the course of a life. Using a multinomial logit, we analyse the impact of individual and country characteristics on the identified career types. The features that can define long-

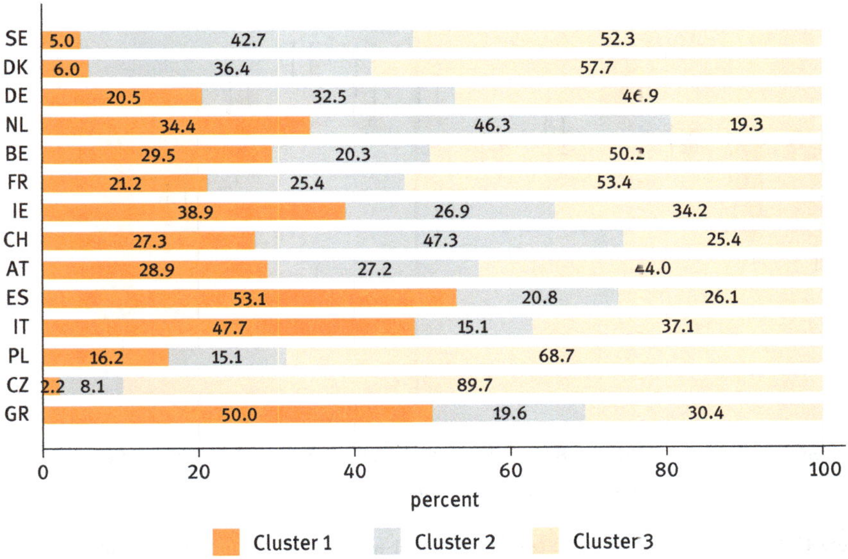

Figure 13.2: Share of women by type of work career in the analysed countries.
Source: SHARE Wave 3 (SHARELIFE) release 6.1.0.

term careers include: number of children, number of years of education, year of birth, marital status at age 50 and country.

Country specificity is very important in both explaining the deviation from the 'uninterrupted' career pattern (cluster 3) to non-work (cluster 1) and part-time (clusters 2). Figures 13.3 and 13.4 below show that taking into account individual features increases the role of the country variable in explaining the difference. Hence, national policies and social norms in countries are important drivers of the type of observed careers.

Individual characteristics are important in explaining the attachment to clusters that identified the 'interrupted' types of work careers. In both cases, the number of children, marriage and education are significant for both women who predominantly did not work or who worked part time. However, there is a significant decline in the probability of being classified as a non-work pattern for younger generations, but this is not the case for the part-time cluster. It is also important that the probability of inactivity (non-work) increases after the second child, whereas the probability of part-time work is significantly higher even after the first child (Table 13.1 summarizes the main results).

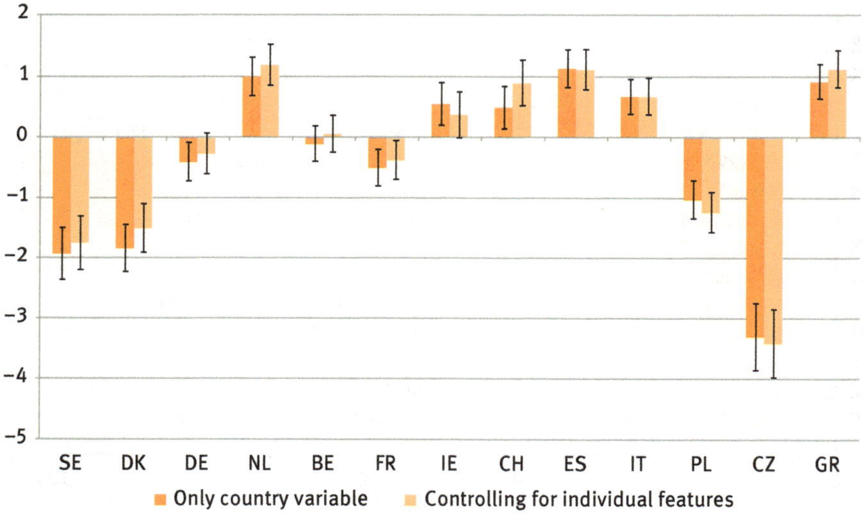

Figure 13.3: Multinomial regression coefficients: 'not-working' vs. 'uninterrupted' career.
Note: reference country: Austria
Source: SHARE Wave 3 (SHARELIFE) release 6.1.0.

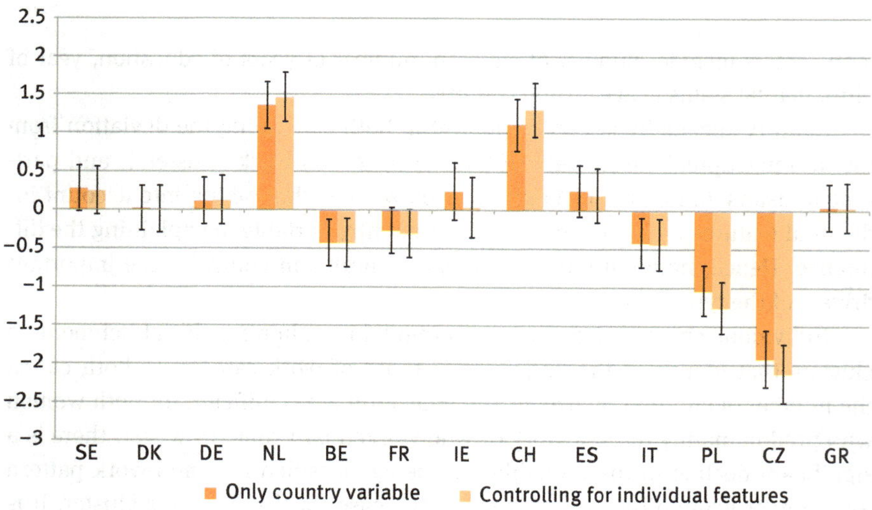

Figure 13.4: Multinomial regression coefficients: 'part-time' vs. 'uninterrupted' career.
Note: reference country: Austria
Source: SHARE Wave 3 (SHARELIFE) release 6.1.0.

Table 13.1: Results of the multinomial regression model (summary).

Variables	Cluster 1 "not-working"	Cluster 2 "part-time"
	(ref Cluster 3 "uninterrupted career")	
Number of children (ref 0)		
1	0.08	0.64***
2	0.48***	1.19***
3+	1.25***	1.70***
Married (ref: single)	1.03***	0.43***
Years in education	−0.37***	−0.03***
Year of birth	−0.06***	−0.01

Significance: *** = 1%; ** = 5%; * = 10%
Source: SHARE Wave 3 (SHARELIFE) release 6.1.0.

13.5 Type of labour market participation impacts socio-economic situation of older women

In this section, we analyse differences in the labour market status, health situation, financial status and life satisfaction of women with full and interrupted labour market patterns and with no labour market activity.

13.5.1 Employment

Current employment is lower among women who belong to the group with little or no labour market attachment in their lifetime which is shown in Figure 13.5. Women who were most likely to have worked part time currently have higher employment levels than those who had full careers. This somewhat surprising result is likely driven by the self-selection of women into part-time work and the types of jobs that offer the possibility of working limited hours.

13.5.2 Health assessment

The dominant perception of health status is good. The share of women who assess their health as very good is largest among those who have had full-time working careers, followed by those with dominant part-time careers. Both of these groups are also least likely to declare bad health as presented in Figure 13.6. Interestingly, women with part-time working careers have more frequent severe and non-severe limitations given their health status relative to women who have worked full time

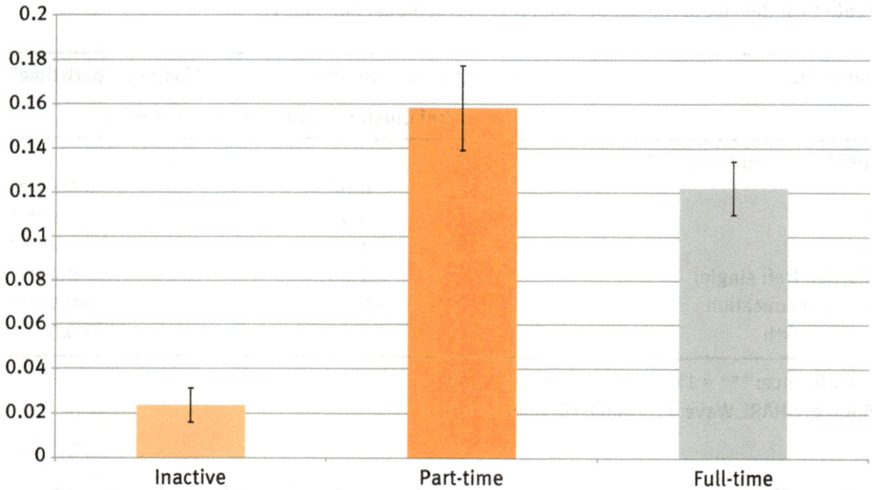

Figure 13.5: Share of employed women by cluster.
Source: SHARE Wave 3 (SHARELIFE) release 6.1.0, Wave 7 release 0.

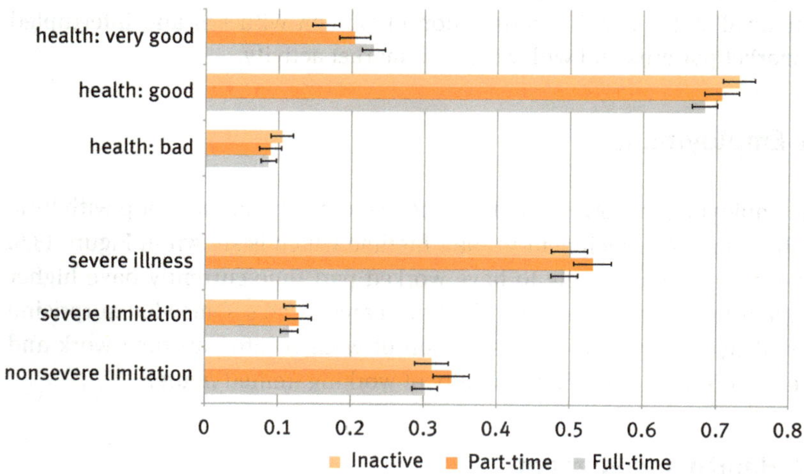

Figure 13.6: Health assessment by cluster.
Source: SHARE Wave 3 (SHARELIFE) release 6.1.0, Wave 7 release 0.

and those who have withdrawn from the labour market. Obviously, these links between current health self-assessment and work history are correlations only and do not imply any causalities. Some full careers may have led to worsening health, but also women with a worse health status in their early careers were likely to have more career interruptions and a lower probability of full-time work.

13.5.3 Financial situation

Women who have withdrawn from the labour market face greater difficulties in making ends meet relative to women who have had full- and part-time working careers. Moreover, the share of women that easily makes ends meet exceeds 47% among women who have worked mostly part time and is slightly higher among women who have worked full time (49%), whereas it is only a third among women with interrupted careers, which is presented in Figure 13.7.

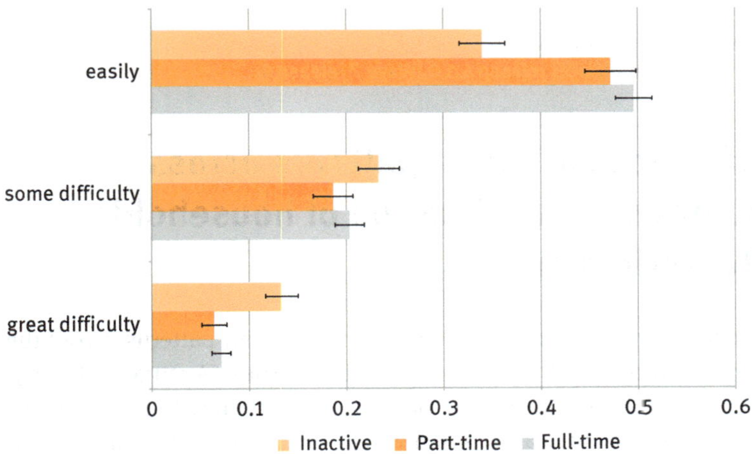

Figure 13.7: Making ends meet by cluster.
Source: SHARE Wave 3 (SHARELIFE) release 6.1.0, Wave 7 release 0.

13.5.4 Life satisfaction

Women who have had working careers (especially part-time) seem to be more satisfied with their lives than women who were mainly inactive. The latter are also less likely to feel that life often has meaning compared to women with full- and part-time working careers as presented in Figure 13.8.

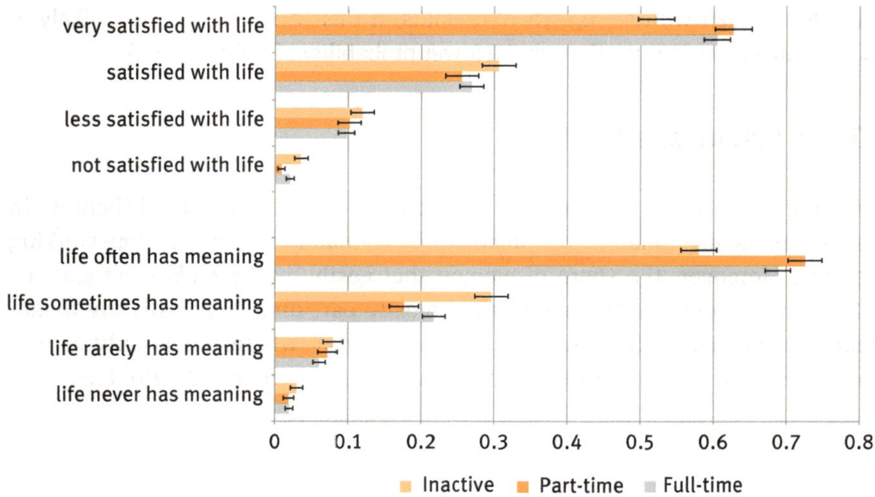

Figure 13.8: Life satisfaction by cluster.
Source: SHARE Wave 3 (SHARELIFE) release 6.1.0, Wave 7 release 0.

13.6 Differences in career patterns across countries affect situation of households after retirement

There are pronounced differences in women's employment patterns across the EU. In southern Europe and some continental countries (Austria, Belgium), women interrupted their labour market activity and withdrew from the labour market for good, whereas in Scandinavian and some continental countries (i.e., Germany, France, Switzerland), women were more likely to continue in part-time careers.

Predominant patterns of interrupted careers affect the current health assessment, life satisfaction, financial situation and labour market activity of women. In particular, women who worked either full- or part-time currently have better overall current financial situations and life satisfaction than women who withdrew from the labour market.

Our results indicate that country policies have an impact on the life course patterns of labour market activity. The choices made during the earlier stages of the life course affect well-being in the later stages. Therefore, the policy developments related to the reconciliation of work and family life today are not only important for today's outcomes but may also affect future outcomes.

References

Antonova, L., L. Aranda, G. Pasini and E. Trevisa. (2014). Migration, family history and pension: the second release of the SHARE Job Episodes Panel. *SHARE Working Paper Series*: 18-2014. Munich: MEA, Max Planck Institute for Social Law and Social Policy

Avendano, M., Berkman, L. F. Brugiavini, A. Pasini, G. (2015). The long-run effect of maternity leave benefits on mental health: Evidence from European countries, Social Science and Medicine. Elsevier Ltd, 132, pp. 45–53. doi: 10.1016/j.socscimed.2015.02.037.

Brugiavini, A., D. Cavapozzi, G. Pasini and E. Trevisan. (2013). Working life histories from SHARELIFE: a retrospective panel. *SHARE Working Paper Series:* 11-2013. Munich: MEA, Max Planck Institute for Social Law and Social Policy.

Brzinsky-Fay, C., U. Kohler and M. Luniak. (2006). Sequence Analysis with Stata. *Stata Journal* 6 (4): 435–460 (26).

Hakim, Catherine. (2003). A New Approach to Explaining Fertility Patterns: Preference Theory. Population and Development Review 29 (3): 349–374. doi:10.1111/j.1728-4457.2003.00349.x.

Kotowska, I. E., J. Stachura, and P. Strzelecki. (2008). Equality of Retirement Benefits Received by Men and Women in Selected European Countries. Childbearing and Future Benefits. AIM WP6, Task 6.4.1 56. ENEPRI Research Reports.

Marco Bertoni, Andrea Bonfatti, Martina Celidoni,
Angela Crema and Chiara Dal Bianco

14 End-of-working-life gender wage gap: The role of health shocks, parental education and personality traits

- We show that intra-occupation wage disparities between men and women account for a large part of the gender wage gap.
- Women sorted into jobs in which they were less discriminated in terms of pay or their characteristics were more rewarded.
- Adding parental education, health shocks and non-cognitive skills helps explain the gap only marginally.

14.1 Introduction

In the last decade, the unadjusted gender pay gap, defined as the raw percentage difference between male and female average gross hourly earnings, decreased in most European Union (EU) countries. Despite this progressive reduction, the average gender wage gap in 2014 in the EU (weighted by the number of employees) still stood at 16.6 per cent, indicating that women earned, on average, 84 per cent of that of men. This figure masks substantial variations across countries: although the gap is relatively narrow in Italy (6.1), Belgium (6.6) and Slovenia (7.0), it becomes significantly larger in countries such as Austria (22.2), Germany (22.3) and Estonia (28.1) (Source: Eurostat).

Starting from the seminal works by Blinder (1973) and Oaxaca (1973), a large body of literature has investigated the gender wage gap to quantify the part that can be explained by differences in individual characteristics, such as education or job experience, and the so-called unexplained part. The latter component can be attributable to gender discrimination, justified by, for instance, a supposedly lower attachment to work by women.

Much of this body of literature has treated the distribution of men and women into different working sectors and occupations as exogenously given. This approach does not acknowledge two potentially relevant factors. First, differences in individual characteristics may lead women to prefer jobs that pay lower wages on average. Second, to some extent, women might be prevented

https://doi.org/10.1515/9783110617245-014

from entering certain top-paid jobs, which might occur even if their skills match those of their male colleagues (gender occupational segregation). Brown, Moon and Zoloth (1980) propose a modified Oaxaca decomposition in which the occupational choice is explicitly modelled.

In this chapter, we estimate the overall gender wage gap at the end of the working life for a set of European countries and quantify the part of the gap that can be explained by parental education, non-cognitive skills and health shocks that occurred during life, in addition to standard individual characteristics. Then, we assess how the explained part of the gap changes when accounting for the endogeneity of occupational attainment.

Our baseline results suggest that the overall end-of-working-life wage gap is approximately 28 per cent, and approximately one-fifth can be explained by standard personal and job characteristics. Adding parental education, health shocks and non-cognitive skills among the explanatory variables only marginally increases the explained share of the gap. Instead, accounting for the endogeneity of job attainment raises the explained part of the total wage gap to about 50 per cent. Interestingly, the actual distribution of women across occupations helps reduce the wage penalty by 22 per cent, suggesting that either preferences or social norms about occupational choices led women to sort into jobs in which their characteristics were more rewarded or less discriminated in terms of pay.

The chapter is organized as follows. The next section describes the data and sample definitions. The following sections illustrate the methodological approach and the decomposition results. The last section concludes.

14.2 Data and descriptive statistics

We use retrospective information on wages collected through SHARELIFE Waves 3 and 7 for 15 European countries. Respondents are asked to report the amount, after taxes and contributions, of their monthly wages at the end of their main job. We restrict our sample to retired employees who reported valid amounts and whose main job corresponds with their last job before retirement.

In SHARELIFE, wages are mostly reported in pre-euro currencies – also for countries currently in the euro area – and refer to different points in time. Therefore, we converted amounts in euro and express them in real terms. To account for cost of living differences across European countries, we used purchasing power parity (PPP)-adjusted exchange rates from Eurostat with Germany as a reference for relative prices (base year 2014).

We obtain hourly wages by dividing monthly wages by average monthly hours worked provided by Eurostat by gender, occupation (the nine aggregate categories in ISCO 2008) and employment contract (full- or part-time).

We eliminate from the sample individuals without information on occupation, whose overall job tenure is longer than 50 years and whose age at the end of their main job is younger than 40 years. We also eliminate those who changed from full-time to part-time (or vice versa) during their careers (approximately 500 individuals, mainly women) and those with no information on parental education and personality traits (the so-called Big Five collected in Wave 7). We end up with a sample of 5,464 observations from Wave 7 and 2,060 observations from Wave 3 for 15 countries (Austria, Germany, Sweden, Spain, Italy, France, Denmark, Greece, Switzerland, Belgium, Czech Republic, Luxemburg, Slovenia, Estonia and Croatia).

Figure 14.1 shows average hourly wages by gender and country. Despite being PPP-adjusted, hourly wages are lower in southern and eastern European countries, and men's wages are statistically significantly higher than women's in most countries. Additionally, Figure 14.1 reports the net hourly wage by gender based on Eurostat and OECD information: we used OECD tax statistics to obtain net hourly wages from Eurostat gross hourly earnings data, in reference

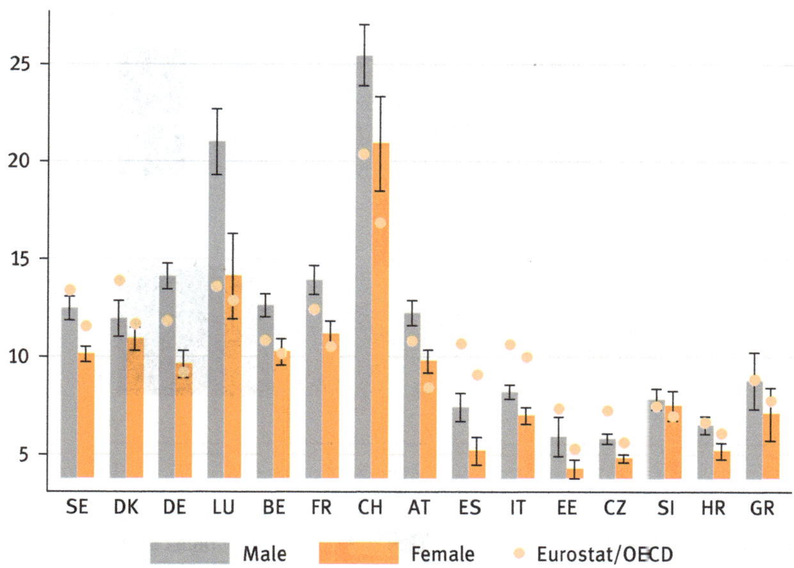

Figure 14.1: Hourly wage (PPP adjusted) by country and gender.
Source: SHARE Wave 3 release 6.1.1, Wave 7 release 0.

to 2014. Although SHARELIFE wages are not directly comparable with those computed from official 2014 statistics because they refer to end-of-working-life wages for older cohorts, Figure 14.1 is somewhat reassuring about the extent of the measurement error in SHARELIFE data due to delayed recall. Most countries ranking high in wage gaps computed by Eurostat for 2014 (Germany and Estonia, for instance) still present some of the largest gaps, whereas others ranking low (Slovenia and Italy) still remain in the lowest part of the distribution of the end-of-working-life wage gap.

Figure 14.2 shows the observed distribution of men and women into four aggregate occupational categories constructed by combining the nine major ISCO 2008 categories according to the type of work (blue or white collar) and skill level required (low or high) to fulfil tasks. The presence of women turns out to be higher with respect to men (about twice as high) in low-skilled, white collar occupations, whereas the proportion of women employed in high-skilled, blue collar occupations is about one-third that of men's. Instead, the proportion of men and women in high-skilled, white collar work is about the same (40%). The distributional differences in the occupations of men and women previously highlighted are not negligible and suggest that explicitly modelling occupational attainment in the decomposition analysis of the wage gap is worthwhile.

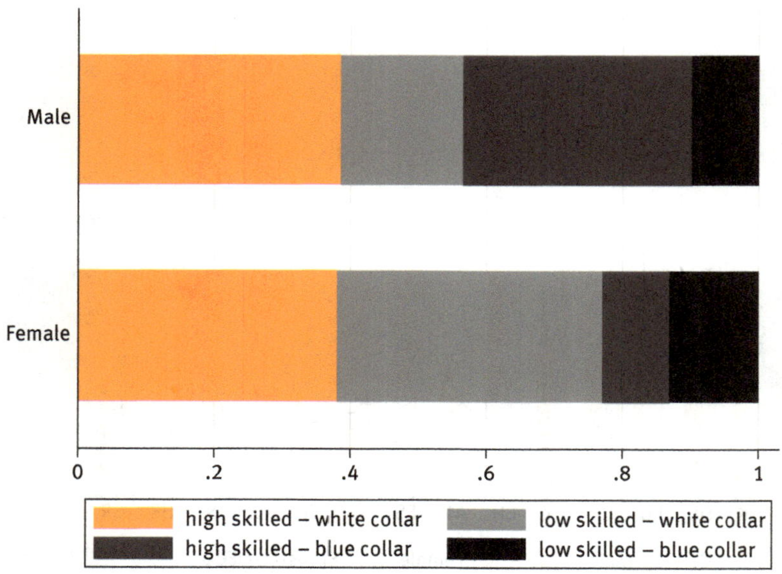

Figure 14.2: Observed male and female occupation distributions.
Source: SHARE Wave 3 release 6.1.1, Wave 7 release 0.

14.3 Empirical methods

The traditional approach to investigating the determinants of the gender wage gap is the Oaxaca (1973)-Blinder (1973) decomposition that distinguishes between the 'explained' and 'unexplained' components of the gap. The former relates to differences in demographic characteristics, human capital and other observables between men and women. The latter can be attributed to discrimination against women in the labour market (Oaxaca and Ransom, 1994).

The standard method entails estimating separate wage equations by gender, where the log-hourly wage is regressed on a set of covariates. In our baseline specification, we include among the controls dummies for education (ISCED categories 3 to 4, and 5 to 6), self-assessed cognitive skills when children (doing better than schoolmates in math or language), being a public employee, being in full-time contracts, having children, living without a partner, number of residence changes, overall job tenure (also squared), cohort and country dummies. We first treat occupational distribution as exogenous and control for occupational categories in the wage equation.

Following Brown, Moon and Zoloth (1980), we then propose an alternative decomposition in which we model occupational attainment by estimating a multinomial logit model. This decomposition allows for disentangling of the intra and inter-occupation explained and unexplained part of the gap. In the occupation equation, we control for education, school performance, cohort and country dummies.

To understand the role of parental education, health shocks and non-cognitive skills in explaining wage differentials, we compare the decomposition results excluding (baseline) and including these controls.

Parental education (two dummies indicating ISCED categories 3 or 4, and 5 or 6 for each parent) and non-cognitive skills are included in both the wage and the occupation equation. Health shocks (left a job because of ill health or disability; took a temporary leave of absence from a job for 6 months or more because of ill health or disability; had a physical injury that led to a permanent handicap, disability or limitations; any other period of ill health or disability that lasted longer than one year) are included only in the wage equation because they do not likely determine individuals' employment in a specific occupation.

14.4 Results

Table 14.1 reports the result of the standard Oaxaca-Blinder decomposition. Approximately 21 per cent of the overall end-of-working-life gender wage gap (which is 0.281) is explained by differences in educational attainment, job characteristics and family structure between men and women. Including parental education, health shocks during working life and non-cognitive skills does not significantly increase the explained wage differential (in line with Cobb-Clark and Tan, 2011).

Table 14.1: Standard Oaxaca-Blinder decomposition.

	Wage gap	Unexplained	Explained
Panel A: Baseline			
Gap	0.281	0.221	0.060
Std. Error	0.012	0.023	0.022
%	100.0	78.78	21.22
Panel B: Including Parental Education, Health Shocks and Non-cognitive Skills			
Gap	0.281	0.219	0.062
Std. Error	0.012	0.024	0.022
%	100.0	77.93	22.07

Note: Bootstrapped standard errors based on 100 replications.
Source: SHARE Wave 1–6 release 6.1.1.

Table 14.2 shows the results of the decomposition when occupational attainments are explicitly modelled. Allowing for an endogenous occupational choice increases the explained component from approximately 21 per cent to 49 per cent (Column 2, Panel A). The wage differential is larger intra-occupation (columns 3 and 4) than inter-occupation (column 5 and 6). The disparity in the characteristics of men and women employed in a specific occupation (column 4, explained intra-occupation wage gap) accounts for 50 per cent of the gap. The unexplained intra-occupation differential in column 3 amounts to approximately 70 per cent, indicating that a large proportion of the wage gap is the result of differences in the wage returns to productivity-related characteristics. The fact that men and women are differently distributed by occupation (see Figure 14.2) is because they have different (observed and unobserved) characteristics that reduce women's wage penalty. More precisely, column 5 (unexplained inter-occupation) shows that the gap decreases mainly because men and women with the same characteristics have very different propensities for entering certain occupations.

Table 14.2: Decomposition modelling of occupation attainment.

	Total			Intra-occupation		Inter-occupation	
	Wage gap	**Unexpl.**	**Expl.**	**Unexpl.**	**Expl.**	**Unexpl.**	**Expl.**
		(1)	**(2)**	**(3)**	**(4)**	**(5)**	**(6)**
Panel A: Baseline							
Gap	0.281	0.142	0.139	0.201	0.140	−0.059	−0.002
Std. Error	0.012	0.026	0.024	0.026	0.024	0.008	0.003
%	100.0	50.57	49.43	71.53	50.02	−20.95	−0.600
Panel B: Including Parental Education, Health Shocks and Non-cognitive Skills							
Gap	0.281	0.137	0.143	0.196	0.145	−0.058	−0.002
Std. Error	0.012	0.027	0.026	0.028	0.025	0.008	0.003
%	100.0	48.98	51.02	69.82	51.73	−20,84	−0.710

Note: Bootstrapped standard errors based on 100 replications.
Source: SHARE Wave 1–6 release 6.1.1.

14.5 Conclusions

Our exercise shows that within occupations' wage differentials the predominant explanation for the overall women's wage penalty and occupational segregation does not represent a disadvantage for women. The portion of the overall gender wage gap that can be explained by differences in men's and women's characteristics increases by including parental education, health shocks and non-cognitive skills. However, regardless of whether occupational attainment is treated as exogenous or endogenous, the increase is modest.

References

Blinder, A. S., 1973. Wage discrimination: reduced form and structural estimates. Journal of Human Resources 14, 436–455.

Oaxaca, R. L., 1973. Male-female wage differentials in urban labor markets. International Economic Review 14 (3), 693–709.

Oaxaca, R. L., Ransom, M., 1994. On discrimination and the decomposition of wage differentials. Journal of Econometrics 61 (1), 5–21.

Brown, R. S, Moon, M., Zoloth, B. S., 1980. Incorporating occupational attainment in studies of male-female earnings differentials. The Journal of Human Resources 15 (1), 3–28.

Cobb-Clark D. A., Tan M., 2011. Noncognitive skills, occupational attainment, and relative wages. Labour Economics 18, 1–13.

Danilo Cavapozzi, Simona Fiore and Giacomo Pasini

15 Family dissolution and labour supply decisions over the life cycle

- Life-history data can clarify the consequences of household split and divorce on the probability of working
- Indeed, employment choices are affected by the occurrence of family dissolution episodes
- The effect is stronger for women
- The magnitude of this effect increases with the presence of children

15.1 Introduction

In this chapter, we look at the association between family dissolution and labour supply decisions during the lifetimes of Europeans aged 50 and over. Family dissolution episodes can be generally observed as a household split, defined as ceasing to live with the partner as a couple, or a divorce. Both such episodes can force individuals, especially women, to enter the labour market to make ends meet and may induce others to leave the labour market given the stress and related psychosocial effects that they produced.

Several studies have looked at the effect of divorce on the labour market participation of former partners (e.g., Bargain et al., 2012). Nevertheless, family dissolution takes place in two steps. First, the household splits. At this stage, couple members usually reach an agreement about income support according to which the couple member at work (or the better-off one) provides income support to the former partner and the children. Whether this agreement is formal or informal depends on the legislation in place in each country and on the decisions taken by the former partners. A household split may or may not lead to a divorce. In the latter case, the agreement about alimonies and childcare generally becomes formal.

The association between household split or divorce, on the one hand, and labour force participation, on the other hand, may differ. In this chapter, we analyse the employment consequences of family dissolution by separately considering household split and divorce. Allowing for this difference in the time perspective is important because the labour supply of individuals might require time to react to the family dissolution episode. As an example, active search

https://doi.org/10.1515/9783110617245-015

attempts are time-consuming activities. Moreover, individuals might opt to use their savings before entering the labour market to make ends meet. After a divorce, alimonies will mitigate the adverse effects of family dissolution on the dependent partner, thus inducing former partners with a low labour market attachment to exit the labour force again. Alternatively, the need to pay for alimonies is expected to increase the employment participation of the former household breadwinner as a result of the augmented expenses that he (she) has to support. Finally, both divorce and household splits are stressful events that undermine the psychosocial well-being of individuals and can compromise their productivity as well as their labour market attachment. Therefore, understanding the sign and magnitude of the association between employment and family dissolution episodes is an important topic.

15.2 How we studied the topic

In our study, we used data from the 18 countries that participated in one or both of the retrospective waves in SHARE (Wave 3 and Wave 7): Sweden, Denmark, Finland, Ireland, Belgium, Luxembourg, Netherlands, France, Germany, Switzerland, Austria, Portugal, Spain, Italy, Malta, Greece, Cyprus and Israel. We excluded the SHARE countries that were part of the eastern bloc because labour market regulations and institutions there, prior to 1989, were not comparable to those in place in western Europe. We structured the data according to the life history approach, which recovers the main events that occurred throughout respondents' lives, looking specifically at family relations, children, health, accommodations and employment. Towards this end, we constructed a retrospective panel, as previously documented by Brugiavini et al. (2013).

Overall, our dataset consisted of 1,609,797 person-year observations. We considered 48,487 individuals (27,100 women and 21,387 men). This data format allowed us to reconstruct individual characteristics at the time of the family dissolution occurrence and to observe their time variation. As an example, if an individual divorced in a given year, the retrospective panel allows for the observation of previous, current and future situations of this individual with respect to a number of characteristics crucial for the analysis, such as employment and number of children. This ability is a clear advantage over standard surveys that retrieve information about the occurrence of family dissolution events but cannot track the time variation of individual characteristics over respondents' lifetimes.

We tracked individuals from the year of their first marriage up to age 60, or until they classified themselves as retired. On average, each respondent had 18 year-observations. The average age at first marriage was 27 years for men and 24 years for women. We observed at least one household split event for approximately 10% of the individuals in our sample, including at least one divorce for approximately 9% of them. The probability of being at work differed widely by gender; 95% of the observations among the men referred to years in which they were at work, whereas this percentage fell to 57% among the women.

We estimated fixed effects linear probability models in which the dependent variable was a binary outcome taking on the value of 1 if the individual worked and 0 if otherwise. Our specifications alternatively investigated how the probability of being employed varies with the occurrence of a household split, described by a dummy variable taking on the value of 1 in the years during which the end of a family relationship was observed and 0 otherwise, and with the occurrence of a divorce, described by a dummy variable taking on the value of 1 in the years during which a divorce was reported. All of the specifications included a set of time-varying explanatory variables consisting of a second-order polynomial of age, a full set of year dummies referring to the calendar years to which observations referred and a dummy variable for the presence of children. The fixed effects panel data technique allows controlling for any time-invariant unobserved individual characteristics. Finally, the analyses were conducted separately by gender.

15.3 Results

On average, the probability of men working only slightly varied in the year of the household split, with a coefficient suggesting an increase by less than 1 percentage point. The men's labour supply response to divorce was higher in magnitude (Table 15.1). In comparison, the employment rate among women rose by 2.5 percentage points in the year of the household split and by 5 percentage points in the year of the divorce (Table 15.2). These are sizeable differences in economic terms given the much lower employment rates of women. This pattern is consistent with the hypothesis that the minimum wage for which individuals, particularly women, experiencing family dissolution are willing to work decreases, which induces them to have stronger labour market attachment. Overall, the positive sign of the coefficient on the household split and divorce dummies suggests that the positive effect on the labour supply of the income channel is stronger than the negative effect potentially induced by the psychosocial problems generated by household dissolution.

Table 15.1: Men, probability of being at work, divorce and household split.

	Coefficient	Standard Error	Coefficient	Standard Error	Coefficient	Standard Error
Panel A						
Year of Split (dummy)	0.008**	(0.004)	−0.004	(0.010)	0.008**	(0.004)
Year of Split X Children (dummy)			0.016	(0.010)		
1 Year before Split (dummy)					0.008*	(0.004)
2 Years before Split (dummy)					0.008*	(0.004)
1 Year after Split (dummy)					−0.002	(0.005)
2 Years after Split (dummy)					−0.003	(0.004)
Panel B						
Year of Divorce (dummy)	0.012***	(0.004)	0.016	(0.010)	0.010**	(0.005)
Year of Divorce X Children (dummy)			−0.006	(0.011)		
1 Year before Divorce (dummy)					0.009**	(0.005)
2 Years before Divorce (dummy)					0.009**	(0.005)
1 Year after Divorce (dummy)					0.004	(0.005)
2 Years after Divorce (dummy)					0.002	(0.005)
No. of observations	679,365		679,365		593,928	
No. of individuals	21,387		21,387		21,296	
Mean of the dependent variable	0.95		0.95		0.95	

Significance: *** = 1%; ** = 5%; * = 10%
Note: Fixed effects linear probability model. The set of explanatory variables includes a second-order polynomial of age, a full set of year dummies referring to the calendar years to which the observations refer and a dummy variable for the presence of children. Standard errors are robust to arbitrary heteroskedasticity in the error term.
Source: SHARE Wave 3 release 6.1.1, Wave 7 release 0.

Table 15.2: Women, probability of being at work, divorce and household split.

	Coefficient	Standard Error	Coefficient	Standard Error	Coefficient	Standard Error
Panel A						
Year of Split (dummy)	0.025***	(0.005)	−0.005	(0.012)	0.031***	(0.005)
Year of Split X Children (dummy)			0.035***	(0.013)		
1 Year before Split (dummy)					−0.003	(0.006)
2 Years before Split (dummy)					−0.002	(0.005)
1 Year after Split (dummy)					0.037***	(0.005)
2 Years after Split (dummy)					0.043***	(0.005)
Panel B						
Year of Divorce (dummy)	0.049***	(0.006)	0.009	(0.015)	0.058***	(0.007)
Year of Divorce X Children (dummy)			0.049***	(0.016)		
1 Year before Divorce (dummy)					0.020***	(0.007)
2 Years before Divorce (dummy)					0.012*	(0.007)
1 Year after Divorce (dummy)					0.057***	(0.007)
2 Years after Divorce (dummy)					0.059***	(0.006)
No. of observations	930,432		930,432		822,213	
No. of individuals	27,100		27,100		26,972	
Mean of the dependent variable	0.57		0.57		0.56	

Significance: *** = 1%; ** = 5%; * = 10%
Note: Fixed effects linear probability model. The set of explanatory variables includes a second-order polynomial of age, a full set of year dummies referring to the calendar years to which the observations refer and a dummy variable for the presence of children. Standard errors are robust to arbitrary heteroskedasticity in the error term.
Source: SHARE Wave 3 release 6.1.1, Wave 7 release 0.

The gender differences in employment participation attributable to family dissolution were also confirmed with respect to the number of children. We added an interaction term between the household split and divorce dummy variables and the presence of children. The interaction was not significant for men but was for women. Specifically, neither household split nor divorce was correlated with the employment decision among women without children but was significant among those with children. A possible explanation is that children are likely to live with their mothers after family dissolution. Despite the availability of alimonies or informal income support arrangements with their former partners, single mothers still need labour earnings to afford expenses related to their children.

As we already pointed out, the labour market effect of household dissolution episodes may not be immediate if, for example, a person decides to use savings to make ends meet or if the job search requires time. Moreover, family dissolution may not be a shock but rather the epilogue of a deteriorating family situation, in which case the effect on the labour market decision might have taken place earlier. People relying on their partner's income may foresee that they are approaching the end of their relationship and anticipate the income effect. If this is indeed the case, we should observe an increase in the probability of working well before the year during which a household split or divorce actually takes place.

To shed light on the prevalent time pattern, we followed the approach of Myrskylä and Margolis (2014) and added two lags and two leads of the household split and divorce dummies to our specifications. This allowed analysis of how the employment decision reacted to past, current and future family dissolution. Strong gender differences were found in this respect as well. The positive association between family dissolution and labour market participation for men is statistically significant in the two years preceding a split and a divorce. The magnitude of this effect is comparable to the one of the exact year of these two events. Regarding women, split and divorce play a different role. We observed an increase in their employment probability in the years following a household split but no effect for the years preceding it. A persistent effect over time is also found for the years following divorce. Nevertheless, it is worth noting that in the case of divorce there is an anticipation effect: women are more likely to be at work also in the years before the formal conclusion of their relationship. This difference in the timing according to which the labour supply of women reacts to household split and divorce events is consistent as divorce necessarily cannot take place before a split.

The analysis in this paper cannot rule out reverse causality and identifies only associations. Therefore, an alternative interpretation is that individuals with a higher labour market attachment are also more likely to leave unhappy marriages (Amato, 2010). Finally, we consistently found lower magnitudes when looking at household splits compared with divorce, for both men and women.

15.4 Conclusions

Our study findings suggest strong gender differences in the effect of household dissolution on employment probability. Whereas household dissolution has a negligible effect on men's employment behaviour, the employment probability of women increases by 4.4 per cent during the year of a household split and by 8.6 per cent during the year of divorce. The effect is driven by women with children. Although both household split and divorce shape women labour supply also after their occurrence, we found an anticipated effect on employment choices only for divorce. This pattern might be driven by the choice of women to undertake job search activities only after they stop living as a couple with their former partners. Finally, we consistently find lower magnitudes when looking at household splits compared with divorce, for both men and women.

The policy implication of these findings is that once within-family income support disappears because a family dissolves, those more at risk – women out of the labour force with dependent children – should be given assistance to manage their work and family responsibilities. Access to childcare services and flexible work arrangements may help smooth the consequences of family dissolution.

References

Amato, P. R., (2010). Research on divorce: Continuing trends and new developments. *Journal of Marriage and Family*, 72 (3): 650–666.

Bargain, O., Keane, C., Ozcan, B., González, L., (2012). Female labor supply and divorce: New evidence from Ireland. *European Economic Review*, 56(8): 1675–1691.

Brugiavini, A., Cavapozzi, D., Pasini G., Trevisan, E., (2013). Working life histories from SHARELIFE: A retrospective panel. *SHARE Working Paper Series*, 11.

Myrskylä, M. and Margolis, R., (2014). Happiness: Before and after the kids. *Demography*, 51: 1843–1866.

Michele Belloni, Raluca Elena Buia, Matija Kovacic
and Elena Meschi

16 Working conditions and health of older workers

- Working conditions are significantly related to health outcomes among older workers in Europe
- General health is correlated with the following work domains: physical environment, work intensity and skills and discretion
- Low job security and uncertain career prospects are associated with mental and behavioural disorders
- An increase in the legal retirement age can have adverse effects on workers' health and should be accompanied by policies aimed to benefit the most vulnerable workers and jobs

16.1 Introduction

Population ageing and the consequent increase in the duration of working life are key features of most European countries. Many studies have investigated the impact of staying longer in the labour force on individual health and well-being (Coe and Zamarro, 2011; Belloni, Meschi and Pasini, 2016; Mazzonna and Peracchi, 2017). Fewer papers have studied the effect of specific job characteristics and working conditions on older workers' physical and mental health.

This chapter analyses the relationship between job characteristics and health among workers aged 50+. We take advantage of the detailed coding of occupations in SHARE Waves 6 and 7 obtained from the new SHARE *jobcoder*. We hypothesise that some occupations are more physically or mentally demanding than others or have more risks that may affect health. To test this hypothesis, we characterise each job category in terms of a set of job quality dimensions measured using data from recent waves of the European Working Conditions Survey (EWCS, Eurofound).

In our model, we explain workers' health in SHARE Waves 6 and 7 by means of several characteristics of their current job, obtained from the EWCS. The fact that we computed measures of job quality from an external source (EWCS) reduces the subjective bias that would exist if job holders were the informants about their jobs' working conditions. In the latter case, the description of job features would be affected by workers' feelings, perceptions, attitudes or values that also correlate with self-reported measures of health.

https://doi.org/10.1515/9783110617245-016

16.2 The data

Our analysis is based on Waves 6 (2015) and 7 (2017) of SHARE, matched to the EWCS Waves 5 (2010) and 6 (2015) by ISCO code and country. These two SHARE waves collected detailed information (ISCO-08 at the 4-digit level, i.e., unit group) on respondents' occupation using a new *jobcoder*. This method allowed us to link respondents' health status to the levels of exposure and risks related to their specific job. We used EWCS job quality indices to summarise working conditions. The matched dataset covered the following European countries included in both SHARE (countries participating in at least one of the two waves) *and* EWCS: Austria, Belgium, Bulgaria, Croatia, Cyprus, Czech Republic, Denmark, Estonia, Finland, France, Germany, Greece, Hungary, Italy, Latvia, Lithuania, Luxembourg, Malta, Poland, Portugal, Romania, Slovakia, Slovenia, Spain and Sweden.

16.2.1 SHARE: Sample selection and health outcomes

Our sample was drawn from all respondents who participated in SHARE for the first time in Waves 6 and 7. Among them, we selected current workers aged 50 to 70 (we excluded retirees from the analysis because their health may have changed due to retirement). In addition, we focused on those working in the same job for at least 10 years to maximise the job impact on health.

The dependent variables were three health measures, specifically:

- self-reported health (recoded as a dummy variable equal to 1 if respondents declared their health status to be fair or poor, and 0 otherwise);
- a general objective health index constructed following the methodology of Poterba et al. (2011). In each wave, we ran a principal component analysis on the variables related to objective health conditions (presence of mobility limitations, at least one limitation in daily life activities, back problems, heart disease, stroke, hypertension, diabetes or cancer; having had a doctor visit, overnight stay in the hospital or in a nursing home and Body Mass Index). The general objective health index was standardised and ranged from 0 (best health) to 100 (worst health); and
- an indicator of mental health equal to 1 if an 'affective or emotional disorder, including anxiety, nervous or psychiatric problems' was diagnosed by the doctor. Note that the EURO-D indicator was not assessed in Wave 7.

16.2.2 European working conditions survey: Job quality indices

To measure working conditions associated with each occupation, we focused on the six job quality indicators developed by *Eurofound* that capture both extrinsic and intrinsic features of the job. The indicators refer to the following categories: physical environment, work intensity, working time quality, social environment, skills and discretion and prospects.

Each index represents an aggregate measure of the proportion of workers exposed to specific hazards in the workplace and is measured on a scale from 0 to 100, where 0 indicates the worst working conditions and 100 indicates the best conditions. The *Physical Environment Index* comprises 13 different indicators related to specific physical hazards, such as posture-related and ambient risks (exposure to vibrations, noise, high and low temperatures, tiring positions, lifting people, carrying heavy loads and repetitive movements) and biological and chemical risks (exposure to inhaling smoke and toxic vapours and handling chemical products and infectious materials). The *Work Intensity Index* measures the level of job workload, such as quantitative demands (working fast), time pressure (having tight deadlines, not having enough time to do the job), frequent disruptive interruptions, pace determinants and interdependency and emotional demands. The *Working Time Quality Index* comprises four dimensions: duration and incidence of atypical working time, the extent to which workers can determine their working time arrangements and how flexible they are to organise their time to balance professional and family life. The *Social Environmental Index* comprises 15 indicators and measures the extent to which workers experience supportive social relationships and (on the negative side) adverse social behaviour, such as bullying, harassment and violence. The *Skills and Discretion Index* builds on 14 indicators and comprises the following dimensions: the skills required in the job (cognitive dimension), autonomy in deciding the manner in which work tasks are performed (decision latitude), worker participation in the organisation and the possibilities for developing job-related skills through training. Finally, the *Prospects Index* considers the continuity of employment as measured by current employment status and type of contract, job security and career prospects.

Although the contents of the indicators are survey elicited (based on individuals' responses), they can be considered objective because they refer to specific observable job quality features and exclude items related to the personal circumstances and quality of the workers. In our current analysis, for each of the six indicators, we took the average by country and ISCO 2-digit over the two waves (2010 and 2015).

16.3 Study results

Table 16.1 reports the descriptive statistics of the variables included in our estimation sample. Approximately 20% of respondents reported that they were in poor or fair health. The health index showed high variability in our sample. Moreover, some 3.2% were diagnosed with an affective or emotional disorder. Among the EWCS work quality indicators, physical environment and working time quality displayed the highest average value (approximately 83). All indicators were characterised by high individual variation.

Table 16.1: Estimation sample and descriptive statistics.

Variable	Obs.	Mean	Std. Dev.	Min.	Max.
Share health outcomes:					
Poor or fair self-reported health	6,740	0.20	0.396	0	1
Objective Health index	6,654	32.8	23.548	1	99
Mental and behavioural disorders	6,740	0.03	0.176	0	1
EWCS work quality indicators:					
Social environment	6,740	77.4	7.3	28.5	100
Physical environment	6,740	82.9	9.0	52.4	97.0
Prospects	6,740	62.2	8.3	29.0	93.8
Work intensity (inverted)	6,740	60.9	10.3	7.3	74.5
Working time quality	6,740	83.0	10.1	39.8	100
Skills and discretion	6,740	64.7	13.5	21.4	91.8

Source: SHARE Wave 6 release 6.1.0, Wave 7 release 0; EWCS Wave 5 and 6.

In the statistical analysis, we used a linear probability model for self-reported health and affective and emotional disorders indicators and an ordinary least square estimator for the continuous objective health index. Our key variables were the six job quality indicators. In the models, we included all work quality indicators jointly because the correlation among them is low (see also Eurofound, 2017, 41). To facilitate comparability among the indices, we reversed the work intensity index such that the higher its value, the lower the work intensity and the better the working conditions. Thus, we expected a negative sign for the estimated coefficients. That is, higher values on the indices reflecting better work conditions should be negatively correlated with worse health.

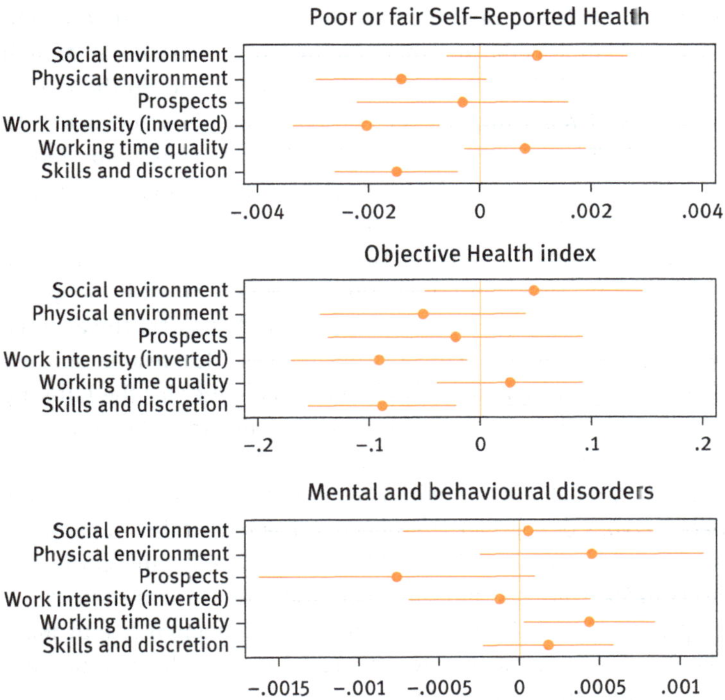

Figure 16.1: Working conditions and health (estimation results)
Note: The figure plots estimated coefficients (dots) and 95% confidence intervals (horizontal lines) of the six job quality indices regressed on self-reported health (upper panel), objective health index (central panel) and mental and behavioural disorders (bottom panel). In all regressions, we controlled for gender, age, education, family status, number of children, country of residence and wave. Standard errors are clustered at the ISCO and country levels.
Source: SHARE Wave 6 release 6.1.0, Wave 7 release 0; EWCS Wave 5 and 6.

Figure 16.1 reports the parameter estimates of the six job quality indices on self-reported health (upper panel), on the health index (central panel) and on mental and behavioural disorders (bottom panel).

The results of the two general health measures (self-reported and objectively measured) were quite similar. Three indices of working quality – *Physical environment, Work intensity* and *Skills and discretion* – showed a significant negative correlation with health. Thus, working in a bad physical environment (i.e., noisy, with high temperatures, breathing in smoke or fumes or carrying or moving heavy loads – among the many items captured by this index) worsened both perceived health (coefficient different from zero at the 10% level) and objective general health.

Work intensity and *Skills and discretion* are negatively correlated with general health. This correlation indicates that, for instance, working at a high speed and under tight deadlines or not having enough time to do the job increases the probability of reporting poor or fair health and is associated with worse objective health. The same occurred in the *Skills and discretion index*, which comprised among its items carrying out complex tasks, having the possibility to choose or change work methods, being involved in improving the work organisation and participating in training. To provide a concrete example, we compared the ISCO group 'Teaching Professionals' (ISCO = 23) with the group 'Stationary Plant and Machine Operators' (ISCO = 81) and consider the average value of the three aforementioned work quality indices. Our results showed that the probability of reporting poor or fair health was higher for the latter by approximately 13 percent. However, we found no evidence that the other four work quality indicators correlated with general health.

Another interesting result was found for *mental and behavioural disorders (including anxiety, nervous or psychiatric problems)*. The probability of being affected by these types of mental health problems was significantly correlated with the *Prospects index*. One may indeed expect that job features such as job security, career prospects and the type of contract affect mental health more than physical health. This statement is even more relevant in the case of older workers for whom losing their job can have severe consequences in terms of future employability and scarcer finances in later life.

16.4 Conclusions

In this chapter, we studied the relationship between working conditions and three health outcomes in a large sample of older workers in Europe. Our results suggest that job quality is an important predictor of individual health and show that some job features are more important than others. For example, physical environment and work intensity are particularly relevant predictors of general health, whereas low job security and uncertain career prospects are significantly associated with affective or emotional disorders.

Our findings have some potentially important policy implications. First, older workers appear sensitive to some specific job features. Therefore, effort needs to be made to monitor and improve these features, and the tasks and duties of the individual worker can be redesigned to reduce physical health risks. Second, policymakers should consider that staying longer in the workforce might have adverse effects on workers' health, especially in occupations characterised by poor job quality. Therefore, any increase in the legal retirement age should be accompanied by policies that benefit the most vulnerable workers and jobs.

We should acknowledge that our empirical strategy does not allow us to determine a causal effect among the variables at this stage. It might be the case that a selection process occurs in which people's health status channels them into certain types of jobs. Therefore, future research should be undertaken to uncover the mechanisms that lie behind the work/health nexus.

References

Belloni, M., E. Meschi and Pasini, G. (2016). The Effect on Mental Health of Retiring During the Economic Crisis. *Health Economics*, 25 (2), pp. 126–140.

Coe N.B. and G. Zamarro (2011). Retirement effects on health in Europe. *Journal of Health Economics*, 30 (1), pp. 77–86.

Eurofound (2017). Sixth European Working Conditions Survey: 2015. Retrieved from https://www.eurofound.europa.eu/surveys/european-working-conditions-surveys/sixth-european-working-conditions-survey-2015.

Mazzonna F., and F. Peracchi (2017). "Unhealthy retirement?" *Journal of Human Resources*, 52(1), pp. 128–151.

Poterba J., S. Venti and Wise, D. (2011). The Composition and Drawdown of Wealth in Retirement. *Journal of Economic Perspectives*, 25(4), pp. 95–118.

Part IV Social transitions and economic crises

Edited by Axel Börsch-Supan

Anikó Bíró and Réka Branyiczki

17 Health gap in post-socialist Central and Eastern Europe: A life-course perspective

- The origins of the health gap between post-socialist central and eastern Europe and western Europe are analysed
- Health disparities existed even before the transition
- Stressful periods, financial difficulties and job losses around the transition are associated with worse health at older ages

17.1 Introduction

The health of the population of post-socialist central and eastern European (CEE) countries lags behind the European Union average. Based on Eurostat data corresponding to the year 2016 and using the EU-28 average as a comparison, life expectancy at both birth and age 65 is approximately 3–6 years shorter than the EU average. These differences are more pronounced among males than among females. Mortality attributable to cancer and ischaemic heart diseases is substantially higher in post-socialist CEE countries than in the rest of the European Union. Laaksonen et al. (2001) argue that the east–west health gap can partly be explained by differences in health behaviours and psychosocial factors. Steptoe and Wardle (2001) arrive at a similar conclusion using a sample of young adults. Health behaviours and psychosocial factors are likely to be related to living conditions during and after the communist era and to the transition itself.

In approximately 1990, the dictatorship of the Communist Party ended in CEE, and the Soviet Union dissolved in 1991. The transition implied a dramatic restructuring of the economy and the social security system. Such major events could have affected not only the healthcare system but also the health status of the population in CEE.

Zatonski (2007) documents that adult mortality rates in post-socialist CEE countries started to diverge from those of western countries in the 1960s. Additionally, during the transition period, adult mortality rose particularly rapidly in post-socialist CEE countries, especially in the Baltics. The dramatic increase in adult male mortality rates during the first years of transition was attributed to

https://doi.org/10.1515/9783110617245-017

the rising incidence of cardiovascular diseases, accidents and violence, indicating the role of stress and social upheaval (EBRD, 1999). In this study, our focus is not on mortality but on the health status and its evolution before and after the transition, conditional on having survived at least approximately 20 years after the transition. Using individual level life history data, we can also increase our understanding of how the transition impacted the health of the population in post-socialist CEE countries. Our analysis also relates to the literature analysing the effect of rapid privatization (as part of the economic transition) on population health and mortality (Azarova et al., 2017; King et al., 2009).

17.2 Data

We use the pre-release data from SHARE Wave 7 (Wave 7 Internal Release 0, April 19, 2018) and data from Wave 3 (Wave 3 Release 6.1.0, March 29, 2018) that include retrospective questions on life history (such as employment history and health at younger ages) of the population older than age 50. Even the youngest cohorts of the sample were already of active age during the transition period, such that the collapse of communism was likely to be a major life event that affected their prospects on the labour market as well. We group the countries into post-socialist CEE countries (Bulgaria, Croatia, Czech Republic, Estonia, Hungary, Latvia, Lithuania, Poland, Romania, Slovak Republic and Slovenia - highlighted with orange in Figure 17.1) and the rest are labelled 'West' (Austria, Belgium, Cyprus, Denmark, Finland, France, Germany, Greece, Ireland, Israel, Italy, Luxembourg, Malta, Netherlands, Portugal, Spain, Sweden and Switzerland).[1] We use questions on health (both current and childhood), timing of stressful periods and financial hardships, employment history and standard demographics.

17.3 Results

17.3.1 Health at old age – 'current' health

Self-reported health (1–excellent to 5–poor) is on average worse in the CEE countries based on Wave 7 data (Figure 17.2). Additionally, most chronic diseases are

1 Although eastern Germany was affected by the transition, we include Germany within the group 'West'. Our results are robust to the exclusion of Germany from the analysis.

Figure 17.1: Post-socialist CEE countries in SHARE Wave 7.

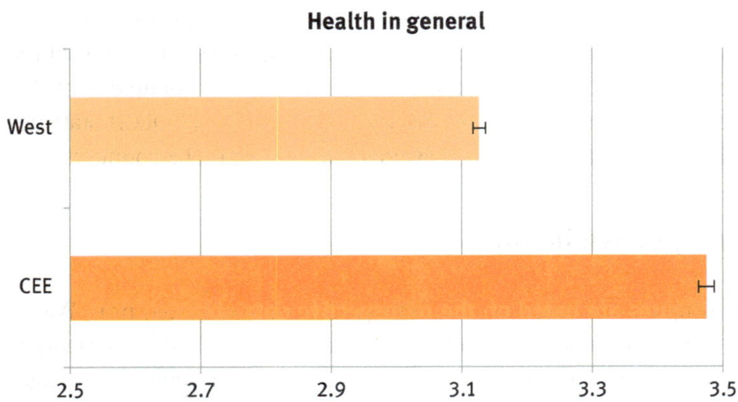

Figure 17.2: Self-reported health in general in CEE and the West.
Note: Average health in general from 1–excellent to 5–poor; 95% confidence interval of the mean is displayed.
Source: SHARE Wave 7 release 0.

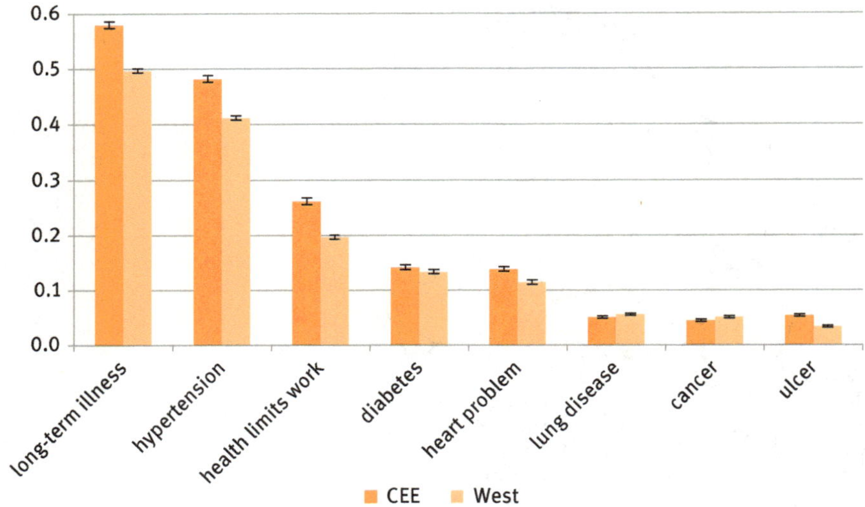

Figure 17.3: Prevalence of health conditions in CEE and the West.
Note: Prevalence of long-term illness, health limits to work, hypertension, diabetes, heart problem lung disease, cancer and ulcer; 95% confidence interval of the mean is displayed.
Source: SHARE Wave 7 release 0.

more prevalent which are known to be influenced by living conditions and lifestyle. In contrast, based on our data, cancer and chronic lung disease are less prevalent in the CEE countries (Figure 17.3). Note that these statistics do not reveal the differences in mortality rates between the country groups. For example, whereas the prevalence of cancer is similar, we know from Eurostat and OECD statistics that the mortality rate due to cancer is on average higher in the CEE countries.

17.3.2. Retrospective health

The subsequent figures are based on the retrospective data obtained from Waves 3 and 7. The overall evaluation of childhood health (1–excellent to 5–poor) is somewhat worse in post-socialist countries. A hospital stay for 1 month or longer during childhood is a rare event but is slightly more prevalent in post-socialist countries (Figure 17.4). The number of ill health periods (0–none to 5–most of the time) is also slightly higher on average in post-socialist countries (Figure 17.5). These differences are moderate in magnitude, albeit statistically significant, indicating that the health gap between CEE and the West may partly originate from periods before the transition.

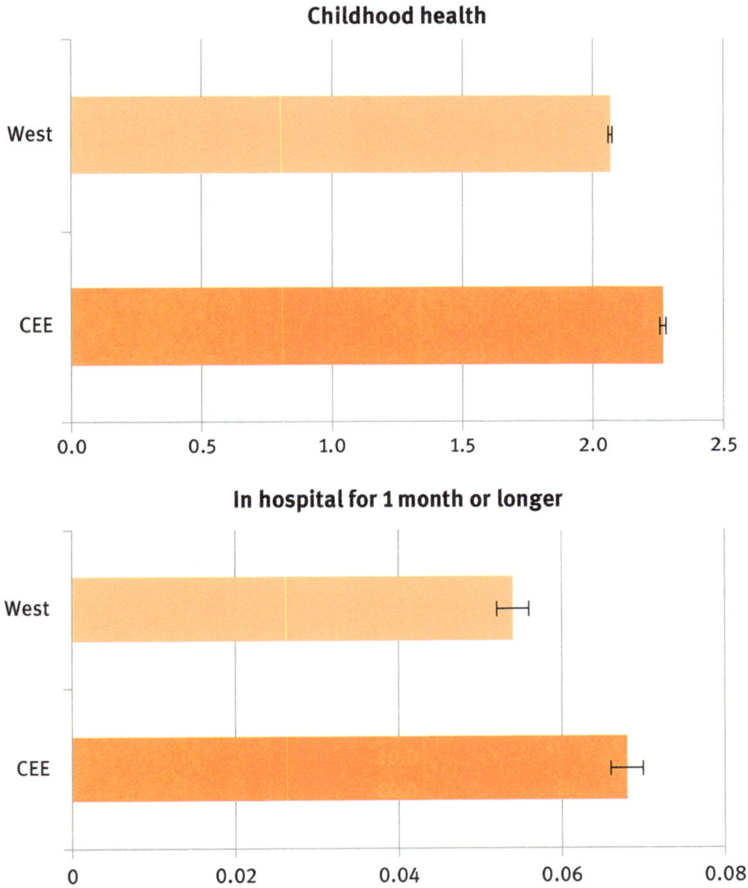

Figure 17.4: Self-reported childhood health and prevalence of hospital stay during childhood.
Note: Average health in childhood from 1–excellent to 5–poor. Prevalence of hospital stay for 1 month or longer during childhood; 95% confidence interval of the mean is displayed.
Source: SHARE Wave 3 release 6.1.0, Wave 7 release 0.

17.3.3 Timing of major health events and hardships

The distribution of the initial year of stressful periods and periods of financial hardship peaked around the transition (1990) in post-socialist countries but not in western countries (Figure 17.6). No such time pattern can be observed for the start of ill periods. In the case of the ill periods, only that period is considered here that is mentioned first. It is likely that there is a time lag between the transition and its potential health impacts.

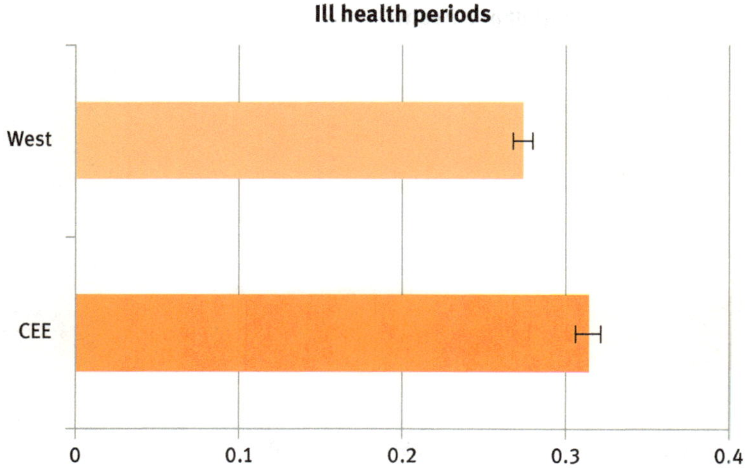

Figure 17.5: Frequency of ill health periods in CEE and the West.
Note: Average value of ill health periods as an adult (hs054) from 0–none to 5–ill or disabled for all or most of my life; 95% confidence interval of the mean is displayed.
Source: SHARE Wave 3 release 6.1.0, Wave 7 release 0.

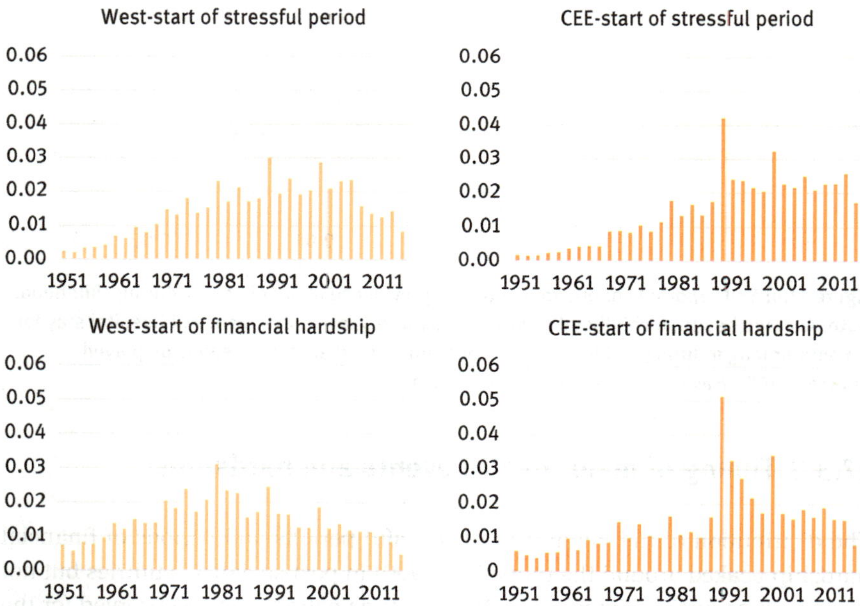

Figure 17.6: Timing of stressful periods and financial hardships in CEE and the West.
Note: Starting year of stressful periods, starting year of financial hardship.
Source: SHARE Wave 3 release 6.1.0, Wave 7 release 0.

The probability that the start of a stressful period or a period with financial hardship falls between 1987–1993 (i.e., around the transition) is 3 percentage points and 8 percentage points higher in post-socialist countries than in the West, respectively (Figure 17.7). These statistics are conditional on having had such hardships. Thus, the cross-country differences in reporting patterns of difficulties or hardships do not affect the estimated differences in the time patterns. The difference reflects the adverse shock of a transformational recession across CEE countries.

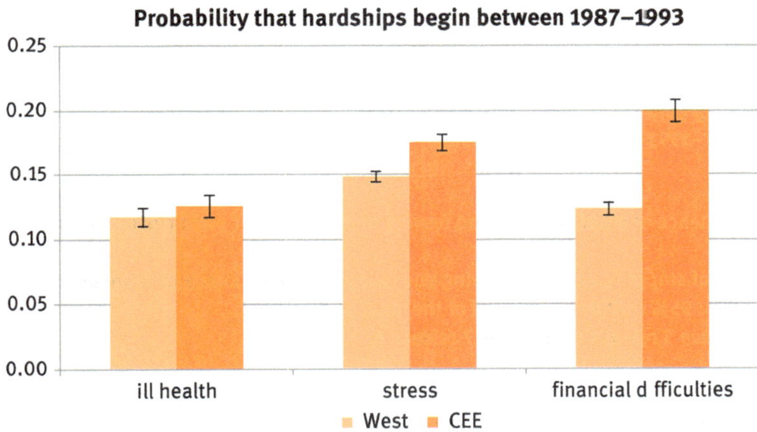

Figure 17.7: Ratio of the hardships beginning during 1987–1993 in CEE and the West.
Note: Probability that the initial year of ill health, stressful periods and financial hardships decline during 1987–1993 conditional on having had such hardship; 95% confidence interval of the mean is displayed.
Source: SHARE Wave 3 release 6.1.0, Wave 7 release 0.

We also observe that people were more likely to stop working in a job around the years of transition (1987–1993) in post-socialist CEE than in the West (Figure 17.8). Additionally, among those who stopped working in a job, the reason for leaving a job such as being laid off or a plant/office shutdown was more prevalent in post-socialist countries. Retiring was also slightly more likely in CEE countries, which may reflect the tendency in some post-socialist countries to transfer the unemployed into early and disability retirement.

17.3.4 Regressions

We estimate, using linear models, how a stressful period around a transition is associated with subsequent health. The sample is restricted to post-socialist

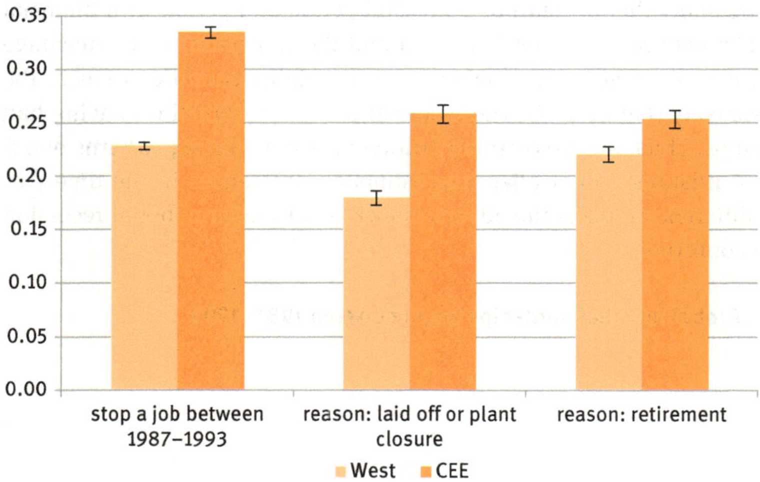

Figure 17.8: Prevalence of stopping a job and leaving due to lay-off or plant closure during 1987–1993.
Note: Prevalence of stopping a job and leaving due to lay-off, plant closure or retirement during 1987–1993; 95% confidence interval of the mean is displayed.
Source: SHARE Wave 3 release 6.1.0, Wave 7 release 0.

CEE countries. We regress various health measures on the binary indicators of a stressful period or financial hardships beginning during 1987–1993. We also add a set of individual controls (age, gender, education dummies, overall childhood health, hospitalization during childhood and country dummies). We observe evidence that such hardships imply worse overall health at older ages and a higher probability of having ever had hypertension or ulcer. We find small and statistically insignificant associations with having ever been diagnosed with cancer or lung disease (not reported in Figures 17.9–17.11).

We also estimate the association between a job change around a transition and later health. The results suggest negative health implications of stopping or changing jobs around a transition.

17.4 Conclusions

Using retrospective data (SHARELIFE), we analysed the origins of the health gap between post-socialist central and eastern Europe, and western Europe. We documented that health disparities existed even before the transition. Additionally,

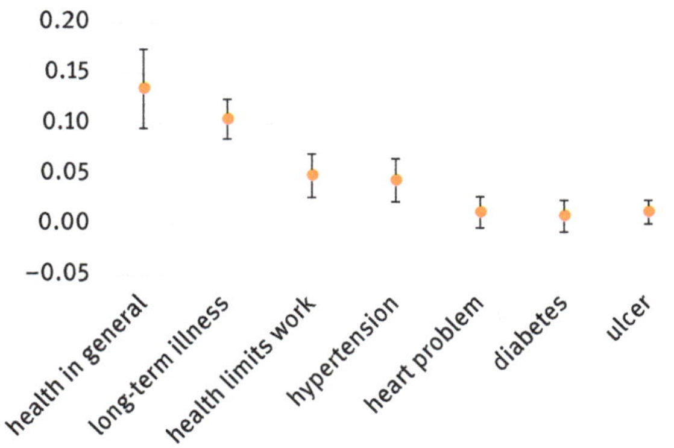

Figure 17.9: Linear regressions – current health and stressful period during 1987–1993.
Note: Estimated coefficient of a stressful period starting during 1987–1993 in separate linear regressions with indicators of current health as a dependent variable (health in general, among others); 95% confidence interval of the point estimate is displayed. Individual controls include age, gender, education dummies (primary, secondary, tertiary), overall childhood health on a scale of 1–5 and hospitalization during childhood dummy.
Source: SHARE Wave 3 release 6.1.0, Wave 7 release 0.

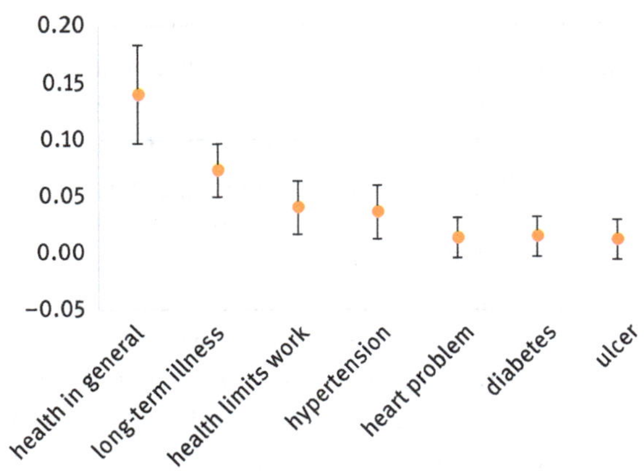

Figure 17.10: Linear regressions – current health and financial hardship during 1987–1993.
Note: Estimated coefficient of financial hardship starting during 1987–1993 in separate linear regressions with indicators of current health as a dependent variable (health in general, among others); 95% confidence interval of the point estimate is displayed. Individual controls include age, gender, education dummies (primary, secondary, tertiary), overall childhood health on a scale of 1–5 and hospitalization during childhood dummy.
Source: SHARE Wave 3 release 6.1.0, Wave 7 release 0.

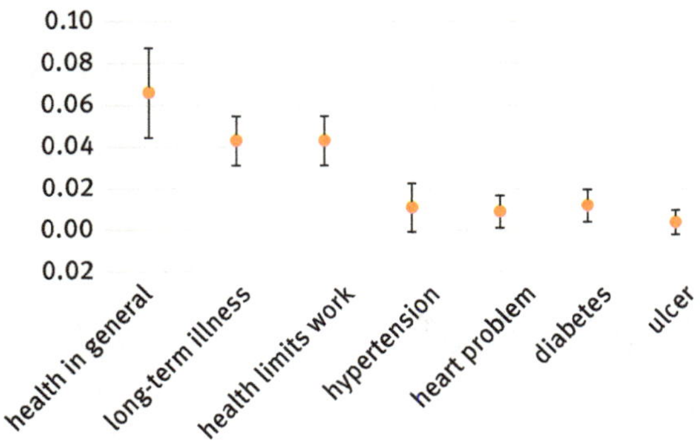

Figure 17.11: Linear regressions – current health and stopping a job between 1987–1993.
Note: Estimated coefficient of stopping a job during 1987–1993 in separate linear regressions with indicators of current health as a dependent variable (health in general, among others); 95% confidence interval of the point estimate is displayed. Individual controls include age in year 2017, gender, education dummies (primary, secondary, tertiary), overall childhood health on a scale of 1–5 and hospitalization during childhood dummy.
Source: SHARE Wave 3 release 6.1.0, Wave 7 release 0.

we showed that the post-socialist transition era was more often associated with the start of stressful periods and financial difficulties in the post-socialist CEE countries than in the West. Finally, with the assistance of a regression analysis, we found evidence that stressful periods, financial difficulties and job loss around the transition period are all associated with worse health at older ages, even after netting out the effect of childhood health and demographic factors. Overall, our results suggest that the post-socialist transition itself increased the health disadvantage of the post-socialist CEE countries.

Our study is subject to a set of limitations. The results are conditional on having survived approximately 20 years after transition; thus, we could not estimate the mortality effects. Health behaviours could not be analysed given data limitations. Additionally, reverse causality is possible from persistent health problems to reporting hardships related to the transition; therefore, our results indicate associations rather than causal effects.

References

Azarova, A., et al. (2017). The effect of rapid privatisation on mortality in mono-industrial towns in post-Soviet Russia: a retrospective cohort study. *The Lancet Public Health*, *2*(5), e231–e238.

EBRD (1999). *Transition report 1999. Ten years of transition*. European Bank for Reconstruction and Development, 1999.

King, L., Hamm, P., and Stuckler, D. (2009). Rapid large-scale privatization and death rates in ex-communist countries: an analysis of stress-related and health system mechanisms. *International Journal of Health Services*, *39*(3), 461–489.

Laaksonen, M., et al. (2001). Do health behaviour and psychosocial risk factors explain the European East-West gap in health status? *The European Journal of Public Health* 11(1),65–73.

Steptoe, A., and Wardle, J. (2001). Health behaviour, risk awareness and emotional well-being in students from Eastern Europe and Western Europe. *Social Science & Medicine*, *53*(12), 1621–1630.

Zatonski, W. (2007). The east-west health gap in Europe – what are the causes? *The European Journal of Public Health*, *17*(2), 121–121.

Ekaterina Markova and Gabriela Yordanova

18 What is hidden behind the 'obvious'? SHARE data raise the curtain about health, early retirement and elderly care of ageing Bulgarians

- The problematic health status of Bulgarians over 50, in line with their inactive relations with the healthcare system, contradicts their relatively high self-assessments of their general health
- Institutionalized long-term elderly care seems to require the full commitment of Bulgarian families that do not use external services or receive support from the community or the state
- A large portion of all employed Bulgarians in SHARE – employees at the end of their working careers and primarily women – seek early retirement, and a third of them have completed their primary or lower education. Forming plans for early retirement depends on their health status

18.1 Introduction

Bulgaria (BG) is the country with the strongest demographic crisis in Europe, and it is also among the oldest populations worldwide (UN, 2015). What is hidden behind the obvious unprecedented ageing in Bulgaria? What research space is open for knowledge-based policies? SHARE data are of significant importance in understanding the ageing impact in eastern Europe relative to the EU, and Bulgaria is an extreme example of a rapidly ageing society.

The chapter describes national data from SHARE Wave 7 that frame together health and attitudes towards early retirement and elderly care:

- General physical health in Bulgaria;
- Early retirement plans; and
- Family networks.

The SHARE data concerning physical health are evaluated through various cross-sectional analyses, such as sex, age, education, source of income and employment status. Special attention is paid to 'employed' respondents seeking early retirement with reference to their gender, age, education and general health self-assessment. To open up space for further research, the national data

https://doi.org/10.1515/9783110617245-018

are observed through a comparative perspective with the central and eastern European countries of Germany (DE), Belgium (BE), Croatia (HR) and Romania RO. The selection of these countries allows a fruitful comparison between developed western democracies as old member states, and post-socialistic EU new-comers.

As an important topic of interest, we find family networks and possible data for use in developing an integrated long-term care policy and overcoming the negative public attitudes towards institutionalized elderly care. Most respondents are living with relatives (parents and/or children) for the purpose of helping each other.

18.2 Health status of ageing Bulgarians

Life expectancy in Bulgaria is among the lowest in the EU (74.7 years, Eurostat 2018). SHARE provides a high-quality opportunity to deeply explore the factors that affect the health behaviour and current health status of Bulgarians (self-assessments and objective measures).

The subjective self-assessment of general health is positive, but the reason for such an estimation could be, in general, the insufficient attention paid by the Bulgarians to their health. Approximately 61 per cent of all Bulgarian respondents report 'good' to 'excellent' health, relative to 68 per cent in Belgium, 57 per cent in Germany, 54 per cent in Croatia and 50 per cent in Romania. The percentage of Bulgarians who positively assess their general health as excellent or very good is higher than the percentages reported in other countries (29% in BG, 25% in BE, 22% in HR, 17% in DE, 13% in RO, Figure 18.1). A comparison of personal self-assessments of general health by country illustrates the serious need for in-depth research beyond the survey data – for example, within the context of national health systems, traditions and health culture.

SHARE data show that every fifth respondent (21.7%) had not discussed his or her health with a medical doctor/nurse in the past 12 months. At the same time, only 25.2 per cent of respondents declared taking no drugs, while 33.3 per cent stated that they took at least 5 different drugs in a typical day. More than two-thirds of respondents (69.1%) stated that they had not seen a dentist in the past year, 26.8 per cent did not suffer from SHARE-listed chronic diseases and half (50.6%) reported a long-term illness. Fully in line with the official statistics, the most reported disease that respondents suffer from is high blood pressure (51.5%), followed by heart attacks (14.3%), diabetes (12.1%) and high

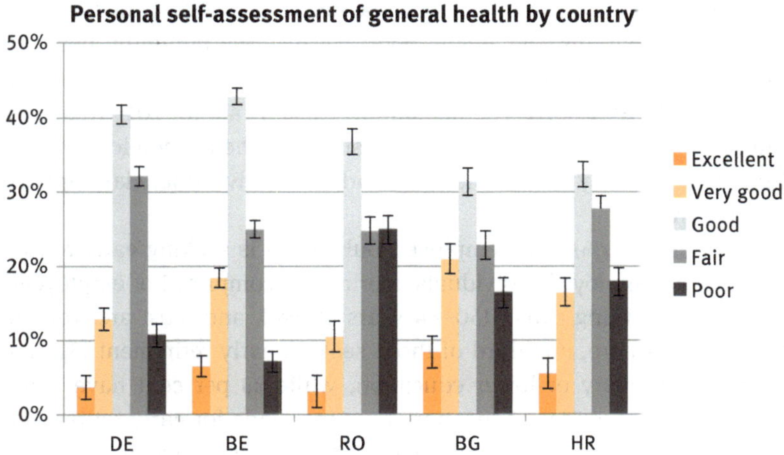

Figure 18.1: Personal self-assessment of general health by country.
Source: SHARE Wave 7 release 0, 95% confidence interval.

blood cholesterol (11.7%). Problematic health causes limitations in daily activities for 44.0 per cent of SHARE respondents; 33.7 per cent had difficulty stooping, kneeling and crouching; 30 per cent had difficulty climbing several flights of stairs; 24.6 per cent had difficulty pulling or pushing large objects; 22.9 per cent had difficulty lifting or carrying weights over 5 kilograms; 15.6 per cent had difficulty getting up from a chair; 14.8 per cent had difficulty climbing one flight of stairs; 16.4 per cent had difficulty walking 100 metres; and 9 per cent had difficulty sitting for two hours.

18.3 Early retirement plans in Bulgaria

The closure of industrial sites in Bulgaria during the change from a planned to a market economy in 1989 forced employees to find any job – even one that did not correspond to their education, experience and qualifications. Many workers became unemployed and, as a result, could not achieve the required age and work experience for retirement. Those who are 50–64 years of age are perceived as vulnerable to unemployment (Holtgrewe, 2015).

From all SHARE respondents in Bulgaria, 27.4 per cent reported being employed or self-employed, 61.7 per cent are retired and 4.7 per cent are unemployed. Of all SHARE respondents, a larger proportion (60.5%) counts on public pensions for the elderly as their main source of income. Retired persons in Bulgaria often engage in undeclared work because of low pensions. We could call retired Bulgarians 'the ageing poor' because the minimum pension for 2017 was EUR 102.28, which was received by 612,437 Bulgarians (National Social Security Institute (NSSI)). The maximum pension rate for 2017 was EUR 465.39, which was received by 53,541 'rich pensioners'. The economic status of retired Bulgarians actually forces them to work or receive financial support from their children.

A large portion (41.6%) of all employed Bulgarians is seeking early retirement. This group of employed individuals is primarily comprised of employees at the end of their working career (50–64 years of age), and most are women (Figure 18.2). Furthermore, one-third of those seeking early retirement (31.3%) report completing primary or lower education, while 33 per cent have completed a professional secondary education. Forming plans for early retirement depends on health status: the general health self-assessment mean is fair, at 3.14; more than half (51.8%) suffer from a long-term illness; 44.2 per cent are limited in activities for health reasons; and 22.5 per cent have health problems that limit their ability to engage in paid work.

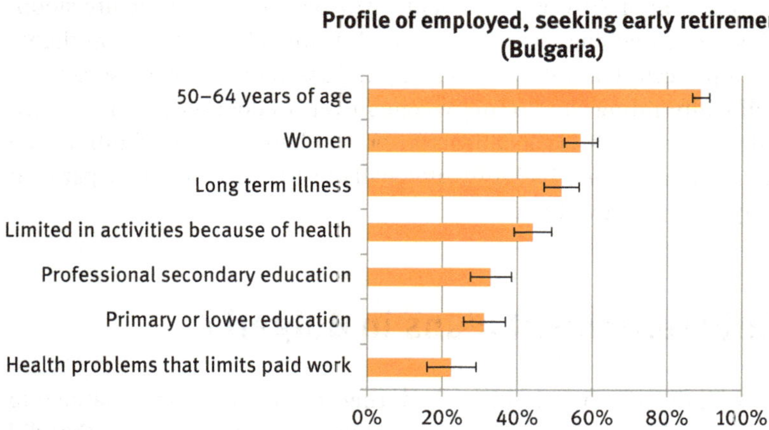

Figure 18.2: Profile of employed, seeking early retirement (Bulgaria).
Source: SHARE Wave 7 release 0, 95% confidence interval.

In line with the context of demographic change in Europe and plans to provide people with better conditions to work longer in good health, the comparative data between countries show that 55 per cent of Romanians and 51 per cent of Germans report a subjective willingness for early retirement relative to 39 per cent in Belgium (Figure 18.3).

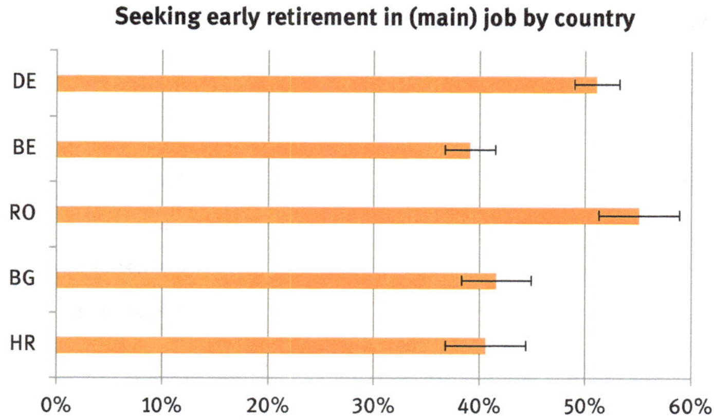

Figure 18.3: Seeking early retirement in (main) job by country.
Source: SHARE Wave 7 release 0, 95% confidence interval.

18.4 Family networks as the main provider of elderly care

A widespread stereotype in Bulgarian society is that elderly care should be taken on by the family. Nursing homes and hospices are considered too expensive. The media often reports that, 'It is shameful and irresponsible to put your parents in such institutions'. SHARE data indicate that 36.1 per cent of respondents are living with parents and parents-in-law in the same household. The main reason for living together is the mutual help provided (more than 70%). The pattern of living with older relatives favours living with parents-in-law (for example, 71.4% live with their mother and 78.2% live with their mother-in-law) because of national traditions. Even those who do not live with their parents maintain a daily relationship with them (42.1% with the mother, 29% with the father). The maximum distance from the parents' home is up to 5 km for most cases (mother's home, 46.6%; father's home, 43.7%). The life history data (Börsch-Supan, 2013) from SHARE show that most Bulgarian respondents were born in small villages and rural areas that are today highly depopulated. Rural areas and villages are inhabited by old persons, whereas the young are seeking a better life and work opportunities in large cities or abroad. Adult children take care of their parents and shape the internal migration of the elderly from villages to cities. The family pattern of living with older parents varies among western and eastern European countries (Figure 18.4).

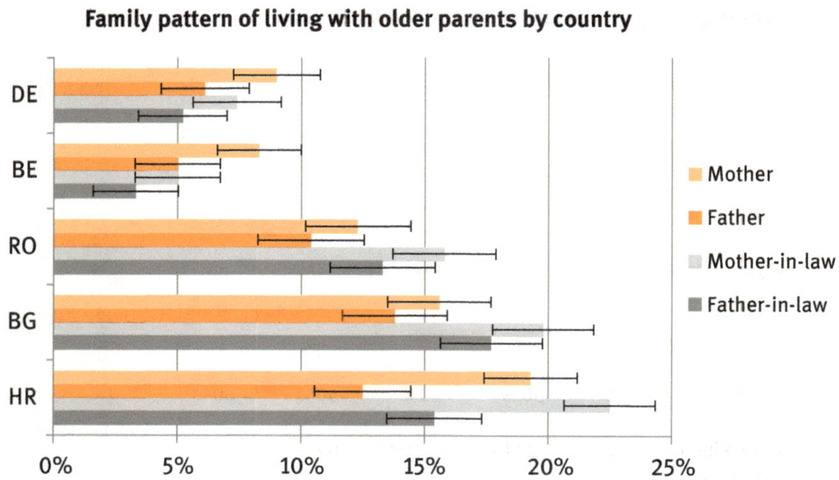

Figure 18.4: Family pattern of living with older parents by country.
Source: SHARE Wave 7 release 0, 95% confidence interval.

Institutionalized elderly care and, in particular, long-term care is generally outside of Bulgarian SHARE respondents' experience: no one contributes to long-term care insurance, and we noted only 3 individuals who were the beneficiaries of nursery home care (1–3 week temporary stay). External professional care has been used by 1–2 per cent of all surveyed households in Bulgaria.

18.5 Conclusions

The preliminary conclusions derived from SHARE data indicate the problematic health status of Bulgarians over 50, which is in line with their inactive relationship with the health care system. From a comparative perspective, the subjective self-assessment of general health provokes our research interest for further analyses: why do Bulgarians demonstrate higher self-assessments than Romanians, Croatians and Germans? Probable explanations might be the tendency of Bulgarians to overestimate their health, to negate health problems and to rarely take preventive health actions.

The early retirement plans of 41 per cent of employed Bulgarians over 50 should be analysed in the context of employment, health and economic policy-making, such as the national programme for increasing the retirement age, ambitions to increase the quality of life of the elderly and a national strategy for demographic development. Among different EU member states, the analysis of the comparative desires for early retirement is of critical importance from a comprehensive and multidimensional perspective within national and EU legislation to create policies that are in line with the personal motives of people who want to leave the labour market earlier.

Long-term elderly care seems to be a full-time commitment for Bulgarian families that do not use external services. Families are entrusted with great responsibility for caring for their sick and elderly parents, and they generally do not receive sufficient support from the community or the state. An open issue is whether – in creating an integrated national long-term care programme – family traditions and stereotypes in Bulgaria would be obstacles or would provide support. In southeast European countries, because the strong family ties and the tradition of living with older parents differ from family networks in western Europe, the long-term care policies should consider national specifics. Moreover, public policies need to be flexible not only at the national and regional levels but also regarding important aspects of historical development, such as how Bulgaria could implement external ideas related to an integrated elderly care policy without exploring strong family networks and stereotypes.

SHARE helps shed light on one additional socio-political dimension of human capital development through its life history data and provides insights into the transition from a centrally planned economy to a market economy and the impact on an individual's lives and their ageing processes. Further research needs to focus on the impact of childhood quality of life on current health status, health literacy and retirement.

References

Börsch-Supan, A., M. Brandt and M. Schröder. (2013). SHARELIFE – One century of life histories in Europe. Advances in Life Course Research. *Advances in life course research*, 18(1).

Eurostat, (2018), Life expectancy at birth, *Statistics Explained*.

Holtgrewe, U., Ramioul, M. and Kirov, V. (2015). *Hard work in new jobs. The Quality of Work and Life in European Growth Sectors*. New York: Palgrawe Macmillan UK.

National Statistical Institute Bulgaria, *Demographic and social statistics 2016*, available at http://www.nsi.bg/en/content/11224/demographic-and-social-statistics

United Nations, Department of Economic and Social Affairs, Population Division (2015). *World Population Prospects: The 2015 Revision, Key Findings and Advance Tables*. Working Paper No. ESA/P/WP.241.

Loretti I. Dobrescu and Alin Marius Andrieș

19 The link to the past and the post-communist welfare state

- Childhood health and cognition have long-lasting effects on the prevalence of dire health and financial circumstances later in life
- Such adverse health effects appear mitigated across various dimensions by the generosity of the welfare state, mostly related to extreme but reversible circumstances (serious – but not long-term or chronic – illnesses, financial hardship or hunger)
- Superior cognitive skills are associated with better chances of making ends meet or avoiding hunger, whereas having experienced financial hardship seems unavoidable given the last 30–40 years of turmoil

19.1 Introduction

Early life provides the foundation for many outcomes in adulthood. How strong is, however, the role of adverse childhood conditions in determining negative adult outcomes for Romanians? And given their current social insurance system, to what extent is this link mitigated by the western-type welfare policies implemented after the 'dawn of democracy' in 1989? Answering these questions will prove an interesting exercise, as Romania's political and social trajectories during the last century have been quite unique. It is an eastern European country with strong Latin origins that emerged three decades ago from an overbearing communist regime. During 'the regime' (i.e., the better part of last century) the *Party* maintained a tight grip on power and control, while also promoting a widespread and quite generous universal social welfare system. The last years have seen the country transitioning to a western-like democracy with several periods of rapid and often chaotic reforms that brought significant social turmoil and economic disparities. So, how does all this matter for the old age Romanians' link with their early life?

The relation between childhood conditions and health or socioeconomic status in later life has been well established (Currie, 2009). For instance, those who experience poor childhood health have significantly worse cognition, health and socioeconomic status as adults (Case et al., 2002; Currie, 2009). Early cognition and education appear as key drivers of socioeconomic success, with nourishing early environments and low exposure to adverse events (e.g. abuse, economic hardship) effectively shaping individual well-being (Heckman et al., 2013).

https://doi.org/10.1515/9783110617245-019

An interesting yet considerably less explored dimension relates to how early-life effects are mediated by national welfare systems and regional economic development. The issue is crucial from a policy standpoint because it provides policymakers and welfare architects with valuable insights into the behaviour of those most vulnerable: the old, the ill and the poor. Despite their key role, however, social welfare policies have not become – theoretically or empirically – a leitmotif of the research into disparities triggered by early life conditions. This has only recently changed through a series of SHARELIFE papers on the link between childhood circumstances and old age health, cognition, income, asset portfolio and risk attitudes (Christelis et al., 2011; Mazzona, 2014).

Numerous adult outcomes can be influenced by childhood health and cognition. This chapter focuses on the prevalence of adverse health and financial circumstances in old age. Once this link is proven, we investigate how it is affected by the welfare state generosity (or stinginess). The analysis is thus particularly relevant in light of the current social and political debate in Romania that has seen the public affected by extreme polarization around two main camps defined by their support for or against the welfare state.

In doing so, we will use Romania's first SHARE wave. Implemented in 2017, SHARE Wave 7 questionnaire included several childhood health, cognition and socioeconomic indicators. To capture the differential effects brought into play by the welfare state, we extend this dataset with several regional level indicators that capture the social insurance system coverage and economic development (e.g., county level social insurance benefits per capita, average individual welfare transfers, total economic surplus).

19.2 Why Romania?

Romania's welfare system is quite a special case: under the communist regime, virtually nobody was on welfare or received social assistance. Since the Iron Curtain fell, Romania became a welfare paradox with pensions and child benefits that rival wages but also the lowest unemployment and social assistance benefits in the European Union. Currently, nearly one in three Romanians (approximately 6.5 million people) receive some form of social benefit (NIS's 'Regional, economic & social benchmarks: Territorial statistics (2018)' – henceforth, NIS, 2018). Particularly interesting is how these benefits are distributed among the vulnerable groups. For instance, the 2016 national public spending on social insurance (health and social benefits) was approximately 19.40 billion EUR, with pensions, medical spending and welfare (or social assistance) accounting for 59.92%, 28.74% and 11.34%, respectively, of this total amount (NIS, 2018). Zooming in on social benefits, we see these funds reaching more than 4.65 million retirees receiving decent public pensions but less than 0.25 million people on welfare (NIS, 2018). These groups represent 27.94% and 1.46% of the country's 15+ population, respectively, and unveil a striking discrepancy considering the 5.90% unemployment rate and 46.30% economic inactivity rate recorded during the same year.

Additionally, Romania exhibits a regional development gradient across its four historic regions (Transylvania, Moldavia-Dobrogea, Muntenia and Banat-Oltenia), largely due to their distinct historical, cultural and economic growth roots. Given the strong socialist philosophy of the communist regime, these territorial discrepancies were less prominent before 1989 but deepened substantially recently. The 'transition' period after 1989 observed imbalances and inequality soaring across the country and, although a number of policies were implemented to diminish poverty and the risk of social exclusion, large regional variations still exist (see NIS's 'Labour force in Romania: Employment and unemployment (2016)' – henceforth, NIS, 2016; NIS 2018). For instance, the 2016 unemployment rate averaged 5.9% nationally, but ranged between 4.7% in Transylvania and 7.6% in Banat-Oltenia (NIS, 2016) (see Table 19.1). This

Table 19.1: Welfare paradox of social benefits.

	Transylvania	Moldavia Dobrogea	Muntenia	Banat Oltenia	TOTAL
Total population	*4,911,312*	*5,707,418*	*5,306,173*	*3,781,626*	*19,706,529*
Number of pensioners	1,190,458	1,275,577	1,281,488	930,185	4,677,708
Share of pensioners	*24.24%*	*22.35%*	*24.15%*	*24.60%*	*23.74%*
Number of unemployed persons	101,000	127,000	178,000	124,000	530,000
Unemployment rate	*4.70%*	*4.80%*	*7.00%*	*7.60%*	*5.90%*
Number of welfare beneficiaries	53,507	91,914	49,028	50,365	244,814
Share of welfare beneficiaries	*1.09%*	*1.61%*	*0.92%*	*1.33%*	*1.24%*

Source: http://www.insse.ro/cms/sites/default/files/field/publicatii/labour_force_in_romania_employment_and_unemployment_2016.pdf.

situation translated into significant differences in welfare beneficiaries' figures, ranging between 0.92% (Muntenia) and 1.61% (Moldavia-Dobrogea). Strikingly, and supporting our previous discussion of the meagre welfare pillar of the Romanian social insurance system, less than half of those unemployed received any form of social assistance (NIS, 2016).

Overall, we expect any link between childhood conditions and current health and financial circumstances to be affected by the dual-dimension of this heterogeneity. The welfare system discrepancies should make a difference for those receiving transfers, mitigating a potential negative association. Economic development further changes the equation of available resources and opportunities, driving different groups of people in the category of social insurance beneficiaries. We subsequently investigate these issues.

19.3 Something old, something . . . current

As mentioned, Romania joined SHARE in 2017 with a questionnaire that included a rich set of questions meant to capture health and cognition in early life. We use four childhood indicators: (i) subjective childhood health status as reported by respondents today and captured by whether one recalls being in fair or poor health; (ii) objective childhood health captured by the number of chronic conditions that one was diagnosed with early in life, and (iii) two cognition indicators on having above-average academic skills in Maths and language relative to one's peers.

Figure 19.1 show a dramatic difference in self-reported health, with Transylvanians reporting bad health almost twice as often than those in Banat-Oltenia (8.23% vs. 4.76%). Those in Transylvania were also the most affected by chronic conditions, as shown by the 18.40% of respondents diagnosed with two or more chronic conditions, whereas the 'objectively healthiest' region in this respect is Muntenia (11.51%). Interestingly, the regional cognition gradient appears less prominent, with the best-performing region (Muntenia) having 45.08% and 51.55% of respondents scoring higher than average in Maths and languages, respectively; Moldavia-Dobrogea is at the lower end of the range in both categories, with only 38.03% and 42.62% of respondents scoring higher than average.

Regarding our outcome variables, we will focus on six adverse conditions in adulthood: (i) whether one has ever had periods of serious illness, (ii) whether one has ever had periods of long-term illness, (iii) whether one is currently diagnosed with two or more chronic conditions, (iv) whether one has ever experienced hunger, (v) whether one has ever experienced financial hardship, and (vi) whether the household can make ends meet.

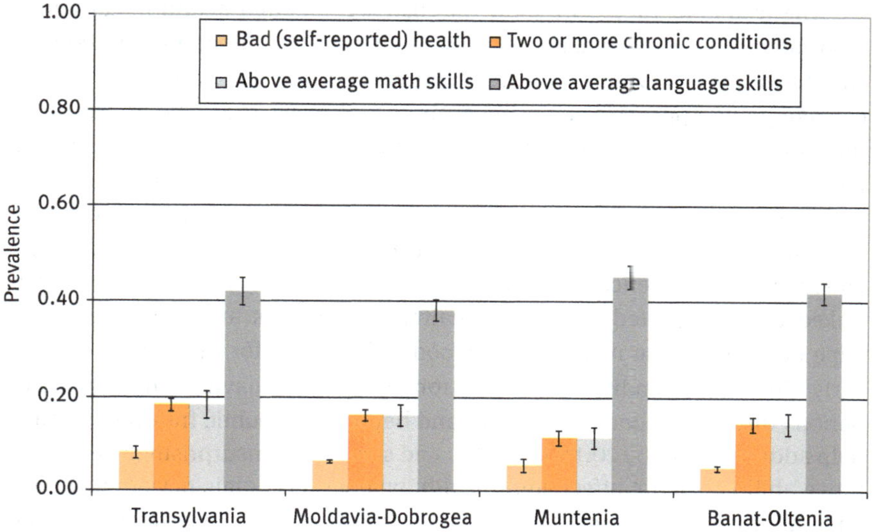

Figure 19.1: Childhood conditions prevalence.
Source: SHARE Wave 7 release 0.

Plotting the mean of every outcome variable by each childhood condition we study shows generally a clear direct association between them (results available on request). Here, we aim to estimate the magnitude of this relation and investigate the extent to which this association is mitigated by the welfare system and economic development. As a result, we include three county-level context variables: (i) per capita monthly amount of social insurance benefits (in health models), (ii) average monthly amount (in 00's) of individual welfare benefits (in financial models), and (iii) per capita total economic surplus (as economic indicator).

For each adult/childhood variable combination, we use a probit model to associate the outcome of interest with the early life health and cognition variables. As mentioned, we also include county-level measures of welfare generosity and economic development, and we interact childhood indicators with such measures to allow for as much differential effects across regions as possible. Our specifications also include respondents' age, gender, education and marital status, as well as two indicators of their childhood socioeconomic status: (i) the number of rooms in the house where respondents lived when they were 10 (adjusted for family size) and (ii) the number of books that their family possessed at that time. Thus, we can estimate childhood effects net of all these factors, which makes them less likely to be spurious.

The results in Table 19.2 show that bad self-reported health in early life is associated with being diagnosed with 2+ chronic conditions in adulthood, as well as with ever having experienced serious or long-term illnesses by 14.4 percentage points (pp), 11.3 pp and 15.4 pp, respectively. The same holds true for the childhood number of chronic conditions that negatively affect all our three measures of adult health, by 8.1 pp, 3.0 pp and 10.2 pp, respectively.

Given these strong direct relations to the past, is there any role for the welfare state in changing these patterns? The answer is yes, with welfare state generosity having beneficial effects for all three adult health outcomes when linked to self-reported childhood health. Such effects are strong enough to wipe out most of the negative childhood links except for those most extreme: early life chronic conditions remain strongly related to having long-term illness periods throughout one's life, above and beyond any public transfers meant to help address them (by 20.1%). Finally, and somewhat unsurprisingly, early cognitive abilities do not affect adult health, whereas economic development matters only for more extreme health circumstances such as long-term or chronic illnesses.

Turning to the relationship between childhood conditions and adult financial circumstances, we find that both our subjective and objective measures of bad childhood health play a key role in making it more likely that one experienced periods of hunger or financial hardship in later life. Bad self-reported health is associated with 3.1 (8.8) pp higher chances of having experienced financial hardship (hunger). Similarly, the effect of chronic conditions in early age is strong for all financial indicators, with the associations ranging from approximately 1.0 to 6.3 pp. Welfare generosity, as captured by social assistance transfers, is once more pretty strong in all models involving financial hardship or hunger. Interestingly, it also slightly mitigates (by 0.2%) the link between dire (objective) health and hunger. This contrasts public transfers making a difference for the current ability of households to make ends meet, which remains negatively associated by 3.1 pp with chronic illnesses experienced more than three decades earlier.

As mentioned, cognitive skills in early life are a key driver of adult socioeconomic status. We confirm this hypothesis, with the ability to make ends meet being strongly associated with higher than average test scores in both Maths (8.8%) and languages (9.0%), a positive and robust result. Interestingly, only superior Maths scores seem to lower the chances of experiencing hunger, even after taking into account social assistance (by 2.2%). This finding is unsurprising though, given the strong link between Maths skills and future earnings (Tyler, 2004). Finally, we find no effect of better cognition on ever having experienced financial hardship, possibly the result of Romania's political and

Table 19.2: Childhood conditions and adult outcomes.

Childhood indicator	Bad (self-reported) health		Two or more chronic conditions		Above averagemath skills		Above average language skills	
Panel A.1. Ever had periods of serious illness								
Childhood Ind	0.113***	0.202	0.030***	0.253***	−0.023	−0.017	−0.012	0.020
Welfare Ind		0.117**		0.035		−0.142**		−0.129**
Child.*Welfare		−0.105		−0.251***		−0.007		−0.036
Econ Dev		−0.001		−0.001		−0.001		−0.001
Panel A.2. Ever had periods of long-term illness								
Childhood Ind	0.154***	−0.194	0.102***	0.201**	0.013	0.005	−0.001	0.151
Welfare Ind		−0.290***		−0.142*		−0.282***		−0.207*
Child.*Welfare		0.373		−0.114		0.007		−0.162
Econ Dev		−0.011***		−0.011***		−0.011***		−0.011***
Panel A.3. Diagnosed with two or more chronic conditions								
Childhood Ind	0.144***	−0.145	0.081***	−0.043	−0.008	0.150	−0.013	0.194*
Welfare Ind		−0.133**		−0.115		−0.064		−0.033
Child.*Welfare		0.318		0.131		−0.169		−0.220*
Econ Dev		−0.013***		−0.011***		−0.013***		−0.013***
Panel B.1. Ever experienced financial hardship								
Childhood Ind	0.088**	0.061	0.063***	0.062***	−0.019	−0.024	0.004	0.006
Welfare Ind		0.007***		0.008**		0.008***		0.011***
Child.*Welfare		0.027***		0.000		0.001		−0.003
Econ Dev		−0.017***		−0.017***		−0.017***		−0.017***

(continued)

Table 19.2 (continued)

Childhood indicator	Bad (self-reported) health		Two or more chronic conditions		Above averagemath skills		Above average language skills	
Panel B.2. Ever experienced hunger								
Childhood Ind	0.031**	0.038**	0.010*	0.012**	−0.018**	−0.024**	−0.006	−0.009
Welfare Ind		0.002**		0.004***		0.000		0.001
Child.*Welfare		−0.007		−0.002**		0.002*		0.001
Econ Dev		−0.001		−0.001		−0.001		−0.001
Panel B.3. Household can make ends meet								
Childhood Ind	−0.032	−0.044	−0.030*	−0.031*	0.088***	0.091***	0.090***	0.089***
Welfare Ind		−0.001		0.000		0.000		−0.001
Child.*Welfare		0.006		−0.001		−0.001		0.000
Econ Dev		0.010**		0.010**		0.010**		0.010**

Note: The sample has 2,045 observations depending on specification, except for B.3 specifications that include 1,362 observations. Childhood Ind is one of the four early life indicators we study; Welfare Ind is the county-level indicator of welfare generosity; Child. *Welfare is the interaction of the aforementioned variables; and Econ Dev is the county-level economic development indicator. *** = 1%; ** = 5%; * = 10%
Source: SHARE Wave 7 release 0.

economic 'transition' climate in the last three decades, dominated by recession, economic and social uncertainty and chaotic reforms. All our respondents have been exposed to this rough 'transition' period; seeing welfare transfers and economic development taking centre stage in determining their chances of having experienced financial hardship is thus not surprising. One peculiar point to note is the positive sign of the welfare indicator in all significant models related to financial hardship and hunger. This could indicate that, although social assistance payments might be relatively less generous than other types of welfare transfers (e.g. public pensions), they are large enough to positively affect the chances of someone reporting dire financial circumstances.

These results make a strong case for early life welfare interventions. Boosting care affordability, promoting preventative health strategies, enforcing higher standards for healthcare providers, establishing programmes that prevent school dropout, striving for higher literacy levels and fostering remedial education for those who fall behind are only a few such policies with tremendous future individual, economic and societal benefits.

References

Case, A., Lubotsky, D., Paxson, C. (2002). Economic status and health in childhood: The origins of the gradient. The American Economic Review 92:1308–1334.

Currie, J. (2009). Healthy, wealthy, and wise: Socioeconomic status, poor health in childhood, and human capital development. Journal of Economic Literature 47(1):87–122.

Christelis, D., Dobrescu, L.I, Motta, A. (2011). The impact of childhood health and cognition on portfolio choice. The Individual and the Welfare State, Springer:59–66.

Heckman, J., Pinto, R., Savelyev, P. (2013). Understanding the mechanisms through which an influential early childhood program boosted adult outcomes. American Economic Review 103(6):2052–2086.

Mazzonna, F. (2014). The long-lasting effects of family background: A European cross-country comparison, Economics of Education Review 40:25–42.

Tyler, J.H. (2004). Basic skills and the earnings of dropouts. Economics of Education Review 23:221–235.

Antigone Lyberaki, Platon Tinios, George Papadoudis and Thomas Georgiadis

20 The economic crisis, fiscal austerity and long-term care: Responses of the care mix in three adjustment countries

- Did austerity in the three southern countries reduce access to long-term care?
- The proportion of needy individuals without any care ('the care gap') *shrank* between 2007 and 2016. Despite austerity, *professional* care and not family based solidarity expanded
- This paradox can be partly explained by the maturation of formal systems and partly by beneficiaries' incomes falling less than the wages of carers in the open market

20.1 Introduction

SHARE Wave 2 was collected in the year immediately preceding the financial crisis; SHARE Wave 6 was collected in the year during which most countries considered the financial crisis to be over. Three southern European countries that participated in both waves (Greece, Spain and Italy) were affected by the financial crisis and implemented deep austerity programmes aimed to, inter alia, control public expenditures (Tinios, 2017). Long-term care (LTC) is an example of a family need that is met by a mix of public, private professional and family care. Given that most formal care is provided by public entities, LTC is likely to be on the receiving end of austerity policies (GBD, 2018). If access to public LTC is affected, the family will be called on to make up any deficit using its own resources. These resources could entail access to bought-in professional services from the private market and could also mean relying on informal solidarity provided by the family or other social networks.

Thus, LTC is an interesting case that lies on the cusp between public and private, formal and informal markets and family. The timing of economic developments is also important because they have occurred when at least two other secular changes were underway: the rapid ageing as the (slightly delayed in southern Europe) baby boom generation advanced in age and the transformation of gender roles as cohorts of women with very different career profiles (better educated, more exposed to paid work) entered retirement.

https://doi.org/10.1515/9783110617245-020

Studying the effects of the crisis during an 8-year period in countries anyway undergoing social change could give us a glimpse into how families marshal their resources – both social and economic – to meet challenges (Lyberaki and Tinios, 2014). Final outcomes on access to care, as well as on the LTC care mix, will be affected by supply (austerity) and demand factors (income falls) and price factors such as co-payments, and the relative price of care may also play a role.

The aim of this chapter is to identify how and whether LTC needs were met. We do so by focusing on three southern European countries that participated in both Wave 2 and Wave 6 (Greece, Italy and Spain) and that share a familial LTC model (Bettio and Plantenga, 2004; Lyberaki, 2011). The focus will be on the care gap (as a measure of unmet need) and the care mix (as a measure of household response). Greece, the country facing the deepest crisis, participated in the first three waves of SHARE, dropped out of Wave 4 and Wave 5 and only rejoined with an enlarged sample in Wave 6. Thus, SHARE affords a unique opportunity to track how a deep and protracted crisis affects the decisions made by older individuals.

20.2 Have needs for care changed?

If ageing is proceeding rapidly, we would expect that the *needs* for LTC are growing if they are largely physiologically determined. We can measure needs conventionally using the reported limitations in Activities of Daily Living (ADL) (e.g., Clark, 2004). If we focus on the group chiefly affected by longevity – those aged over 80 years – we *should* see an increase in care needs as reflected in the demand for care.

Figure 20.1 confounds easy expectations. The care needs of those over 80 between 2007 and 2015 were certainly *not* increasing and, at least for some women, may have *declined* considerably. This decline was particularly marked for Greece, where the needs of women clearly diverge from those of men.

20.3 Did the crisis leave more needs unmet?

The indicator we examine next could be called the 'care gap' – the people who, having declared that they cannot fulfil more than two ADLs, appear not to receive *any* care, whether formal or informal. Given the austerity narrative, our central expectation is that care gaps would *increase*. Again, we see that these

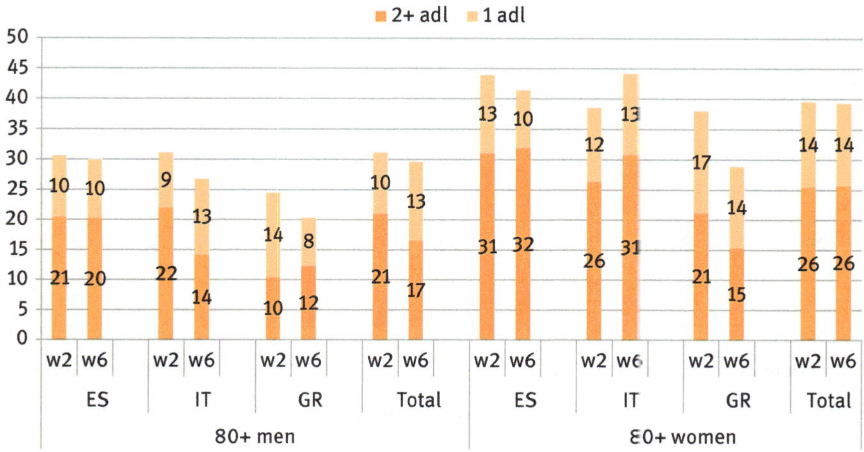

Figure 20.1: Persons with ADL limitations, by gender, persons 80+, Wave 2 and Wave 6.
Note: 'Total' refers to the 12 countries that participated in both Wave 2 and Wave 6.
Source: SHARE Wave 2 and 6 release 6.1.0.

expectations are not confirmed (Figure 20.2). Care gaps do not increase but, in contrast, appear to *decrease* – substantially for those older than 80 years of age. The decline is largest in Greece, the country hardest hit by austerity – in direct opposition to expectations. Comparing our southern European picture with other countries in the SHARE sample, we see that the decline in gaps (especially for the older group) is a European phenomenon that most likely results from the maturation of LTC as a social policy sector (the most dramatic declines occur in Scandinavia and eastern Europe).

20.4 Type of care received

SHARE distinguishes care as professional (*both* public and bought-in, but supplied by professionals) and informal, which is typically supplied free by members of social networks (mainly within the family).

The austerity narrative predisposes declines in *formal* care; state provisions were continuously under threat, whereas family incomes were severely squeezed. Again, the opposite holds. Figure 20.3, which shows changes in the care mix between 2007 and 2015, indicates that *formal* care and *not* informal care is increasing. This situation is particularly noticeable for those 80+ years

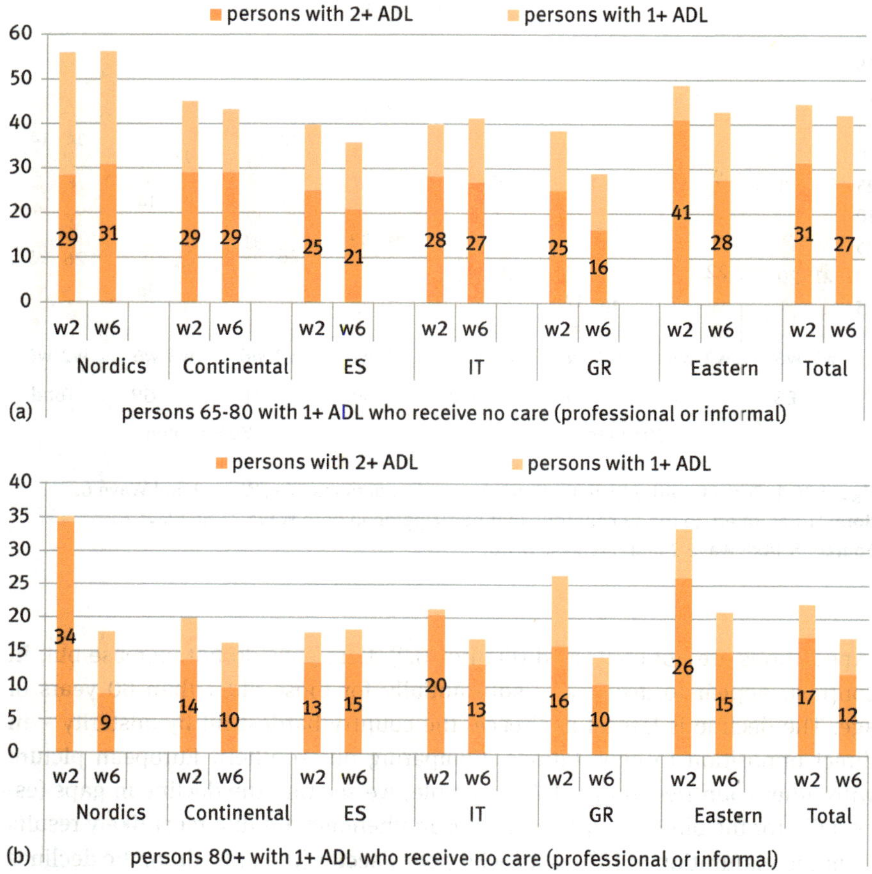

Figure 20.2: Care gaps, by number of ADL and age group, cross section, Wave 2 and Wave 6.
Source: SHARE Wave 2 and 6 release 6.1.0.

of age. Although informal care in the southern countries remains the dominant channel to meet needs, the care mix shifted in favour of exclusively formal care in Italy and an increase in the combination of formal and informal care in Greece and Spain. *Total* formal care increased everywhere.

A further point to note is the coincidence of formal and informal. Informal care is important even in systems that heavily rely on formal care, which signals complementarities between the two types: when both types are available, many people would probably choose both. However, this is not to say that the austerity narrative, in which formal care is *either* withdrawn *or* no longer affordable, is not applicable.

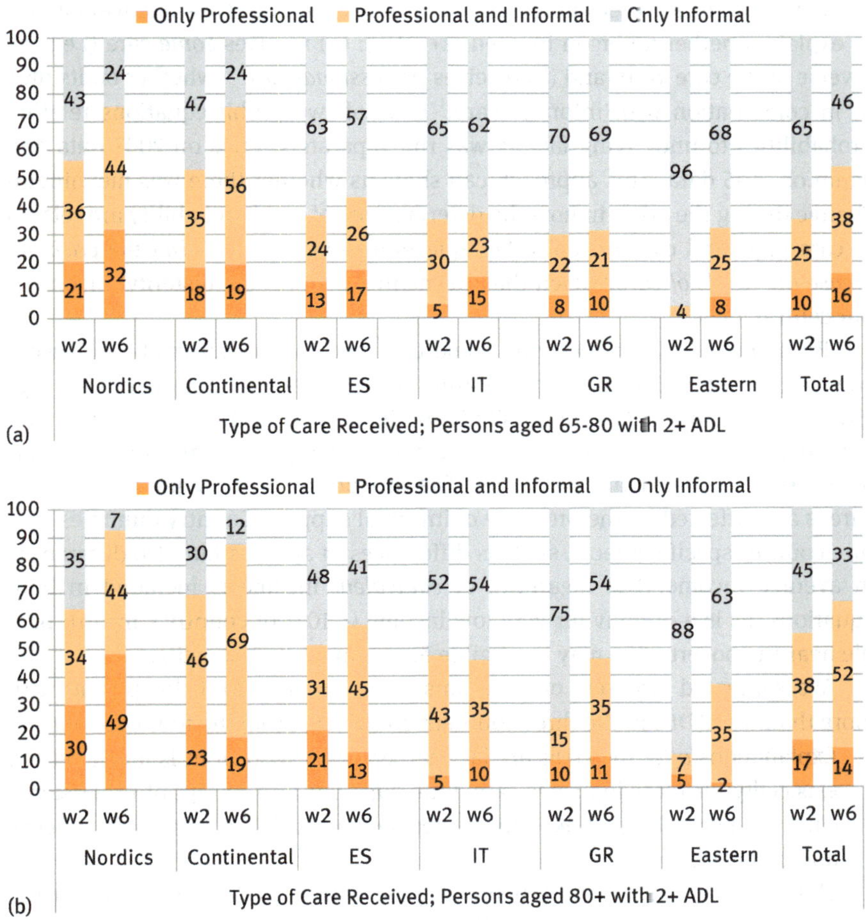

Figure 20.3: Type of care received, persons with 2+ ADL by age group, cross section, Wave 2 and Wave 6.
Note: 'Total' refers to the 12 countries that participated in both Wave 2 and Wave 6.
Source: SHARE Wave 2 and 6 release 6.1.0.

20.5 Seeking explanations: Individuals and LTC in Wave 2 and Wave 6

The aggregate picture does not conform to the austerity narrative. Easy expectations were disproved, leaving many issues unanswered. We deal with these by exploiting the 'added value' of SHARE – the possibility of directly approaching the individual experience.

For the three southern European countries, we set up two statistical models to explain whether a person in need (2+ ADL): (a) receives *some* care (i.e., the reverse of the care gap); and (b) receives *professional care* – whether on its own or in combination with informal care.[1] Each of two probit equations relating probabilities to underlying factors was run separately, once on 2007 data and again on 2015 data. This approach can show us whether there was meaningful change during the crisis in how the determinants of need and ability are related to care gaps and care mix. The key question to be asked is, *Did the crisis increase the needs of care?* Given that our main interest is on austerity, income is our central focus.

Both equations (for receiving some care and for professional care) use a common set of variables. Some capture need (demand): three bands for age (50–65, 65–80, 80+); ADL>3; possibility of depression (EURO-D); dementia and poor health (SPH bad). Others capture access (supply): rural living; gender; lives alone; childless and pensioner. The probability of receiving professional care is also affected by the presence of informal support. Country dummies capture country-specific effects, such as differences in systems but also differences in average income. The logarithm of *equivalent* income is included in both equations, as is a dummy for very low income (< 10% of country's mean); people near the poverty line may be eligible for means-tested benefits.

We estimated two sets of equations, for 2007 and 2015, for people with more than two ADLs in the three southern countries. From the four equations:

- Explanations *after* the crisis are far sharper (the statistical fit is much better), especially for receiving *some* care. Care gaps but also receipt of professional care, are more closely linked to the explanatory variables – individual needs and potential.
- The fact that outcomes are better aligned with *needs* could mean that the mechanisms in place are more discerning. This could be the result of either *formal* LTC systems (which were being reformed) coming into maturity *or* that austerity could be forcing prioritisation.
- The institutional maturation hypothesis – that formal systems are better at discerning need – receives support from three indirect observations: living in a rural area is not linked to less professional care, dementia begins to be important only in 2015 and the presence of informal care reduces the probability of professional care in only 2007 and not 2015. Professional and informal care may now operate less as substitutes and more as complements.

1 We use the entire sample from age 50, as long as ADL limitations are >2.

- Certain influences with roles of equal significance confirm the continuing familial character of the systems: age, health, being childless, being a woman.
- Country effects show that most of the transformation is taking place in Greece. In terms of the care gap, Greece is significantly *more* likely to face one (after allowing for other effects). In terms of *professional* care, Greek exceptionalism is reversed: whereas a needy Greek person was *less* likely to access that type of care in 2007 (by approximately 20%), country differences disappear in 2015.

Therefore, it is clear that income plays a key role. Although it played *no* part in 2007 in predicting receiving care, it becomes important and positive in 2015. The growth in influence is more notable in the explanation of professional care, where it exercises three times the effect than before. Being poor *becomes* important in explaining access but adds *less* to simply having low income in predicting professional care.

Figures 20.4 and 5 convey the complex influence of income by looking at how it affects predicted probabilities in the two years. We calculate the probabilities for a reference individual (Greek, 65, alone; in poor health, income

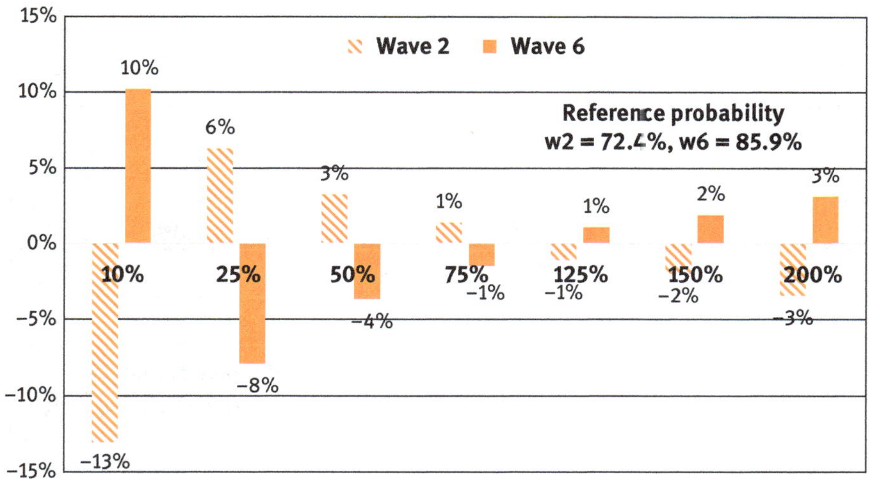

Figure 20.4: Difference in the predicted probability of receiving *some* care by persons with 2+ ADL; by income (% of mean income).
Note: Reference: 65–80, poor health, alone, rural; income at GR W2 mean (€10k)W2 coefficients not statistically significant.
Source: SHARE Wave 2 and 6 release 6.1.0.

equal to the 2007 Greek average). The income of that individual is then varied, which alters predicted probabilities. At 10% of the average income, the separate effect of poverty kicks in. The two figures report *differences* in probabilities relative to the reference individual as income is varied in the seven steps of the Wave 2 average, from 10% to 200%).

Figure 20.4 shows the predicted probability of *not* suffering a care gap given a need for care. In 2015, a well-defined relationship existed: at very low incomes, people suffer *less* from care gaps that then decline as income rises. The 2007 relationship is shaded because it is not significant. We should note that the reference point involves a significant general *decline* in care gaps.

Figure 20.5 equivalently charts the influence of income on *professional* care, which in Greece means mostly out-of-pocket care from unregulated markets. We see a strong link with income, which operates on top of a *doubling* of the overall levels of professional care for the reference individual (from 19% to 43%). Professional care rises across the board but more decisively for the better off.

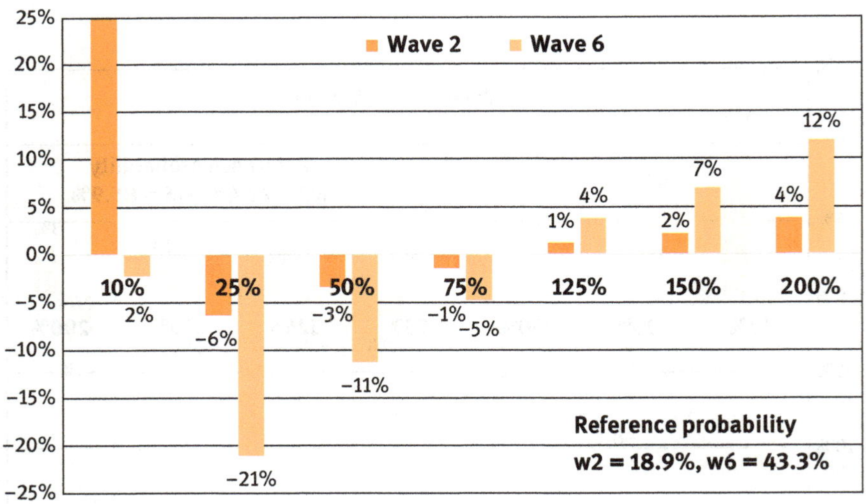

Figure 20.5: Difference in the predicted probability of receiving *professional* care by persons with 2+ ADL; by income (% of mean income).
Note: Reference: 65–80, poor health, alone, rural; income at GR W2 mean (€10k), has access to informal care.
Source: SHARE Wave 2 and 6 release 6.1.0.

20.5 Conclusions

Easy expectations can be deceptive. Far from austerity affecting LTC, southern Europe seems to suggest the opposite, despite the deepest recession since the Second World War. It was *not* the family that adapted but the provision of professional services. This phenomenon could be the result of formal systems becoming better at discerning need; however, the influence of income – in enabling access to bought-in services from the open, unregulated market – plays a key role.

Why should households whose average income declined by a quarter decide to spend *more* to buy LTC services? Such behaviour is understandable if the *prices* of care services declined. Such a decline could be a byproduct of the 'internal devaluation' that was implemented in Greece but also – to a smaller extent – elsewhere. For instance, minimum wages in Greece declined by far more than pensions, which pensioners perceived as a decrease in relative prices and the possibility of buying more LTC despite their falling incomes.

References

Bettio, F., and Plantenga, J. (2004). Comparing care regimes in Europe. *Feminist economics*, 10(1), 85–113.

Clark, R. L. (2004). *Economics of an Aging Society*. Oxford: Blackwell Publishing.

Global Burden of Disease-Greece Collaborators (GBD) (2018). The burden of disease in Greece, health loss, risk factors, and health financing, 2000–16. *Lancet Public Health* 2018;

Lyberaki, A. (2011). Migrant women, care work, and women's employment in Greece. *Feminist economics*, 17(3), 103–131.

Lyberaki, A., and Tinios, P. (2014). The informal welfare state and the family: Invisible actors in the Greek drama. *Political Studies Review*, 12(2), 193–208.

Tinios, P. (2017). Greece: Forced transformation in a deep crisis. In B. Greve (Ed.) *Long-term care – challenges and perspective* (pp. 93–106). New York: Routledge.

Ela Ostrovsky-Berman and Howard Litwin

21 Financial and non-financial transfers from parents to adult children after the economic crisis

- The economic crisis has had a long-term effect on financial and non-financial transfers from older Europeans to their adult children
- Large financial transfers from parents aged 65 years and older to their adult children increased dramatically during the crisis and remained higher than they were before the crisis
- The frequency of looking after grandchildren has decreased since the crisis and continues to be lower than it was before the crisis

21.1 Financial shocks and interfamilial exchange

Do financial shocks have long-term consequences for the interfamilial exchange of resources and for intergenerational solidarity? The great financial crisis that struck Europe in 2008 provides a unique opportunity to address this important research question. Towards this aim, this chapter presents analyses using data from SHARE to consider the effects of the economic crisis on the parental provision of financial and non-financial assistance to adult children. The longitudinal SHARE data, which span some six waves of data collection from 2004 to 2015, make it possible to examine the trends in private familial transfers before and after the crisis.

In recent decades, a unique confluence of financial constraints among young adults, psycho-social circumstances, cultural factors and family norms has emerged to motivate older parents to continue to provide help to their adult children well into their lives (Albertini et al., 2007). The economic crisis in 2008 has exacerbated this trend given the increased instability that it caused in the labour market, fear of changes in social protection policies and deterioration in terms of pension funds, as well as the increase in financial distress that many adult children have experienced. Major financial shocks, such as the 2008 crisis, thus create dissonance and require adaptation in saving and consumption behaviour. They also affect intergenerational redistribution.

https://doi.org/10.1515/9783110617245-021

Much of the financial literature focuses on the impact of the economic crisis on household wealth. In this regard, it is suggested that macroeconomic shocks impact household welfare via the labour market, the product market and the financial markets. For example, the consequences of the recession in 2008 in the Euro area included an increase in unemployment from 7.2% in March 2008 to 9.5% in May 2009, a shrinkage of GDP by 4% during 2009 and a decline in the value of financial assets. It has also been shown that households' net wealth as a percentage of disposable income was hit sharply during the crisis in most European countries (Cavasso and Weber, 2014). According to the European Central Bank, the average net wealth in the Eurozone fell by 10%. Changes in household wealth can lead to adjustments in the consumption behaviour of individuals, affecting in turn direct financial support to adult children as well as indirect support via assets such as property that might be used as collateral and, thus, affect households' ability to access credit.

The financial literature on intergenerational solidarity focuses mostly on the effect of the financial crisis on monetary or 'in kind' transfers. However, it is equally important to consider the effect of the crisis on the provision of non-financial assistance. Such non-financial transfers can be considered as indirect financial support because they affect the labour market and capital accumulation for both providers and receivers. Moreover, the increasing number of women in the labour market increases the need for time-related transfers. By looking after their grandchildren, older parents enable their adult children to invest more time in career development and to decrease their childcare expenses. However, investing time into looking after grandchildren might limit the chances of older parents of pre-pension age to keep their jobs or to find new ones, as well as increasing their everyday expenses. These consequences are even more serious during a financial crisis. Consequently, in the current study, we take both financial and non-financial transfers into account. Moreover, insofar as a substitution effect may exist between financial transfers and non-financial transfers (Attias-Donfut et al., 2005), we also consider the relationship between the two.

Towards this end, we consider two types of financial transfers from parents to adult children: large (more than 5,000 euros) and small (at least 250 euros) financial assistance. We also examine two types of non-financial transfers: non-financial transfers (practical help) and looking after the grandchildren. For financial transfers, we observe the provision of the transfer (yes, no). For non-financial assistance, we consider the volume of the transfers (i.e., their frequency).

The main aim of the enquiry is to clarify whether macroeconomic shocks indeed have long-term effects on the provision of private transfers from older parents to their adult children. An additional aim is to shed light on the interrelationship between financial and non-financial transfers following an economic crisis. In this regard, we seek to clarify whether there are, in fact, mutual effects of the two types of transfers or whether one substitutes for the other in times of deep financial distress.

21.2 Sample and data

SHARE studies households in Europe with persons aged 50 and older. Because the present study focuses on the provision of financial and non-financial assistance from parents to adult children, the study samples for most of the analyses include only respondents with children. The samples for the examination of grandchild care are further limited because they necessarily include only respondents whose children have children. The data for the analyses were collected biennially and span some 12 years. We use data from Wave 1 (2004) and Wave 2 (2006), which were administered before the financial crisis of 2008, and data from Waves 4–6 (2011, 2013 and 2015, respectively), which were gathered after the crisis. (It should be noted that the SHARE Wave 3 data (2008) were not used in the present analysis insofar as the questionnaire did not include the relevant transfer measures.)

21.3 Transfers before and after the economic crisis

Figure 21.1 describes the distribution of parental providers of large or small financial help (respectively). The figure compares the trends among three age groups: 50–64 (pre-retirement), 65–74 (early post-retirement) and 75+ (late post-retirement). Overall, parents aged 50 and older are observed to provide small financial help more frequently than they provide more sizeable help to their adult children. These results hold for all age groups. To examine the changes in the tendency to provide financial help to adult children, we tested whether the differences between the respective waves were significant. The results indicated that, before the crisis (i.e., changes between Wave 1 and Wave 2), there was a significant increase in the tendency to provide both large and small financial help among all age groups.

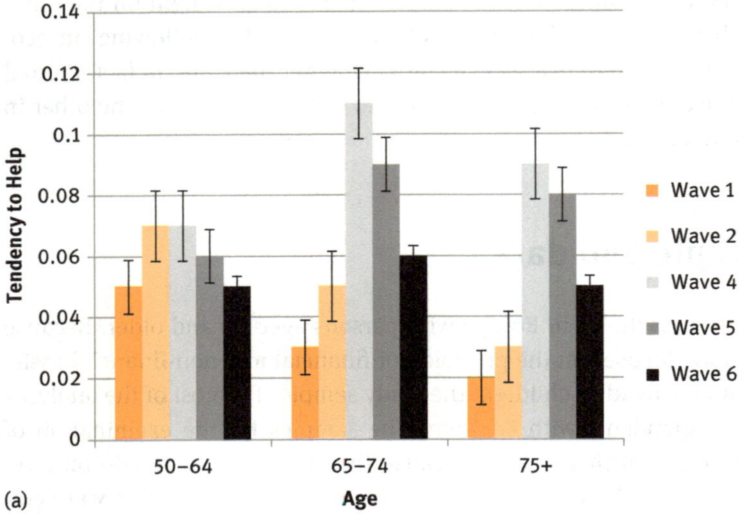

Figure 21.1.a: Tendency to provide sizeable financial help to adult children before and after the financial crisis.
Source: SHARE Wave 1, 2, 4, 5, 6 release 6.1.1.

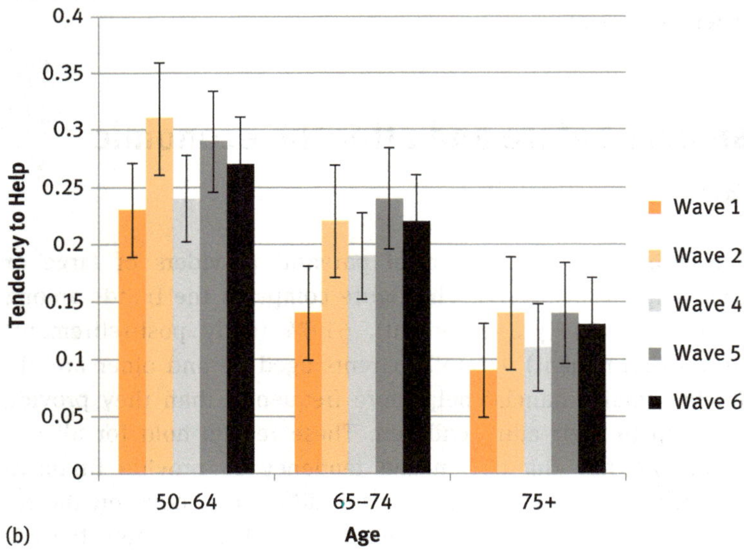

Figure 21.1.b: Tendency to provide small financial help to adult children before and after the financial crisis.
Source: SHARE Wave 1, 2, 4, 5, 6 release 6.1.1.

However, the response immediately after the financial crisis differed among age groups and in relation to the extent of the support. Specifically, whereas parents aged 50–64 years maintained a similar level of sizeable financial help, the tendency of parents aged 65 years and older increased immediately after the crisis and was maintained over time, albeit to a decreasing degree. The decrease notwithstanding, the tendency to provide sizeable financial help at Wave 6 was significantly higher than before the crisis. Hence, the economic crisis seems to have affected the tendency to provide sizeable financial help in both the short term and the long term. In contrast, the tendency to provide small financial help decreased immediately after the crisis but recovered during the fifth and sixth waves. In particular, the propensity to support adult children through small financial gifts among parents aged 65+ returned to the level found in the second wave.

The changes in the non-financial transfers to adult children are presented in Figure 21.2. We observe the frequency of the provided help in two categories: (a) practical help to children, and (b) looking after the grandchildren. Overall, parents aged 75 and older gave such help to their adult children less frequently than their younger counterparts did. For rates over time, no significant changes were found in either category when comparing the first and second waves. However, after the crisis, the frequency of providing practical help

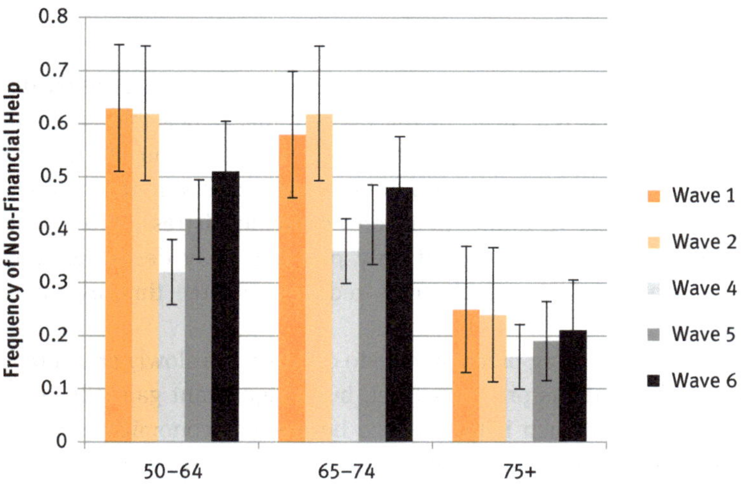

(a)

Figure 21.2.a: Changes in the frequency of non-financial help to adult children before and after the financial crisis.
Source: SHARE Wave 1, 2, 4, 5, 6 release 6.1.1.

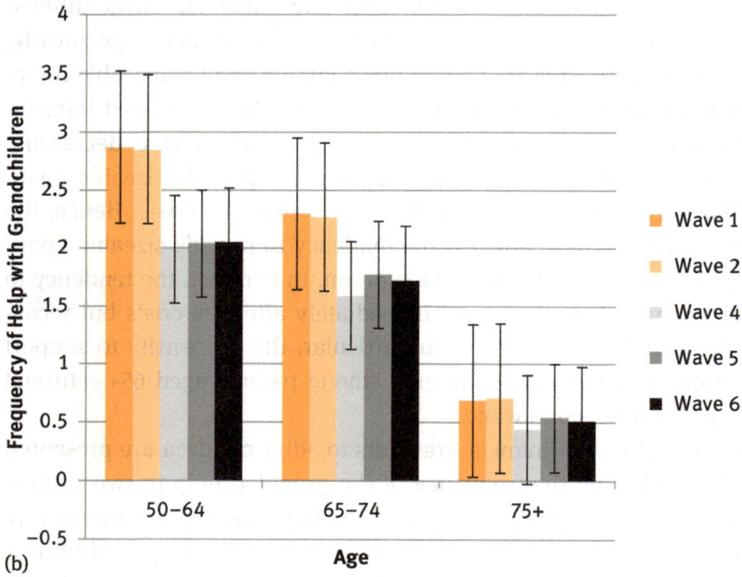

Figure 21.2.b: Changes in the frequency of help to adult children by looking after grandchildren before and after the financial crisis.
Source: SHARE Wave 1, 2, 4, 5, 6 release 6.1.1.

sharply decreased, as did looking after grandchildren, albeit to a lesser degree. These changes occurred in all of the age groups. A possible explanation for this finding is that when experiencing instability in the labour market, a vulnerable population such as older employees will work longer hours to keep their jobs. In addition, given economic distress, those who were unemployed, retired or employed only part-time may decide to fully join the labour market. Taking such steps reduces the free time available to help adult children.

The frequency of providing practical help to children has slowly and subsequently recovered towards its pre-crisis level, but a significant gap still exists between the frequency of such help provided before the economic crisis and the level six years after the crisis. In comparison, the rate of recovery in the frequency of looking after children has progressed only to a small degree. Thus, here also, the economic crisis has had (and continues to have) a long-term effect. Economic shocks impact the provision of both financial and non-financial transfers from parents to their adult children.

21.4 The inter-relationship between financial and non-financial transfers

The next step of the study was to explore the effects of the respective transfer variables on each of the four transfer outcomes, controlling for key demographic variables and economic distress. The analyses were done separately for the second wave (before the crisis), the fourth wave (immediately after the crisis) and the sixth wave (as an indicator for long-term impact). Two of the four transfer variables showed significant results in relation to the long-term effect of the crisis: (1) sizeable financial help and (2) looking after grandchildren.

First, we regressed sizeable financial help on non-financial transfers and small financial help. The coefficients, as presented in Figure 21.3, show a

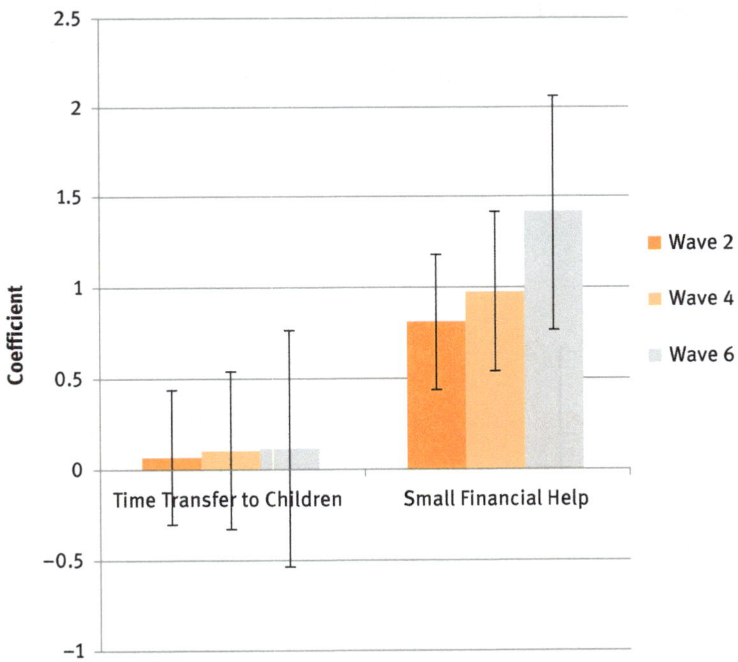

Figure 21.3: Transfer predictors of large financial transfers.
Note: The figure illustrates the effect of non-financial transfers and small financial help to adult children on the provision of sizeable financial help to adult children, as predicted by means of the logistic regression, controlling for age group, gender, education, marital status, number of children and financial distress.
Source: SHARE Wave 2, 4, 6 release 6.1.1.

significant positive effect of the propensity to provide small financial help to children, and of non-financial transfers to a lesser degree on the propensity to provide sizeable financial help. Hence, supporting adult children in everyday matters by providing small financial help and personal/practical help increases the tendency to provide large financial support. The results of a Wald test to compare the coefficients among the waves showed that the effect of small financial help increased significantly after the financial crisis and continued to rise in the long term (wave 6). Thus, sizeable financial help does not substitute for small financial help or non-financial help but supplements such assistance.

Next, we regressed the frequency of looking after grandchildren on the respective transfer variables. The coefficients are presented in Figure 21.4. The results show that before the crisis, the association between sizeable financial help and looking after grandchildren was insignificant, but the correlation increased positively after the crisis. The correlation of small financial help also increased. In comparison, the provision of non-financial transfers (practical help) remained a predictor of looking after grandchildren even after the crisis, but to a lesser degree. Thus, here too, there is little evidence of a substitution effect.

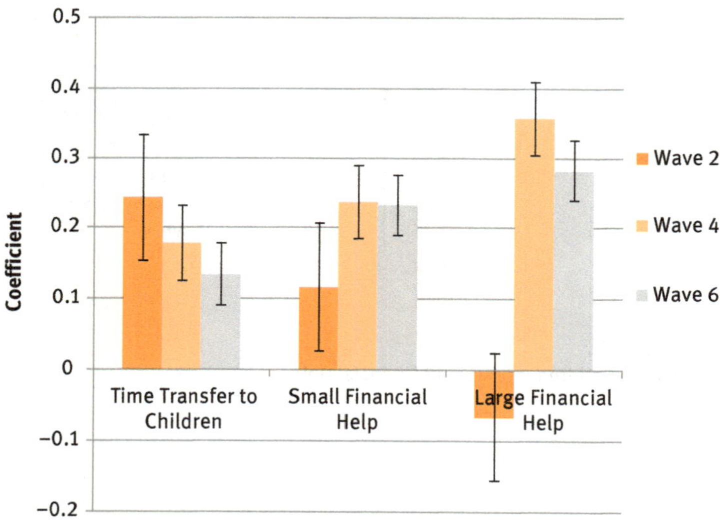

Figure 21.4: Transfer predictors of looking after grandchildren.
Note: The figure illustrates the effect of non-financial transfers, small financial help and sizeable financial help to adult children on the frequency of looking after grandchildren, as predicted by means of logistic regression, controlling for age group, gender, education, marital status, number of children and financial distress. This regression is restricted to respondents that have grandchildren.
Source: SHARE Wave 2, 4, 6 release 6.1.1.

21.5 Conclusions and policy implications

This study clarified that financial shocks, such as the economic crisis of 2008, have long-term effects on private parental transfers to adult children. This study also showed that despite the crisis, little evidence exists for a substitution effect in the balance between financial and non-financial transfers to adult children. Thus, major economic recessions do indeed constitute a serious risk factor for the private exchange of assistance and weaken parents' ability to provide financial and non-financial transfers to their adult children. Nevertheless, many older parents continue to assist their children both financially and practically, even if to a lesser degree given the tribulations imposed by the economic recession.

References

Albertini, M., Kohli, M. & Vogel, C., 2007. Intergenerational Transfers of Time and Money in European Families: Common Patterns – Different Regimes?. *Journal of European Social Policy*, 17(4), pp. 319–334.

Attias-Donfut, C., Ogg, J. & Wolff, F.-C., 2005. European Patterns of Intergenerational Financial and Time Transfers. *European Journal of Ageing*, 2(3), pp. 161–173.

Cavasso, B. & Weber, G., 2014. The effect of the great recession on the wealth and financial distress of 65+ Europeans. In: A. Börsch-Supan, M. Brandt, H. Litwin & G. Weber, eds. *Active Ageing and Solidarity between Generations in Europe – First Results from SHARE after the Economic Crisis*. s.l.: De Gruyter, pp. 27–36.

Part V Social context and health

Edited by Howard Litwin

Ella Schwartz and Howard Litwin

22 Changes in social networks and cognitive decline

- Cognitive performance declines as older adults remove social ties, particularly if relationships are excluded for an extended period
- Adding close ties to the social network is beneficial for cognition, similar to the effects of continuously including these ties
- Changes in the relationships with children and friends are particularly meaningful for cognition, but the inclusion of the spouse in the social network is not

22.1 Cognition and social networks in late life

Cognitive functioning is a meaningful part of well-being in older age. Evidence suggests that social relationships can play a protective role in maintaining cognition in later life and mitigating cognitive decline. Social ties can provide stimulating 'cognitive exercise', buffer the effects of stress, encourage health-promoting behaviours and build cognitive reserves (Kelly et al., 2017). Moreover, evidence generally indicates that larger social networks and more frequent contact with social ties are related to better cognition (Kelly et al., 2017).

Older adults commonly report having close social ties but also experience losses and gains in these relationships as they age. They may add new ties to their close circle or diminish their existing relationships with close ties as a result of life events or changes in their social preferences (Cornwell et al., 2014). However, many studies do not differentiate between persons who have maintained a stable level of social connections over the years and those whose social ties have transformed. For example, a small social network can indicate no contact with close friends over an extended period, reflecting a long-lasting lack of cognitive stimulation. Conversely, a small network may also indicate that regular contacts have only recently diminished and, thus, might have weaker effects on cognition. The distinction between stable and changed ties is important because persons who have few social ties over longer periods may be at a higher risk of cognitive decline.

The nature of the social tie may also have significant implications for the cognitive function. For example, friends might provide more leisure activities, whereas children tend to provide more emotionally meaningful support in the

https://doi.org/10.1515/9783110617245-022

face of stress. However, the findings are mixed regarding the role of family and friends in cognitive function (Aartsen et al., 2004; La Fleur and Salthouse, 2016). Therefore, this chapter examines changes in four different types of social ties that are prevalent among older adults – spouse, children, other relatives and friends – in relation to older adults' cognitive function. This chapter also examines the role of stability versus change over time in the availability of these four types of social ties.

22.2 Data and methods

The analyses presented in this chapter are based on the fourth and sixth waves of SHARE, collected in 2011 and 2015, respectively. These analyses focus on adults aged 65 and older. Cognitive performance is represented by a summary score combining three tests: immediate recall, delayed recall and fluency. The first test consists of reading ten words and asking respondents to repeat them. The second measure asks respondents to repeat the same word list after a ten-minute interval. The third probe reflects the number of animals that participants can name in one minute. The scores from these three tests were standardized and their mean score was used as a general measure of cognitive performance.

Social networks were measured by asking respondents to name up to seven people with whom they discuss important matters and to request additional information about them (Schwartz, Litwin and Kotte, 2017). The networks were assessed in two separate waves, enabling us to distinguish between stable availability or unavailability of different types of social ties (spouse, children, relatives and friends) and temporary availability or unavailability of these same types of ties, such as citing versus not citing friends in both waves or removing friends who were only cited in Wave 4 versus adding friends in Wave 6. The spousal and child relationships included a fifth category of not having a spouse or children at all. For spouses, this category also included participants whose spouse died between the study waves. This scenario indicated that persons who 'removed' their spouse from the network still had a spouse but no longer mentioned him or her as a close social network member. The study sample numbered 13,411 adults who had full information on all study variables.

The analyses began with a description of the change patterns experienced by the older adults. We then regressed the changes in cognitive performance on changes in social networks and controlled for key covariates: age, gender, education, financial adequacy, self-rated health, mobility limitations, hearing ability and country of residence. The analyses were weighted to account for the sample design and for respondents' differential probabilities of participating by using the Wave 4 weights. These baseline weights were then adjusted for attrition (Cornwell et al., 2014).

22.3 Stability and change of confidant availability

Figure 22.1 presents the patterns of change among the ties nominated as close social network members. The figure indicates that most respondents either mentioned a spouse in their social network in both measurements (42%) or lacked a spouse (40%). Between 5 and 7 per cent did not mention once or twice their spouse as a close social tie. Half of the respondents cited their children as social network members at both measurements. They were also slightly more likely to add children to their networks over time (16%) than to remove them (10%) or not to ever cite them (13%). Approximately half of the respondents (52%) did not mention any relatives at either measurement, whereas almost

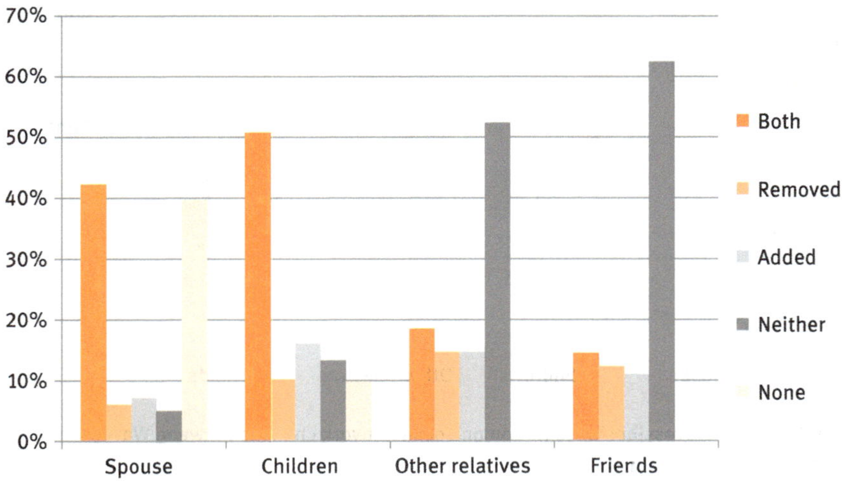

Figure 22.1: Change patterns in confidant relationships between Wave 4 and Wave 6 (weighted).
Note: Both – in SN in both waves; Removed – removed from SN in Wave 6; Added – added to SN in Wave 6; Neither – not mentioned in SN in both waves; None – respondent does not have a spouse\child.
Source: SHARE Wave 4 and 6 release 6.1.0.

one-fifth mentioned relatives at both measurements (18%). Close to one-sixth (15%) had a change in the naming of relatives. Finally, almost two-thirds of respondents (62%) did not mention friends at either time point, whereas the rest mentioned friends at both time points (14%), removed friends (12%) or added friends (11%) over time.

We next analyse the network data in relation to changes in the cognition score over time. For this purpose, we ran an OLS regression model (Figure 22.2). The reference category for the social network variables was respondents who continuously cited the social network member in each relationship category at both measurements. The results revealed that a decline in the cognition score

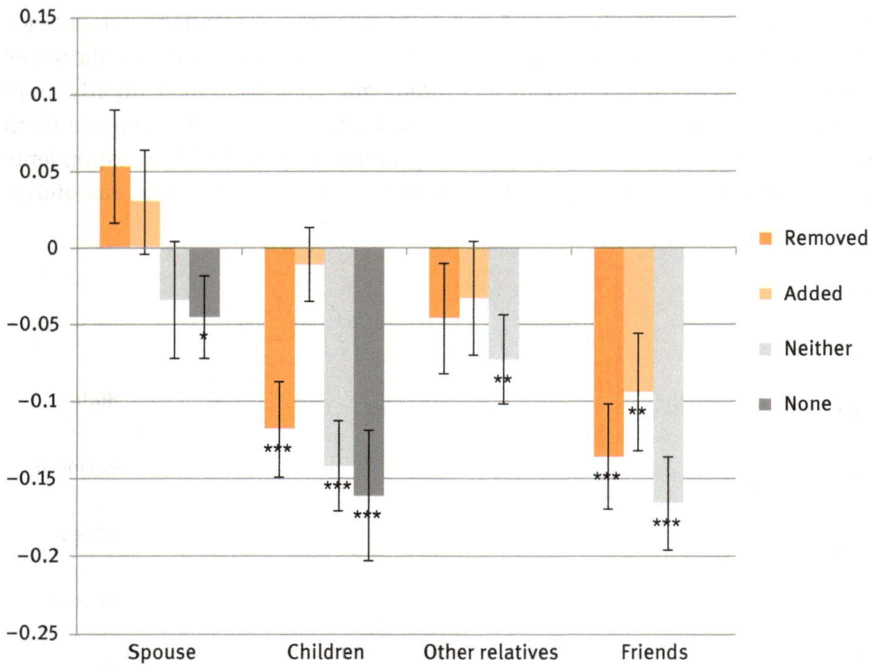

Figure 22.2: OLS regressions of cognition on social network changes between Waves 4 and 6 (weighted).

Significance: *** = 1%; ** = 5%; * = 10%.

Note: The effects presented are compared with citing the person in the social network in both waves. Controlled for baseline cognition, age, gender, education, financial adequacy, self-rated health, mobility limitations, hearing and country.

Removed – removed from SN in Wave 6; Added – added to SN in Wave 6; Neither – not mentioned in SN in either wave; None – respondent does not have a spouse\child.

Source: SHARE Wave 4 and 6 release 6.1.0.

was associated with not having a spouse at all relative to continuously citing the spouse as a network member. We note that this category included persons whose spouse passed away between the two measurements; therefore, cognitive decline may also be associated with being widowed. Changes in the naming of the spouse as a social network member did not differ in their effects on cognition from that of the reference category. Changes in the naming of children among one's close social ties had a negative association with cognition, such that removing children from the close network and not citing them continuously was associated with lower cognition. Adding children to the network did not differ from continuously citing children in the associations with cognition.

Turning to relatives in the social network, changes in their inclusion in the network had similar associations with cognition as did continuously citing them as close ties. Only continuously not citing relatives as confidants was related to worse cognitive consequences. In comparison, changes in the inclusion of friends in the network had the most consistent associations with cognition scores. Both the addition and the removal of friends from the close network was related to worse cognition relative to continuously citing them. Not having friends as confidants at either time point was also related to poorer cognition.

22.4 Discussion

This study explored how changes within older adults' social networks are related to cognitive functioning in old age. The results indicate that cognitive performance declines as older adults remove social ties and that cognition is particularly sensitive to continuously excluding persons from one's social network. The identity of the excluded confidants also emerged as important, such that changes in the relationships with children and friends were particularly meaningful to cognitive decline.

Older adults seem to be particularly vulnerable to cognitive decline when they suffer from a continual lack of social ties – when excluding children, relatives and friends from their close ties for long periods. Such a distancing of social ties may imply less social interactions and less cognitive stimulation over time, possibly contributing to the more detrimental effect. However, even changes that occurred in a shorter timeframe – mentioning children and friends at Wave 4 and excluding them four years later – had negative implications. Thus, even a few years without these close ties seem to entail negative effects. These findings suggest that practitioners should pay attention to adults who are chronically lacking close family and friendship ties and to those who seem to lose touch with their children and friends.

On a more positive note, the findings generally indicate that adding close ties had as strong an impact as continuously citing them in the network. Therefore, even relatively new additions to one's close social network are positively related to cognition. These findings imply that, even in old age, the addition of ties can favourably affect cognitive functioning, perhaps resulting from having more frequent, meaningful and cognitively stimulating interactions. Thus, practitioners should encourage their older patients to improve and strengthen their close ties.

The current study also draws attention to the nature of older adults' social ties given that different types of close ties were found to differ in their association with cognition. Friends and children were shown to be especially meaningful for cognitive functioning, whereas spousal ties had almost no association with cognition outcome. That friends and children provide more frequent and/or more cognitively stimulating interactions is possible. Friendship ties, for example, might involve more leisure activities and more novel topics of conversation. Close children might encourage health-promoting behaviours and assist in coping with stress (Kelly et al., 2017). Thus, looking at the general patterns of social losses and gains is not enough; knowing who is being lost or gained is also necessary.

The lack of a spousal tie seemed related to cognition only if no spouse existed or if the spouse passed away. However, excluding one's spouse from the network while still having a spouse was not related to cognition. In such cases, the spouse may still be available as a source of mental stimulation even if he or she was not viewed as a source of emotional support.

We should note that the findings from this study might also indicate that older adults who suffer from cognitive decline are more likely to remove close ties instead of removing ties leading to cognitive decline. Previous findings have shown that both processes may be at play (Kelly et al., 2017). Whatever the case, the findings nevertheless suggest that attention should be paid to adults who remove close ties, particularly friends and children, because they might face an increased risk of cognitive decline.

References

Aartsen, M. J., van Tilburg, T., Smits, C. H. M. and Knipscheer, K. C. P. M. (2004) 'A longitudinal study of the impact of physical and cognitive decline on the personal network in old age', *Journal of Social and Personal Relationships*, 21(2), pp. 249–266. doi: 10.1177/0265407504041386.

Cornwell, B., Schumm, L. P., Laumann, E. O., Kim, J. and Kim, Y.-J. (2014) 'Assessment of social network change in a national longitudinal survey.', *The Journals of Gerontology, Series B: Psychological Sciences and Social Sciences*, 69(8), pp. S75–S82. doi: 10.1093/geronb/gbu037.

La Fleur, C. G. and Salthouse, T. A. (2016) 'Which aspects of social support are associated with which cognitive abilities for which people?', *The Journals of Gerontology, Series B: Psychological Sciences and Social Sciences*, 72(6), pp. 1006–1016. doi: 10.1093/geronb/gbv119.

Kelly, M. E., Duff, H., Kelly, S., McHugh Power, J. E., Brennan, S., Lawlor, B. A. and Loughrey, D. G. (2017) 'The impact of social activities, social networks, social support and social relationships on the cognitive functioning of healthy older adults: A systematic review', *Systematic Reviews*, 6(1), p. 259. doi: 10.1186/s13643-017-0632-2.

Schwartz, E., Litwin, H. and Kotte, M. (2017) 'Measuring social network and network changes in SHARE Wave 6', in Malter, F. and Börsch-Supan, A. (eds) *SHARE Wave 6: Panel innovations and collecting Dried Blood Spots*. Munich: MEA, Max Planck Institute for Social Law and Social Policy, pp. 22–39.

Liili Abuladze and Luule Sakkeus

23 The role of social networks and disability in survival

- Having abundant social networks protects from dying earlier among people with everyday activity limitations and those without as well
- People with everyday activity limitations who have no friends in their social network die earlier
- Having children in the social network does not increase survival of people with activity limitations

23.1 Introduction

Disability involves functional decline and/or difficulties in performing roles or activities. The possibility of developing a disability and the risk of death both increase in late life. However, social relations may prevent or alleviate disability by providing information, giving personal or practical support, promoting self-affirmation and encouraging self-efficacy. Social ties can also modify individual biological processes that may lead to disability-related health conditions. Thus, social relations constitute an important factor in the disablement process (Verbrugge and Jette, 1994).

23.2 Social networks and disability

Social networks are the collection of ties that people variously maintain over their life course. Larger network size is positively related to health and survival. However, the number of members in the network can decline with age. If the size reduction is voluntary, it can have a positive effect on health. However, network reduction may negatively affect one's well-being, which, in turn, lowers one's chances of survival. Interestingly, networks may grow in the initial stages of a member's functional impairment. Nevertheless, these same ties may disappear over time due to difficulties in maintaining relationships when disabled (Tough, Siegrist and Fekete, 2017).

The quality and type of the relationships can compensate for having few social ties. Strong ties, often represented by close family members, generally

https://doi.org/10.1515/9783110617245-023

remain in the network when a person is disabled. Weak ties, on the other hand, do not usually provide long-term care (Granovetter, 1973) and may drop out of a network when activity limitations require the receipt of greater practical support.

Low frequency of contact with the network is related to a greater risk of functional decline (Stuck et al., 1999). However, contact frequency may also increase when disability emerges, due to the need for daily support or supervision (Cornwell, 2009). This latter phenomenon may be associated with an increased mortality risk. Given the importance of social ties in relation to the disability/ mortality nexus, the study reported in this chapter sought to clarify which social network characteristics affect the timing of death among disabled older people.

23.3 Data, variables and method

We focused on people interviewed in Wave 4 of SHARE (2010–2011) and studied how their social networks were related to survival up to the end of Wave 7 (2017), according to disability status. Due to overlapping social networks within couples, we included only one respondent from each couple in the analysis (n = 32,145). A total of 11.4 per cent (3,650) of respondents died during the observation period. The dependent variable in the study was timing of death, measured in years. For the survivors, the last interview time was calculated as the exit time. For 314 of those who had died, the time of death was not identified from the interview, and this was imputed based on the country-specific age and sex-based average probability of dying.

First, we analysed people with all social network sizes (0 – 2+) in the survival models (32,145 individuals, 3,650 deaths, excluding those for whom information on study variables was missing). The second set of models was run for those having at least one network member (30,613 individuals, 3,334 deaths).

The main stratifying variable was disability status, indicating having everyday activity limitations or not. Independent social network variables were derived from the SHARE name generator of one's closest ties and included the following: network size, number of children in the network, emotional closeness with the closest member, contact frequency with family, and having friends in the network. We also included the following variables as controls: gender, age, partnership status, education. All these variables were measured at Wave 4.

Cox survival regression analysis was used to explore the timing of death between Wave 4 and Wave 7, including interactions between disability status and network. The 12 countries that participated in all four waves were classified into five regions: Germanic (Austria, Germany, Switzerland), Nordic (Denmark, Sweden), southern European (Spain, Italy), French-speaking (Belgium, France), and eastern European (the Czech Republic, Slovenia, Estonia).

23.4 Descriptive results

The southern and eastern European regions had the highest proportions of deaths. People with limitations had almost three times the likelihood of dying (16%) compared to those without limitations (6.2%). Among those with at least one network member, the difference in the proportions of deaths between those with everyday activity limitations and those without limitations was approximately 40 per cent (13.8% and 9.7%, respectively). The largest share of deaths in the full sample occurred among people without any network members (20.3%), followed by respondents with one network member (13.8%) and those with two or more members (9.8%).

People with one child in their network had the largest proportion of deaths (12.4%), followed by those with two or more children in the network (11%). Additionally, people who reported being only somewhat close (or less) to the closest member had a larger proportion of deaths (15.3) than those who were very or extremely close (10.6%). Respondents with no reported contact frequency or no reported family members had the greatest proportion of deaths (15.5%), followed by those with only seldom contact with family members (13.7%). More people with no friends in the network (12.3%) died than people with friends (8.3%).

Figure 23.1 describes the proportion of survivors and deceased people by everyday activity limitations and network size. Figure 23.2 presents the respective survival curves by activity limitation (or not) and network size.

23.5 Network and disability dynamics in survival

The survival time of people from the eastern European region was the shortest, but it did not differ statistically from that of the Nordic group (Table 23.1). Southern Europeans followed in their survival time. The French-speaking countries had the longest survival time.

People with no limitations in Wave 4 died later than those with limitations. In terms of network size, the smaller the network, the earlier the time of death. Respondents reporting no network members had the earliest time of death.

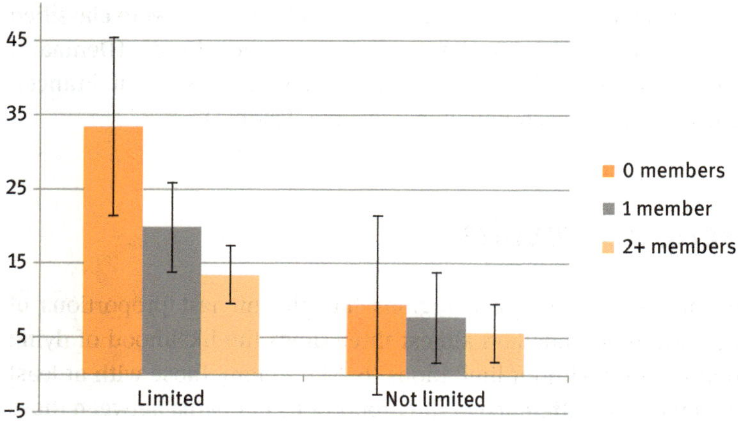

Figure 23.1: Proportion of deceased individuals by everyday activity limitations and network size.
Note: n = 32,145, death events = 3,650.
Source: SHARE Wave 1, 2, 4, 5, 6 release 6.1.0, Wave 7 release 0.

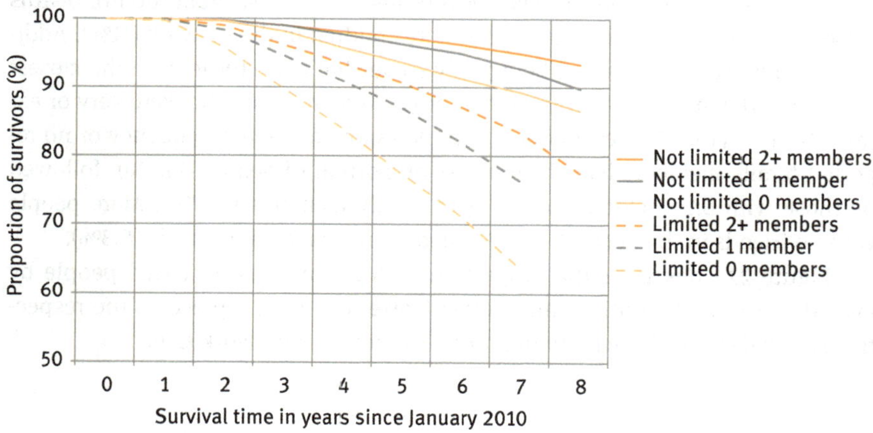

Figure 23.2: Kaplan-Meier survival curve by everyday activity limitations and network size.
Note: n = 32,145, death events = 3,650.
Source: SHARE Wave 1, 2, 4, 5, 6 release 6.1.0, Wave 7 release 0.

Interactions between disability and network size indicated that those with no limitations and abundant networks (2+ members) were best off in terms of survival, followed by respondents with no limitations and one network member. People with limitations and two or more members did not differ in their survival

Table 23.1: Cox survival regression results of timing of death between 2010 and 2017 for all people.

Variables	**Cox**	
	Hazard Ratio	Standard Error
Age (65–79)	2.911***	(0.137)
Age (80+)	9.773***	(0.050)
Gender (female)	0.556***	(0.020)
Education (secondary)	0.866***	(0.035)
Education (tertiary)	0.648***	(0.036)
Education (in school/ other)	0.868	(0.211)
Partner in household (yes)	0.682***	(0.026)
Region (Germanic)	0.668***	(0.049)
Region (Nordic)	1.004	(0.060)
Region (South)	0.879**	(0.050)
Region (French)	0.656***	(0.048)
Limitations (none)	0.513***	(0.020)
Network size (0)	1.570***	(0.097)
Network size (1)	1.239***	(0.045)
Interaction		
No limitations * 0 members	0.813	(0.096)
No limitations * 1 member	0.642***	(0.039)
No limitations * 2+ members	0.507***	(0.025)
Limitations * 0 members	1.558***	(0.110)
Limitations * 1 member	1.229***	(0.053)

Significance: *** = 1%; ** = 5%; * = 10%.
Note: n = 32,145, death events = 3,650.
Reference categories: Age (50–64), Gender (male), Education (basic), Region (Eastern), Limitations (yes), Network size (2+), Limitations (yes)*Network size (2+).
Source: SHARE Wave 1, 2, 4, 5, 6 release 6.1.0, Wave 7 release 0.

outcomes from those with no limitations, but no network members. Respondents with limitations and no network members died the earliest.

Separate Cox survival regression models for respondents with at least one network member helped to clarify the role of other network characteristics besides size in survival. Beyond the basic size associations reported earlier, these analyses showed that having two or more children in one's social network was not related to dying later. Respondents without limitations had half the risk of dying earlier compared to people with limitations and two or more children in the network. At the same time, those with limitations and any other number of children in the network did not differ from the reference group. Thus, the number of children in one's network did not influence the timing of death by disability status among those having at least one network member.

Respondents who had only somewhat or less close ties and who had limitations had the highest hazard of dying earlier, but it was not significantly different from those with extreme closeness and limitations. Again, respondents with no limitations had half the risk of dying earlier than the reference group, irrespective of the closeness intensity. It seems, therefore, that level of closeness with network members did not make a difference in the timing of death.

Contact frequency with family members also did not make a difference in the timing of death. In this case, what mattered most was having limitations or not. However, those not limited in their everyday activities and communicating with their family members several times a week or more did have the best survival chances. Those with limitations and daily communication, on the other hand, had the highest hazard of dying earlier, twice higher the risk of those with no limitations and daily contact frequency (HR 2.01, CI 1.80 – 2.24).

Finally, respondents with limitations and no friends in their network had a higher risk of dying earlier (HR 2.02, CI 1.77 – 2.29) than those with friends in their network (HR 1.74 CI 1.51 – 2.00). For people without limitations, however, having friends did not make a difference.

23.6 Conclusions and policy implications

We found that the survival outcomes by different network characteristics follow, to a large extent, similar patterns as general health outcomes reported in the research literature. In general, larger networks protect from dying earlier among those with activity limitations as well as those without. Moreover, people with health concerns benefit from having more confidants around, but not to the same extent that non-limited persons with one or more confidants do. Having confidants nearby may be beneficial because they point to or motivate better health behaviour. In terms of having children in one's network, the findings suggest that children appear in one's network when one develops serious health concerns.

The level of closeness with network member(s) does not explain survival differences between those with or without limitations. We should point out that the results in this indicator may be partly biased due to the method of recording social networks in SHARE – these tend to be strong personal ties with whom satisfaction and closeness is relatively high anyway, and therefore closeness does not vary a lot. Finally, results for friends suggest that they drop out when one has more advanced activity limitations, perhaps due to higher need in their interactions or peers dying. In any case, people with limitations and no friends in their network tend to have the highest risk of dying earliest.

Developing home-based long-term care services for disabled older people, especially those in advanced stages, can reduce the care burden of children and others, such as friends. This will enable the closest network members to reduce their daily physical care responsibilities and free them to provide emotional support and affection, which they most likely can do better. In addition, developing more community-centred activities may help people with disabilities to stay involved in social activity longer, meet new people and develop new ties.

Acknowledgements: The research leading to these results has received support from the Estonian Research Council (grant PRG71).

References

Cornwell, B. (2009). Network bridging potential in later life: life-course experiences and social network position. *Journal of Aging and Health*, 21(1), pp. 129–54.

Granovetter, M. (1973). The strength of weak ties. *American Journal of Sociology*, 78(6), pp. 1360–1380.

Stuck, A., Walthert, J., Nikolaus, T., Buela, C., Hohmann, C. and Beck, J. (1999). Risk factors for functional status decline in community-living elderly people: a systematic literature review. *Social Science and Medicine*, 48(4), pp. 445–469.

Tough, H., Siegrist, J. and Fekete, C. (2017). Social relationships, mental health and wellbeing in physical disability: a systematic review. *BMC Public Health*, 17(414), pp. 2–18.

Verbrugge, L. and Jette, A. (1994). The disablement process. *Social Science and Medicine*, 38(1), pp. 1–14.

Melanie Wagner and Ina Holdik

24 Social embeddedness of care recipients and their spousal caregivers

- Care recipients and their spousal caregivers have larger, closer and more family-oriented core social networks than couples who neither provide nor receive care
- Partner care decreases the relationship quality among caregivers but not among care recipients
- Partner care intensifies the relationship to one's social network contacts outside the partnership for both the spousal caregiver and the care recipient

24.1 Introduction

Because of population ageing, western societies are challenged by a steadily increasing need for long-term care. In Europe, a large part of such care is provided within families. Providing care to a family member can be a stressful experience that leads to emotional or physical problems (Carretero et al., 2009). Furthermore, caring for one's partner is particularly burdensome because the care provided is usually more intense than the care given to an older parent. In addition, the burden of care interweaves with concerns for and worries about the partner (Bobinac et al., 2010). In contrast, receiving such care is a distressing event that is exacerbated by the concern of being a burden to the caregiver partner (McPherson et al., 2010). As a result, the partnership can lose its balance. Therefore, in such partner caregiving situations, the social networks in which caregivers and care receivers are embedded may play an important role in dealing with the difficulties of the caregiving situation (Litwin et al., 2015). An intensification of social contacts is associated with improved health (Cornwell and Laumann, 2015) and might, therefore, be essential to protect both caregivers and care recipients.

This chapter presents a study that examined the partnerships and social networks (hereafter referred to as SNs) of Europeans aged 50 and older who are involved in the provision or receipt of spousal care. In our study, we investigated whether and how partner relationship characteristics and SN characteristics adapted to the care situation among those who became caregivers and those who became care dependent. For this purpose, we used data from SHARE Waves 4 and 6. Given the aim of the enquiry, we restricted our sample to

https://doi.org/10.1515/9783110617245-024

SHARE respondents who live with their spouse or partner and to those who were interviewed in both waves of the data collection. Consequently, the study sample included 37,864 persons aged 50 years or older from 13 European countries. From this sample, 1,879 identified themselves as spousal caregivers and 1,066 as cared-for by their spouse. The lower number of care recipients compared with caregivers was the result of a higher rate of non-response among the care recipients who may no longer have been able to take part in the SHARE survey.

24.2 Results

The data revealed differences in the socio-demographic characteristics, the partner relationship and the SNs of the respective samples of caregivers, care recipients and those who neither provide nor receive spousal care (Table 24.1). The p-value of the F statistic (analysis of variance) shows the group differences that are significant.

Table 24.1: Socio-demographic characteristics of caregivers, care recipients and people neither giving nor providing spousal care.

Variables	**(1)**	**(2)**	**(3)**	**p-values[a]**		
	Care-givers	**Care recipients**	**Neither**	**1 *vs.*2**	**1 *vs.* 3**	**2 *vs.* 3**
Age[b]	69.1	70.3	65.3	0.00***	0.00***	0.00***
Chronic diseases[c]	2.09	3.12	1.60	0.00***	0.00***	0.00***
(I)ADL[d]	0.65	3.81	0.24	0.00***	0.00***	0.00***
Female	0.54	0.51	0.50	0.42	0.009**	1.00
Education[e]	10.2	9.8	10.8	0.11	0.00***	0.00***
Working	0.15	0.07	0.27	0.00***	0.00***	0.00***
Monthly household income[f]	36,858	38,180	48,264	1.00	0.00***	0.00***
Household size[g]	2.34	2.33	2.45	1.00	0.00***	0.00***
Observations	1,879	1,066	34,856			

Significance: *** = 1%; ** = 5%; * = 10%.
Note: [a] With Bonferroni correction; [b] 50–97 years; [c] 0–6; [d] 0–13 difficulties; [e] 0–25 years; [f] 1,292–1,167,696 Euro; [g] 2–12.
Source: SHARE Wave 4 and 6 release 6.1.0.

The comparison shows that respondents who provided or received care were on average older and more likely to have chronic diseases than respondents who neither provided nor received care. While care recipients had on average only one more chronic disease than their caregiving partners, they had far more difficulties with the basic and instrumental activities of daily living. Furthermore, only 15 per cent of caregivers and seven per cent of care recipients were engaged in employment, whereas 27 percent of those who neither provided nor received care were employed or self-employed. Accordingly, perhaps, the average annual household income was higher for non-caring couples than for caregivers or care recipients.

Table 24.2 compares how the partner relationship characteristics and the SN characteristics were perceived by caregivers, care recipients and those neither providing nor receiving partner care. With regard to the partner relationship, three-quarters of the caregivers named their partner as a confidant, that is, as a member of their personal SN, whereas 86 percent of care recipients

Table 24.2: Partner relationship and SN characteristics of caregivers, care recipients and people neither giving nor providing partner care.

Variables	(1)	(2)	(3)	p-values[a]		
	Caregivers	Care recipients	Neither	1 *vs.*2	1 *vs.* 3	2 *vs.* 3
Partner relationship characteristics						
Partner named as confidant[b]	0.75	0.86	0.85	0.00***	0.00***	0.78
Emotional closeness to partner[c]	2.70	3.08	3.05	0.00***	0.00***	1.00
SN characteristics						
SN size[d]	2.18	1.97	1.90	0.00***	0.00***	0.53**
Emotional closeness to SN[e]	2.89	2.67	2.62	0.00***	0.00***	0.70
Observations	1,879	1,066	34,856			

Significance: *** = 1%; ** = 5%; * = 10%.
Note: [a] With Bonferroni correction; [b] Dummy for whether partner named as member of the social network; [c] 0 = Partner not named as confidant, 1 = Not very close – 4 = extremely close; [d] 0–7; [e] 0 = Nobody named in SN, 1 = Not very close – 4 = extremely close.
Source: SHARE Wave 4 and 6 release 6.1.0.

regarded their partner as a confidant. Among respondents who did not provide or receive any care, 85 per cent counted their partner as a confidant. In addition, emotional closeness to the partner was rated lower for those who provided care (2.70) than it was for those who received it (3.08) or who neither provided nor received care (3.05).

Whereas caregivers named on average 2.18 other people (besides the partner) within their SN, care recipients named only 1.97 other SN members. Those who did not provide or receive care named, on average, 1.90 SN members other than their spouse. The mean emotional closeness to one's SN was higher for caregivers (2.89) than for care recipients (2.67) and those who do not provide or receive any care (2.62).

The results thus far reveal differences between the groups of caregivers and care recipients. Because these differences might also be explained by socio-demographic differences, such as the higher age of caregivers and the care recipients compared with the non-carers or other unobserved differences, the next analyses show how partner relationship characteristics and SN characteristics changed *within* subjects over time. We estimated longitudinal models and calculated subject-specific means for those who became caregivers or care recipients, controlling for variables that can independently affect changes in one's partnership or one's SN (age, working status, income and household size). Time-constant characteristics, such as gender or education, are differenced-out and, thus, were automatically controlled for in the design chosen. Figure 24.1 shows by how many scale points partner relationship characteristics and SN characteristics changed for people who became partner caregivers or care recipients. The lines to either side of the dots display the 90 per cent confidence intervals. If these intervals exclude the zero axis, the plotted changes are significant. If they span the zero axis, the results are insignificant.

Regarding partner relationship characteristics, we found that caregivers named their cared-for partner as a confidant less often when they started providing care for him or her, which occurred in approximately four per cent of the cases. We also saw a decrease in emotional closeness to the partner. The closeness score declined by approximately 0.13 points on a scale from zero to four. However, no such changes were found among the recipients of care. In their case, the coefficients were positive but included the zero axis, meaning that the subjective quality of the partner relationship did not change significantly for those who became care dependent on their partner.

In contrast, the results for the SN characteristics revealed that the SNs changed in rather similar ways for caregivers and care recipients. We found an increase in the size of the SN for both groups. The SNs of caregivers increased by 0.24 scale points, which means that one out of four caregivers

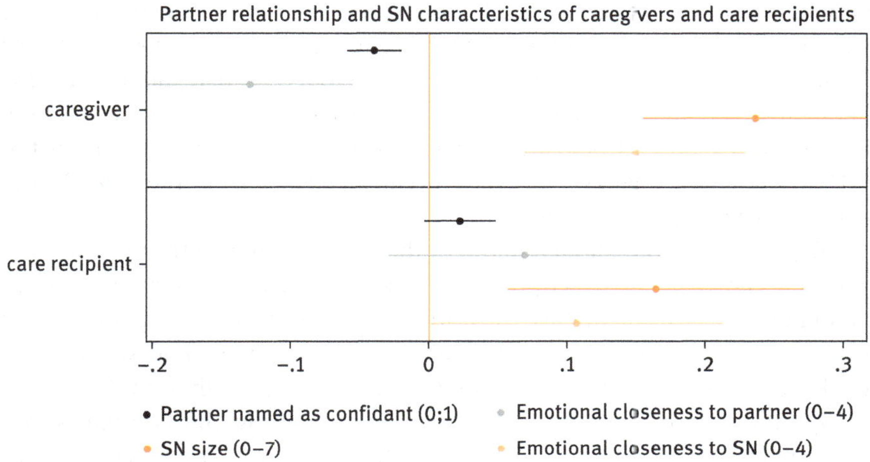

Figure 24.1: Changes in partner relationship characteristics and SN characteristics of caregivers and care recipients.
Significance: 90% confidence intervals displayed as the lines to either side of the dots.
Note: 37,864 observations; Marginal effects based on fixed-effects estimation; Control variables: age, employment, income, household size.
Source: SHARE Wave 4 and 6 release 6.1.0.

added someone to their SN. For care recipients, the SN increased by 0.16. Both groups also intensified their emotional closeness to their SN.

24.3 Discussion

Comparisons of spousal caregivers, care recipients and partners without any care provision or receipt showed differences in the partner relationship characteristics. Caregivers rated the relationship to the partner as less intense, whereas care recipients rated their relationship to their partner in similar ways as couples in which no care was provided or received. Additional longitudinal analysis supported the finding by showing that (some) caregiving partners stopped naming their partner as a confidant and that the perceived emotional closeness to the cared-for partner was rated lower on average after they started to provide care. These changes may arise from a changed distribution of roles within the relationship. The caregiving partner may no longer be able to carry on extensive conversations or participate in social activities with the care-dependent partner. Nevertheless, we should point out that, although statistically significant, these changes were rather small in size. In contrast, partners who became care-dependent did not show significant changes in their relationship to their partner. From their perception, the partner relationship did not change. However, it has to be noted that these results reflect the responses from care recipients who could still participate in the SHARE interview; changes may later occur among them, if they should become more impaired or dependent.

Regarding the SN characteristics of the other persons in the network (besides the partner), the descriptive results showed that caregivers had larger and emotionally more intense networks than care recipients or couples for whom no care was provided. Although the care recipients had smaller networks than the caregivers, the longitudinal analysis showed that both groups intensified their social contacts after entering the care situation, which contradicts the concept of social isolation of caregivers and care recipients. Caregiving partners seem to compensate for the burdens of the caring situation by intensifying close contacts outside the partner relationship to find social support and distract from possibly stressful duties of care and worries about the spouse. Regarding the care-receiving partner, relationships outside the partnership might gain importance by providing additional social support in dealing with their reduced capabilities and their dependence on the partner. However, further research is required to understand how more distant social contacts are affected because the present analysis focused only on the core SN.

In sum, the results show that caregivers experience a slight deterioration in the relationship with the care dependent partner but not vice versa: the partnership relationship does not change from the view of the care recipient. Furthermore, the larger network (outside the partner relationship) is intensified for caregivers and care recipients alike. The intensification of social contacts might be essential to sustain caregivers' and care recipients' health and well-being and, hence, the quality of the long-term care provided by the spouse. Therefore, greater attention should be paid to how caregivers and care recipients can be supported in the maintenance of existing social network ties and the cultivation of new ones.

References

Bobinac, A., van Exel, N. J., Rutten, F. F. and Brouwer, W. B. 2010. Caring for and caring about: Disentangling the caregiver effect and the family effect. *Journal of Health Economics*, 29, 549–556.

Carretero, S., Garcés, J., Ródenas, F. and Sanjosé, V. 2009. The informal caregiver's burden of dependent people: Theory and empirical review. *Archives of Gerontology and Geriatrics*, 49, 74–79.
Cornwell, B. and Laumann, E. O. 2015. The health benefits of network growth: New evidence from a national survey of older adults. *Social Science & Medicine*, 125, 94–106.
Litwin, H., Stoeckel, K. J. and Schwartz, E. 2015. Social networks and mental health among older Europeans: Are there age effects? *European Journal of Ageing*, 12, 299–309.
McPherson, C. J., Wilson, K. G., Chyurlia, L. and Leclerc, C. 2010. The balance of give and take in caregiver–partner relationships: An examination of self-perceived burden, relationship equity, and quality of life from the perspective of care recipients following stroke. *Rehabilitation Psychology*, 55, 194–203.

Fátima Barbosa, Cláudia Cunha, Gina Voss
and Alice Delerue Matos

25 The impact of living alone on physical and mental health: Does loneliness matter?

- The number of people living alone is increasing among those aged 50 and older in Europe, but the proportions vary across countries
- Loneliness is a key factor in explaining the impact of living alone on health
- When loneliness is taken into account, solo living is not necessarily detrimental to the health

25.1 Living alone, health and loneliness after 50

Living alone is an increasingly common phenomenon in ageing populations. The death of a spouse and the tendency of older people and their adult children to maintain independent lifestyles are noted as the main causes for this gradual increase in solo living in recent decades (Victor *et al.*, 2000). However, the impact of living alone on the physical and mental health of older people is still unclear.

Research on this subject shows that older people who live alone have a high risk of experiencing loneliness (Park et al., 2017). As noted by Shiovitz-Ezra (2015), loneliness is defined as a feeling of distress that stems from the perception that the quantity and/or the quality of one's social ties is/are insufficient. A review of several studies concluded that loneliness is associated with poor physical and mental health (Courtin and Knapp, 2017; Shiovitz-Ezra, 2015). Given the increase in solo living among older Europeans, it is important to study the impact of living alone on their physical and mental health, taking into account the role of loneliness in this relationship over time.

25.2 Study methods

Our study sample included Europeans aged 50 years and older residing in the 16 European countries that participated in SHARE Waves 4, 5 and 6

https://doi.org/10.1515/9783110617245-025

(Austria, Germany, Sweden, Netherlands, Spain, Italy, France, Denmark, Switzerland, Belgium, Czech Republic, Poland, Luxembourg, Portugal, Slovenia and Estonia) and in Israel. Because Luxembourg and Israel did not participate in Wave 4, the baseline measurement for these countries is Wave 5.

Our independent variable of primary interest – living alone – was categorized as 0 if the respondent's household size was two or more and 1 if the household size was one. The dependent variables were physical and mental health. For physical health, we created a latent continuous measure based on the procedures employed by Ploubidis and Grundy (2011). This measure combines an objective health indicator (maximum grip strength) and six self-reports. The self-reports were self-perceived health (a 5-point ordinal scale that ranged from poor (1) to excellent (5); the presence of long-term illness, coded 0 if yes and 1 if no; limited activities due to poor health: coded 1 if severely limited, 2 if limited but not severely and 3 if not limited; and three health conditions: (a) heart attack, (b) stroke and (c) chronic lung disease – all coded 0 if yes and 1 if no. According to Ploubidis and Grundy (2011), this indicator is less subject to measurement error and has greater reproducibility and reliability compared with individual health indicators used separately. To construct this variable, we used the statistical programme MPLUS, version 7, WLSMV estimator. The combined SHARE-based health indicator revealed a good model fit in all waves (RMSEA = 0.03 in Wave 4, 0.03 in Wave 5 and 0.03 in Wave 6; CFI = 0.99 in Wave 4, 0.99 in Wave 5 and 0.98 in Wave 6; and TLI = 0.98 in Wave 4, 0.98 in Wave 5 and 0.97 in Wave 6).

Mental health was assessed using the EURO-D scale that counts up to 12 depressive symptoms, such as irritability, tearfulness and loss of enjoyment during the last month. The range of this scale is 0–12. We employed a dummy dichotomous variable in which a EURO-D score of greater than three indicated clinical depression (1) and a score equal to or less than three indicated no depression (0).

This study was carried out in several stages. First, at baseline, we examined the percentages of individuals aged 50+ who lived alone in each country. Second, to assess the differences in physical and mental health at baseline between respondents living alone and those not living alone, we applied statistical tests for a two-group comparison (t-test (t); chi-square tests (X^2)). Effect size measures (Hedges' g/Phi) were used to complement these analyses. Lastly, two longitudinal linear mixed models were tested to analyse the effect of loneliness vis-à-vis the impact of living alone on the physical and mental health of the 50+ population.

The first longitudinal model was adjusted for the following variables: age at the time of the interview, gender, retirement status (retired was coded as 1 and all other categories as 0 (employed or self-employed, unemployed, permanently sick or disabled, homemaker and other) and financial distress (with a range from (1), 'makes ends meet easily', to (4) 'makes ends meet with great difficulty'). Educational level was divided into three categories based on the International Standard Classification of Education (ISCED): primary schooling or less (ISCED-97 score = 0–2), secondary education (ISCED-97 score = 3) and post-secondary education (ISCED-97 score = 4–6). Also included in the model were the number of visits to the doctor in the previous month; physical inactivity (coded 1 if the respondent never practised moderate or vigorous physical activity and 0 if otherwise) and the number of activities done in the last year. Combining data from Waves 4, 5 and 6, for this first model, we have 175,717 observations for 99,021 individuals.

The second model was adjusted for all previously mentioned variables plus loneliness, assessed on the revised UCLA scale. The scale measures three general feelings of loneliness or feeling left out, lack of companionship and isolation. Each item was scored on a 3-point Likert scale (1 = Hardly ever or never; 2 = Some of the time; 3 = Often). Hence, the total scale score ranged from 3 to 9. For the second model, we have 163,412 observations for 93,632 individuals.

25.3 Results of the study

Figure 25.1 shows a variation in living alone across the countries at baseline. Sweden (37%), Estonia (32.8%), Austria (32.2%) and the Netherlands (30.7%) were the countries with the highest percentage of people aged 50+ and living alone. Portugal (11.1%), Poland (17.6%), Spain (19.3%) and Israel (19.4%) had the lowest percentage.

Regarding physical health outcome, in all countries, people living alone had poorer health compared with those living with others (t-test, sig. < 0.001). However, when considering effect size, which measures the magnitude of the differences found, only in Austria (0.27), Sweden (0.28), Italy (0.21), Denmark (0.35) and Switzerland (0.26) were the differences in physical health between these two types of living arrangements significant (for the t-test, the effect size used is Hedges' g: small effect ≥ 0.20 but less than 0.50). In terms of mental health, in all countries, people living alone showed more severe depression (chi-square, sig < 0.10). Nevertheless, the effect size was significant only in Spain (0.11), Italy (0.12), Israel (0.11) and the Czech Republic (0.11). (For chi-square, the effect size used is Phi: small effect ≥ 0.10 but less than 0.30.)

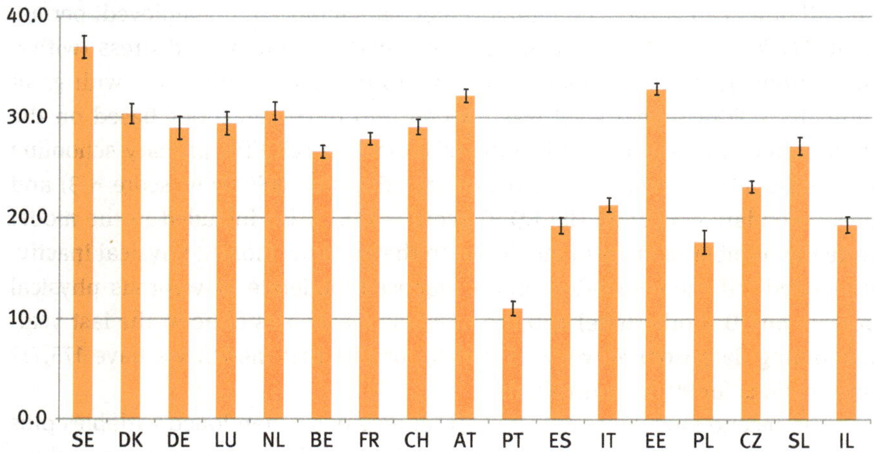

Figure 25.1: Percentage of people aged 50+ and living alone by country (weighted) at baseline.
Note: Brackets denote standard errors, N = 57,955 (unweighted). Wave 4 data used for countries AT, DE, SE, NL, ES, IT, FR, DK, CH, BE, CZ, PL, PT, SL and EE; Wave 5 data for countries IL and LU.
Source: SHARE Wave 4 and 5 release 6.1.0.

The results of the longitudinal analysis are shown in Table 25.1. As may be seen, when loneliness was not taken into account, living alone in five countries was associated with poor physical health (Austria (β –0.04, p = 0.007), Germany (β –0.04, p = 0.034), Sweden (β 0.05, p = 0.006), Denmark (β 0.05, p = 0.009) and Belgium (β –0.03, p = 0.014)) and in three other countries with better physical health (Spain (β 0.03, p = 0.061), Slovenia (β 0.04, p = 0.034) and Estonia (β 0.04, p = 0.001)). When loneliness was included in the longitudinal regression, living alone had a positive effect on physical health in five countries (Spain (β 0.06, p > 0.001), Italy (β 0.05, p = 0.003), France (β 0.03, p = 0.033), Slovenia (β 0.05, p = 0.009) and Estonia (β 0.05, p > 0.001)). Thus, there are important differences when loneliness is introduced. In Austria, Germany, Sweden, Denmark and Belgium, living alone initially had a negative effect on physical health. However, when loneliness was considered, this effect was no longer significant. In Spain and Estonia, the effect continued to be significant. In addition, the effect of living alone in France and Italy became positively significant when loneliness was introduced and, in Slovenia, the positive effect remained.

Regarding mental health, living alone was significantly associated with having depression in 15 countries when loneliness was not yet taken into account (Model 1). After taking loneliness into account in Model 2, a significant negative association emerged in five countries (Austria, Sweden, Spain, Italy and France); that is, living alone, net of loneliness, was related to less risk of depression.

Table 25.1: Effects of living alone on physical and mental health: Longitudinal linear mixed models by country.

	Model 1		Model 2	
	Physical health	Mental health	Physical health	Mental health
Country	**b**	**OR**	**b**	**OR**
SE	−0.05 **	1.28**	−0.01	0.83*
DK	−0.05 **	1.34**	−0.03	0.89
DE	−0.04 **	1.27**	−0.01	0.86
LU	0.03	1.46**	0.05	1.07
NL	−0.01	1.85	−0.00	1.56
BE	−0.03 **	1.59***	−0.01	1.08
FR	0.01	1.12*	0.03 *	0.88*
CH	−0.01	1.16	0.01	0.89
AT	−0.04 **	1.21**	−0.02	0.86*
PT	−0.02	1.31*	0.00	0.85
ES	0.03 *	1.69***	0.06 ***	0.84**
IT	0.02	1.41***	0.05 **	0.85*
EE	0.04 **	1.23***	0.05 ***	1.01
PL	0.01	1.33**	0.03	1.01
CZ	−0.01	1.41***	0.01	1.08
SL	0.04 **	1.42***	0.05 **	1.12
IL	−0.01	1.39**	−0.01	1.20

Significance: *** = 1%; ** = 5%; * = 10%.
Note: Mixed models; Model 1: 175,717 observations for 99,021 individuals; Model 2: 163,412 observations for 98,632 individuals. Model 1: adjusted for age, gender, retirement status, financial distress, ISCED, health, number of visits to the doctor, physical inactivity, number of activities done and living alone; Model 2: adjusted to variables of Model 1 plus loneliness.
Source: SHARE Wave 4, 5, 6 release 6.1.0.

In the remaining 10 countries that presented risk of depression when loneliness was not considered, living alone became non-significant with the introduction of this variable. Consequently, when loneliness is adjusted in the model, living alone does not have a negative effect on mental health, and in some countries, it even has a protective role.

25.4 Conclusions

Our results show a wide variation in the prevalence of solo living among older Europeans. Solo living is more prevalent in northern, western and eastern countries, in contrast to southern countries, Poland and Israel. Moreover, the longitudinal regressions revealed that when loneliness is considered, living alone is not necessarily detrimental to health, specifically mental health. Thus, the findings underscore the important role of loneliness in the association between solo living and health.

In conclusion, these findings have implications for public policies in Europe and Israel. They make it clear that living alone at an older age is a public health concern. However, they also suggest that the negative effect of living alone is driven primarily by loneliness. Therefore, attention should be paid to older people living alone and, especially, to the feelings of loneliness that might be experienced by the older population. European countries should develop and implement public programmes and policies that are geared to reducing the sense of loneliness in ageing cohorts. Reducing loneliness can promote better physical and mental health among older people, improve their quality of life and help reduce burgeoning healthcare costs.

References

Courtin, E. and Knapp, M. (2017). Social isolation, loneliness and health in old age: a scoping review. *Health & Social Care in the Community*, 25(3),pp.799–812.

Park, N., Jang, Y., Lee, B. and Chiriboga, D. (2017). The relation between living alone and depressive symptoms in older Korean Americans: do feelings of loneliness mediate? *Aging & Mental Health*, 21(3),pp.304–312.

Ploubidis, G. and Grundy, E. (2011). Health Measurement in Population Surveys: Combining Information from Self-reported and Observer-Measured Health Indicators. *Demography*, 48(2),pp.699–724.

Shiovitz-Ezra, S. (2015). Loneliness in Europe: do perceived neighbourhood characteristics matter? In: A. Börsch-Supan, T. Kneip, H. Litwin, M. Myck and G. Weber, ed., *Ageing in Europe – Supporting Policies for an Inclusive Society*. Berlin: de Gruyter.

Victor, C., Scambler, S., Bond, J. and Bowling, A. (2000). Being alone in later life: loneliness, social isolation and living alone. *Reviews in Clinical Gerontology*, 10(4),pp.407–417.

Stipica Mudražija, Šime Smolić and Ivan Čipin

26 Living alone in Europe and health behaviours

- Living alone in old age is an indicator of higher risk of adverse health behaviour
- Older adults living alone smoke more and eat less healthy food than those living with others, but they are also less likely to drink excessively
- Living arrangements and related health behaviours vary substantially across countries
- Thus, although policy should promote a healthy lifestyle among older adults living alone, a one-size-fits-all approach is suboptimal

26.1 Introduction

Living alone is an integral part of the population ageing process. Single-person households are particularly widespread in older ages in many developed countries. In fact, such households are often considered the most visible sign of societal ageing (Reher and Requena, 2018). This phenomenon stems from the second demographic transition (Van De Kaa, 1987) that altered population trends in the latter half of the twentieth century. Single living in later life may result from preferences or circumstances, including available resources, health status, kin or partner availability and social and family support. Although some older adults choose to live alone and keep their personal autonomy – and are well prepared to do so – others are substantially more vulnerable than older persons who live with someone.

A particular challenge in this area of interest is the link between living alone and health behaviours. Some research evidence, such as the UK study by Kharicha and colleagues (2007), suggests that those who live alone tend to smoke more and consume less fibre-rich foods such as fruits and vegetables. These and other adverse health behaviours are linked to negative health outcomes (Segovia et al., 1989; Abuladze et al., 2017) which, in turn, adversely affect the fiscal sustainability of healthcare systems.

However, variations exist in the association between solo living and health behaviour. Such differences stem from the diversity of experiences that shape the living arrangements of older adults. Public policies that affect personal circumstances and preferences add a further layer of complexity to the relationship.

https://doi.org/10.1515/9783110617245-026

This chapter explores how living alone is associated with health behaviours across countries, taking into account key demographic and socioeconomic characteristics that distinguish those living alone from those who reside with others. We explore how living alone is associated with four key indicators of health behaviour (smoking, drinking, physical inactivity and unhealthy diet) among people aged 60 and older in Europe and Israel. In addition, we consider possible age differences and, in particular, whether living alone in advanced old age has greater adverse effects on health behaviours than among the younger old. Finally, we examine whether and how different national contexts shape the relationships between living alone and health-related behaviour.

26.2 Study methodology

We used individual-level data from SHARE Waves 4–6 to explore the health behaviours of older adults. The *outcome variables* were a set of health risk behaviours from the behavioural risks (BR) module. They included smoking (respondents who reported smoking at the time of the interview), excessive drinking (7 and 14 or more alcoholic drinks during the last 7 days for women and men, respectively), physical inactivity (never engaged in vigorous or moderate physical activity) and unhealthy diet (whether consumed fruits and vegetables less frequently than daily). The *key independent variable* was a dichotomous measure that indicated whether the respondent was living alone or with others. To explore the predictors of health behaviours, we analysed their prevalence by country and then employed a logistic regression analysis of the predictors of health behaviours, controlling for a collection of potentially *confounding variables*. These variables were as follows: gender, age (60–69, 70–79 and 80 years and older), years of education, number of living children (including natural, foster, adopted or step-children), child distance (if any child lives within 30 minutes), urban or rural area, depression (score of 4 or more on the EURO-D depression scale), total equivalized household income (classified into quintiles by individual country) and welfare regime (continental (AT, DE, FR, CH, BE, LU), social democratic (SE, DK), Mediterranean (ES, IT, GR, PT), eastern European (CZ, PL, SI, EE, HR) and mixed (IL)).

26.3 Study results

We first compared differences in health-related lifestyle factors by living arrangements and country to explore whether respondents aged 60 and older who live alone were more likely to engage in risky health behaviours. In general, not accounting for any compositional differences between the two groups, older adults living alone appear to smoke more than those living with others, are less physically active and eat less healthy but are less likely to drink excessively.

The lowest proportion of respondents aged 60 and older who reported smoking at the time of the interview were from Portugal and France (10%), and the highest was from Poland (22%), followed by the Czech Republic (19%) and Greece (18%). Older adults living alone in Austria, Germany, Denmark, Sweden and Slovenia had statistically higher chances of smoking ($p < 0.05$) than those living with others, with differences ranging from 2.6 percentage points in Slovenia to 8.7 percentage points in Denmark (Figure 26.1).

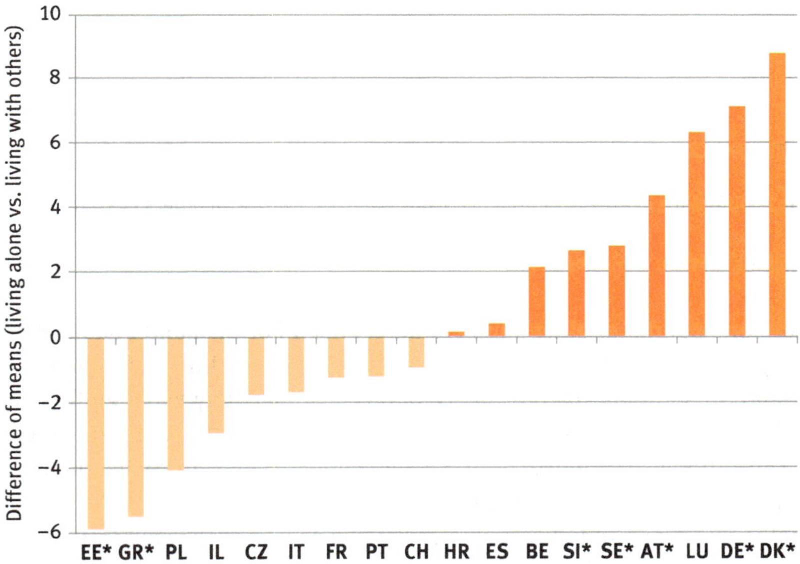

Figure 26.1: Difference in smoking, living alone vs. living with others by country.
Note: * p < 5%.
Source: SHARE Wave 4, 5, 6 release 6.1.1.

The proportion of older adults who drank excessively ranged from less than 1 per cent in Israel to approximately 25 per cent in Belgium, France and Portugal, and approximately 30 per cent in Denmark. Respondents who lived alone were significantly less likely to experience excessive drinking in Belgium, Germany, France, Denmark, Sweden, Greece, Italy, Portugal, Czech Republic and Slovenia ($p < 0.05$), with differences ranging from 2.2 percentage points in Sweden to 15.6 percentage points in Portugal (Figure 26.2).

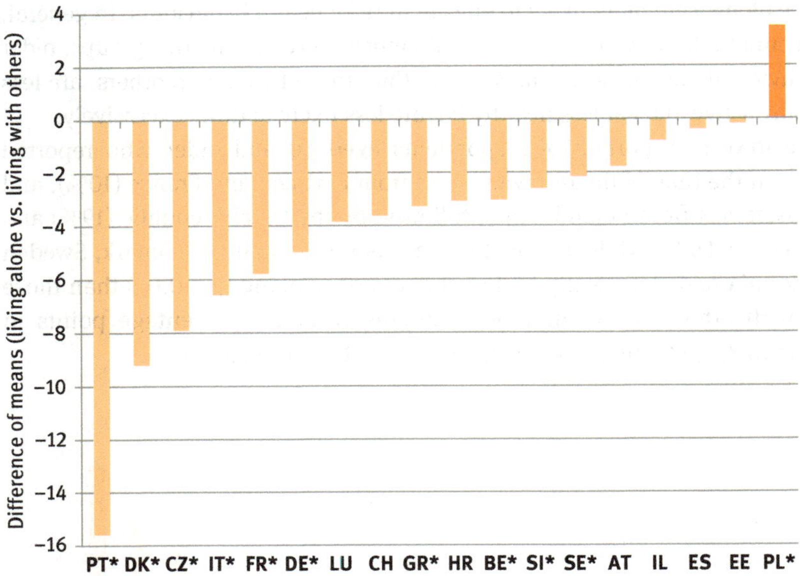

Figure 26.2: Difference in excessive drinking, living alone vs. living with others by country.
Note: * p < 5%.
Source: SHARE Wave 4, 5, 6 release 6.1.1.

About one-quarter of older adults in Italy, Israel, Portugal and Poland were physically inactive relative to only one in seventeen older adults in Sweden and Switzerland. In addition, the prevalence of physical inactivity was significantly higher for respondents who lived alone than for others in all countries except Israel. The differences ranged from 5.2 percentage points in Switzerland to 12 percentage points in Poland (Figure 26.3).

Finally, about one in ten French and Belgian respondents aged 60+ exhibited unhealthy eating habits relative to approximately 30 percent of respondents in the Czech Republic, Estonia, Greece and Israel, and almost one-half in Poland. Respondents who lived alone in Austria, Belgium, Denmark, Italy, Croatia and Estonia were significantly more likely to practice unhealthy eating relative to their peers who lived with others (Figure 26.4).

We estimated logistic regression models for the outcome variables. In Model A, we estimated each health behaviour by living arrangement (living alone). In Model B, we added the control variables and in Model C we included interactions of age and welfare regime with the variable 'living alone'. Figure 26.5 highlights the results for the main predictor of interest – living alone. Model C (the grey bar) shows that older adults living alone had a 1.2 times greater

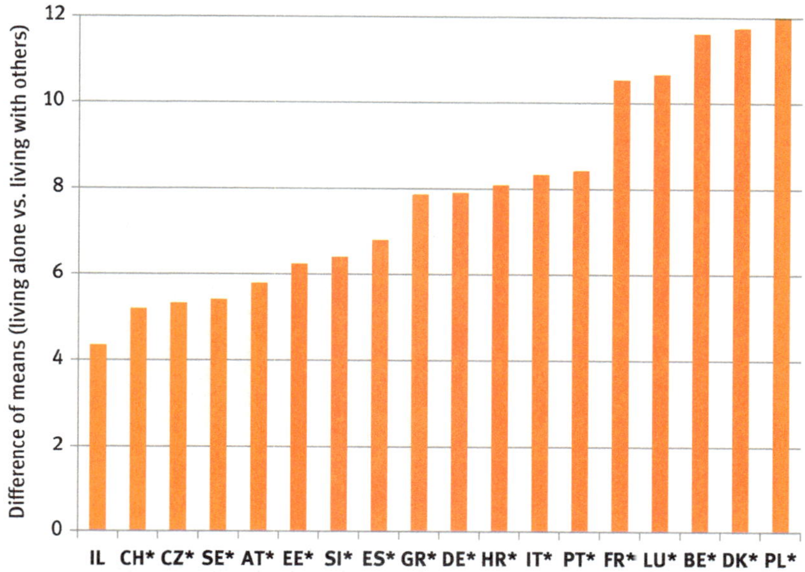

Figure 26.3: Difference in physical inactivity, living alone vs. living with others by country.
Note: * p < 5%.
Source: SHARE Wave 4, 5, 6 release 6.1.1.

probability of reporting that they smoked at the time of the interview and a 1.3 times greater likelihood of eating unhealthy food every day. No significant difference existed in physical activity by living arrangements after the controls and interactions were considered. Conversely, those who lived alone were approximately 25 per cent less likely to report excessive drinking.

Regarding the other predictors included in the model, age was negatively associated with smoking, excessive drinking and eating unhealthy foods, and positively related to physical inactivity. However, the results of the interaction of age and living alone suggest that no difference exists in the age–health behaviours relationship by living arrangements (results not shown).

The predictive margins of probability of various health behaviours by living arrangement type across different welfare regimes (Figures 26.6–26.9) showed a complex pattern of relationships of welfare regime types and outcomes of interest. Living alone in continental and social democratic regimes was associated with a stronger adverse relationship with smoking than in the Mediterranean and eastern European regimes, whereas no adverse relationship was observed in the mixed regime. Similarly, whereas living alone was associated with a higher probability of physical inactivity in the continental and social democratic welfare

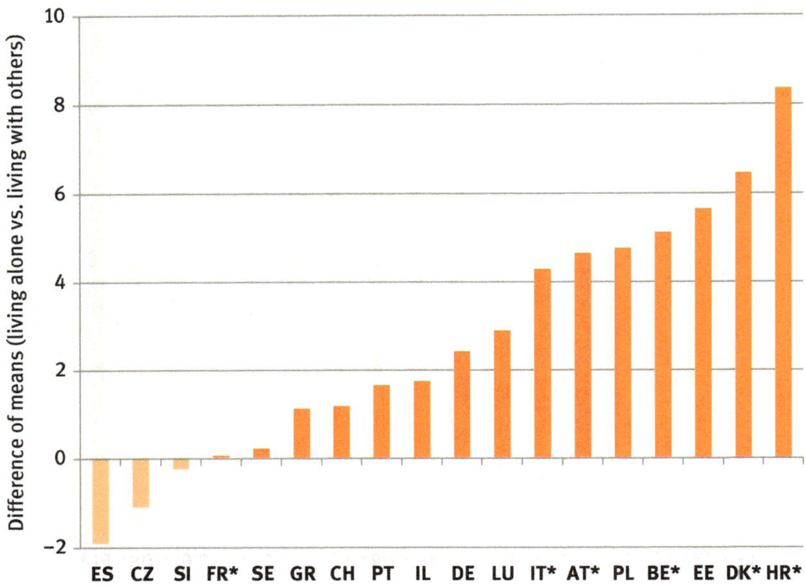

Figure 26.4: Difference in unhealthy diet, living alone vs. living with others by country.
Note: * $p < 5\%$.
Source: SHARE Wave 4, 5, 6 release 6.1.1.

regimes, either no or a negative relationship existed across other welfare regimes. Conversely, although the probability of having an unhealthy diet varied across welfare regimes, the relative difference in living arrangements appeared approximately constant. Finally, the probability of drinking exhibited the clearest welfare regime gradient, from the highest in the continental to the lowest in the mixed welfare regime, with the negative impact of living alone relative to living with others particularly pronounced in the Mediterranean regime.

26.4 Discussion and conclusion

The analysis tentatively confirms the previous finding from the literature that living alone in old age is associated with more adverse health behaviours than living with others. However, the analysis also highlights some differences between countries, suggesting that national contexts potentially play an important role. Bivariate analysis showed that persons aged 60 or older and living alone were, in general, less likely to drink excessively than their peers who

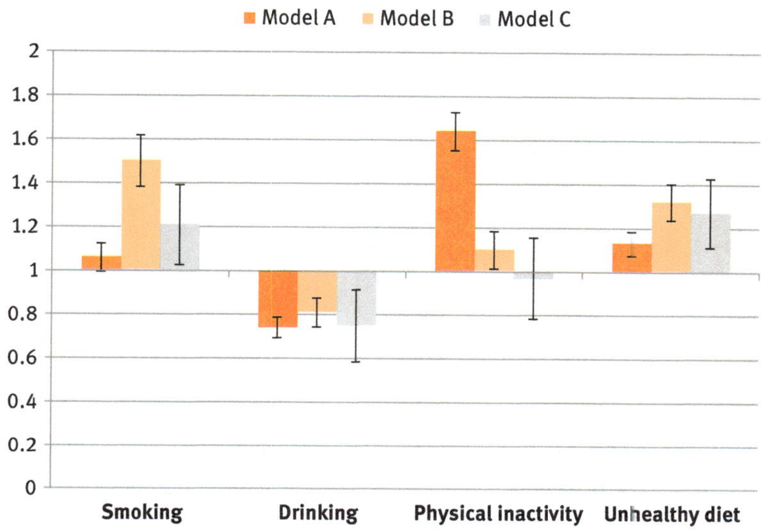

Figure 26.5: Odd ratios for the variable of main interest 'living alone .
Notes: *Model A* included only the predictor variable 'living alone'; *Model B* controlled for the rest of the independent variables; *Model C* included controls and interactions.
Source: SHARE Wave 4, 5, 6 release 6.1.1.

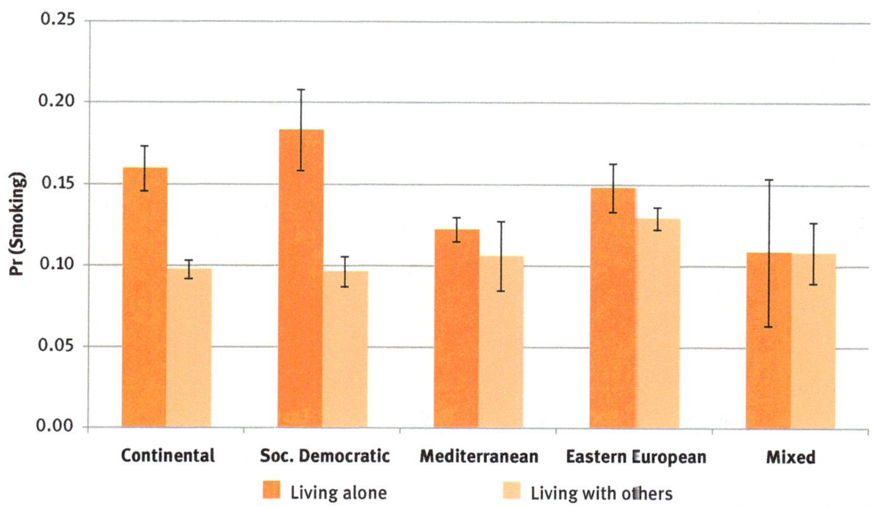

Figure 26.6: Predictive margins of probability of smoking by living arrangement and welfare regime.
Source: SHARE Wave 4, 5, 6 release 6.1.1.

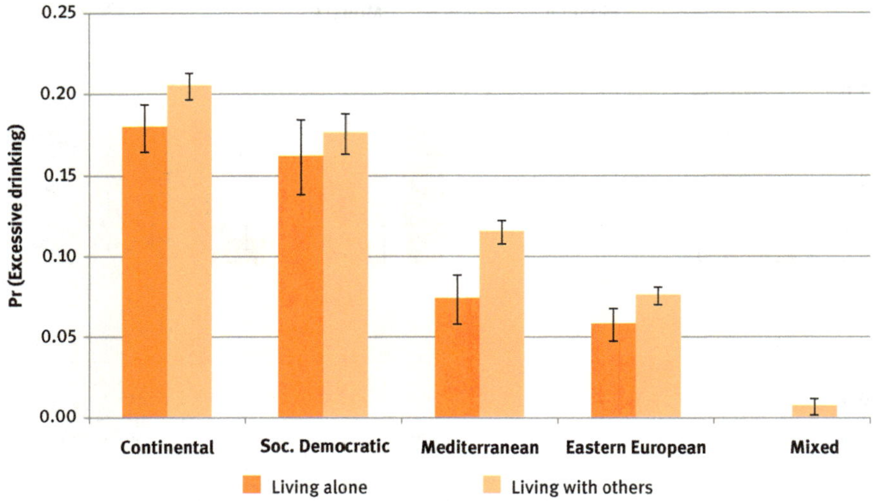

Figure 26.7: Predictive margins of probability of drinking excessively by living arrangement and welfare regime.
Source: SHARE Wave 4, 5, 6 release 6.1.1.

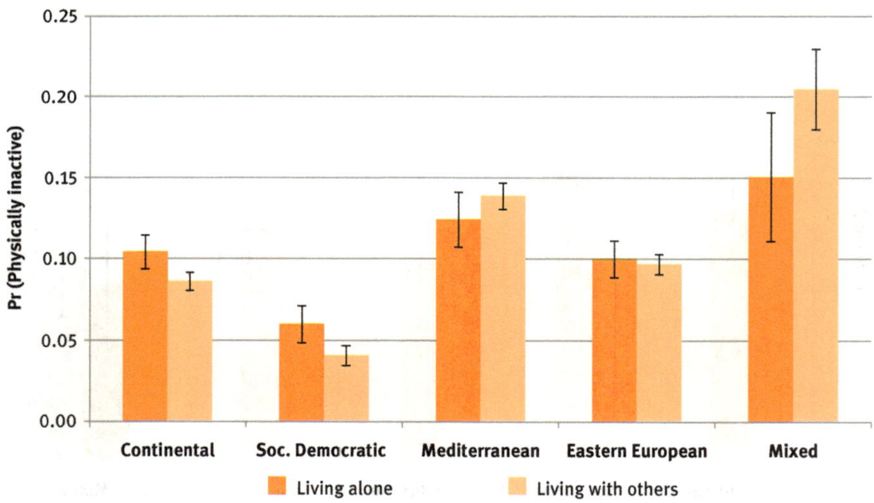

Figure 26.8: Predictive margins of probability of being physically inactive by living arrangement and welfare regime.
Source: SHARE Wave 4, 5, 6 release 6.1.1.

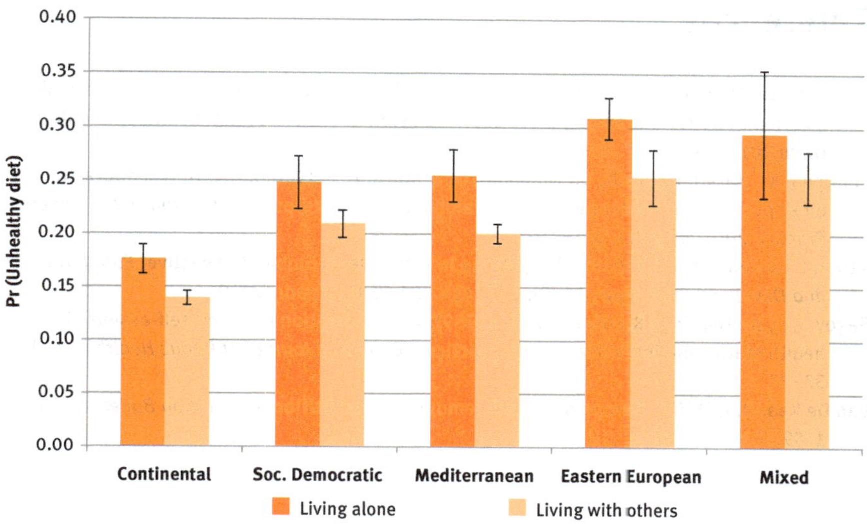

Figure 26.9: Predictive margins of probability of having an unhealthy diet by living arrangement and welfare regime.
Source: SHARE Wave 4, 5, 6 release 6.1.1.

lived with others. In northern European countries, as well as in Germany, Austria and Slovenia, older persons living alone were more likely to smoke. In addition, in all countries except for Israel, older persons living alone were significantly less physically active. Econometric analysis further confirmed that the link between living alone and smoking and physical inactivity varied significantly across different welfare regimes. In contrast, whereas age is correlated with health behaviours, we found no evidence that it also modifies the link between living alone and health behaviours. In other words, regardless of their living arrangement, older adults exhibit similar differences in health behaviour by age.

Overall, our analysis supports two main conclusions. First, living alone is an important indicator of higher risk of adverse health behaviour for older adults. Therefore, developing targeted public policies for this population that focus on promoting a healthy lifestyle is appropriate. Second, living arrangements and related health behaviours vary substantially across countries, implying that policy priorities and solutions from one country may be informative but not necessarily readily applicable or effective in other countries. Although scope exists for interventions across Europe, a one-size-fits-all policy approach is likely suboptimal. Future research should explore the issue of pathways into living alone because this information can complement the insights of the present analysis and provide a foundation for a set of country-specific policy recommendations.

References

Abuladze, L., Kunder, N., Lang, K. & Vaask, S. (2017). Associations between self-rated health and health behaviour among older adults in Estonia: a cross-sectional analysis. *BMJ Open* 2017; 7:e013257. doi: 10.1136/bmjopen-2016-013257.

Kharicha, K., Harari, D., Swift, C., Gillmann, G. & Stuck, A. E. (2007). Health risk appraisal in older people 1: are older people living alone an 'at-risk' group? *British Journal of General Practice* 2007; 57 (537): 271–276.

Reher, D. & Requena, M. (2018). Living Alone in Later Life: A Global Perspective. *Population and Development Review*; 44 (3): 427–454. doi:10.1111/padr.12149.

Segovia, J., Bartlett R. F. & Edwards A. C. (1989). The association between self-assessed health status and individual health practices. *Canadian Journal of Public Health*; 80 (1): 32–37.

Van De Kaa, D. J. (1987). Europe's second demographic transition. *Population Bulletin*; 42 (1): 1–59.

Yarine Fawaz and Pedro Mira

27 Bereavement, loneliness and health

- When a spouse or close confidant dies, loneliness and depressive symptoms increase
- The death of a confidant reduces one's satisfaction with one's social network
- Policymakers should pay extra attention to bereavement in old age given its effect on loneliness and health

27.1 Introduction

Loneliness and social isolation are important public health issues. A recent meta-analysis of research on the subject, mostly from the medical literature, concludes that being lonely and socially isolated – i.e., lacking social connections – may be at least as devastating to a person's health and survival as being obese or a heavy smoker (Holt-Lunstad et al. 2015). Using SHARE cross-sectional data, Deindl et al. (2013) found a positive correlation between one's degree of integration in social networks and one's self-assessed health.

Spousal bereavement – known as the 'widowhood effect' in the literature – also has potential health impacts. For example, a meta-analysis by Moon et al. (2011) found a positive association between widowhood and mortality. Moreover, the death of close relations or friends is likely to impact loneliness and social isolation. These issues are important because individuals are increasingly exposed to bereavement as they age.

The study reported in this chapter uses SHARE data to investigate the consequences of bereavement for loneliness, social isolation and health. We exploit longitudinal data on health outcomes and loneliness, as well as information on respondents' social networks. Our study considers two explanatory variables. First, we examine indicators of whether or not a respondent lost a spouse in the interval between any two consecutive waves. Second, we study the death of a confidant in a person's social network between Waves 4 and 6, when the network data were collected. We look at the effect of both of these events on selected health outcomes, measures of loneliness and the quality of the social network. We hypothesize that bereavement is associated with: (1) more loneliness and lower quality networks and (2) worse health outcomes through its effect on loneliness and isolation.

https://doi.org/10.1515/9783110617245-027

27.2 Data and analysis

Sample: We included all SHARE respondents aged 60+ who were observed in more than one wave between Waves 1–6. Because our analysis is longitudinal, a unit of observation contains information on a respondent in two waves, referred to here as initial and subsequent waves. For example, a respondent observed in Waves 4, 5 and 6 contributed one observation with initial information obtained from Wave 4 and subsequent information obtained from Wave 5, and a second observation where Waves 5 and 6 were the initial and subsequent waves, respectively. We pooled multiple observations for the same respondent.

Health outcomes: We focused on three variables that capture different dimensions of health. Mental health was measured using the EURO-D score, which is the sum of 12 depressive symptoms in older adults. Physical health was measured using an index of frailty (Fried et al. 2001) that combines the following conditions: unintentional weight loss, self-reported exhaustion, weakness (grip strength), slow walking speed and low physical activity. Functional health was measured by summing the difficulties in activities of daily living (ADLs) and in instrumental activities of daily living (IADLs) in a single measure. The descriptive statistics of these health outcomes in the latest wave (Wave 6) are displayed in Table 27.1 (the data for other waves are similar). All health variables were coded such that greater values reflect worse outcomes.

Social Isolation and Loneliness: The Social Network (SN) module available in Waves 4 and 6 of SHARE uses a name generator to identify and describe a person's network of confidants (Litwin et al. 2013). In our analysis, we employed variables that measure the quality of this network as markers of isolation. They included: 1) the size of the SN (the number of confidants) other than the spouse; 2) satisfaction with respect to one's SN measured on a scale from 0 to 10, where 10 indicates 'completely satisfied' and 3) frequency of contact with the most frequently contacted confidant measured on an ordinal scale from 1 (never) to 7 (daily), again excluding the spouse. Loneliness, or 'felt' isolation, was measured using the short form of the RUCLA loneliness scale. We combined the three items of the scale into a single measure that reflected how often respondents felt: a) a sense of being left out, b) a lack of companionship and c) isolation. The total RUCLA index score ranged from 3–9, with a higher score indicating a more intense feeling of loneliness.

Bereavement: We considered two types of personal losses that are prevalent in the lives of older people. First, the death of a spouse between two consecutive waves was experienced by 2,639 respondents, or an incidence of 3.7% per wave. Second, we examined the death of confidants in the SN between Waves 4 and 6. In Wave 6, survey participants who did not mention a confidant who was cited

Table 27.1: Variable descriptions.

	Mean	Sd	Min	Max	N
Health Outcomes					
Frailty	1.06	1.18	0	5	21,119
Limitations	0.83	2.16	0	15	23,462
EURO-D	2.46	2.22	0	12	23,088
Loneliness and Social Isolation					
RUCLA	3.87	1.34	3	9	21,483
SN size	2.16	1.61	0	7	23,489
SN satisfaction	8.96	1.30	0	10	21,847
SN contact frequency	6.22	0.96	1	7	15,551
Bereavement incidence					
Widow	0.04	0.19	0	1	72,217
SN: dead	0.05	0.23	0	1	23,896
SN: dead close	0.01	0.11	0	1	23,896
SN: dead not close	0.04	0.20	0	1	23,896

Note: SHARE Wave 6 for health outcomes, loneliness and social isolation. SHARE Waves 1–2, 2–4, 4–5, 5–6 for the spousal bereavement variable (widow), SHARE Waves 4–6 for the non-spousal bereavement variables (deaths within one's social network).
Source: SHARE Wave 1–6.

earlier in Wave 4 were asked why that person was not named again. We used a binary indicator to indicate the death of at least one member of the individual's SN – excluding the spouse. As displayed in Table 27.1, 5% of our sample – i.e., 1,311 individuals out of 23,896 observed in Waves 4 and 6 – experienced this type of network confidant loss. We also used information on how close the deceased SN person was to the respondent. In this case, we defined indicators for 'death of an SN member who was extremely close' (n = 272), 'death of an SN member who was less than extremely close' (n = 1,048) and 'no confidant died between W4 and W6' (n = 22,585). We note that the first two categories are not mutually exclusive.

Analysis: First, we regressed health outcomes in the subsequent wave on the bereavement indicators in the initial wave. We entered a set of controls into the procedure because they are potential confounders. They included the respective initial health outcome, the duration between initial and subsequent interviews, gender, age, age squared, being in a couple, having children, education (categories), working status, income and wealth quartiles and country. Second, we regressed measures of loneliness and social isolation in the subsequent wave on the bereavement indicators. We included the same baseline controls as in the previous regression, adding the initial loneliness or SN outcome and replacing the initial health outcome by initial self-assessed health. In the regressions that used the death of a confidant, we added initial SN size; in the regressions that used the death of a close confidant, we included both SN size and the number of close confidants. To isolate the effect of the death of a spouse, which we report, the corresponding regressions included binary indicators for 'widow in subsequent wave', 'widow in initial wave' and their interaction, in addition to 'in couple' and other controls. Given the extensive set of controls and our use of longitudinal data, the regression design can be considered quasi-experimental, such that a causal interpretation of the bereavement coefficients is warranted.

27.3 Results and discussion

Table 27.2 reports the coefficients of the bereavement events in the regressions of the health outcomes.

Table 27.2: Effect of widowhood transitions and death of an SN member on health outcomes.

	(1)	(2)	(3)
	Frail	**Limitations**	**EURO-D**
Widow	0.139***	0.187***	1.013***
	(0.020)	(0.034)	(0.037)
SN: dead	0.039	0.043	0.115**
	(0.029)	(0.051)	(0.055)
SN: dead close	0.085	−0.024	0.259**
	(0.062)	(0.107)	(0.117)

Significance: *** = 1%; ** = 5%; * = 10%.
Note: Standard errors in parenthesis. SHARE Waves 1 to 6 for widowhood, Waves 4 and 6 for the SN bereavement indicators. Controls at baseline: (lagged) health outcome, gender, age, age squared, being in a couple, having children, education categories, working status, income and wealth quartiles and country dummies. The second panel includes baseline SN size as a control; the third panel includes baseline SN size and number of extremely close confidants.
Source: SHARE Wave 1–6.

The coefficients for ‘widow’ in the first row measure the effect on health, conditional on past health, of becoming a widow in the interval between two consecutive waves as opposed to remaining married. The coefficients show that becoming a widow is associated with modest detrimental effects on our measures of physical and functional health. Moreover, we find a large detrimental effect on mental health. The coefficient for the EURO-D depression score implies a relative increase by more than 1 point. This increase is substantial because the threshold for clinical depression is 4 or more depressive symptoms. Adding 1 to the EURO-D score of every respondent would increase the prevalence of depression from 31% to 44%.

The other rows of Table 27.2 show the effect of the death of a confidant who is not a spouse. Almost all of the coefficients point to a small negative effect of this event on health but few are statistically significantly. However, non-spousal bereavement leads to a significant 0.12-point increase in the EURO-D depression score. Moreover, when the confidant who died was extremely close to the respondent, the coefficient more than doubles, increasing the EURO-D by 0.26 points or equivalent to a quarter of the large effect of spousal bereavement.

In Table 27.3, we show how bereavement affects loneliness and several indicators of quality of the social network. The results show that becoming a widow leads to a substantial increase in feelings of loneliness. In contrast, widows seem to respond to the death of their spouses by adding confidants to their network and increasing their frequency of contact. Losing their spouse may allow them to expand their social network by leaving them with more free time, or they may increase their social contact to make up for that loss. There is no effect on satisfaction with the network of confidants; however, note that the deceased spouse may or may not have been a confidant.

The remaining rows of Table 27.3 point to the death of a confidant as having a detrimental effect on the person’s feeling of loneliness and satisfaction with his/her social network. If the deceased confidant was close, these effects are again much larger. However, non-spousal bereavement does not seem to imply any change in the SN size or contact frequency.

27.4 Conclusion

We found that the death of a spouse or a close confidant is correlated with an increase in loneliness and the number of depressive symptoms. In addition, the death of a confidant reduces the quality of a person’s social network in terms of satisfaction, all the more so when the confidant was extremely close to the respondent.

Table 27.3: Effect of bereavement and social isolation on loneliness and SN quality.

	(1)	(2)	(3)	(4)
	RUCLA	**SN Size**	**Satisfaction**	**Frequency**
Widow	0.856***	0.636***	0.075	0.142***
	(0.041)	(0.057)	(0.055)	(0.044)
SN: dead	0.083**	−0.053	−0.068*	−0.007
	(0.034)	(0.041)	(0.038)	(0.027)
SN: dead close	0.178**	0.099	−0.191**	−0.008
	(0.073)	(0.089)	(0.080)	(0.059)

Significance: *** = 1%; ** = 5%; * = 10%.
Note: SHARE Waves 5 and 6 for column (1), Waves 4 and 6 for columns (2) to (4). Controls at baseline: lagged outcome, self-assessed health, gender, age, age squared, being in a couple, having children, education categories, working status, income and wealth quartiles and country dummies. Columns (2) to (4) include controls for baseline SN size (2nd panel), baseline SN size and number of extremely close confidants (3rd panel).
Source: SHARE Wave 1–6.

Our analysis of the effect of bereavement is limited to fairly short-term intervals: 1-wave intervals for widowhood and 2-wave intervals for the death of confidants. Future research should explore the effects at longer horizons, controlling for time since bereavement. Whether we would find stronger effects over longer horizons or that, instead, individuals adjust to the death of spouse and confidants remains to be seen.

In sum, the SHARE data confirm the high incidence of bereavement in old age. Our findings suggest that policymakers concerned with loneliness and social isolation as a public health issue should pay special attention to bereavement as an important factor in the nexus between social connectedness (or the lack thereof) and health.

References

Deindl, C., Hank, K. and Brandt, M. (2013). 26. Social networks and self-rated health in later life. In Börsch-Supan, A. (Ed.), Brandt, M. (Ed.), Litwin, H. (Ed.), et al. (2013). *Active ageing and solidarity between generations in Europe. First results from SHARE after the economic crisis*. Berlin, Boston: De Gruyter. pp 301–310.

Fried, L., Tangen, C., Walston, J., Newman, A., Hirsch, C., Gottdiener, J., Seeman, T., Tracy, R., Kop, W., Burke, G. and McBurnie, M. (2001). Frailty in Older Adults: Evidence for a

Phenotype. *The Journals of Gerontology Series A: Biological Sciences and Medical Sciences*, 56(3). pp. M146–M157.
Holt-Lunstad, J., Smith, T., Baker, M., Harris, T. and Stephenson, D. (2015). Loneliness and Social Isolation as Risk Factors for Mortality. *Perspectives on Psychological Science*, 10(2). pp. 227–237.
Litwin, H., Stoeckel, K., Roll, A., Shiovitz-Ezra, S., and M. Kotte (2013). Social network measurement in SHARE wave four. In Malter, F. and A. Börsch-Supan (Eds.) (2013). *SHARE Wave 4: Innovations & Methodology*. Munich: Munich Center for the Economics of Aging (MEA). pp. 18–37.
Moon, J., Kondo, N., Glymour, M. and Subramanian, S. (2011). Widowhood and Mortality: A Meta-Analysis. *PLoS ONE*, 6(8), p.e23465.

Part VI Healthcare and health behaviour

Edited by Florence Jusot

Hendrik Jürges and Luca Stella

28 The social dynamics of unmet need, catastrophic healthcare expenses and satisfaction with health insurance coverage

- Substantial heterogeneity exists in access to healthcare and health insurance coverage across Europe, with Greece and Italy being the countries in Waves 6 and 7 with the most serious deficiencies
- Unmet healthcare needs over the life cycle are most prevalent among former eastern European countries, whereas the educational inequalities in unmet needs are mostly concentrated in southern Europe
- Low-educated, sick or disabled or divorced individuals have a greater risk of suffering from 'chronic' difficulties related to access to care

28.1 Introduction

In this chapter, we investigate how access to healthcare – as a crucial dimension of social inclusion – varies across European countries and over time. To this end, we focus on social inequality in access to healthcare in SHARE Waves 5, 6 and 7 data among the elderly population along three relevant dimensions: subjective unmet need, catastrophic out-of-pocket (OOP) healthcare expenses (relative to annual household income) and dissatisfaction with basic health insurance (HI) coverage.

Using cross-sectional data from SHARE Wave 5, Jürges (2015) has already shown that access to healthcare varies largely across Europe, with Estonia, Italy and Israel being the countries with the most serious deficiencies. The contribution of this chapter is to extend this analysis in several dimensions. By adding data collected in Waves 6 and 7, we are able to not only describe barriers to access to care and health insurance coverage in a larger set of countries but also document unmet need retrospectively (as elicited from the life-history data in Wave 7) and, perhaps more importantly, analyse the dynamics in barriers to healthcare access. An important aspect of our analysis is to understand whether and the extent to which limited access to healthcare is a persistent phenomenon or just transitory, that is, whether the individuals reporting

https://doi.org/10.1515/9783110617245-028

unmet need, catastrophic OOP healthcare expenses or dissatisfaction with health insurance coverage in Wave 6 and/or 7 are the same individuals in Wave 5 ('chronic' deficiency) or whether they are different individuals from one wave to another ('temporary' deficiency). Substantial consensus exists that the persistent or long-term share of poverty – among which limited access to healthcare is included – should receive more attention than the temporary share (Biewen, 2006).

To measure subjective unmet need, catastrophic OOP expenses and dissatisfaction with health insurance coverage, we follow Jürges (2015) and, thus, rely on the detailed information collected in the healthcare module. Specifically, regarding subjective unmet need, we asked respondents the following questions: 'Was there a time in the past 12 months when you needed to see a doctor but could not because of cost?'; 'Was there a time in the past 12 months when you needed to see a doctor but could not because you had to wait too long?'; 'In the last twelve months, to help you keep your living costs down, have you postponed visits to the dentist?' In Wave 7, respondents were also asked the following question: 'Was there a time in the past 12 months when you needed medication but could not afford it because of costs?' Regarding OOP expenses, SHARE provides information on respondents' annual out-of-pocket expenses and the corresponding amount of the deductible (if any) for five types of medical care or care-related illnesses: doctor visits, dentist visits including prostheses, prescription and over-the-counter drugs, hospital and other inpatient stays (including temporary stays in nursing homes) and at-home care (personal care, wheels-on-meals and others). OOP expenses are computed as the sum of the deductibles paid, direct payments to healthcare providers and co-payments. Moreover, to compare the financial burden of OOP expenses on households across countries, we compute the percentage of annual household income spent out-of-pocket on healthcare. As in Jürges (2015), we use 15 per cent of net annual household income as the threshold to define catastrophic healthcare expenses (see, for example, Wyszewianski, 1986). Finally, the healthcare module contains self-reported information on satisfaction with health insurance coverage. The following question is asked to the respondents: 'Overall, how satisfied are you with your own coverage in your basic health insurance/national health system?'

One important innovation of our analyses is that we use the retrospective interview in SHARE Wave 7, which contains four self-reported questions on unmet need suffered by respondents not only during their adult life but also during their childhood and youth. In particular, respondents were asked whether during their life they '*ever needed to see a doctor but you did not because you could not afford it*', '*ever needed to see a doctor but you did not because you could not afford it*', '*ever postponed a dentist visit to help you keep your living costs down*' and '*ever foregone taking medication which you could not afford because of cost*'.

28.2 Cross-country differences in unmet need, out-of-pocket expenses and satisfaction with health insurance coverage in waves 6 and 7

In this section, we provide a cross-national comparison of the level of unmet need, catastrophic OOP expenses and dissatisfaction with health insurance coverage among European elderly. In particular, Figure 28.1 illustrates – for each country in Wave 6 – the percentage of respondents who declare at least one unmet need (see Panel A), the fraction of households with catastrophic OOP healthcare expenses (see Panel B) and the proportion of respondents who report dissatisfaction or significant dissatisfaction with the coverage in their basic health insurance (see Panel C). Overall, Figure 28.1 shows that the cross-national heterogeneity in terms of the three indicators is remarkable. For example, approximately 40 per cent of respondents in Greece and Estonia reported at least one unmet need in the last 12 months, whereas in countries with the lowest levels of unmet need, such as Austria and Switzerland, this proportion is approximately 5 per cent. Moreover, although more than 15 per cent of households in Portugal, Poland, Greece, Italy and Israel faced catastrophic healthcare expenses, this proportion drops to less than 5 per cent in a number of countries, including Belgium, Czech Republic, Switzerland, Luxembourg, Germany, France, Denmark and Sweden. Figure 28.1 also shows the presence of a significant gap in terms of dissatisfaction with HI coverage, ranging from approximately 55 per cent in Greece to approximately 5 per cent in Switzerland. However, the countries under investigation are noted as having very different cultural histories, labour market institutions and social characteristics. Such differences may play a relevant role in explaining the substantial heterogeneity in the access to healthcare and health insurance coverage across Europe. At the same time, these cross-country differences can be partly explained by the consequences of the recent financial crisis, which were particularly severe for Greece and the other southern European countries, such as Italy and Portugal.

Figure 28.2 shows a similar pattern of healthcare access in the longitudinal sample of Wave 7 (Note: We drop countries with very few observations in one of the three indicators, including Portugal, Estonia and Croatia).

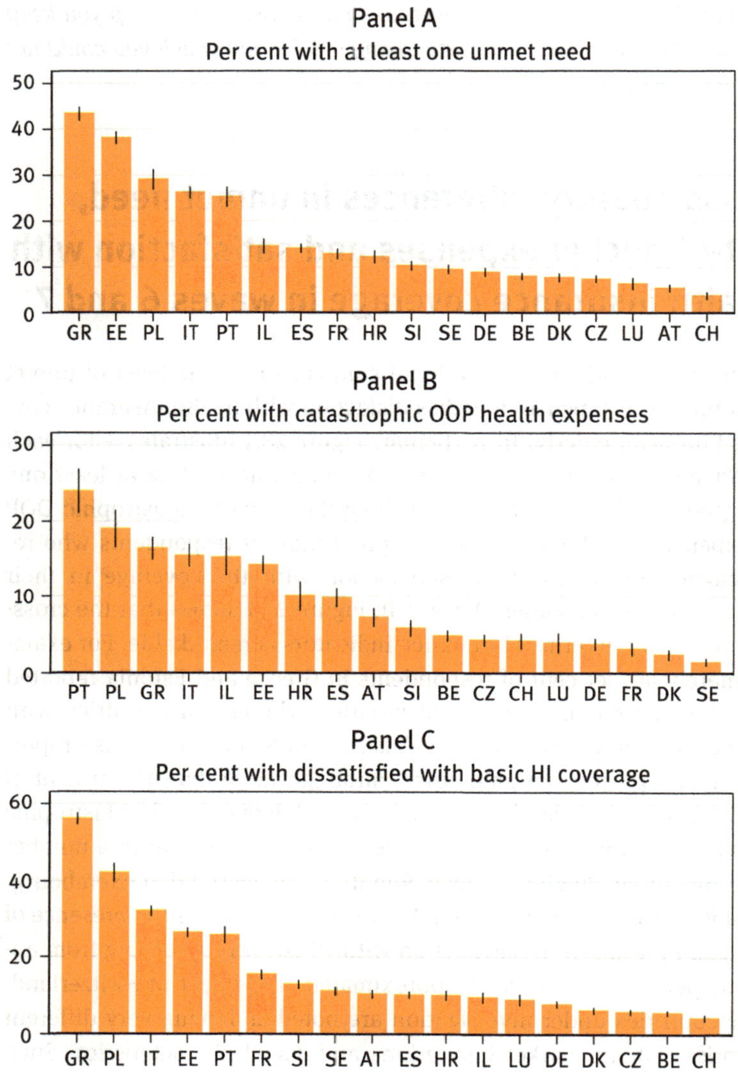

Figure 28.1: Percentage of respondents in Wave 6 reporting at least one unmet need, catastrophic OOP health expenses, dissatisfaction with basic HI coverage, by country. Vertical lines show 95 per cent confidence intervals.

Note: N = 67,226.

Source: SHARE Wave 6 release 6.1.0.

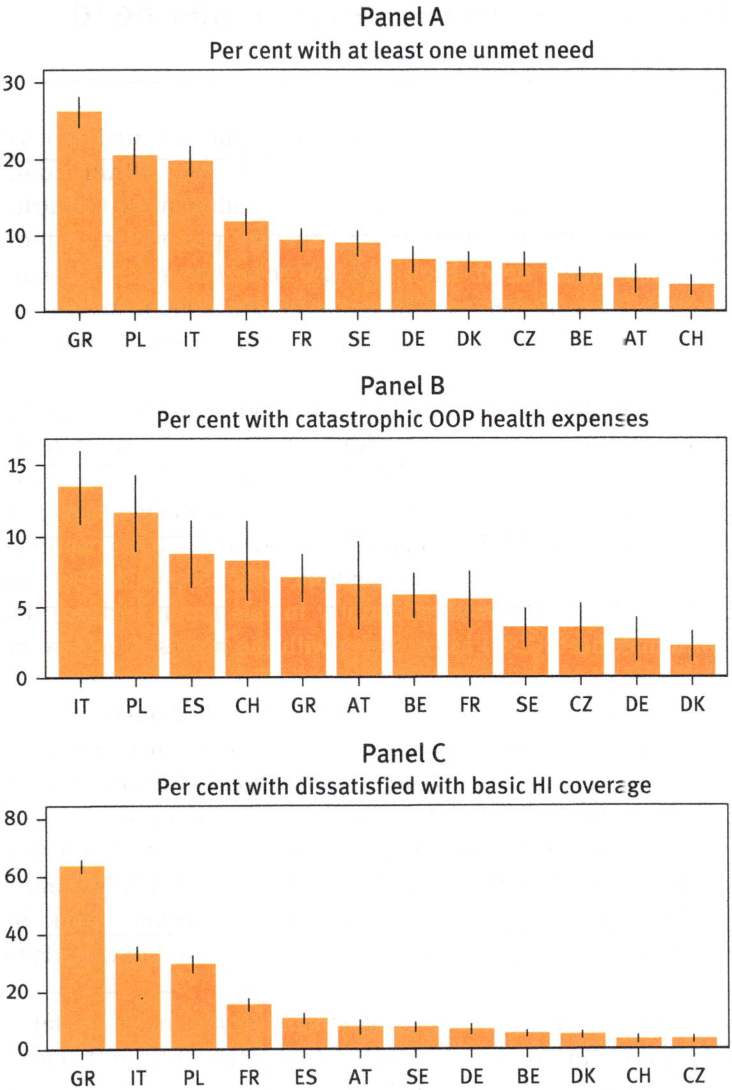

Figure 28.2: Percentage of respondents in Wave 7 reporting at least one unmet need, catastrophic OOP health expenses and dissatisfaction with basic HI coverage, by country. Vertical lines show 95 per cent confidence intervals.

Note: N = 54,824 (longitudinal respondents).

Source: SHARE Wave 7 release 0.

28.3 Cross-country differences in unmet need over the life cycle

Figure 28.3 illustrates the percentage of individuals who reported at least one unmet healthcare need over their life cycle across the SHARE countries, separately for high versus low education for individuals. Countries are first grouped regionally, and then by the average percentage of individuals who reported unmet need. High and low education refers to being in the top versus bottom 50 per cent in terms of educational attainment in a specific country. Education itself was measured by the ISCED 1997 classification.

The data show substantial differences in reported unmet healthcare needs across the SHARE countries, overall and within the four European regions. Overall, respondents in the former eastern European countries report the highest levels, but the range is broad. For example, the country with the largest proportion of reported unmet need is Romania (37%), whereas the three countries with the lowest proportions are the Czech Republic (9%), Slovenia (9%) and Slovakia (7%). Interestingly, the median country in this group (Poland) has similar levels of unmet need (22%) as countries with the highest levels in the three other European regions.

In southern Europe, the country with the highest level of unmet need is Greece (29%), probably reflecting the consequences of its financial crisis. In northern Europe, Finland (24%) stands out in comparison to the other Nordic countries, such as Denmark and Sweden. The lowest levels of self-reported unmet need can be found among the western European countries, but with a substantial gap that ranges from 8 per cent in Austria to 21 per cent in France. The 'top performing' countries in the other three European regions should be noted as having levels of unmet need that are as low as those in Switzerland and Austria.

Whereas educational differences in experiencing unmet need are fairly low in several countries (in 14 out of 27 countries, the educational differences are up to 2 percentage points, which is neither statistically nor substantively significant), a group of countries (i.e. Greece, Italy, Portugal, Luxembourg, Israel and Bulgaria) present substantial inequalities in unmet healthcare needs, ranging from 7 percentage points in Luxembourg and Portugal to 10 percentage points in Israel. Taken together, this evidence suggests that educational inequalities in access to healthcare are mostly concentrated in southern European countries.

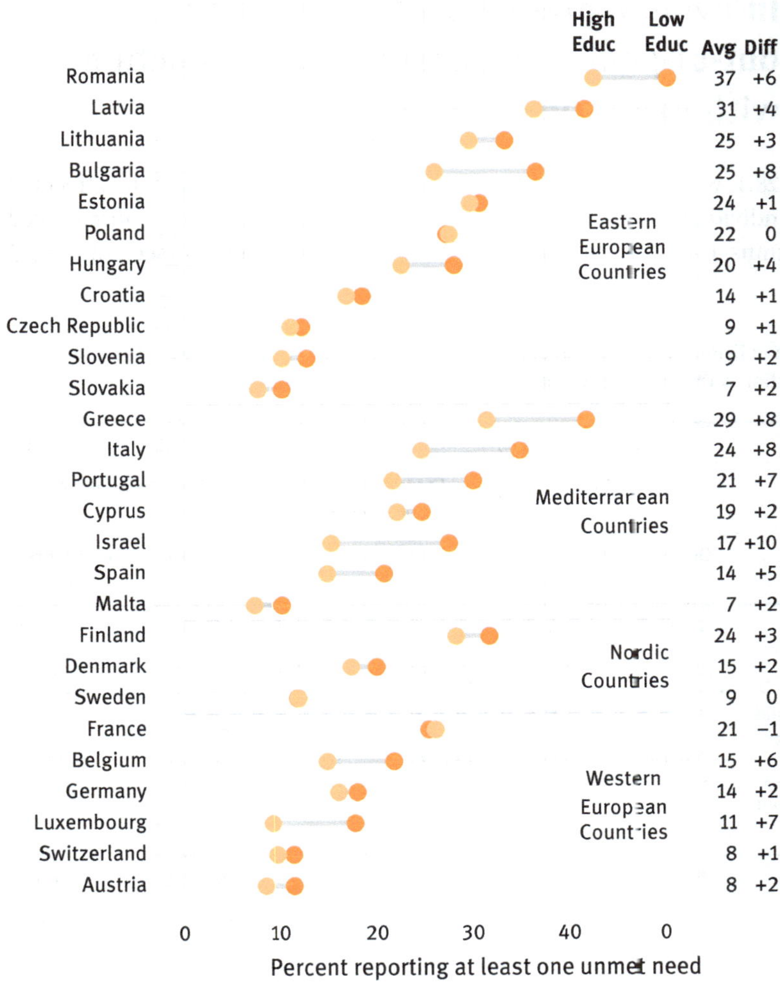

Figure 28.3: Percentage of respondents in Wave 7 reporting at least one unmet healthcare need over their life, by country and educational attainment. Low and high education are measured by the relative within-country rank (bottom versus top 50 per cent of sample respondents). Confidence intervals around proportions are approximately plus/minus 2 percentage points.
Note: N = 73,578 observations.
Source: SHARE Wave 7 release 0.

28.4 Individual predictors of unmet need, out-of-pocket expenses and satisfaction with health insurance

In Table 28.1, we use Waves 5, 6 and 7 and report the estimates of the effects of a set of individual covariates on our outcomes of interest, that is, unmet need (see columns 1 and 2), catastrophic OOP healthcare expenses (see columns 3

Table 28.1: Individual predictors of unmet need, catastrophic OOP health expenses and dissatisfaction with basic HI coverage.

	(1)	(2)	(3)	(4)	(5)	(6)
Outcome:	**Unmet need**		**Catastrophic OOP expenses**		**Dissatisfaction with HI**	
Group:	**One wave**	**Two or three waves**	**One wave**	**Two or three waves**	**One wave**	**Two or three waves**
Female	1.311***	1.219***	1.044	1.062**	1.118***	1.108***
	(0.040)	(0.023)	(0.036)	(0.029)	(0.042)	(0.021)
Having a child	1.237***	1.196***	0.875**	0.815***	1.042	1.014
	(0.070)	(0.042)	(0.054)	(0.038)	(0.074)	(0.036)
Never married – ref.						
Married	0.711***	0.707***	1.485***	0.922	0.841*	0.966
	(0.057)	(0.031)	(0.138)	(0.059)	(0.086)	(0.044)
Divorced	1.012	1.432***	1.375***	1.138*	1.174	1.254***
	(0.094)	(0.071)	(0.150)	(0.083)	(0.139)	(0.064)
Widowed	0.886	0.817***	1.270**	1.039	0.759**	0.929
	(0.079)	(0.041)	(0.133)	(0.073)	(0.087)	(0.048)
Low-educated – ref.						
Medium-educated	0.815***	0.755***	1.023	0.958	1.008	0.992
	(0.029)	(0.016)	(0.043)	(0.030)	(0.044)	(0.022)

Table 28.1 (continued)

	(1)	(2)	(3)	(4)	(5)	(6)
Outcome:	**Unmet need**		**Catastrophic OOP expenses**		**Dissatisfaction with HI**	
Group:	**One wave**	**Two or three waves**	**One wave**	**Two or three waves**	**One wave**	**Two or three waves**
Highly educated	0.740***	0.770***	0.884***	0.838***	0.856***	0.847***
	(0.031)	(0.020)	(0.040)	(0.031)	(0.043)	(0.023)
Other employment – ref.						
Retired	0.875	0.577***	1.069	0.703***	0.760**	0.760***
	(0.102)	(0.040)	(0.155)	(0.074)	(0.102)	(0.059)
Employed	0.756**	0.491***	0.719**	0.519***	0.753**	0.833**
	(0.094)	(0.035)	(0.108)	(0.057)	(0.108)	(0.067)
Unemployed	1.788***	1.323***	0.969	0.718**	1.010	1.164
	(0.259)	(0.110)	(0.196)	(0.100)	(0.186)	(0.109)
Sick or disabled	1.599***	1.379***	1.172	1.344**	1.239	1.278***
	(0.223)	(0.110)	(0.211)	(0.160)	(0.208)	(0.116)
Homemaker	0.839	0.717***	1.049	0.778**	0.854	0.863*
	(0.104)	(0.052)	(0.165)	(0.087)	(0.122)	(0.072)
Observations	102,927	102,927	70,153	70,153	98,431	98,431

Note: Multinomial logit estimations; relative-risk ratios reported. The referent group is given by zero waves. Robust standard errors are reported in parentheses. All regressions include age indicators (in 10-year intervals), wave dummies and county fixed effects.
Significance: *** = 1%; ** = 5%; * = 10%.
Source: SHARE Wave 5 and 6 release 6.1.0; Wave 7 release 0.

and 4) and dissatisfaction with basic health insurance coverage (see columns 5 and 6). These outcomes may occur in different groups of waves, which we operationalize as follows: no waves (referent group), one wave (see columns 1, 3 and 5) and more than one wave (see columns 2, 4 and 6). Importantly, by considering people who reported any condition in two or three waves, we aim to provide an assessment of the individuals who face 'chronic' difficulties in healthcare access and, thus, shed light on the persistent phenomenon of limited access to healthcare.

Specifically, each equation is estimated using a multinomial logit model, and the results are presented in terms of relative risk ratios.

What emerges is that, irrespective of the chosen outcome, highly educated individuals (ISCED ≥ 5, tertiary education) are significantly less likely to report deficiencies in healthcare access. Notably, this result also holds for the respondents who reported any condition in two or three waves, thereby suggesting that low-educated people have a greater risk of suffering from 'chronic' deficiencies in access to healthcare. We interpret this result as evidence that education plays a key role in explaining the lasting inequalities in access to healthcare services.

We also find that employed people exhibit a substantially lower probability of suffering from persistent unmet needs, catastrophic OOP expenses or being dissatisfied with basic HI coverage. In contrast, being sick or disabled is positively associated with these outcomes, especially for individuals who reported the condition in two or three waves. Divorced individuals appear to be at greater risk of reporting 'chronic' difficulties in healthcare access, suggesting that family disruptions represent a relevant determinant of our outcomes. Consistent with this idea, we find that being married reduces the likelihood of reporting unmet need and being dissatisfied with HI coverage, although the effect on catastrophic OOP expenses varies between one versus two or three waves and is significant only in the former case. Moreover, females appear to be particularly vulnerable to insufficient access to healthcare services.

References

Biewen, M. (2006). "Who are the chronic poor? An econometric analysis of chronic poverty in Germany". *Research on Economic Inequality*, Volume 13, pp. 31–62 .

Jürges, H. (2015). "Health insurance coverage and access to care among European elders: cross-national differences and social gradients". In: Börsch-Supan A., Kneip T., Litwin H., Myck M., Weber G. (eds). *Ageing in Europe-Supporting Policies for an Inclusive Society. de Gruyter, Boston,* pp. 301–312.

Wyszewianski, L. (1986). "Financially catastrophic and high-cost cases: definitions, distinctions, and their implications for policy formulation". *Inquiry* 23(4), pp. 382–394.

Simona Fiore, Matija Kovacic and Cristina E. Orso

29 Differences in healthcare use between immigrant and local older individuals

- This chapter studies the utilization of health services and the health-related expenditures of immigrants aged fifty or older among residents of Europe
- The results suggest that immigrants' health-related behaviour differ with respect to that of locals
- Specifically, the two groups do not have the same capacity to afford health-related expenditures, even when demographic controls and healthcare needs are considered

29.1 Introduction

Immigration to Europe has increased dramatically during the past thirty years, and it is very unlikely that this trend will diminish or reverse in the near future. Although the literature includes extensive studies on the effect of immigration on many economically relevant dimensions (such as the labour market, politics, fiscal contributions and demography), scant rigorous evidence exists on how immigrants perform in host countries in terms of health.

Surprisingly, we know very little about health conditions, access to health services and health-related expenditures of immigrants relative to locals. Closing this gap is important from a public health perspective given that the immigration process might contribute to changing trends in health and health behaviours and that host countries need to handle the fiscal burden and the social cost of these changes (Moullan et al., 2014; Pace, 2010; Rechel et al., 2011).

In this chapter, we analyse the utilization of health services and the health-related expenditures of immigrants and assess how their health-related behaviours differ with respect to locals. We control for a rich set of need factors related to aspects of individuals' health status and other socio-demographic variables that may affect the use of healthcare services.

Data from SHARE are especially suitable for this scope because they represent a rich set of individual information on healthcare utilization and out-of-pocket expenditures for health-related services. In particular, the sixth and seventh waves gather information on polypharmacy (i.e. the concurrent use of multiple medications), which is considered an emerging public health issue, especially for older

https://doi.org/10.1515/9783110617245-029

people. By combining this specific information with demographic and socio-economic variables, we are able to compare immigrants' and locals' outcomes by controlling for factors that may influence both immigration status and health-related behaviours (i.e. among others, age, education and marital status and specific contemporaneous and past healthcare needs).

29.2 Healthcare utilization and health-related expenditures: Does immigration status matter?

To investigate whether immigration status may affect the utilization of healthcare services and health-related expenditures and behaviours, we pool observations from the 6th and the 7th Waves of SHARE. We estimate a set of *probit* models for health-related behaviours as a function of (i) demographics (such as age, gender and marital status), (ii) socio-economic characteristics (education and occupational status) and (iii) healthcare needs (self-assessed health, chronic conditions, presence of limitations in ADL and IADL). Regarding the dependent variables considered in the analysis, we focus on a set of dummies that approximate, respectively, (i) the utilization of health services (i.e., 'Postpone doctor's visits due to financial difficulties', 'Seen the dentist in the last twelve months', and 'Polypharmacy') and the (ii) out-of-pocket medical expenditures (i.e., 'Paid anything yourself for aid/appliances in the last 12 months', and 'Paid anything yourself for ambulatory in the last 12 months').

Our variable of interest, i.e., respondents' immigration status, is defined as a binary variable that assumes the value of 1 if the individual was born abroad and 0 otherwise.

The following figures present descriptive statistics on our sample.

Figure 29.1 shows that, on average, immigrants represent approximately 10 per cent of the surveyed population in destination countries. However, a significant heterogeneity exists across countries, with the lowest shares of immigrants at approximately 2 per cent in Italy and Hungary and the highest shares in Estonia and Luxembourg (respectively, approximately 20 per cent and 30 per cent). Israel is an extreme case because most of the actual population living in the country was born abroad. The presence of immigrants is balanced in terms of gender, with similar shares of immigrant men and women in each country (Figure 29.1).

Figure 29.2 plots the macro area of immigrants' origin by country of destination. Most of the immigrants in the SHARE sample come from Europe, with a

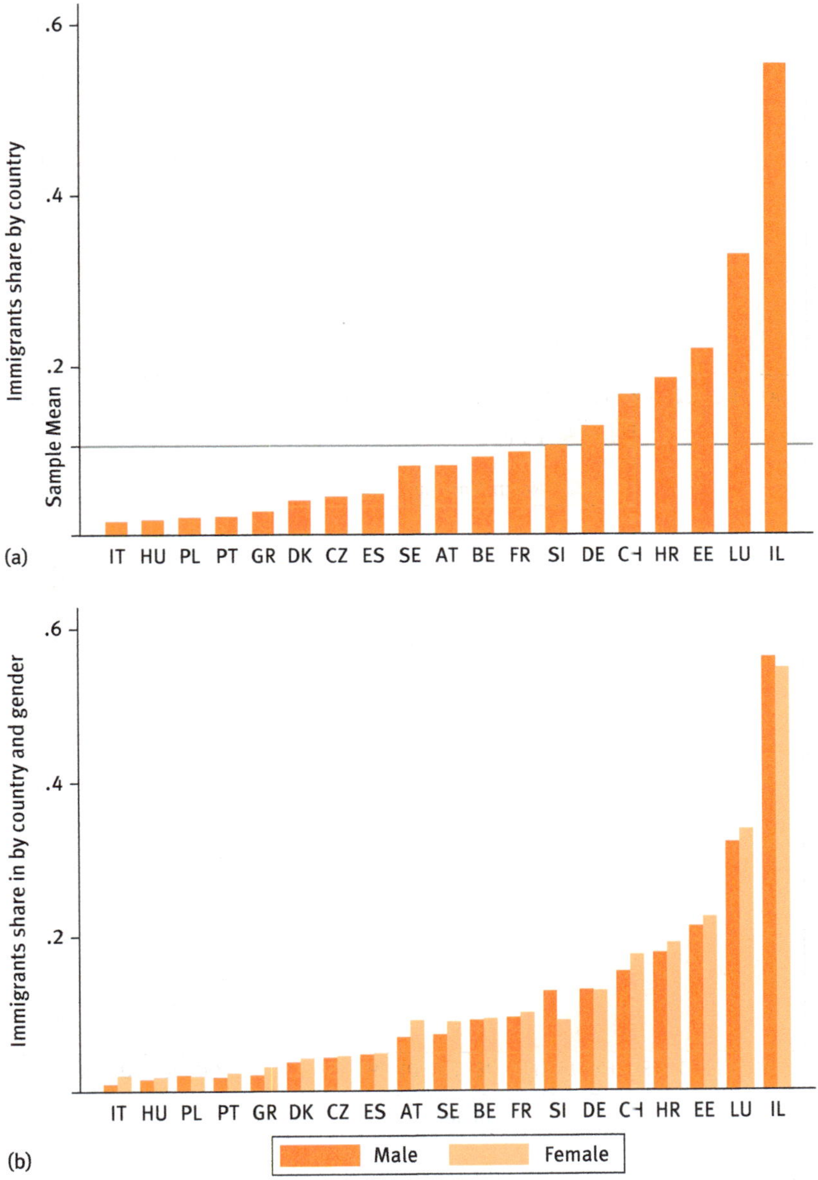

Figure 29.1: Immigrants' Share in Destination Countries.
Source: SHARE Wave 6, Wave 7 release 0.

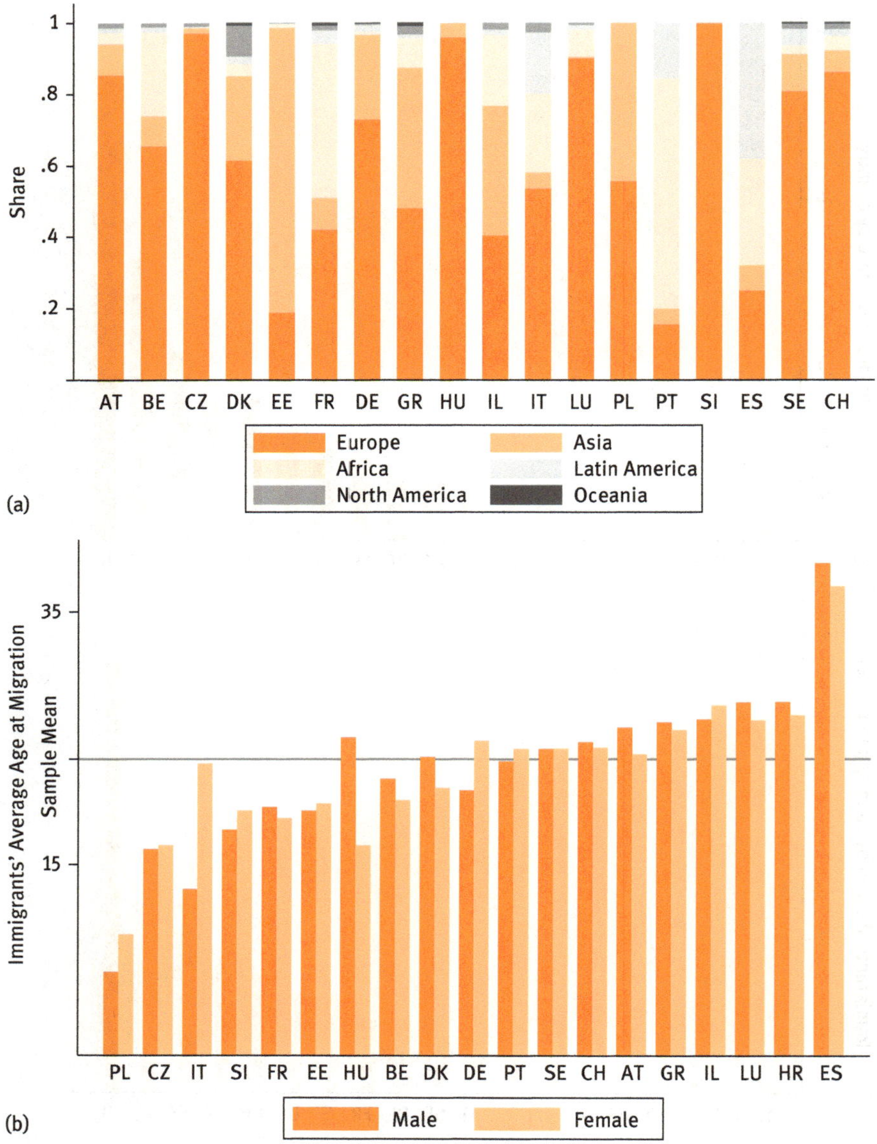

Figure 29.2: Immigrants' Origin and Age at Migration.
Source: SHARE Wave 6, Wave 7 release 0.

sizable share from Africa and Asia (in countries such as Portugal, Spain, France and Estonia). The average age at migration for the sample is approximately 23 years, with some heterogeneity across countries (Figure 29.2). Overall, most immigrants spent many years in the country of destination and more than 70 per cent acquired citizenship in the country in which they reside, such that they can have access to the country-specific healthcare system.

In Panel A of Table 29.1, the average value of the control variables used in the regression are reported for locals and immigrants. reports the p-values associated with a t-test on the mean difference. Significant differences among the two groups of individuals are found with respect to age, share of females and the probability of being married. The difference between the two groups is small but statistically significant, suggesting that (i) immigrants are slightly

Table 29.1: Descriptive Statistics.

PANEL A. Control Variables	Locals	Immigrants	P-value of the difference
Age (years)	70.023	70.373	0.0001
Female (dummy)	0.566	0.584	0.0001
Ever Married (dummy)	0.845	0.832	0.0001
High Edu (dummy)	0.212	0.291	0.0000
Low Edu (dummy)	0.391	0.334	0.0000
IADL[(a)] (discrete)	0.965	1.063	0.0000
ADL[(b)] (discrete)	0.673	0.700	0.0016
Chronic[(c)] (discrete)	1.845	2.000	0.0000
Self-perceived Health Status (discrete)	3.176	3.332	0.0000
PANEL B. Outcomes Variables (all dummies)	**Locals**	**Immigrants**	**P-value of the difference**
Polypharmacy[(d)]	0.292	0.326	0.0000
Doctor Cost[(e)]	0.045	0.045	0.9691
Dentist[(f)]	0.510	0.507	0.5032
Aid[(g)]	0.049	0.055	0.0168
Ambulatory[(h)]	0.096	0.102	0.1161

Note: [(a)]Limitations with instrumental activities of daily living; [(b)]Limitations with activities of daily living; [(c)]Number of chronic diseases; [(d)]Taking at least 5 different drugs on a typical day; [(e)]Could not see a doctor because of cost; [(f)]Seen a dentist/dental hygienist in the last 12 months; [(g)]Paid anything yourself for aids/appliances in the past 12 months; [(h)]Paid anything yourself for ambulatory therapies in the past 12 months.

Source: SHARE Wave 6, Wave 7 release 0.

older, (ii) there are fewer women in the local population than in the local immigrant and (iii) immigrants are less likely to have ever been married than locals are. Moreover, immigrants in our sample have significantly higher levels of educational attainment with respect to locals. When observing the health status variables, the two groups are also significantly different: locals' self-perceived health status is better than that of immigrants and, indeed, immigrants experience more limitations in daily activities and suffer from more chronic diseases.

In Panel B of Table 29.1, the groups of immigrants and locals are compared with respect to utilization of health services and health-related expenditures (i.e., the outcomes variables used in the regression). A simple comparison of the mean does not reveal much difference among locals and immigrants. However, to assess whether significant differences exist between locals and immigrants in terms of the utilization of health services and health-related expenditures, a more rigorous analysis is needed because the two groups differ on a number of observable dimensions (Table 29.1, Panel A). In the next section, we compare immigrant and local health behaviours in a regression framework.

29.3 Results

The results of the regression analysis are provided in Table 29.2. The coefficients for our main variable of interest ('Immigrant') suggest that being an immigrant is positively associated with the probability of postponing doctor visits due to financial difficulties and is negatively correlated with out-of-pocket expenditures for medical aids and appliances. This evidence is interesting because immigrants significantly differ in terms of health services utilization and expenditures even when compared with locals with similar health profiles (defined in terms of healthcare needs). For instance, among individuals with similar self-assessed health conditions, chronic conditions and limitations in ADL and IADL, those born abroad are more likely to postpone doctor visits due to financial difficulties and less likely to sustain out-of-pocket medical expenditures. One could argue that the latter evidence may be due to relatively lower immigrants' income or wealth or to the relatively lower educational attainment of the immigrant population. However, the average level of education among immigrants is significantly higher relative to the local population (Table 29.1, Panel A) which, given that education is positively correlated with individual financial conditions, does not help explain the differences in health services utilization and expenditures. Indeed, the sign and the direction of the effects of

Table 29.2: Probit Model, Marginal Effects.

Outcome	Polypharmacy	Doctor Cost	Dentist	Aid	Ambulatory
Immigrant (d)	−0.002	0.010***	−0.015	−0.010***	−0.005
	(0.006)	(0.004)	(0.013)	(0.003)	(0.005)
Female (d)	−0.016***	0.011***	0.070***	0.009***	0.048***
	(0.006)	(0.002)	(0.005)	(0.002)	(0.003)
Age	0.002***	−0.002***	−0.005***	0.001***	−0.002***
	(0.000)	(0.000)	(0.000)	(0.000)	(0.000)
SAH	0.087***	0.015***	−0.024***	0.017***	0.018***
	(0.004)	(0.001)	(0.003)	(0.001)	(0.002)
ADL	0.002	−0.002	0.028***	0.006***	0.009***
	(0.003)	(0.002)	(0.003)	(0.001)	(0.002)
IADL	0.017***	0.001	−0.032***	0.006***	−0.000
	(0.003)	(0.000)	(0.002)	(0.001)	(0.002)
CHRONIC	0.088***	0.008***	0.008***	0.006***	0.013***
	(0.002)	(0.001)	(0.002)	(0.000)	(0.001)
Ever Married (d)	−0.006	−0.007**	0.057***	−0.004**	0.007**
	(0.005)	(0.003)	(0.005)	(0.002)	(0.003)
Low-Education (d)	0.010*	0.013***	−0.099***	−0.007***	−0.034***
	(0.006)	(0.002)	(0.005)	(0.002)	(0.005)
High-Education (d)	0.005	−0.006**	0.082***	0.004**	0.024***
	(0.004)	(0.003)	(0.006)	(0.002)	(0.003)
Retired (d)	0.057***	0.004	0.003	−0.006**	−0.010**
	(0.007)	(0.002)	(0.011)	(0.003)	(0.005)
Unemployed (d)	0.009	0.041***	−0.096***	−0.009	−0.029***
	(0.009)	(0.009)	(0.018)	(0.007)	(0.007)
Disabled (d)	0.136***	0.019***	−0.051***	0.017***	0.007
	(0.014)	(0.004)	(0.010)	(0.006)	(0.010)
Homemaker (d)	0.044***	0.012**	−0.054***	−0.013***	−0.027***
	(0.007)	(0.005)	(0.012)	(0.003)	(0.005)

Table 29.2 (continued)

Outcome	Polypharmacy	Doctor Cost	Dentist	Aid	Ambulatory
Country dummy	*Yes*	*Yes*	*Yes*	*Yes*	*Yes*
Continent dummy	*Yes*	*Yes*	*Yes*	*Yes*	*Yes*
No. of observations	100453	78942	129769	78849	78860

Note: All reported coefficients are marginal effects. Standard errors, reported in parenthesis, are clustered by country. Reference categories: Male, Never married and not in civil union, Medium Education, Employed.
Significance: *** = 1 %; ** = 5 %; * = 10 %.
Source: SHARE Wave 6, Wave 7 release 0.

education are correct: highly educated individuals have significantly higher health service expenditures and utilization.

In addition to healthcare needs and educational variables, we also control for an individual's occupational status. The coefficients suggest that unemployed individuals and homemakers have significantly lower healthcare utilization and expenditures. The effect of immigration status, even in the presence of these additional controls, remains significant in columns 2 and 4, indicating that immigrant and local populations may have different healthcare preferences and behaviour.

29.4 Concluding remarks

In this chapter, we analyse the use of health services and the health-related expenditures of immigrants and assess how their health-related behaviour differs from that of locals, after controlling for healthcare needs and socio-demographic variables. The study uses SHARE data from Waves 6 and 7 and exploits information on healthcare utilization and out-of-pocket expenditures for health-related services, along with the new variable on polypharmacy. The results reveal that foreign-born individuals are more likely to postpone doctor visits due to financial difficulties and display a lower probability to incur out-of-pocket expenditures for medical aids and appliances. These results are consistent with prior findings, suggesting that immigrants are more likely to use emergency care services and less likely to regularly visit general practitioners and specialists and use preventive care (see Devillanova et al., 2016). One plausible explanation may be that immigrants face specific barriers to accessing doctors and specialists, which in turn may lead to a late diagnosis and/or care of acute and chronic disorders. A deeper investigation of these mechanisms would be desirable to introduce appropriate policy tools.

References

Devillanova, C., Frattini, T. (2016). "Inequities in immigrants' access to healthcare services: disentangling potential barriers" *International Journal of Manpower*, 37(7), pp. 1191–1208.

Moullan, Y., Jusot, F. (2014). "Why is the 'healthy immigrant effect' different between European countries?" *European Journal of Public Health*, 24 (1), pp. 80–86.

Pace, P. (2010), "What can be done in EU member states to better protect the health of the migrants?" *Eurohealth*, 16 (1), pp. 5–10.

Rechel, B., Mladovsky, P., Deville, W., et al. (2011). "Migration and Health in the European Union. European Observatory on Health systems and Policies Series", Mc Graw Hill, Open University Press, New York.

Marco Bertoni, Andrea Bonfatti, Martina Celidoni,
Angela Crema and Chiara Dal Bianco

30 Life expectancy and health investments

- Life expectancy has a positive causal effect on health investments.
- One reason that longer lives do not necessarily imply a longer time spent in poor health is individuals' investments in healthy behaviours.

30.1 Introduction

During the last 15 years, life expectancy at age 65 in the European Union has increased by 2.2 years, reaching 18.2 years for males and 21.6 years for females in 2016 (source: Eurostat). The steady increase in life expectancy has not yet approached a maximum (Oeppen and Vaupel, 2002); consequently, in the next decades, population ageing is bound to decrease the proportion of individuals in their active life spans and increase the proportion of retirees. This imbalance threatens the sustainability of public health and long-term care programmes. Will population ageing be accompanied by an extended period of good health and a longer working life, or will it be associated with a longer period of morbidity?

Recent empirical evidence (see, e.g., Felder et al., 2010) has in fact shown that proximity to death is a more important determinant of health expenditures than ageing per se because morbidity is compressed at the end of life. However, little is known about the mechanisms behind such a result. An important role in answering this question is played by the adoption of individual health-promoting behaviours, which can be viewed as investments to improve future well-being (Grossman, 1972). How much individuals are willing to invest in health depends on their discount rates or – in other words – on the value of life.

According to standard economic models, expectations of a longer life span may generate an incentive to invest in health to increase the quality of life when old because a longer planning horizon increases returns on investment. However, such expectations might also provide a disincentive to invest in health because the marginal value of additional years of life is lower (Fang et al. 2007).

In this chapter, we investigate the effect of a longer life expectancy on health investments across SHARE countries to provide additional evidence on which of the two channels prevails. Life expectancy is measured as the

https://doi.org/10.1515/9783110617245-030

subjective probability of living past age 75. The health behaviours we consider are body weight, nutrition, exercise and smoking.

We find a positive bivariate association between life expectancy and health investment. Because healthier individuals are likely to live longer and to invest more in health, we assess the robustness of this result when controlling for health endowment. Additionally, health investments are likely to have a direct effect on life expectancy; therefore, we apply an instrumental variable strategy to provide a causal interpretation of the positive effect of life expectancy on health investments. The results show that life expectancy has indeed a causal positive effect on all measures of investments that we consider. The effect of an increase in the subjective survival probability is especially strong on the probability of not being overweight and of being a non-smoker. A longer life span increases the incentive to invest in health to improve the quality of life when older, with positive consequences for the sustainability of public health systems.

The next section presents data and descriptive evidence. The following section describes the empirical strategy and the last section reports the main findings and conclusions.

30.2 Data and descriptive statistics

We use data on individuals aged 50 to 65 who were interviewed in SHARE Wave 4, Wave 5 and refreshers of Wave 6 because nutrition questions were not asked of panel respondents in Wave 6. We end up with a sample of 16 European countries and 18,097 observations without missing values for the set of variables considered in the analyses. The average age is 58 years and 56 per cent of subjects are females. Life expectancy is given by the answer to the question 'What are the chances that you will live to be age 75 or more?' In our sample, the average subjective probability of living past age 75 shows large variability across countries, ranging from values lower than 70 per cent in the Czech Republic, Croatia and Estonia, and higher than 80 per cent in Denmark (see Figure 30.1).

We consider among health behaviours body weight, nutrition, physical activity and smoking. We define a binary variable that takes the value of one when the Body Mass Index is lower than 25, that is, when individuals are not classified as overweight. We measure eating habits using a binary variable that takes the value of one when the individual reports consuming fruits and vegetable daily, as recommended by the World Health Organization (WHO) for a healthy diet. According to the WHO (http://www.who.int/nutrition/topics/ageing/en/index1.html), older

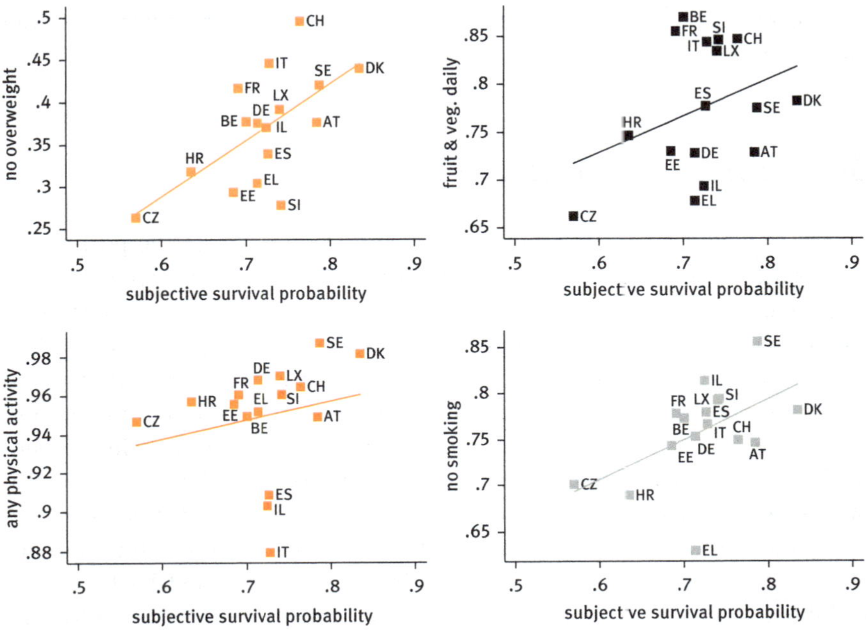

Figure 30.1: Correlation between subjective survival probability and health investments.
Source: SHARE Wave 4, 5 and 6 release 6.1.0.

individuals are vulnerable to malnutrition associated with a higher risk of bad health outcomes (e.g., premature mortality, coronary heart disease, hypertension and weight gain). Our measure of physical activity takes the value of one if the individual reports doing any physical activity, either vigorous or moderate, and zero otherwise. Not smoking takes the value of one if the respondent currently does not smoke and zero otherwise. On average, 37 per cent of our sample is not overweight, and the lowest percentage is found in the Czech Republic and Slovenia (approximately 27 per cent) and the highest in Switzerland (50 per cent). Approximately 78 per cent of the sample reports consuming fruits and vegetables every day; the percentage is lower for Czech Republic, Greece and Israel (approximately 68 per cent) and is higher than 85 per cent for France and Belgium. Approximately 95 per cent do some kind of physical activity, with little variability across countries. Finally, Greece and Croatia have the lowest percentages of non-smokers (slightly lower than 70 per cent) and Sweden and Israel the highest percentages (higher than 80 per cent).

As shown in Figure 30.1, an increase in the subjective probability of surviving to age 75 or older is positively associated with a higher probability of not being overweight, eating fruits and vegetable daily, doing any physical activity and not smoking.

30.3 Empirical methods

To assess whether we can provide a causal interpretation of the positive bivariate associations between life expectancy and health investments, we estimate a linear probability model and account for the potential sources of endogeneity, i.e. omitted variable and reverse causality. The individual health endowment is likely to be correlated with both life expectancy and health investment. Therefore, we control for the current health of the respondent by including among the regressors a binary indicator for being in poor health, the number of limitations with Activities of Daily Living and Instrumental Activities of Daily Living, the number of diagnosed chronic conditions, the EURO-D score measuring depressive symptoms and the presence of reduced muscle strength. We further include in our model health during childhood (self-reported health evaluation and whether the individual missed school for a month or more because of a health condition) and parents' educational attainment to control for long-run health determinants. Finally, the model controls for cohort-by-country-by-gender fixed effects that implicitly also account for pension eligibility rules and for a set of individual characteristics, such as education, household composition and household income and wealth.

The other relevant source of endogeneity that we need to account for is reverse causality because investments in health have a positive effect on life expectancy. To address this concern, we rely on an instrumental variable strategy. Specifically, we need an instrument that affects health behaviours only by modifying individuals' subjective assessment of their life expectancy. Following Fang et al. (2007), we use as instruments two binary variables indicating whether the respondent's mother and father are alive at the time of the interview, conditional on mother and father cohort fixed effects (this information is derived from the current age if the parent is alive or from parental year of death – asked in Wave 7 – if deceased).

The correlation between the instruments and life expectancy is reported in Figure 30.2. It also reports on the x-axis the fraction of respondents having at least one parent alive by country and the countries' average subjective probability of surviving to age 75 or older on the y-axis. The results suggest that the instruments are informative.

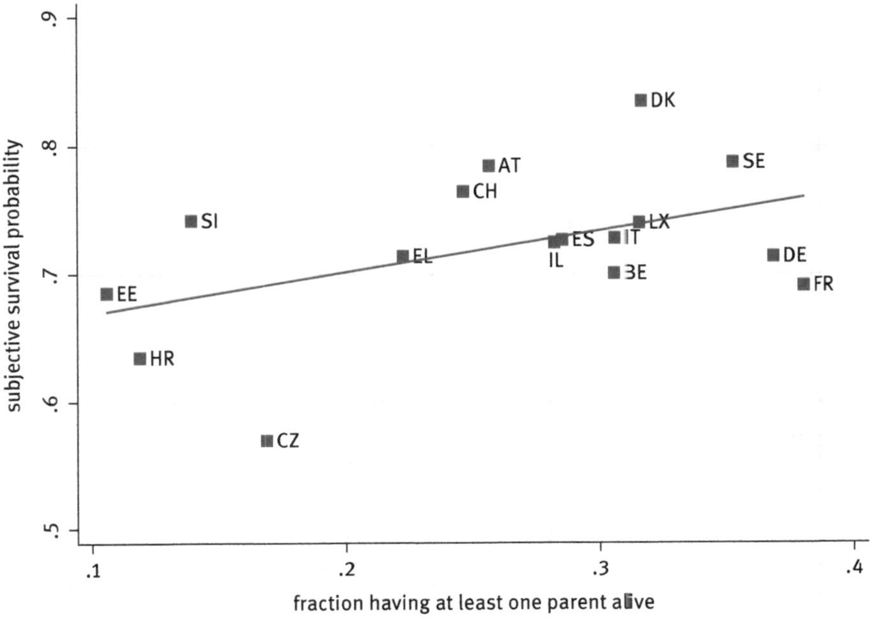

Figure 30.2: Correlation between subjective survival probability and fraction having at least one living parent.
Source: SHARE Wave 4, 5 and 6 release 6.1.0.

The validity of our identification strategy relies on the assumption that, conditional on our set of controls (including parents' year of birth fixed effects), investments in health are conditionally mean independent of the genetic health endowment. Additionally, we need to rule out the possible direct effect of parental death on health investments. We do so in a robustness test (not reported) through which we verify that our results are robust when we drop from our sample respondents whose parents died recently for whom there might be a stronger direct connection between parental bereavement and the adoption of health behaviours.

30.4 Results

Table 30.1 shows our main results. We report the parameter for the subjective probability of surviving past age 75 (which is standardised to have a mean of zero and a standard deviation equal to one) for each investment measure and for two different specifications. For each outcome, the first column provides the

Table 30.1: Linear probability model estimates.

Variables	No overweight		Fruit and veg. daily		Any physical activity		No smoking	
	(1)	(2)	(3)	(4)	(5)	(6)	(7)	(8)
	OLS	IV	OLS	IV	OLS	IV	OLS	IV
Subj. prob. of living to age 75+	−0.001	0.297***	0.025***	0.139**	0.006***	0.054*	0.030***	0.342***
	(0.004)	(0.077)	(0.004)	(0.058)	(0.002)	(0.029)	(0.004)	(0.073)
Observations	18,097	18,097	18,097	18,097	18,097	18,097	18,097	18,097
Hansen p-value		0.875		0.713		0.932		0.515
Weak identification		29.973		29.973		29.973		29.973

Significance: * p < 0.1, ** p < 0.05, *** p < 0.01.
Note: The following controls are included in all models: household composition, education, household income and wealth, health indicators, health during childhood, parental education and year of birth-country-gender fixed effects. The Weak identification test statistic is the Kleibergen-Paap rank Wald F-statistic, with Stock and Yogo (2005) critical values for 10 per cent maximal IV size equal to 19.93. Standard errors are clustered at the individual level in parentheses.
Source: SHARE Wave 4, 5 and 6 release 6.1.0, Wave 7 release 0.

ordinary least squares (OLS) estimate of the association between expectations to live past age 75 and health investments, net of the effect of all covariates listed in the previous section. The subjective probability of living past age 75 is not significantly associated with not being overweight but is positively and significantly associated with consuming fruits and vegetables daily, doing any physical activity and refraining from smoking. In most cases, the coefficients related to the control variables (not reported for brevity but available from the authors) have the expected sign.

The OLS estimates reported in the odd-numbered columns of Table 30.1 do not necessarily identify a causal relationship because they suffer endogeneity attributable to reverse causality (see the discussion in the previous section). The estimation results from our instrumental variable (IV) approach, which uses two dummies for whether the respondent's mother and father are alive as instruments, are reported in the even-numbered columns of Table 30.1. For each specification, we report the p-value of the Hansen test, which shows that the overidentifying restrictions are not rejected, and the weak identification F statistic, which shows that the instruments are informative. Subjective life expectancy is highly significant for all outcomes, and the point estimates imply that OLS greatly understates the strength of the effect. In particular, a one standard deviation increase in the subjective probability of living to age 75 or older increases the probability of not being overweight by 29.8 per cent, the probability of consuming fruits and vegetable daily by 13.8 per cent, the probability of doing any physical activity by 5.4 per cent and the probability of not smoking by 34 per cent. We have also performed the same analysis using alcohol consumption, for which we can derive a consistent indicator only for Waves 4 and 5 (a binary variable that is equal to one if the respondent does not drink alcohol daily and zero otherwise), but both estimates are close to and not significantly different from zero.

30.5 Conclusions

This chapter investigated whether longer subjective life expectancy has a causal effect on investment in healthy behaviours. The theoretical predictions behind this relationship are ambiguous because expectations of a longer planning horizon increase returns to investment in health on the one hand, while a longer lifespan reduces the marginal value of additional years of life on the other hand.

Our empirical analysis based on the instrumental variables suggests that the first channel prevails given that we observe positive effects of a longer lifespan on most health behaviours that we have considered.

In summary, our results provide an economic mechanism behind the so-called 'compression of morbidity' hypothesis because they show that one reason longer lives do not necessarily imply a longer time spent in poor health is individuals' investments in healthy behaviours.

References

Fang, H., Keane, M., Khwaja, A., Salm, M., and Silverman, D. (2007). Testing the mechanisms of structural models: The case of the Mickey Mantle effect. *American Economic Review*, 97(2), pp.53–59.

Grossman, M. (1972). On the Concept of Health Capital and the Demand for Health. *Journal of Political Economy*, 80(2), pp.223–255.

Oeppen, J. and Vaupel, J. W. (2002). "DEMOGRAPHY: Enhanced: Broken Limits to Life Expectancy". *Science*, 296 (5570), pp.1029–31.

Felder, S., Werblow, A., and Zweifel, P. (2010). Do red herrings swim in circles? Controlling for the endogeneity of time to death. *Journal of Health Economics*, 29, pp.205–212.

Andrej Srakar and Valentina Prevolnik Rupel

31 Multiple chronic conditions in older people in European countries: A network analysis approach

- European countries differ in their distribution of comorbidities of older people
- The differences largely follow Esping Andersen's welfare regime typology
- Strong connections among diseases are found in eastern European countries in which this issue should receive additional attention from policymakers

31.1 Introduction

The presence of multiple coexisting chronic diseases (i.e., comorbidities) in individuals and the expected rise in chronic diseases over the coming years are increasingly being recognized as major public health and healthcare challenges of modern societies (Glynn et al., 2011). Individuals with multiple conditions are presumed to have greater health needs, higher risk of complications and more difficulty managing treatment regimens. Therefore, comorbidity is associated with worse health outcomes, more complex clinical management and increased healthcare costs. At present, the main healthcare model is disease-focused rather than person-focused; therefore, the involvement of several different healthcare providers in managing multiple disorders is inevitable and often results in competing treatments, sub-optimal coordination and communication between care providers and/or unnecessary replication of diagnostic tests or treatments. As a consequence, the common belief is that persons with multiple diseases have high rates of healthcare utilization, which is confirmed by international studies (Glynn et al., 2011; Barnett et al., 2012).

We use a dataset based on the SHARE Wave 6 survey, which includes data on 18 European countries: Austria, Germany, Sweden, Spain, Italy, France, Denmark, Greece, Switzerland, Belgium, Israel, the Czech Republic, Poland, Luxembourg, Portugal, Slovenia, Estonia and Croatia. We model the presence of comorbidities as a two-mode (affiliation) network analysis problem using cluster analysis techniques developed for network analysis (for more, see, e.g., Doreian, Ferligoj and Batagelj, 2005). This approach has special scientific

https://doi.org/10.1515/9783110617245-031

relevance because, to our knowledge, network analysis has been rarely used to date to study this problem and very seldom (if ever) before in analyses using SHARE data. In our case, the diseases form one mode of connections and the respondents having them form the second mode. By transforming such two-mode affiliation networks into one-mode networks with diseases as nodes and weights on the lines to measure the frequency of connections between any chosen pair of diseases, we can study the distribution of comorbidities in older age across the included European countries.

We study the following two main research questions: 1) which are the most frequent groupings of diseases that can be characterized from the data for older people in Europe; and 2) does the grouping of diseases differ across Europe (are comorbidities more frequent in some countries than in others and are some health systems more exposed to comorbidities). In the following section, we provide basic information on the data and methods used. In the third section, we discuss the results. In the final section, we provide conclusions and recommendations.

31.2 Data and method

This paper uses the dataset on the Survey of Health, Ageing and Retirement in Europe (SHARE) Wave 6. The final included sample, which encompasses only individuals aged 50 years or older, includes 67,346 respondents.

In our analysis, we primarily use only one variable, ph006, and ask 'Has a doctor ever told you that you had/Do you currently have any of the conditions on this card? With this we mean that a doctor has told you that you have this condition and that you are either currently being treated for or bothered by this condition. Please tell me the number or numbers of conditions'.

Given comparability with other waves, we use the following 17 diseases (we exclude chronic kidney disease as a special category, first asked in Wave 6) as answers to this question:

- A heart attack including myocardial infarction, coronary thrombosis or any other heart problem including congestive heart failure
- High blood pressure or hypertension
- High blood cholesterol
- A stroke or cerebral vascular disease
- Diabetes or high blood sugar
- Chronic lung disease, such as chronic bronchitis or emphysema

- Cancer or a malignant tumour, including leukaemia or lymphoma but excluding minor skin cancers
- Stomach or duodenal ulcer, peptic ulcer
- Parkinson's disease
- Cataracts
- Hip fractures
- Other fractures
- Alzheimer's disease, dementia, organic brain syndrome, senility or any other serious memory impairment
- Other affective or emotional disorders, including anxiety, nervous or psychiatric problems
- Rheumatoid arthritis
- Osteoarthritis or other rheumatism
- Other diseases (including children's kidney disease)

We separate countries by welfare regimes into five clusters based on an updated Esping Andersen typology (1990), as follows:
- Continental countries: Austria, Germany, Switzerland, Belgium, France and Luxembourg
- Socio-democratic countries: Denmark and Sweden
- Mediterranean countries: Greece, Italy, Portugal and Spain
- Eastern European countries: Czech Republic, Estonia and Poland
- Mixed model countries: Israel

We use a cluster technique for network analysis called VOS (visualization of similarities), which was proposed by Van Eck and Waltman (see, e.g., 2009). In VOC clustering, the optimization is over the VOS quality function, where the following expression is maximized:

$$V = \frac{1}{2m} \sum_{i,j} [s_{ij} - \gamma] \, \delta (c_i, c_j) \qquad (31.1)$$

where:

m – the total number of edges in a network
s_{ij} – association strength between vertices i and j
γ – resolution parameter
δ – a function that yields 1 if the vertices are in the same community and 0 otherwise
C – respective community

The optimal number of clusters according to the VOS technique is found when the aforementioned function is maximized. To derive the optimal number of clusters, information provided by the Cramers' V statistic, Rajski's Index and the Adjusted Rand Index is also used and studied in a separate paper to be applied to the SHARE Working Paper Series.

31.3 Results

We present the results of the analysis by included countries and welfare regimes. In Figure 31.1, we present the results of the cluster analysis for six continental countries. In most countries, two clusters are visible, one with the diseases that strongly link each other (the 'connected' cluster) and encompass heart attacks, high blood pressure, high cholesterol, diabetes, cataracts and – in most cases – arthritis and osteoarthritis. In the other cluster are all remaining diseases that appear very weakly connected. Interestingly, judged by weights on the lines (shown as widths of the connections on the graph – the widths are normalized by the size of the sample), most of the connections in certain countries (e.g., Switzerland, Belgium) are rather weak; they seem stronger and have the greatest disparity between the two clusters in the Benelux countries and France.

In Figure 31.2, we present the results of the analysis for socio-democratic countries. Interestingly, the connections (and, consequently, the comorbidities) appear rather weak. Again, we find the presence of two large clusters – the 'connected' and the 'unconnected' ones – for which the diseases in both largely follow the distribution in the continental countries.

Figure 31.3 shows the comorbidities for Mediterranean countries. Interestingly, in most cases, three clusters come to the fore, with very unstable positions of arthritis and osteoarthritis relative to the previous sets of countries. Nevertheless, five main diseases appear as the most 'connected' and stable: heart attack, high blood pressure, high cholesterol, diabetes and cataracts. Furthermore, in most countries, the comorbidities appear not very strong, which holds in particular for Italy and Spain.

Relative to the previous sets of countries, in most eastern European countries (Figure 31.4), the comorbidities appear very strong – this finding holds for all countries except Poland (which also has one of the smallest samples of all included countries). In particular, in the Czech Republic, Croatia and Slovenia (and, to a certain extent, Estonia), the cluster of 'connected' diseases – again encompassing the same set of 'stable' diseases – that is, heart attack, high

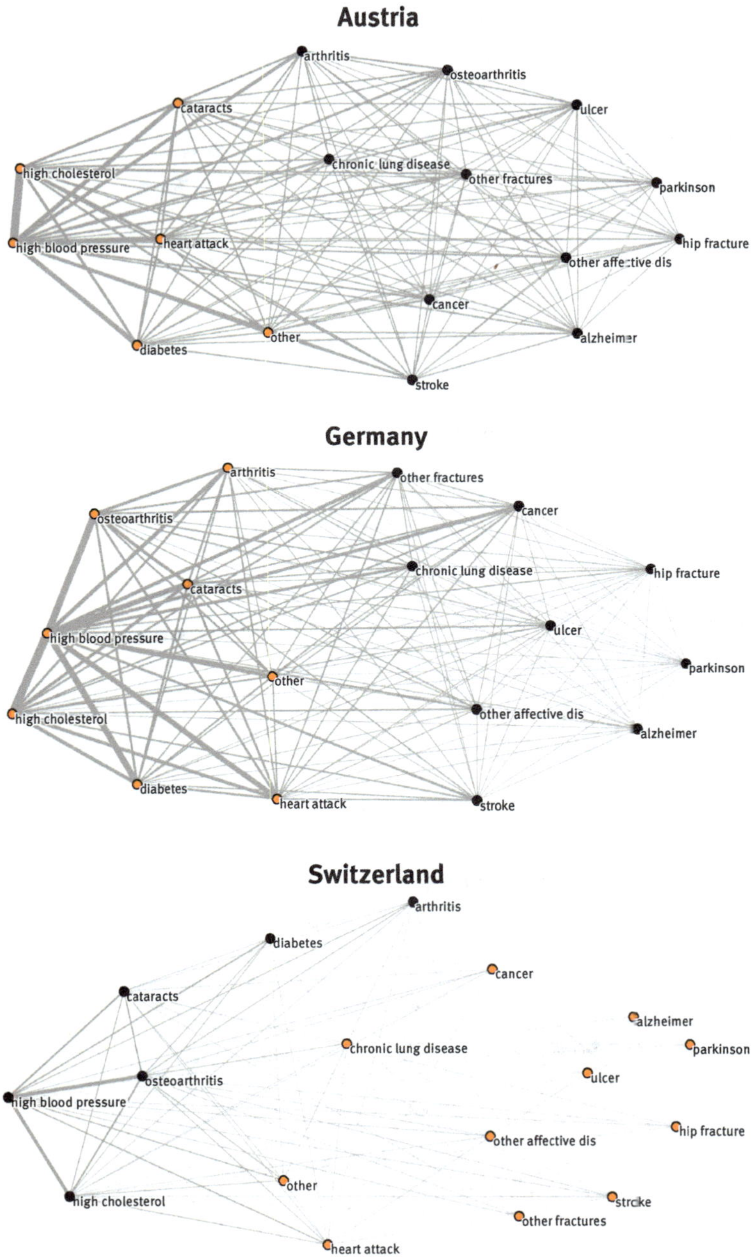

Figure 31.1: Clusters of comorbidities among continental countries.
Source: SHARE Wave 6 release 6.1.0

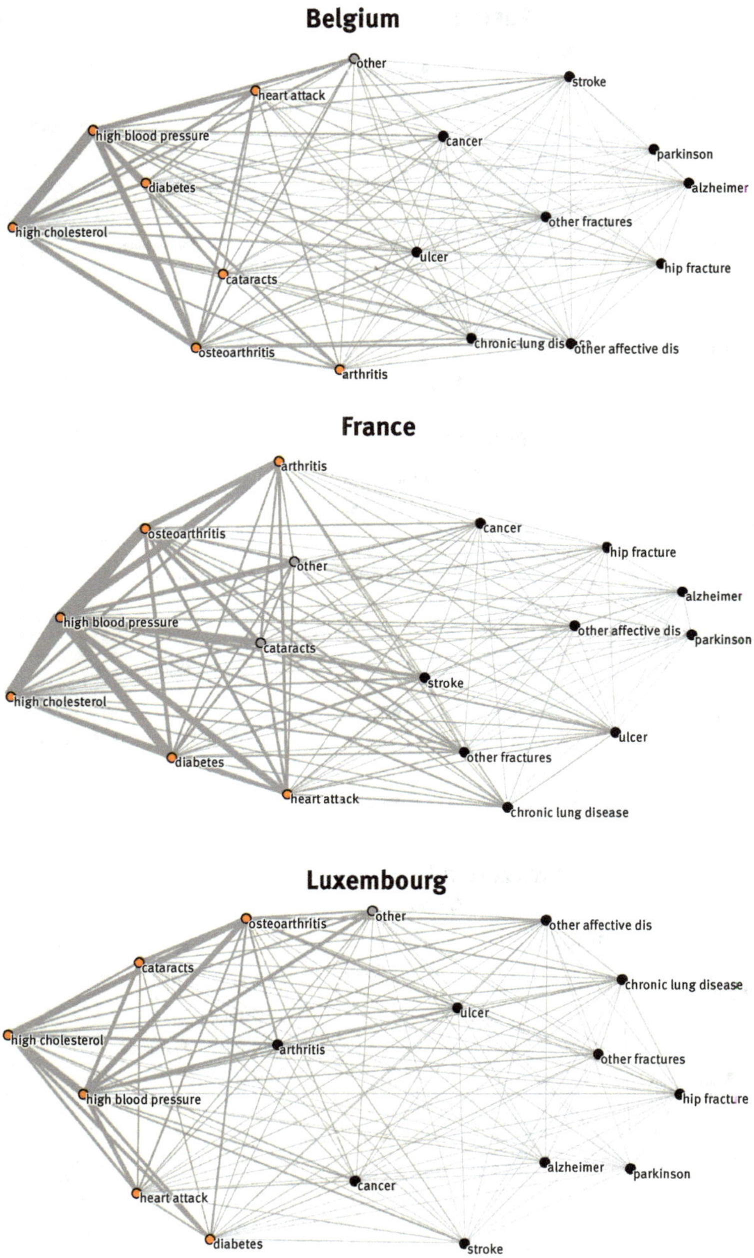

Figure 31.1 (continued)

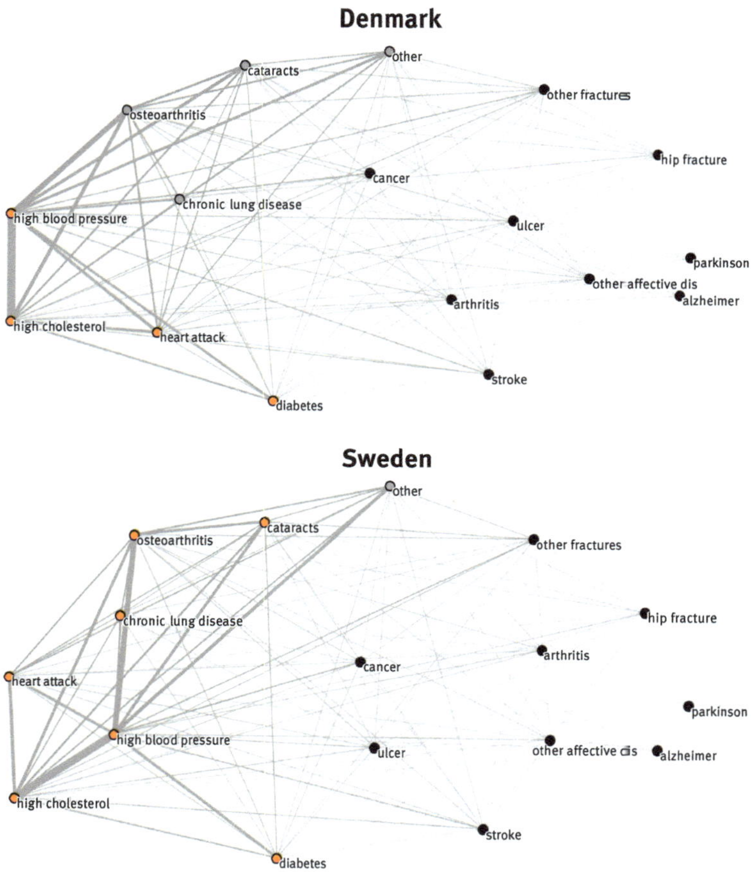

Figure 31.2: Clusters of comorbidities among socio-democratic countries.
Source: SHARE Wave 6 release 6.1.0.

blood pressure, high cholesterol, diabetes and cataracts, also arthritis and osteoarthritis (with the exception of Slovenia, where the distribution seems more complex and unclear), is very strongly connected.

Of the countries in the mixed model (Figure 31.5), only Israel is included in the study. For Israel, similar to most of the studied countries, three clusters are observed that have an unstable position of arthritis and osteoarthritis but a stable 'connected' cluster of four diseases – heart attack, high blood pressure, high cholesterol and diabetes.

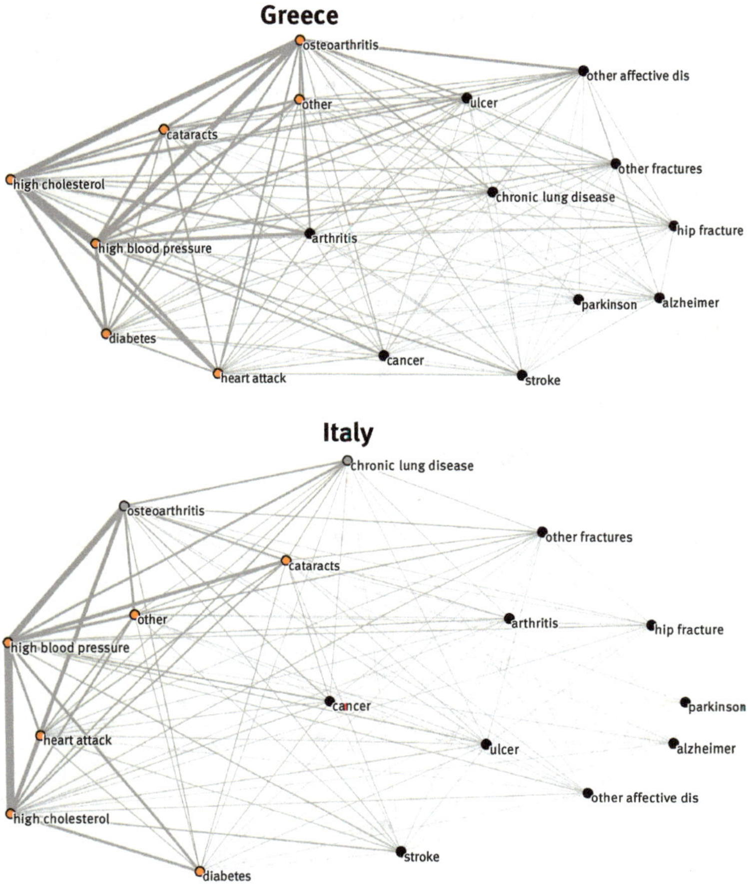

Figure 31.3: Clusters of comorbidities among Mediterranean countries.
Source: SHARE Wave 6 release 6.1.0.

31.4 Conclusion

Comorbidities are an extremely weakly studied problem, and not many empirical and statistical studies have been done to date to study this problem in comparative terms. We provide a new approach – network analysis – to study the problem that has to date not been used with SHARE data. We use the VOS cluster analysis technique to derive clusters of comorbidities across countries, which can be to a significant extent labelled 'connected' and 'unconnected' clusters. We find that the connected cluster with the most

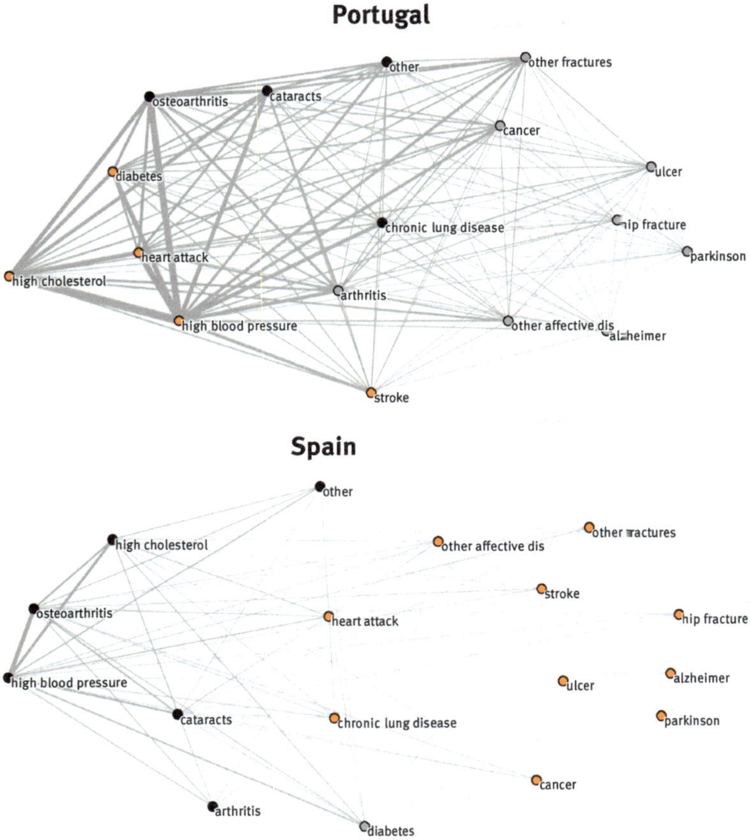

Figure 31.3 (continued)

comorbidities encompasses, in most cases, the following set of diseases, with variations across the countries: heart attack, high blood pressure, high cholesterol, diabetes, cataracts, arthritis and osteoarthritis. We also establish the extent to which the comorbidities seem the largest in eastern European countries relative to other welfare regime typologies. Furthermore, the distinctions between the connected and unconnected clusters seem clear and highly present in this regime.

The analysis also carries an important policy message. Systems that already suffer from healthcare problems, including eastern European countries, are likely to suffer even more in the future given the prevalence of comorbidities. Because the question of comorbidities brings worse health

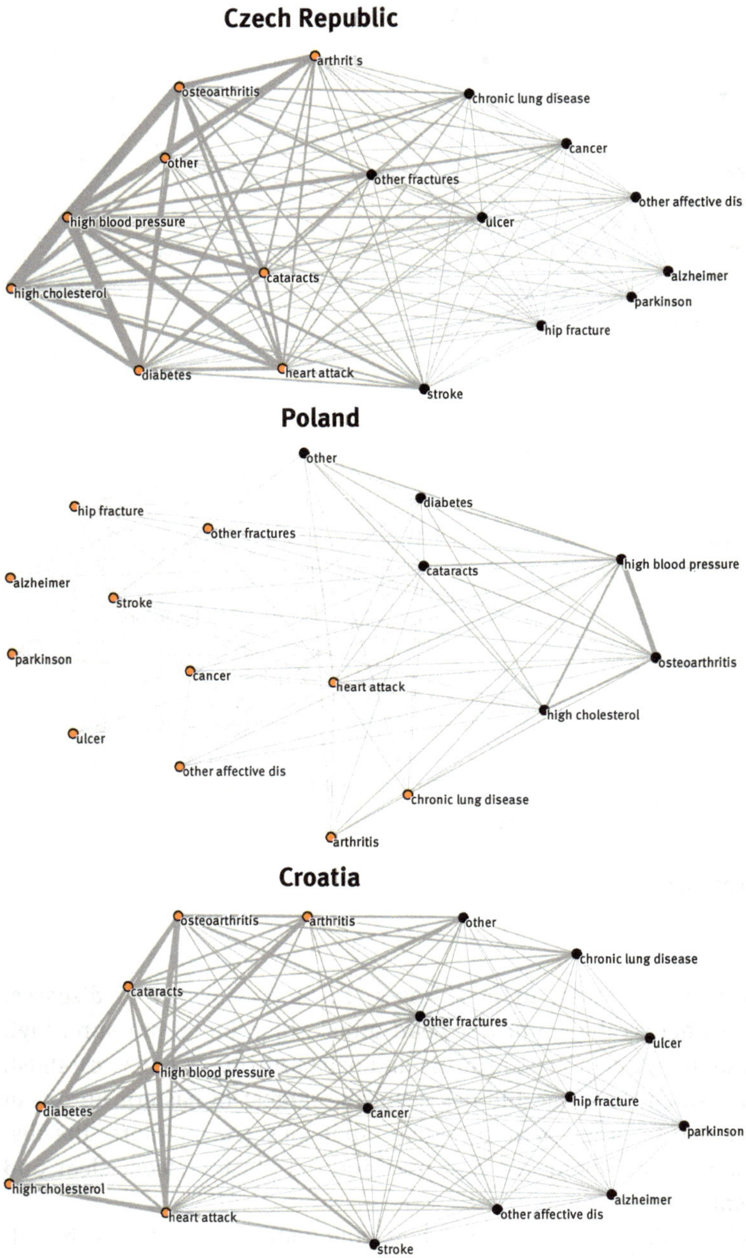

Figure 31.4: Clusters of comorbidities among eastern European countries.
Source: SHARE Wave 6 release 6.1.0.

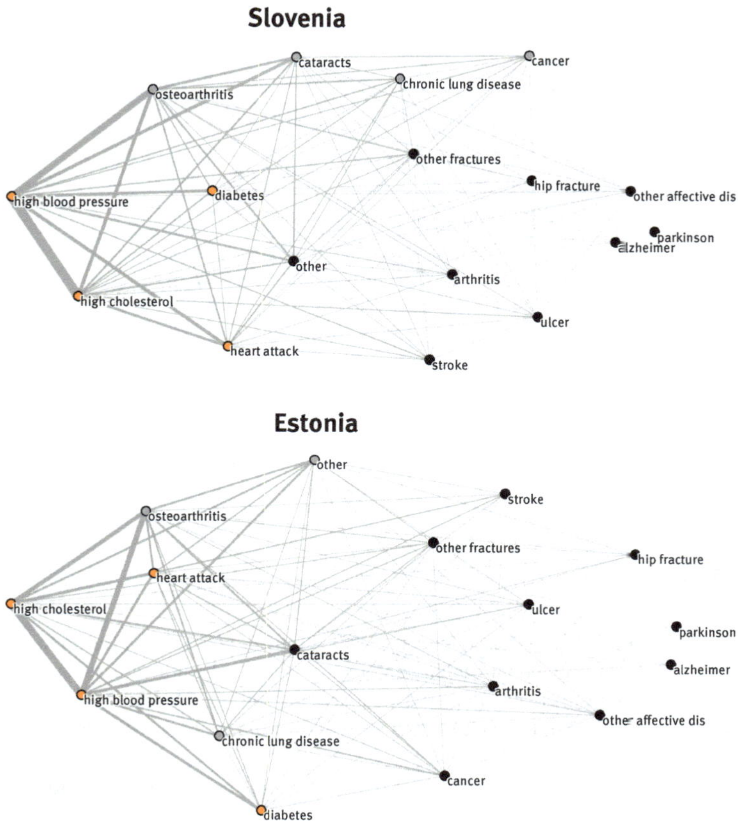

Figure 31.4 (continued)

outcomes, more complex clinical management and increased healthcare costs (as noted in the introduction to the article), the analysis points to the types of diseases of older people that should be most looked on in this respect when acting through policy means, as well as the countries in which the problem seems most pressing. We must also point to the research gap: this analysis represents an initial exploration, and significantly more work must be invested to research the issue in greater detail, such as estimating the costs of the presence of comorbidities in older people and their effects on healthcare utilization. We hope that this issue will receive more focus in future studies, also through the use of SHARE data (and different research approaches).

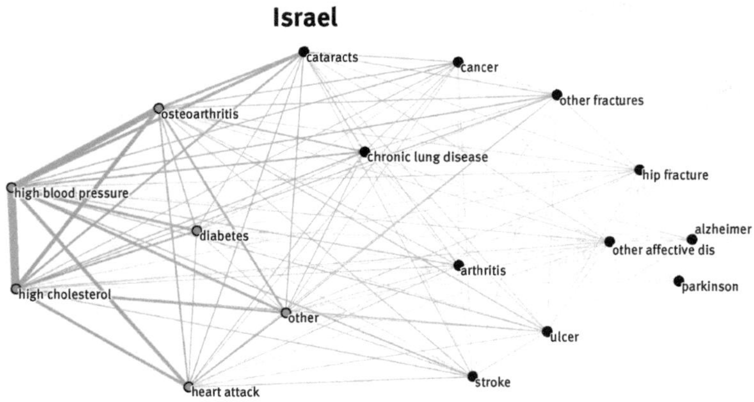

Figure 31.5: Clusters of comorbidities in Israel.
Source: SHARE Wave 6 release 6.1.0.

References

Barnett, Karen, Mercer, Stewart W., Norbury, Michael, Watt, Graham, Wyke, Sally, Guthrie, Bruce (2012). Epidemiology of multimorbidity and implications for health care, research, and medical education: a cross-sectional study. *Lancet*, 380 (9836), 37–43.

Doreian, Patrick, Batagelj, Vladimir, Ferligoj, Anuška (2005). *Generalized Blockmodeling*. Cambridge: Cambridge University Press.

Esping-Andersen, Gøsta (1990). *The Three Worlds of Welfare Capitalism*. Cambridge: Polity Press.

Glynn, Liam G., Valderas, Jose M., Healy, Pamela, Burke, Evelyn, Newell, John, Gillespie, Patrick, Murphy, Andrew W. (2011). The prevalence of multimorbidity in primary care and its effect on health care utilization and cost. *Family Practice.*, 28 (5), 516–523. DOI: 10.1093/fampra/cmr013.

Van Eck, Nees Jan, Waltman, Ludo (2009). How to normalize cooccurrence data? An analysis of some well-known similarity measures. *Journal of the American Society for Information Science and Technology*, 60(8), 1635–1651.

Part VII Objective health

Edited by Karen Anderson-Ranberg

Luzia M. Weiss, Judith Kronschnabl, Thorsten Kneip
and Michael Bergmann

32 Changes in body mass and cognitive decline – disentangling a seeming paradox

- On average, women with a higher BMI perform cognitively worse than women with a lower BMI, but this is not true of men. However, the relation is non-monotonous: cognitive performance is highest for women at the lower end and men at the upper end of the normal weight range
- Individual changes in BMI over time are positively related to changes in cognitive performance. This association is driven by weight loss
- We find no evidence of a link between weight changes unrelated to illness and cognitive performance
- Our findings suggest that the obesity paradox in cognition results from disregarding (partially unobservable) factors that affect both BMI and cognition. Hence, any naïve interpretation of the obesity paradox ('a modest weight gain is beneficial') should be dispelled

32.1 The obesity paradox in cognition

According to the World Health Organization, the prevalence of obesity in later life has increased dramatically throughout the world, a trend that poses serious challenges to public health and healthcare systems. At the same time, obesity is a well-known risk factor for poorer health in later life. Obesity is related to several diseases, including diabetes mellitus, hypertension, cardiovascular diseases and mortality (Peeters et al., 2003). However, evidence also suggests that being overweight might actually be a protective factor against cardiovascular and all-cause mortality (Uretsky et al., 2007). This phenomenon is discussed in the literature as the obesity paradox or 'jolly fat'. First discussed against the background of cardiovascular diseases, the obesity paradox is now present in the literature with respect to different causes of mortality and with respect to cognitive decline.

Cross-sectional studies conclusively show that, for children and adults, obesity is positively associated with poorer cognitive performance; however, the relationship between obesity and cognition is less clear and more complex in the older population. In such populations, a higher body mass seems to

https://doi.org/10.1515/9783110617245-032

preserve health, and extra weight appears to benefit cognition (Smith et al., 2011). Based on longitudinal data, Memel and colleagues (2016) find that, although an elevated initial BMI is detrimental to cognitive performance, *changes* in weight and cognitive performance are positively correlated. However, they do not account for diseases that might affect both weight loss and cognitive function. This issue raises the question of whether a higher BMI is truly protective against cognitive decline in old age or whether the obesity paradox in cognition is a mere artefact when taking into account relevant confounding variables. In other words: is being overweight in old age truly healthier or must the common naïve interpretation of the obesity paradox in cognition – that a (modest) weight gain is beneficial – be dispelled?

32.2 Possible explanations

The current literature measures obesity almost exclusively by BMI. Part of the obesity paradox could be the result of the fact that BMI is not informative about body composition. This lack of information is particularly important when observing the elderly because aging is accompanied by changes in body composition (sarcopenia), including an increase in fat mass and, at the same time, a decline in skeletal muscle mass (Ades and Savage, 2010). Thus, BMI might underestimate adiposity. To account for differences and changes in body composition, other measures might be better indicators, such as waist circumference or grip strength, as a measure of skeletal functioning muscle mass (Iliodromiti et al., 2018). Furthermore, weight loss and cognitive impairment may co-occur with other morbidities, particularly in older age. Thus, confounding health conditions might induce a spurious correlation between obesity and cognition. Moreover, the existing literature mostly lacks information on recent weight changes and whether weight changes were intentional or the result of chronic diseases.

Data from the Survey of Health, Ageing and Retirement in Europe (SHARE) can help mitigate these issues by providing a rich set of relevant longitudinal variables, including repeated measurements of isometric hand-grip strength. To that end, the obesity paradox in cognition could be disentangled and might disappear when the aforementioned problems are considered. Against this background, this chapter revisits the obesity paradox in cognition. After replicating the findings that people of higher BMI perform cognitively worse on average but BMI change is positively related to cognitive performance, we show that the latter is driven by weight loss and not by weight gain. We do not expect weight change to directly influence cognition. In fact, we suggest that the association between BMI and cognition is driven by unobserved confounding variables, such as severe diseases, leading to weight loss or a change in body composition and cognitive impairment. In line with this hypothesis, we find that a significant part of the association can be explained by controlling for severe diseases and that BMI change that is not the result of illness is unrelated to cognitive performance.

32.3 Data and method

The following analyses use longitudinal data from SHARE Waves 1, 2, 4, 5 and 6. Restricting the sample to respondents with non-missing information on all relevant measures leaves us with 195,046 observations. The data offer the possibility to both assess whether and how people with different levels of BMI differ in terms of cognitive performance (between-comparison) and study intra-individual change (within-comparison). We use fixed-effects and first-difference methods to assess whether a person experiencing a *change* in BMI also experiences a *change* in cognitive performance. These methods use each individual as his/her own control, alleviating the problem of unobserved individual characteristics related to the outcome, which would otherwise lead to biased results.

To measure respondents' cognitive performance, we created an index by adding the scores for immediate as well as delayed word recall and verbal fluency (see Memel et al., 2016). BMI is calculated as $\text{BMI} = \frac{\text{weight(kg)}}{\text{height(m)2}}$ using self-reported weight and height after carefully correcting for obvious errors by utilizing the available information from all waves. To capture the difference between weight loss attributable to a reduction in body fat or muscle mass, we used respondents' grip strength as a proxy for unobserved conditions associated with a detrimental reduction in lean body mass. As possible confounders, that is, factors that might lead to (unintentional) weight loss *and* cognitive decline, we identified certain observed health conditions, namely, Parkinson's Disease, stroke, some types of (severe) cancer and dementia. We account for the possible enduring or cumulative effects of these conditions by adding the elapsed time since its first reporting. In our last model, we examine only respondents with self-reported weight loss who were asked for underlying reasons. Answers were collapsed into two categories that distinguish between reasons related to versus unrelated to illness. Finally, we include a quadratic function of age in our models to account for the fact that cognitive decline might accelerate with age. All models are calculated separately for women and men.

32.4 Results

On average, a higher BMI in our sample is significantly associated with lower cognitive performance for women, but no such significant association exists for men. This relationship can be split in a within- and between-effect and is largely driven by the between-variation in the data. The latter is described in Figure 32.1, which illustrates the predicted cognition score over the BMI range using a piecewise linear specification ('splines'), taking into account that the relationship might be non-linear. The used cut-off points correspond to the WHO cut-offs for the BMI categories 'underweight' (BMI<18.5), 'normal weight' (18.5–24.9), 'overweight' (25–29.9), 'obesity class I' (30–34.9), 'obesity class II' (35–39.9) and 'obesity class III' (≥40).

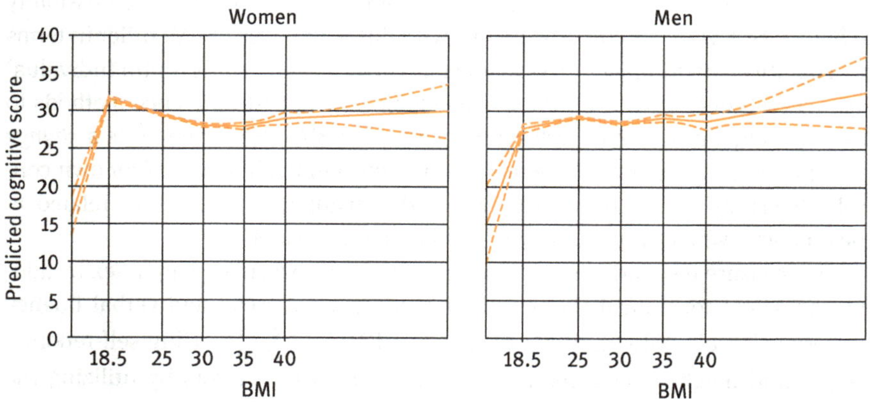

Figure 32.1: Cognition profiles over the BMI range (between-comparison).
Source: SHARE Wave 1– 6 release 6.0.0.

Figure 32.1 shows how the relationship between cognitive function and BMI score varies over BMI categories. For both sexes, the average (linear) association is driven by the BMI categories 'normal' and 'overweight' because the majority of the respondents (approximately 80% of both women and men) belongs to these categories. Similar to the aforementioned average coefficients, the association is negative for normal weight and overweight women but is inversely U-shaped for men within this BMI range. In the 'underweight' category, the association is in the opposite direction for both sexes: we observe lower cognitive function scores with lower BMI scores. Although only a few respondents were underweight, the association is strong and significant. For higher BMI categories (obesity classes

I–III), although based on a larger number of respondents, no significant association can be found.

The picture looks different when investigating the within-effect of BMI changes (Figure 32.2). Here, an increase in BMI is associated with an overall increase in cognitive function for men and women. The relation is not linear but still fairly monotonous. No conclusion can be drawn for the highest obesity class III (i.e., BMI > 40) because estimates for the relating spline are rather imprecise.

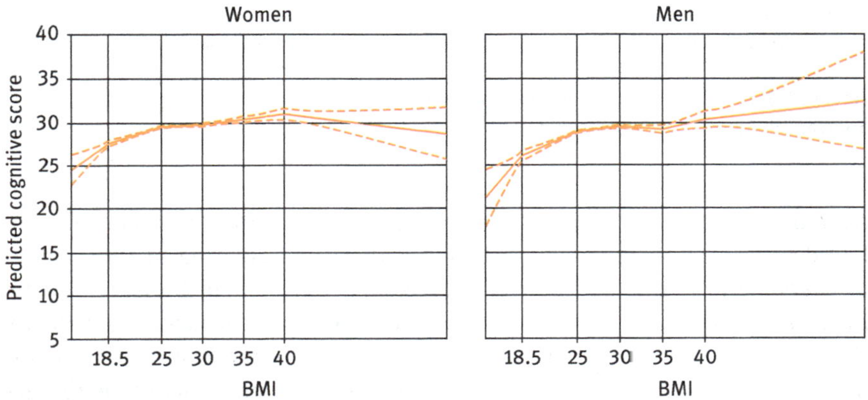

Figure 32.2: Cognition profiles over the BMI range (within-comparison).
Source: SHARE Wave 1–6 release 6.0.0.

As a shortcoming, the model forces the estimated function to be symmetric: an increase in BMI is assumed to promote cognitive performance by the same amount as a decrease reduces it. Because we hypothesize that this association (leading to the observed obesity paradox) is primarily driven by weight loss, we distinguish by the direction of the weight change between two consecutive waves ('first differences') in Figure 32.3. The first bar of each graph shows the regression coefficient for the BMI-score estimated in a model without further controls. Here, weight gain is not significantly correlated with changes in the cognition score, whereas weight loss is associated with cognitive decline. However, this association can be significantly reduced by adding possible confounders, such as age (second bar), grip strength (third bar) and the diseases previously described (fourth bar). The observed pattern holds for both genders but is stronger for men.

Although accounting for observed conditions significantly reduces the BMI-cognition association, it cannot completely explain this association. The

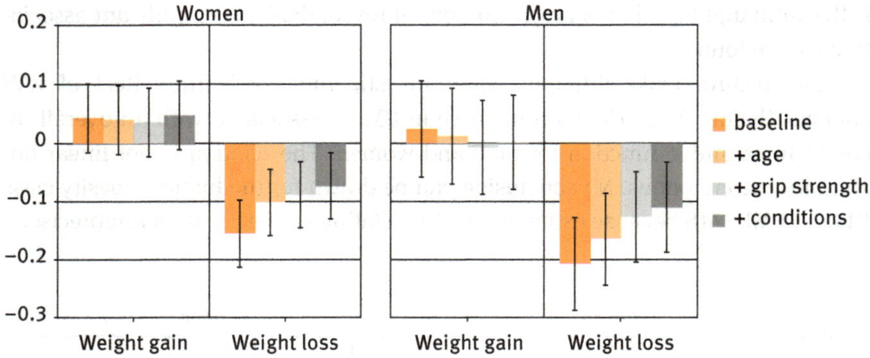

Figure 32.3: Effects of BMI gain vs. loss on change in cognition.
Source: SHARE Wave 1–6 release 6.0.0.

remaining correlation might, however, persist because the included confounders cannot be precisely measured. Other (undiagnosed or unreported) diseases might lead to weight loss and cognitive decline. Furthermore, the duration and severity of the included diseases may not be measured satisfactorily: even if we know when a disease was reported for the first time, we know neither when the diagnosis occurred nor when the actual onset of the disease took place. To address this concern, we include the self-reported reason for weight loss (Figure 32.4). Although not available for all cases, this information offers a straightforward approach to identifying (unintentional) weight loss attributable to illnesses as opposed to other reasons (e.g., physical activity or

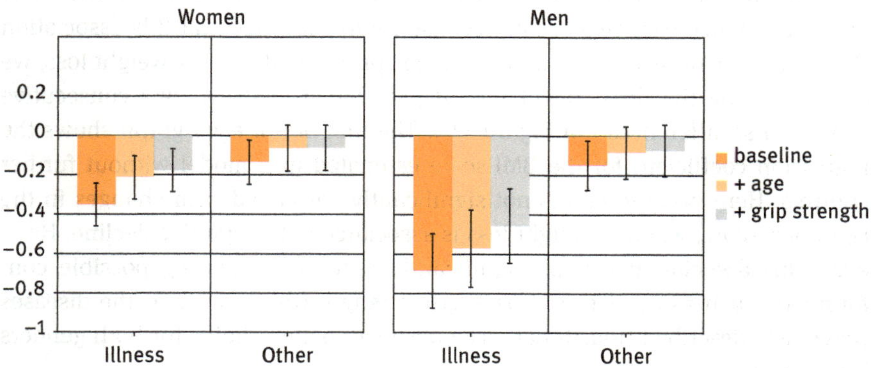

Figure 32.4: Effects of BMI decrease on change in cognition by reason for weight loss.
Source: SHARE Wave 1–6 release 6.0.0.

diet). Again, we first ran a baseline model containing only the amount of weight loss and successively added age and grip strength.

In case of reasons for weight loss other than illness (right part of each box), the negative effect on cognition vanishes when controlling for age and grip strength. In contrast, the association between weight loss and cognitive decline is much stronger for respondents reporting an illness as a reason for losing weight and remains significant under all model specifications (left part of each box). Again, the pattern is stronger for men than for women.

32.5 Conclusion

Our results question previous findings that suggest that higher body mass becomes protective in older age and, hence, preserves health and cognition. Whereas recent studies also assume that BMI decrease is an indicator of cognitive decline in old age, we find no evidence for an adverse effect of weight loss unrelated to illness. Rather, the obesity paradox in cognition can be traced back to a spurious association attributable to partially unobserved health conditions affecting both body weight and cognitive performance.

Although the within-estimators used in our analyses do not suffer from attrition of respondents with certain (time-constant) cognitive predispositions, selective drop out given omitted time-varying variables could potentially distort our findings. However, additional tests (not shown) do not reveal a substantial bias in our estimates for BMI decrease resulting from selective attrition and, thus, do not challenge our general findings.

References

Ades, P. A., Savage, P. D. (2010). 'The obesity paradox: perception vs knowledge', *Mayo Clinic Proceedings*, 85(2), pp. 112–114.

Iliodromiti, S., Celis-Morales, Carlos A., Lyall, Donald M., Anderson, Jana, Gray, Stuart R., Mackay, Daniel F., Nelson, Scott M., Welsh, Paul, Pell, J. P., Gill, Jason M. R., Sattar, Naveed (2018). 'The impact of confounding on the associations of different adiposity measures with the incidence of cardiovascular disease: a cohort study of 296 535 adults of white European descent', *European Heart Journal*, 39(17), pp. 1514–1520.

Memel, M., Bourassa, K., Woolverton, C., Sbarra, D. A. (2016). 'Body mass and physical activity uniquely predict change in cognition for aging adults', *Annals of Behavioral Medicine: a Publication of the Society of Behavioral Medicine*, 50(3), pp. 397–408.

Peeters, A., Barendregt J. J., Willekens F., Mackenbach J. P., Al Mamun A., Bonneux L.; NEDCOM, the Netherlands Epidemiology and Demography Compression of Morbidity

Research Group (2003). 'Obesity in adulthood and its consequences for life expectancy: a life-table analysis', *Annals of Internal Medicine*, 138(1), p. 24–32.
Smith, E., Hay, P., Campbell L., Trollor, J. N. (2011). 'A review of the association between obesity and cognitive function across the lifespan: implications for novel approaches to prevention and treatment' *Obesity Reviews: an Official Journal of the International Association for the Study of Obesity*, 12(9), pp. 740–755.
Uretsky, S., Messerli F. H., Bangalore S., Champion A., Cooper-Dehoff R. M., Zhou Q., Pepine C. J. (2007). 'Obesity paradox in patients with hypertension and coronary artery disease', *The American Journal of Medicine*, 120(10), pp. 863–870.

Jens Elmelund Rise, Linda Juel Ahrenfeldt, Rune Lindahl-Jacobsen and Karen Andersen Ranberg

33 The association between self-reported physical activity and physical performance: Does advancing age matter?

- Older people who engage in moderate or vigorous physical activities have better muscle strength than their physically inactive peers
- The benefits of physical activity increase with advancing age

33.1 Physical activity and physical function at older ages

Ageing is associated with declines in physical functional performance, partly due to reductions in muscle mass and muscle fibres and a shift from faster (type 2) to slower muscle fibres (type 1). These changes are related to muscle weakness and lower speed of movement, thereby affecting muscle performance. However, intervention studies reveal that exercise training improves muscle strength and, consequently, physical performance. Moreover, more intense physical activity results in a better outcome (Paterson, Jones and Rice, 2007).

Physical performance is a prerequisite for physical independence. Such independence is the hallmark of satisfying healthy ageing. Physical activity also reduces the risk of age-related morbidities and mortality. However, although we know that physical activity is important for maintaining muscle performance and improving physical functioning, little is known about the magnitude at which physical activity affects muscle performance in advanced age.

Insofar as physical activity is important for healthy and disability-free living, the SHARE survey collects self-reported data on respondents' engagement in physical activity and the intensity of such activity. SHARE also collects an objective measure of hand grip strength. This particular measure is not only a good marker of physical performance – it is inversely correlated with all-cause

https://doi.org/10.1515/9783110617245-033

mortality in middle and older adulthood and predicts disability among older adults (Andersen-Ranberg et al, 2009).

The relationship between the level of physical activity and hand grip strength in older adults has been studied in only two small studies and with partly contradicting results. A cross-sectional study showed that, although no association exists between grip strength and physical activity among 50–64-year-olds, a significant association was observed among those aged 65 and older (Hwang et al, 2016). Moreover, the association was strongest among the oldest participants, that is, those older than 75 years of age. A similar pattern was described in another study using the five sit-to-stand test (Landi et al., 2018). Gómez-Cabello et al. (2014) also showed that higher levels of physical activity were associated with greater grip strength among those aged 65+ and that the difference in grip strength was greatest in the youngest age group and became progressively lower with advancing age

Good health is important to individuals and society. Insofar as physical activity is associated with good health, it is essential to know more about the benefits of physical activity in the rapidly ageing European population. Therefore, the current chapter considers how different levels of self-reported physical activity are related to hand grip strength across older age groups in Europe.

33.2 The study

We used a *pooled* sample of data from SHARE Waves 1 to 6 (excluding Wave 3, which collected retrospective life histories). The first six waves of SHARE cover the time period from 2004 to 2015. The number of participants by wave and country is shown in Table 33.1. Physical activity levels were assessed by the following questions in the computer-assisted personal interview: 'How often do you engage in vigorous physical activity, such as sports, heavy housework or a job that involves physical labour?' and 'How often do you engage in activities that require a moderate level of energy, such as gardening, cleaning the car or doing a walk?'. In both questions, the answer categories were 'More than once a week', 'Once a week', 'One to three times a month', or 'Hardly ever or never'. For our analysis, we dichotomized the answer categories into 'active' and 'inactive', where 'active' reflected those who answered 'More than once a week' or 'Once a week' and 'inactive' represented those answering 'One to three times a month' or 'Hardly ever or never'.

Participants were divided into age groups (50–59, 60–69, 70–79 and 80+ years) and geographic regions because we have previously found a geographic variation in grip strength in gender and height-adjusted peers (Andersen-Ranberg et al, 2009). The northern Europe category included respondents from Denmark and Sweden; western Europe reflected those from Austria, Germany, France, the Netherlands, Switzerland, Belgium, Ireland and Luxembourg; southern Europe grouped participants from Spain, Italy, Greece and Portugal; and Eastern Europe included those from the Czech Republic, Poland, Hungary, Slovenia, Estonia and Croatia.

Table 33.1: Overview of number of participants per country in each wave.

	Wave 1	Wave 2	Wave 4	Wave 5	Wave 6
Sweden	2,958	2,694	1,922	4,484	3,863
Denmark	1,583	2,463	2,172	4,016	3,640
Ireland	0	989	0	0	0
Germany	2,910	2,514	1,576	5,536	4,326
Luxembourg	0	0	0	1,580	1,539
Netherlands	2,810	2,564	2,683	4,092	0
Belgium	3,583	3,050	4,954	5,477	5,649
France	2,881	2,797	5,437	4,390	3,851
Switzerland	932	1,429	3,544	2,980	2,767
Austria	1,506	1,167	4,928	4,252	3,343
Portugal	0	0	1,659	0	1,644
Spain	2,175	2,272	3,262	6,457	5,521
Italy	2,480	2,895	3,489	4,635	5,177
Estonia	0	0	6,666	5,625	5,518
Poland	0	2,383	1,661	0	1,785
Czech Republic	0	2,609	5,258	5,486	4,778
Hungary	0	0	2,926	0	0
Slovenia	0	0	2,646	2,884	4,151
Croatia	0	0	0	0	2,376
Greece	2,633	3,179	0	0	4,759

Source: SHARE Wave 1–6.

Using linear regression analysis with robust standard errors, we compared grip strength between physically inactive and physically moderately or vigorously active participants for all countries combined, stratified by age groups and gender. The grip strength difference was measured in both absolute (kilograms) and relative (percentage) terms. The robust model employed clustering from repeated measurement of the participants over several different SHARE waves. All regression analyses included an interaction between age group and physical activity (moderate physical activity and vigorous physical activity) and were adjusted for SHARE wave, limitations in daily activities for the past 6 months due to a health problem, height and European region. A Holm-Bonferroni adjustment was carried out on each subdivision when evaluating the difference between physically active and inactive participants. Participants younger than 50 years were excluded from the analyses, as were those with missing information.

33.3 Key results

In this study, 50,690 (45%) men and 61,048 women (55%) were included, corresponding to 240,820 observations. Table 33.2 shows the distribution across age groups among participants and their mean grip strength. Both moderately and vigorously physically active participants had higher grip strength compared with the inactive participants, which was the case for both genders (Figure 33.1).

Table 33.2: Feasibility of grip strength (GS) test by age group and gender.

	Grip Strength							
Age group	**Men**				**Women**			
	Enrolled	**Completed**	**Missing GS**	**GS mean**	**Enrolled**	**Completed**	**Missing GS**	**GS mean**
years	**N**	**N**	**%**	**KG**	**N**	**N**	**%**	**KG**
50–59	31,254	29,475	6%	48.7	40,993	38,767	5%	29.7
60–69	38,355	36,136	6%	44.5	44,403	41,535	6%	27.3
70–79	26,594	24,455	8%	38.4	31,278	27,911	11%	23.6
80+	11,436	9,619	16%	31.5	16,507	12,652	23%	19.3

Note: Grip strength (GS), number of participants (N).
Source: SHARE Wave 1–6.

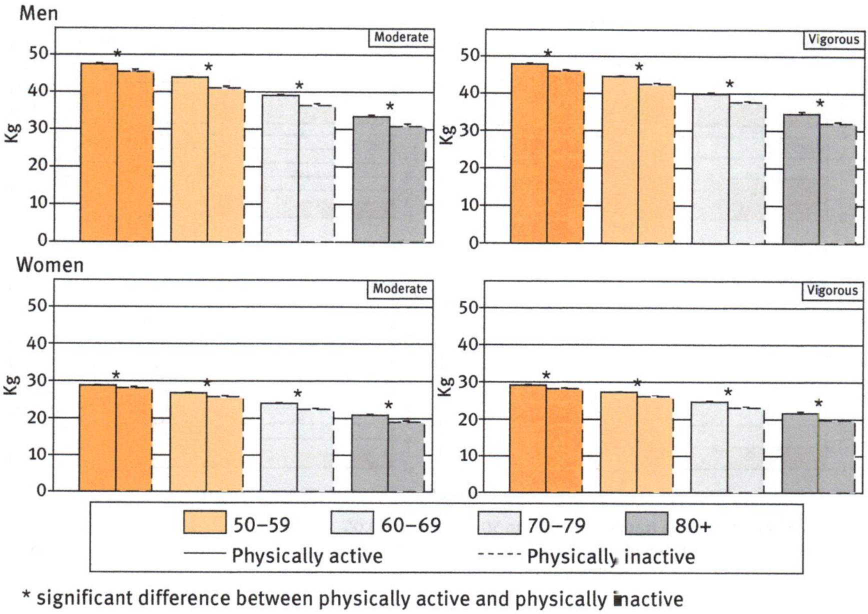

Figure 33.1: Grip strength for physically active and physically inactive (moderately or vigorously) participants by age groups and gender.
Note: Error bars are shown as confidence intervals.
Source: SHARE Wave 1–6.

For absolute grip strength (kg), we found an interaction for women between age and physical activity; that is, the difference in grip strength between physically inactive and physically active women differed by age (Figure 33.2). Thus, for the group of moderately physically active women aged 70–79 and 80+ and vigorously physically active women aged 80+, there was a larger difference in grip strength between the physically active and the physically inactive compared with the age groups 50–59 and 60–69. Likewise, for the group of vigorously physically active women aged 70–79, there was a larger difference in grip strength compared with the age group 50–59.

The relative changes were largest in the oldest age groups. Hence, moderately and vigorously physically active men and women aged 80+ showed significant differences in relative grip strength (%) compared with those aged 50–59 and 60–69 years. Moreover, both genders had significantly higher relative grip strength when comparing the 80+ year-old age group with the 70–79 years-old age group, and likewise when comparing the 70–79 years-old age group with the 50–59 and 60–69 years-old groups.

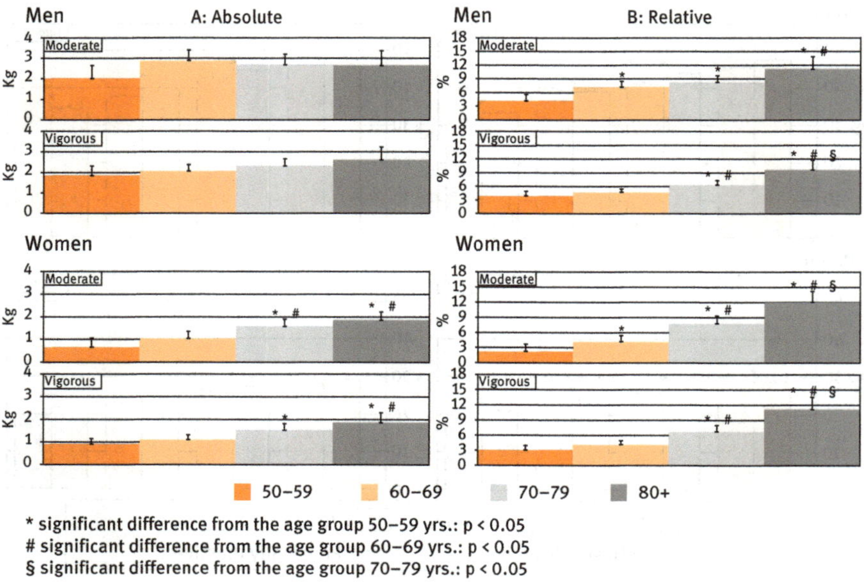

Figure 33.2: Grip strength differences between physically active and physically inactive (moderately or vigorously) participants by age group and gender.
Note: Grip strength difference is shown in absolute kilograms (A) and relative percentage change (B). Error bars are shown as confidence intervals.
Source: SHARE Wave 1–6.

33.4 What we learned

Using grip strength as a proxy indicator of good health, our analysis confirms that physical activity is associated with good health. Moreover, the findings underscore the increasing health benefit of physical activity with advancing age. Therefore, a physically active lifestyle is important even in very old age.

Our findings are in line with the works of Hwang et al. (2016), and Landi et al. (2018), both of whom showed that the health benefits from physical activity seem to increase with age. However, as recalled, Gómez-Cabello et al. (2014) found an increasingly smaller difference between the active and the inactive along with advancing age. This contradiction might be explained by differences in methodology in the respective studies, as Gómez-Cabello et al. (2014) used a different physical activity scale that includes both duration and intensity. The SHARE probe asks two basic questions on physical activity level. However, despite the methodological differences, all studies showed that physical inactivity has a strong negative effect on health.

It is difficult to explain why the biggest difference in grip strength is seen in the oldest age group, but one explanation might be that higher relative workload leads to increased muscle strength. Given the general ageing-associated decline in muscle performance, a given physical exercise (for example, walking up a flight of stairs) yields a higher workload in the oldest age group relative to the youngest age group.

We should point out that, although SHARE collects data from a representative population sample, the possibility exists that survey participants in the oldest cohort are somewhat healthier than their non-participating counterparts. Nevertheless, the selection effect among those aged 80+ years notwithstanding, we still show that active participants have better grip strength than inactive ones. Thus, it is plausible that the difference in grip strength in the general population may be even larger.

We also note that the current inquiry employed a cross-sectional analysis because a sufficiently large number of survey participants with unknown vital status are lost to follow-up. This phenomenon occurs particularly among those in the oldest age groups because they suffer from the highest mortality risk and drop out more frequently due to morbidities. Thus, we cannot demonstrate a direct causal effect of the health benefits of vigorous and moderate physical activity with advancing age.

33.5 Conclusion

The results in this study show that, relative to physically inactive individuals, older people who engage in moderate or vigorous physical activity have better muscle strength. Moreover, the muscle strength difference between the active and the inactive is higher in the oldest age groups relative to the middle and younger ages. Because grip strength is highly correlated with mortality, morbidity and disability, the results of this study corroborate prior findings that physical activity has a positive health effect on older adults and that this effect may even be strongest in the oldest age groups. This knowledge should be used to set a policy agenda that focuses on discouraging a sedentary and inactive lifestyle and facilitates physical activity among all age groups, especially among older adults. Implementation of such initiatives may reduce the adverse outcomes of ageing-associated diseases and increase independent life expectancy and quality of life.

References

Andersen-Ranberg, K., Petersen, I., Frederiksen, H., Mackenbach, J.P. and Christensen, K. (2009), Cross-national differences in grip strength among 50+ year-old Europeans: results from the SHARE study, European Journal of Ageing, 6(3), pp. 227–236.

Gómez-Cabello, A., Carnicero, J. A., Alonso-Bouzón, C., Tresguerres, J. Á., Alfaro-Acha, A., Ara, I., Rodriguez-Mañas, L. and García-García, F. (2014). Age and gender, two key factors in the associations between physical activity and strength during the ageing process. Maturitas, 78(2), pp. 106–112

Hwang, A. C., Zhan, Y. R., Lee, W.J., Peng, L. N., Chen, L. Y., Lin, M. H., Liu, L. K., and Chen, L. K. (2016). Higher Daily Physical Activities Continue to Preserve Muscle Strength After Mid-Life, But Not Muscle Mass After Age of 75. Medicine (Baltimore), 95 (22),p.e 3809.

Landi, F., Calvani, R., Picca, A., Tosato, M., Martone, A. M., D'Angelo, E., Serafini, E., Bernabei, R., and Marzetti, E. (2018). Impact of habitual physical activity and type of exercise on physical performance across ages in community-living people. PLoS One, 13(1), p.e 0191820.

Paterson, D. H., Jones, G. R. and Rice, C. L. (2007). Ageing and physical activity: evidence to develop exercise recommendations for older adults. Can J Public Health, 98 (2), pp. 69–108.

Pedro Pita Barros, Fernando Pimentel-Santos
and David Dias Neto

34 Grip strength across Europe –North/ South and East/West divides

- The north/south divide in handgrip strength found in previous SHARE waves, still persists in the 7th wave
- The enlargement of the set of countries participating in SHARE reveals an east/west divide in handgrip strength as well
- Country differences in handgrip strength are stable over age groups
- Country differences in handgrip strength are not concentrated at the bottom or at the top levels of handgrip strength

34.1 Introduction

One syndrome associated with the ageing process is sarcopenia. This syndrome can be defined as loss of muscle mass, muscle strength and muscle function. Sarcopenia leads to several health and disability outcomes, including functional limitations, lower quality of life and premature death. We use grip strength as a proxy for the probable presence of sarcopenia in the European population according to the most recent definition of sarcopenia (Cruz-Jentoft et al., 2018). The measurement of low muscle strength by grip strength provides an indication of probable sarcopenia, while confirmation of sarcopenia requires additionally low muscle quantity and muscle strength or function.

Ageing populations increase the relevance of identifying the variables associated with sarcopenia. We use the Survey on Health, Ageing and Retirement in Europe (SHARE) database, to assess the existence and prevalence of probable sarcopenia by using grip strength as a proxy. Our analyses use SHARE Wave 7 data and thereby extends the number of countries covered by previous waves of SHARE (Andersen-Ranberg et al, 2009; Franzese, 2015). These previous analyses of earlier waves of SHARE established relevant differences across European countries, with an emphasis on the north–south divide, with higher grip strength in the north than in the south. Other regularities found in these previous studies were that grip strength declines with advancing age in all countries, and in both genders.

https://doi.org/10.1515/9783110617245-034

The more recent inclusion of new SHARE countries mainly from the eastern European region allows us to look at grip strength from a broader perspective. Using SHARE Wave 7 data we are able to compare grip strength not from the north to the south of Europe and also from east to west. The 11 countries included in the analysis by Andersen-Ranberg et al. (2009), using data collected in the first wave of SHARE in 2004, were Austria, Belgium, Denmark, France, Germany, Greece, Italy, Netherlands, Spain, Sweden, and Switzerland. The 7th SHARE wave, with data from 2017, covers in addition 17 more countries: Israel, Czech Republic, Poland, Luxembourg, Hungary, Portugal, Slovenia, Estonia, Croatia, Lithuania, Bulgaria, Cyprus, Finland, Latvia, Malta, Romania and Slovakia. One country, the Netherlands, is not part of the 7th wave of SHARE. The expanded set of countries allows SHARE to now include eastern Europe, have an expanded southern European set of countries, and have Finland added to the north Europe group. We consider four groups of countries: northern Europe (Denmark, Finland, Sweden, Estonia, Latvia and Lithuania), southern Europe (Cyprus, Greece, Israel, Italy, Malta, Portugal and Spain), eastern Europe (Bulgaria, Hungary, Poland and Romania) and western and central Europe (Austria, Belgium, Croatia, Czech Republic, France, Germany, Luxembourg, Slovakia, Slovenia and Switzerland). We will concentrate our discussion below on northern, eastern and southern Europe.

34.2 Data and computations

The main variable from SHARE that allows addressing the presence of probable sarcopenia is handgrip strength. A proxy for the onset of sarcopenia is defined using criteria based on thresholds for grip strength (different for men and women), already available in the literature (Cruz-Jentoft et al., 2018). Handgrip strength is one of the criteria pointed out and the other is muscle mass or muscle function (for which no measurements exist in recent SHARE waves). Therefore, we concentrate on the first part of the algorithm set in Cruz-Jentoft et al. (2018), with an assessment of grip strength, to help identifying probable sarcopenia.

Our main variable of interest is handgrip strength, which is measured in the SHARE survey. Our measure of handgrip strength is the maximum value over two measurements in each hand. The indicator of probable sarcopenia is defined as 1 if handgrip strength, as previously defined, is less than 27 kg for men and 16kg for women (Cruz-Jentoft et al., 2018).

Simple probit models that regress our proxy for probable sarcopenia on individual characteristics (age and gender) and country fixed effects provide the main source of data analysis. A complementary analysis based on a linear regression that directly uses handgrip strength directly is also performed. The two approaches represent different ways of treating the information on grip strength. The indicator of probable sarcopenia, which transforms the measurement of grip strength into a simple indication of probable sarcopenia (indicator value of 1) or no probably sarcopenia (value of 0) according to cut-off values proposed in Cruz-Jentoft et al. (2018) has the advantage of a simplifying the data – a male respondent with a measurement of 26 kg in handgrip strength is treated equally relative to another male respondent with 24 kg and differently from another male respondent with 32 kg of handgrip strength (the cut-off used is 27 kg). Thus, small variations in measurement are, to some extent, neutralized and the results can be expressed in terms of the probability of a positive indicator for probable sarcopenia. The disadvantage is that the indicator variable has less information than the underlying measurement. Both approaches are subsequently reported, allowing for a cross-check of whether, or not, the option of using one or the other changes the comparison across countries.

34.3 Handgrip strength across Europe in Wave 7

Figures 34.1a and 34.1b present the estimated probability of probable sarcopenia for men and women, respectively, organized by quartiles, after controlling for age effects. Table 34.1 reports the underlying values. Figures 34.1a and 34.1b show that both men and women in eastern Europe and men in Spain have the highest probability of low handgrip strength. The northern countries have the lowest probability of poor handgrip strength, with the southern countries

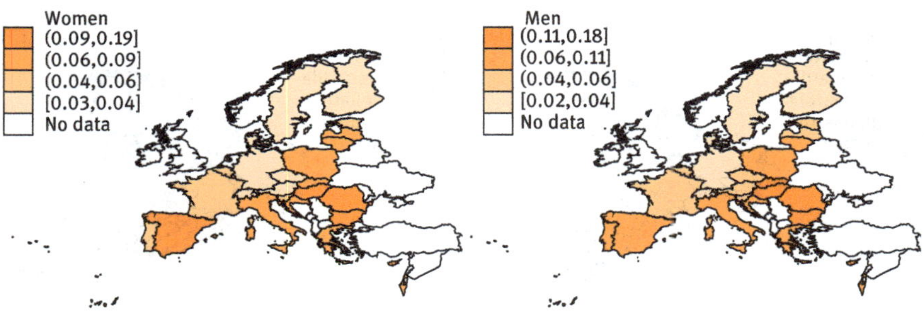

Figure 34.1: Probable sarcopenia.

Note: Numbers report the estimated probability of handgrip strength lower than the threshold for probable sarcopenia (Cruz-Jentoft, 2018).

Source: SHARE Wave 7 release.

Table 34.1: Differences by Age Group (country fixed effects).

	Men (50–59)	Men (60–69)	Men (70–79)	Men (80+)
Average absolute deviation	2.818	2.394	2.559	2.518
Standard deviation	3.408	2.856	2.962	2.954
	Women (50–59)	**Women (60–69)**	**Women (70–79)**	**Women (80+)**
Average absolute deviation	1.529	1.487	1.744	1.686
Standard deviation	1.939	1.791	1.978	1.930

Source: SHARE Wave 7 release 0.

having a higher probability of probable sarcopenia, confirming the previous finding of a north versus south divide. The broad features do hold for men and women, which are estimated separately.

The measure of probable sarcopenia is based on the measurement of handgrip strength, as previously defined. This approach treats all values lower (or higher) than the cut-off as being equal and, naturally, has less information than the actual measurement value of handgrip strength. Thus, checking that our main insight – the existence of an east/west divide – holds is also important if handgrip strength in kg is used as the relevant continuous variable. The linear regression model allows computation of average values across countries, after accounting for age and gender differences between countries. These values are then used to build the quartiles over average handgrip strength, leading to Figure 34.2, in which a

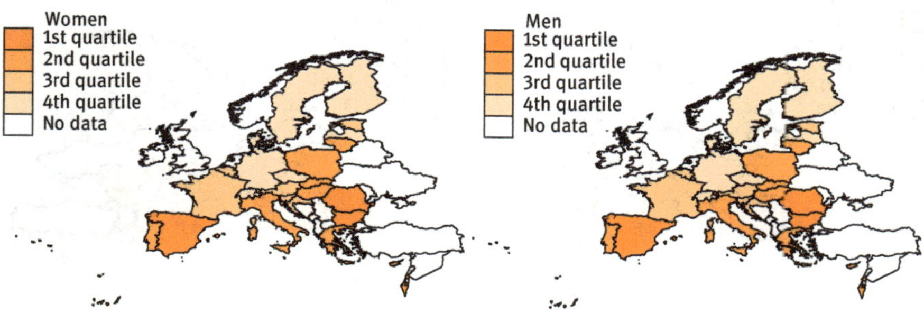

Figure 34.2: Handgrip strength.
Note: Darker colours indicate weaker grip strength.
Source: SHARE Wave 7 release 0.

darker colour refers to higher likelihood of probable sarcopenia (weaker grip strength).

Overall, the countries added to SHARE since Wave 1 confirm the north-south distinction found in previous waves and studies (Andersen-Ranberg et al., 2009). The new countries in the south and north Europe (Finland) groups fit into the previous pattern found more than a decade ago. Additionally, the SHARE Wave 7 data shows that an east-west split exists as well, with most eastern European countries (Bulgaria, Hungary, Romania) plus Slovakia showing weaker grip strength and higher probabilities of sarcopenia than their more western and northern peers, and southern Europe, apart from Spain. In contrast, central European countries on are closer to the north Europe group (and western and central European countries).

The cut-off values for handgrip strength have changed recently. To confirm that the broad divides identified are not the result of the particular cut-off points for handgrip strength, the analysis was replicated using the old cut-off values, as defined in the initial proposal of Cruz-Jentoft et al. (2010). The new cut-off values, as indicated in Cruz-Jentoft et al. (2018), have lower values, meaning that some cases of hand grip strength that would be classified as probable sarcopenia under the 2010 criterion are not classified as such under the new 2018 criterion. Nevertheless, the same divides emerge (full results available from the authors upon request).

34.4 Country differences across groups

The north/south and the east/west divides in hand grip strength were assessed to this point on average values, even if these values were adjusted for elements such as age and gender.

An interesting aspect is whether these differences across countries are stable over the entire age range (as previously found in Andersen-Ranberg et al. (2009) in the comparison of north to south countries) or are driven by a particular age group. Differences between countries may widen at older ages. If that is the case, then attention should be paid to what motivates such a divergence. However, differences may also remain stable among age groups, or may even decline at older ages (through a convergence effect). The implications for international comparisons and learning from health policies related to frailty and sarcopenia detection and associated interventions are distinct.

To assess this (potential) effect, we split the sample according to age groups, along decades: 50–59 years of age, 60–69 years, 70–79 years of age and 80 years or older. Then, we proceed to re-estimate the relationship between the handgrip measurement and age and country fixed effects, with separate samples for men and women. We now have to set a criterion to assess whether differences across countries are increasing or decreasing over age groups. We use two different ways to measure these changes. The first one is to consider the sum of the absolute deviations to the mean (of the country fixed effects). The closer the value is to zero, the more similar are the countries. Thus, if this indicator has a smaller value for older age groups countries' populations have more similar handgrip strength at these older ages.

A second indicator is the standard deviation of the country fixed effects. This indicator has a similar interpretation, and the difference from the previous indicator is of significant importance to extreme differences.

As a brief technical note, in all regressions performed as the first step to compute the two indicators, we take Austria's country fixed effect to be normalized to zero (without loss of generality).

The results for the two indicators and the four age groups are reported in Table 34.1.

The differences across age groups do not seem to have any particular pattern for either men or women. For men, the dispersion of country fixed effects seems larger for the younger age group (50–59 years old). For the other groups, no systematic difference seems to exist. Thus, handgrip strength differences are present for all age groups in, essentially, a similar manner. Country differences are stable over age groups. This in line with the previous findings of Andersen-Ranberg et al. (2009) for the differences between north and south populations across the age range. We interpret this as reflecting permanent features of the population and of health systems.

Figures 34.3 and 34.4 present the quartiles of handgrip strength per age group (decade). Despite some changes from age group to age group, the broad divide of north, south and eastern Europe clusters is apparent. The values in Table 34.1 reveal that underlying variations among countries do not change significantly across age groups.

34.5 Final remarks

The main implication from the analysis performed is the existence of persistent differences in handgrip strength across several dimensions. North Europe countries have populations with a lower risk of probable sarcopenia, when measured by handgrip strength. The analysis by age groups reveals that these

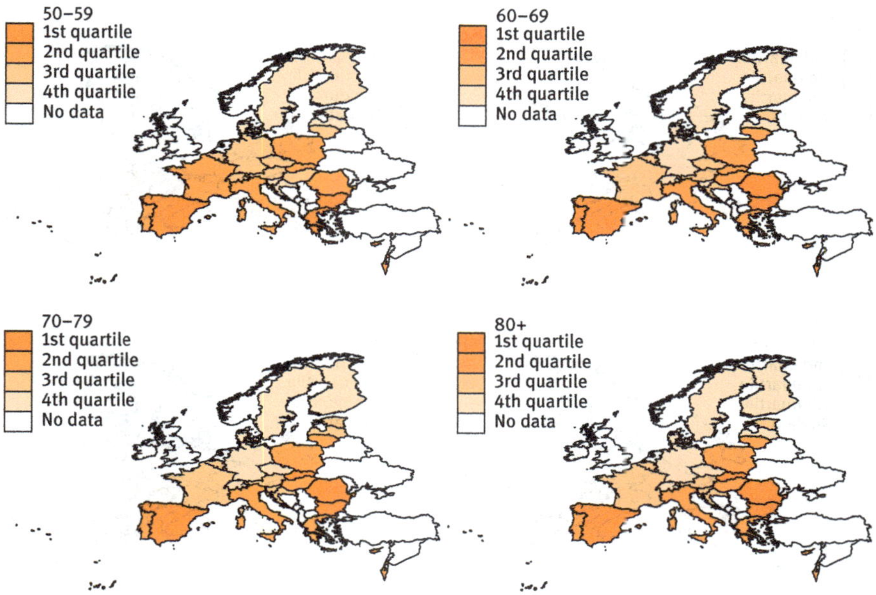

Figure 34.3: Handgrip strength, men by age group.
Note: Darker colours indicate weaker handgrip strength.
Source: SHARE Wave 7 release 0.

differences are stable across age groups and across handgrip strength (country-level) quartiles in the population (taking the lowest/highest 25 per cent of the population ordered by handgrip measurement in each country). Differences are not driven by age or by the weakest or strongest members of the population in terms of handgrip strength.

The three groups of European countries we focus on (eastern, northern and southern Europe) are different environmentally, socio-culturally, and institutionally. Eastern European countries tend to be, on average, less economically developed than northern and southern Europe countries, which can be associated with differences in access to healthcare and in healthy lifestyles by the population.

Southern European countries are more mixed in this respect, with important differences within this group with regard to income (GDP per capita) and in the design of the healthcare systems. However, southern Europe has several countries with higher life expectancy, even at older ages, than northern Europe countries. Higher handgrip strength is generally associated with less disability, lower morbidity and higher survival, which suggests that factors other than age must be present and relevant to explain cross-country differences in handgrip strength.

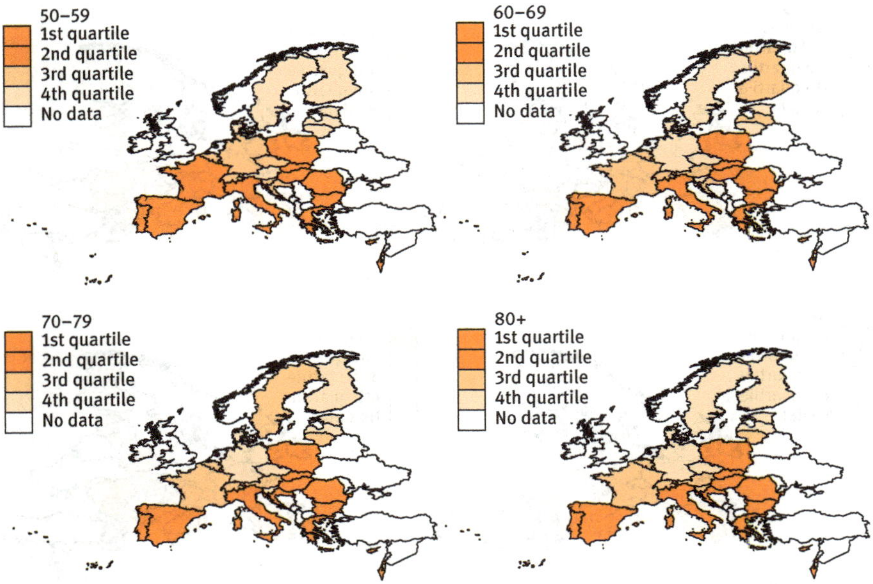

Figure 34.4: Handgrip strength, women by age group.
Note: Darker colours indicate weaker handgrip strength.
Source: SHARE Wave 7 release 0.

More important to our discussion is the possibility of different mechanisms behind the lower grip strength in eastern Europe and southern Europe. Unveiling the contribution of these and other characteristics will help to address concerns about the best approach to reduce the onset of sarcopenia, as well as improving and substantiating novel health policy recommendations that can positively affect the health and function of millions of Europeans. We leave for future exploration the role that exercise and physical activity as well as nutrition and the complex interplay between these factors, play with respect to sarcopenia. To understand the impact of physical activity it will be important to characterize type of exercise (aerobic vs resistance), frequency and intensity in different countries. Nutrition and typical diet of each country can also play a role, although full discussion requires information on eating habits of the population in each country. It will be of interest to evaluate levels of energy intake and contents of different nutrients in particular proteins, vitamin D and polyunsaturated fatty acids to speculate about the impact of nutrition in muscle strength and sarcopenia. The establishment of patterns of physical activity and nutritional habits will allow the identification of specific targets with respect to the relevant variables to prevent or delay sarcopenia. An early intervention will have an enormous social impact contributing for frailty prevention and their associated risks including falls and fractures (major determinant of reduced quality of life and life survival). Other variables should be evoked to complement these complex interplays. Cultural factors and architectural design of public spaces and cities favouring more physical exercise in some countries than in others may contribute to such differences. The role of other conditions, such as depression and diabetes for example, in fostering differences in grip strength across countries should be explored as well. These insights will inform health policies to tailor health promotion strategies, which may include changes in life styles related to exercise and nutrition. Our first results from SHARE wave 7 provide an initial step in better understanding sarcopenia distribution and its drivers across Europe.

Acknowledgements: We thank Karen Andersen-Ranberg for extremely useful suggestions and very thoughtful discussions. The usual disclaimer applies.

References

Andersen-Ranberg, K., Petersen, I., Frederiksen, H., Mackenbach, J., Christensen, K., 2009, "Cross-national differences in grip strength among 50+ year-old Europeans: results from the SHARE study". In: European Journal of Ageing 6. No. 3, p. 227–236."

Beaudart, C:, R. Rizzoli, O. Bruyére, J-Y Reginster and E. Biver, 2014. Sarcopenia: burden and challenges for public health, Archives of Public Health, 72: 45.

Cruz-Jentoft, AS, JP Bayens, JM Bower, Y Barie, T Cederholm, F Landi, FC Martin, JP Michel, Y Roland, SM Schneider, E Topinkova, M Vandewoude, M Zamboni (EWGSOP), 2010, Sarcopenia: European consensus on definition and diagnosis: report of the European Working Group on Sarcopenia in older people, Age & Ageing, 39 (4):412 –423.

Cruz-Jentoft, AS, G Bahat, J Bauer, Y Boirie, O Bruyère, T Cederholm, C Cooper, F Landi, Y Roland, AA Sayer, SM Schneider, C Sieber, E Topinkova, M Vandewoude, M Visser, M Zamboni (EWGSOP2), 2018, Sarcopenia: revised European consensus on definition and diagnosis, Age and Ageing; 0: 1–16. doi: 10.1093/ageing/afy169.

Franzese, F., 2015, Slipping into poverty: effects on mental and physical health, Chapter 12 in: Axel Borsch-Supan et al. "Ageing in Europe – Supporting policies for an inclusive society"139–149, Walter de Gruyter GmbH, Berlin/Boston.

Hendrik Jürges, Anne Laferrère and Adèle Lemoine

35 End of life and palliative care in Europe: An exploration of SHARE data

- The proportion of deceased that had needed help with pain, breathing or anxiety was 80 per cent, twice that of those deemed to need palliative care (41%)
- Palliative care was less needed in Slovenia, Hungary, Austria, Poland, the Czech Republic and Germany. However, the need for help with pain, breathing and anxiety did not differ by country
- Thirty-one per cent received adequate palliative care, or 75 per cent of those who needed it. Controlling for needs, a higher income increased palliative care reception
- Care was less likely to be rated very good or excellent when palliative care was not available or when ailments were not properly addressed. Care was rated the highest in Austria, Greece, Switzerland, Spain, Croatia, Israel and the Czech Republic

35.1 Introduction

What is a good life? Is there a good death? The two questions sum up philosophy, literature and religion. As a more down to earth tool, the Survey on Health, Ageing and Retirement in Europe (SHARE) provides information on how Europeans and their families face old-age ailments. The survey also addresses death. A member of the family or a knowledgeable person is asked questions about the former respondent's last year of life. Inspired by Gawande (2014), questions about palliative care were added in Wave 7.

The 3 per cent who died in a hospice were assumed to have received palliative care (PC) there. For the others, the survey asked if they died in a PC unit and, if not, the following question: 'In the last four weeks of his/her life, did [Name of the deceased] have any hospice or palliative care?' A definition was provided: '*By hospice care we mean palliative care for terminally ill or seriously ill patients, delivered at home or in an institution. According to the WHO definition, palliative care is an approach that improves the quality of life of patients and their families facing the problem associated with life-threatening illness, through the prevention and relief of suffering by means of early identification and impeccable assessment and treatment of pain and other problems, physical, psychosocial and spiritual*'. Note that the definition of palliative care was only provided after previous questions used the term or a synonym. For the 50 per cent

https://doi.org/10.1515/9783110617245-035

who died in a hospital, the question was 'Was that in a *palliative care* or *inpatient hospice unit?*', for the 9 per cent who died in a nursing home, the question was 'Was that in an *inpatient hospice unit?*' and for the 3 per cent who died in a residential home, it was '*Was the residential housing provided by hospice?*' Until recently, in many European languages, a hospice meant a home for the sick or poor. Hence, that PC was overestimated is possible.

Fortunately, additional questions were asked, such as whether the deceased had suffered from pain, trouble breathing (dyspnoea), and anxiety, and how these ailments were dealt with. Leaving out those for whom no answer (2%) or a 'don't know' answer (5%) was provided for PC or care provision, 2,998 observations remained. Of the deceased, 58 per cent had needed pain medication, 44 per cent had needed breathing assistance and 46 per cent had felt anxiety (all figures are unweighted). Pain relief in case of need was widespread (87%), as was help for breathing (89%). Anxiety seems to be somewhat less dealt with (82%). Receiving PC is expected to be synonymous with receiving help for these three ailments, if needed. However, there is a gap between both aspects.

Using a first definition of palliative care (dying in a hospice, in an inpatient hospice unit within a hospital or institution or having any hospice or PC in the last four weeks of life), the proportion receiving PC was surprisingly large, at 38 per cent (Table 1, col.4). For 59 per cent, PC was deemed not needed. The remainder is divided between when PC was not available (2%) and when it was too expensive (1%).

In 64 per cent of cases, all three needs were fulfilled, 20 per cent had none of the three ailments and 16 per cent had at least one of them unmet (Table 35.1, last line). Comparing PC reception and the satisfaction of the three needs leads to the creation of a stricter definition of palliative care, excluding from having had PC the 7 per cent for whom anxiety, pain or dyspnoea were not adequately cared for. The proportion of adequate palliative care provision plummets to 31 per cent and inadequate care increases to 10 per cent. In what follows, we analyse PC, adequate PC and whether the three needs (pain, dyspnoea, anxiety) were met.

35.2 Cross-national differences in palliative care

Needing and receiving PC depends on the cause of death. People who died from a long-term disease, such as cancer, represented a quarter of the deceased and nearly 40 per cent of those who had PC, and 58 per cent of those who died from cancer received PC. Significant differences in need for palliative care are observed among countries. Controlling for age and cause of death, countries

Table 35.1: Palliative care and the satisfaction of needed help with pain, breathing and anxiety.

	All 3 needs	At least one need	None of the 3	Total	Corrected definition
Declared...	**were fulfilled (1)**	**was unfulfilled (2)**	**Needs (3)**	**(4)**	**(5)**
... deceased had palliative care	27.1	7.1	3.5	37.7	37.7−7.1 **=30.6**
...palliative care was not available or too expensive	1.4	1.1	0.5	3.0	**3.0**
Quality of palliative care was poor					**+7.1**
...palliative care was not needed	35.0	8.0	16.3	59.3	59.3
Total	63.5	16.2	20.3	100.0	100.0

Note: In per cent. n = 2,998.
Source: SHARE Wave 7 release 0.

with the lowest needs were Slovenia, Hungary, Austria, Poland, the Czech Republic and Germany, where less than 30 per cent needed PC. The need for relief from pain, breathing and anxiety differed much less by country (Figure 35.1). When palliative care was deemed needed, only 7 per cent answered that it was not available or too expensive, but 29 per cent in Hungary did so.

To study access to care, we control for the need for care. We assume that the cause of death influences the need for PC or care and determines access only through this selection channel. Figure 35.2 presents the proportion receiving PC and that receiving adequate PC (excluding from adequate PC the cases for which pain, dyspnoea or anxiety were not taken care of) by country. Receiving adequate PC was more likely in Italy and Spain and less likely in Slovenia, Hungary or Israel.

Turning to the adequacy of care for pain, dyspnoea and anxiety, the best countries are again Italy and Spain but also Switzerland and Austria (Figure 35.3).

Conditional on needs, being married, the presence of children, relationship with proxy respondent, area of living, time spent with illness before death and the level of income or education could influence PC or care provision, either positively or negatively. We proceed with Heckman's two-step method. Table 35.2 presents the results. The first step estimates the need for PC (col. 1) and that of facing at least one of the three ailments (col. 4). Dying from cancer increases the

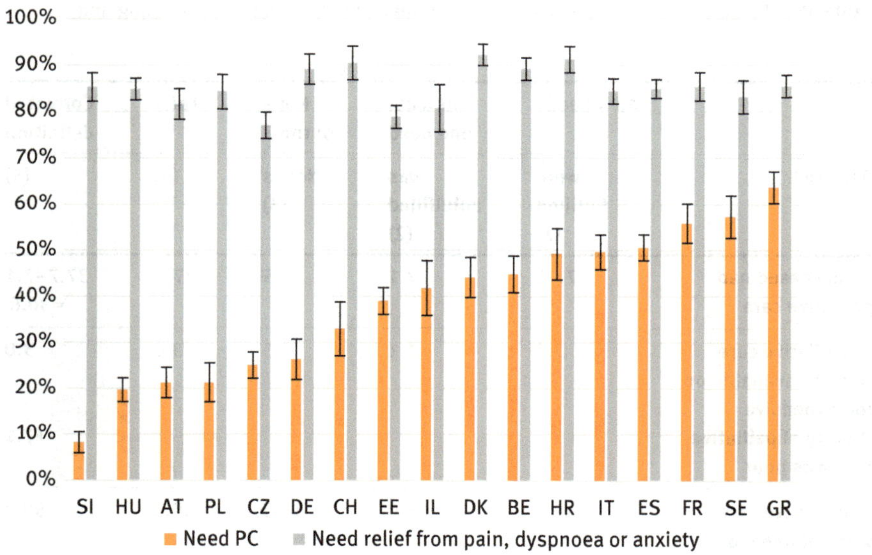

Figure 35.1: Need for palliative care or relief from pain, dyspnoea or anxiety by country.
Note: Adjusted for age and cause of death. Bars represent standard errors. n = 2,998.
Source: SHARE Wave 7 release 0.

probability of needing PC or help with pain, breathing or anxiety relative to other causes of death. Severe infections and respiratory diseases increase the probability of needing help for at least one of the three ailments, even relative to cancer. The positive relation between age of death and the need for PC supports the notion that the growing life expectancy might increase future needs for palliative care (Seale, 2000). Age is only significant at the 15 per cent level when the need for ailments relief is considered.

The second step (Table 35.2, col 2, 3, 5) estimates what affects receiving end-of-life care. The first specification (col. 2) uses the initial definition of PC, the second (col. 3) refers to the stricter definition of adequate PC and the third (col. 4) focuses on the proper relief of pain, anxiety and dyspnoea. Conditional on needs, dying older is positively related, while dying at home is negatively related, to receiving PC or adequate care. Sex has no effect. The presence of a spouse has no effect on receiving PC but positively affects the relief of pain, dyspnoea or anxiety. Being in the top income quartile facilitates receiving proper PC by 6 percentage points relative to those in the other income quartiles. Not being in the lowest level of education is positively correlated with adequate dealing with pain, dyspnoea or anxiety. Hence, a possible inequality in end-of-life care related to income and education, which may be linked to information about care.

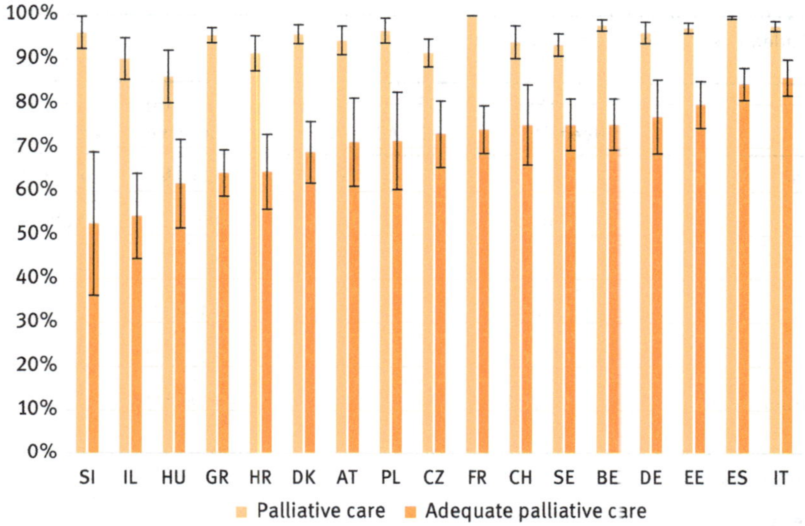

Figure 35.2: Quality of palliative care in case of need.
Note: Controlling for PC need. Adjusted for sex and age at death. Bars represent standard errors. n = 1,220 needing PC.
Source: SHARE Wave 7 release 0.

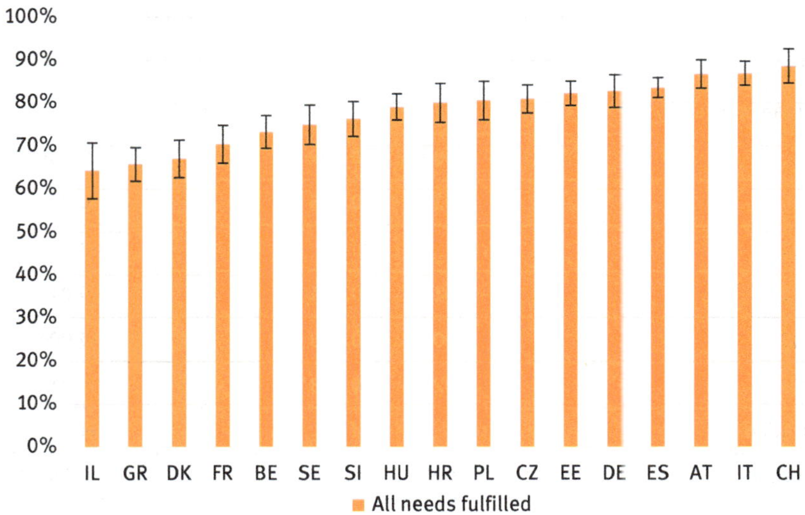

Figure 35.3: Relief from pain, dyspnoea or anxiety.
Note: Controlling for need for relief from pain, dyspnoea or anxiety. Adjusted for sex and age at death. Bars represent standard errors. n = 2,390 needing relief from at least one of the three ailments.
Source: SHARE Wave 7 release 0.

Table 35.2: Heckman probit: need for palliative care or relief from ailments, and determinants of PC, of adequate PC and of relief of ailments.

	(1) Need PC	(2) PC	(3) Adequate PC	(4) Need relief	(5) Met needs
Age at time of death	0.002**	0.002**	0.006***	0.001§	0.006***
Female	0.013	0.014	0.028	0.015	0.026
Cancer	ref			ref	
Heart attack	−0.342***			−0.181***	
Stroke	−0.160***			−0.173***	
Other cardiovascular disease	−0.190***			−0.145***	
Respiratory disease	−0.182***			0.046**	
Digestive system disease	−0.095*			−0.104**	
Infectious disease	−0.169***			0.047**	
Accident	−0.417***			−0.177*	
Degenerative disease	−0.143***			−0.193***	
Other	−0.126***			−0.159***	
Ill less than one month	−0.237***			−0.241***	
Ill more than one year	0.007			0.017	
Married		0.004	0.009		0.046**
No child		0.024	0.055		0.003
Income Q1		ref	ref		ref
Income Q2		−0.017	−0.051		−0.018
Income Q3		0.008	0.023		−0.006
Income Q4		0.026µ	0.063*		−0.014
Low education		ref	ref		ref
Mid education		0.005	0.040		0.052**
High education		0.034*	0.067§		0.090**
Big city		ref	ref		ref

Table 35.2 (continued)

	(1) Need PC	(2) PC	(3) Adequate PC	(4) Need relief	(5) Met needs
Outskirt of big city		0.001	−0.004		0.012
Large town		−0.034*	−0.041		0.014
Small town		−0.001	0.021		0.041§
Rural area		−0.031*	−0.004		0.051*
Area missing		−0.027	0.014		−0.007
Proxy non-relative		−0.031§	0.018		0.016
Nb years since death		0.002	−0.010		−0.012*
Died at home		−0.048**	−0.105**		−0.032*
N	2981	2981	2981	2981	2981

Note: Marginal effects. Other controls not shown: country dummies. *** p < 0.01, ** p < 0.05, * p < 0.10, § p < 0.15.
Source: SHARE Wave 7 release 0.

35.3 Determinants of care rating

The estimated probabilities of rating end-of-life care as very good or excellent are presented in Figure 35.4. Seventy-two per cent judged the care as excellent or very good, and this figure was 80 per cent or more in Austria, Israel, Switzerland, Greece, Croatia and Spain but 60 per cent or less in Hungary, Poland and Estonia. Clearly, having had inadequate care significantly reduces the rating to 58 per cent when PC was not available or too expensive, to approximately 67 per cent in the case of lack of pain relief, to 63 per cent in the case of lack of help with breathing and to 52 per cent when anxiety was not properly addressed. Having a spouse was favourable, as was dying at home. Having more income improved the care rating by 6 percentage points when income was higher than the median relative to the lowest quartile.

To summarize, receiving palliative care seems to be linked to care quality. The relief of pain or dyspnoea and, even more importantly, of anxiety helped people judge that care was excellent or very good. The links among anxiety, place of death and the rating of care should be further explored.

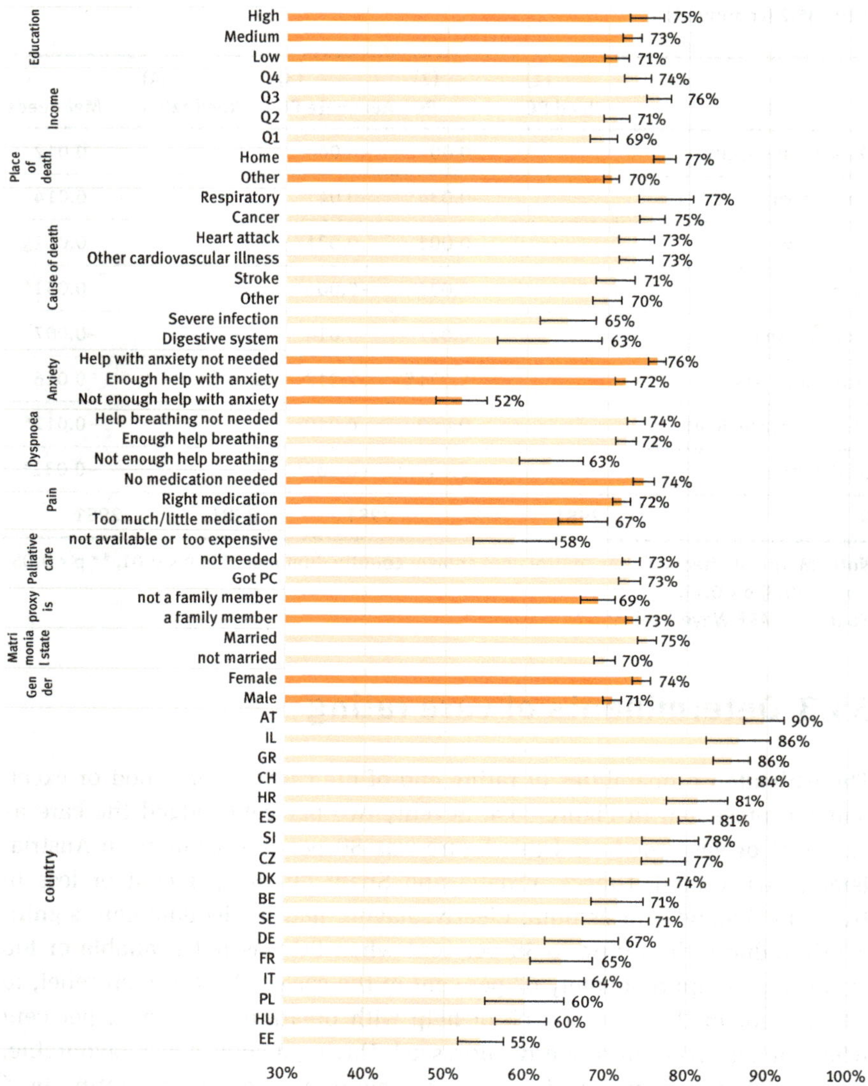

Figure 35.4: Estimated probabilities of rating care as excellent or very good.
Note: Logit model. Predictive margins. Bars are for standard errors. n = 2,892.
Source: SHARE Wave 7 release 0.

References

Gawande, Atul (2014): Being Mortal. Illness, Medicine and What Matters in the End, Profile book, Wellcome Collection.

Seale, C. (2000): "Changing patterns of death and dying", *Social Science & Medicine* 51, 6, pp. 917–930.

Part VIII Dried blood spot samples

Edited by Axel Börsch-Supan

Axel Börsch-Supan, Martina Börsch-Supan and Luzia M. Weiss

36 Dried blood spot samples and their validation

- Laboratory results from the DBS assays cannot be directly compared with the results that would be obtained from assays of venous plasma samples using standard laboratory methods
- Nevertheless, we can reliably measure A1c, HDL, CysC and CRF from DBS samples. Taking into account the blood type and the various treatment effects is very important
- Total cholesterol is by far the weakest of the seven analytes, but the qualitative information contained in the total cholesterol values is still useful

36.1 Introduction

The key innovation of Wave 6 was the sampling of dried blood spots (DBS) in the large international population survey of SHARE using lay interviewers. This endeavour was truly cutting-edge.

From a laboratory point of view, venous blood samples are best suited for analysing blood biomarkers. However, collecting venous samples in very large community-based settings in as many countries as in SHARE entails major logistical challenges related to collection, transportation and timely laboratory analyses, as well as significant expenses for venipuncture by certified health professionals. Moreover, a venipuncture is invasive and may harm the individual. Venipuncture may also be regarded as intrusive by respondents, thus yielding higher proportions of non-participation.

Instead of drawing venous samples, SHARE decided to collect blood using a method more adaptable to the circumstances of a very large international population survey. The DBS sampling is such a method. DBS samples are drops of capillary whole blood collected on filter paper from a simple finger prick. One of the best-known DBS applications is the screening test for phenylketonuria in new-borns for which DBS sampling is a minimally invasive method relative to collecting venous blood. In new-borns, the drop of blood is collected from the heel, but the same technique can be applied to adults' fingertips and may be carried out in a home setting by trained survey interviewers. Blood collected on filter cards can be shipped by regular mail to a laboratory and stored at −20°C (some store them at −80 °C) until analyses, making DBS samples ideally suited for large population-based studies such as SHARE.

https://doi.org/10.1515/9783110617245-036

SHARE has chosen two sets of biomarkers to be assayed from the DBS samples. Priority in the selection process was given to their relevance in evidencing typical diseases at older age, such as cardiovascular disease (CVD), cancer, diabetes and cognitive decline. Additional criteria were the existence of suitable assays (i.e. reagents and procedures to detect the biomarker) and the availability of comparative population values from (inter)national health registers (e.g. the Robert-Koch-Institute in Germany, Eurohealth or WHO) and other population surveys, including HRS and its sister studies. Selection was also guided by the ability to share a DBS extract across multiple analyses, thereby limiting the amount of blood needed. The first set contains markers used in routine blood analyses. For these markers, reference values from venous blood samples are well established and include the following.

1. *Glycosylated haemoglobin* (HbA1c or A1c) is a marker for diabetes. An excess of sugar molecules in the blood irreversibly bind to haemoglobin. The so-formed A1c signals longstanding and chronically high levels of blood sugar.

2–4. *High density lipoprotein* (HDL) cholesterol, (total) cholesterol (TC) and triglycerides (TG) are molecules of the lipid panel and important players in lipid metabolism, such as serving as building blocks for cells and transport molecules for lipids. Imbalances in lipid metabolism lead to various diseases of the cardiovascular system.

5. *Cystatin C* (CysC) is a marker for kidney function and CVD. CysC, though a measure for the clearance of degradation products from blood, also signals risk of CVD. Those with elevated cystatin C levels have been shown to be at highest risk for CVD, even when kidney dysfunction is mild; those with the highest levels of CysC are older and have hypertension, dyslipidaemia, high BMI and higher levels of CRP.

6. *C-reactive protein* (CRP) marks the general level of inflammation in the body caused by acute infections or chronic diseases. Inflammatory processes are involved in CVD, diabetes, obesity and cognitive decline.

7. *Total haemoglobin* (tHb) is a marker of anaemia that indicates a decrease in red blood cells or haemoglobin, thereby lowering the ability to carry oxygen in the blood. Anaemia may arise from loss of blood, pathological removal of blood cells, diseases of the haematopoietic system, chronic inflammatory diseases, kidney disease, wasting diseases (e.g. cancers) and more.

Approximately 8,000 probes from SHARE respondents were assayed in the United States at the University of Washington (UW) in Seattle for these markers.

The second set of biomarkers is more innovative and was assayed at the *Statens Serum Institut* (SSI) in Copenhagen. This set is mainly comprised of a large set of cytokines, which are small blood-based proteins prominently involved in inflammatory processes. Their selection and importance is described by Borbye-Lorenzen and Börsch-Supan in Chapter 39 of this volume.

8–12. The proteins *IL-8, IL-16, IL-18, IL-12/23p40* and *MCP-1* indicate an inflammation occurring in the body; all are pro-inflammatory markers but act in different tissues. Elevated blood levels of either one or several of these cytokines will better inform us about the type of inflammation and its degree; they may confirm the report of, for example, CVD or atherosclerosis by a respondent or point to yet undetected inflammation, cancer and/or (onset of) cognitive impairment.

13–14. *Vascular epithelial growth factor (VEGF) and epidermal growth factor (EGF)* are proteins involved in normal and pathologic cell and tissue growth. They are needed in healing (e.g. in blood vessels) but may also indicate proliferating tissue in the case of cancer.

15. *Brain-derived neurotrophic factor (BDNF)* is another growth factor. BDNF acts on neurons of the central and peripheral nervous system, supports the survival of neurons and encourages growth of neuronal tissue. BDNF is involved in learning and memory. Its level increases with exercise and social embeddedness. In turn, the BDNF blood level is lowered in cognitive decline.

16. *Apolipoprotein E (ApoE)* belongs to a class of proteins involved in the metabolism of fats in the body and is a component of the lipid panel. ApoE mediates the cholesterol metabolism, transports cholesterol to neurons and is the principal cholesterol carrier in the brain. ApoE is important in Alzheimer's and cardiovascular diseases.

17. *Clusterin* has the general vital function in the organism to clear misfolded proteins or cell debris; through this function, clusterin is involved in ageing and many diseases related to oxidative stress, including neurodegenerative and inflammatory diseases and cancers.

18. *Vitamin D (VitD)* is essential for several biological processes. Being deficient is associated with mortality and diseases, among them CVD but also functional loss from lower muscle function and muscle mass (sarcopenia), affecting postural stability. Additionally, osteoporosis can be caused by low VitD because it is essential for the absorption of calcium from the diet.

Laboratory results from the DBS assays cannot be directly compared with the results one would obtain from assays of venous plasma samples using standard laboratory methods (Crimmins et al. 2013; Karvanen 2003), which is particularly relevant for the first set of markers for which well-established thresholds exist. Although 'gold standard' values also have measurement variations, DBS values of, for example, total cholesterol – known to be particularly difficult to measure from DBS samples – have both a larger mean and a larger variance, systematically influenced by many laboratory and fieldwork-related factors. Figure 36.1 shows how these differences are generated.

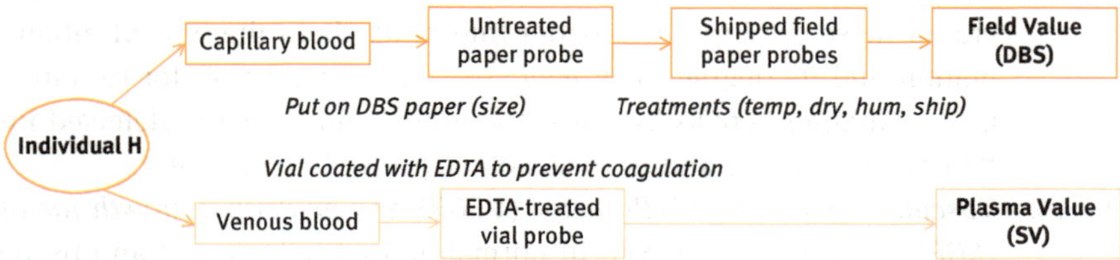

Figure 36.1: DBS fieldwork setting versus gold standard clinical setting.
Source: Own illustration.

In the centre of Figure 36.1 is a donor with characteristics *H* (e.g. health, age, sex) who donates both venous blood and capillary blood. The upper part of Figure 36.1 refers to the process of how capillary blood samples donated by the SHARE respondents were collected in the field and then shipped to be analysed in the two laboratories (UW and SSI): the capillary blood from the finger prick is dropped on paper, dried and later shipped to the lab under potentially unfavourable conditions *T* (e.g. temperature, humidity, drying time, shipment time, spot size). The sample is finally analysed to yield a value called DBS. The lower part refers to the collection of venous blood in a typical clinical setting. The venous blood from the donor is collected in a vial coated with EDTA (ethylendiaminetetraacetic acid, a chemical that prevents the coagulation of blood) and is then analysed in the lab, yielding a value SV, considered the gold standard of medical measurement.

The field-measured value of DBS is not equal to the gold-standard value of SV for three reasons. First, the DBS samples collected in the field have different sizes and are exposed during shipment to varying temperatures, humidity and other factors, called 'fieldwork effects'. Second, the capillary blood of the donor is dried in the field and then re-liquefied in the lab, potentially creating chemical changes called the 'dry-liquefy effect'. Finally, capillary blood given for DBS is a more heterogeneous mixture of arterial and venous blood, interstitial fluid and red blood cells, whereas venous blood from venipuncture is treated with EDTA to prevent coagulation, and most markers are analysed from only plasma. We call this difference the 'blood-type effect'.

36.2 Fieldwork effects

We tested the influence of different fieldwork circumstances using data from the UW assays of approximately 8,000 probes that were linked to the SHARE data. Details are given in Chapter 37 of this volume. We regressed DBS on fieldwork conditions and donor health. We included interviewer fixed effects to isolate the fieldwork effects that hold across different interviewers or regions. Figure 36.2 shows that the influence of field conditions or sample quality is significant and differs among assays. Small spot size is the main challenge in the field, especially for TC and A1c, but not for TG, CysC or CRP. TC is also sensitive to high outside temperatures and long shipment times. HDL is sensitive to the combination of long shipment times and insufficient humidity protection. TG and CysC are also sensitive to short drying times. CRP and tHb seem relatively robust to field conditions and sample quality.

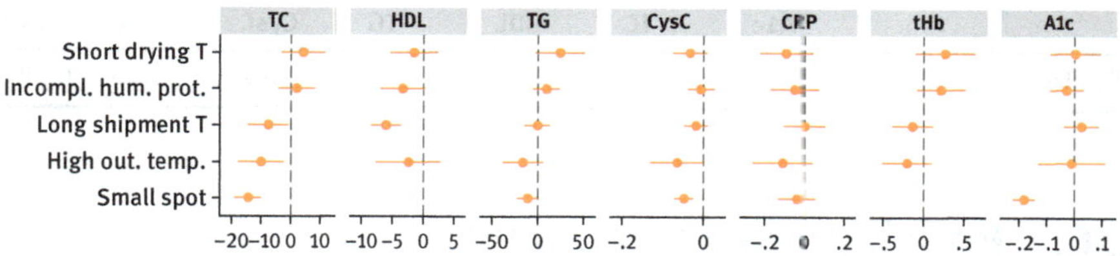

Figure 36.2: Influence of SHARE fieldwork conditions (N ~ 8,000).

36.3 Dry-liquefy effect

In previous studies, the dry-liquefy effect has been studied extensively at UW (e.g. Crimmins et al. 2013); the effect is small. UW has collected venous blood samples in EDTA tubes. Those samples were then analysed using conventional clinical chemistry analysers. In parallel, blood from each EDTA tube was dropped onto filter paper to create artificial DBS samples and then analysed similar to field-collected DBS. The relation is linear and tight Table 36.1.

Table 36.1: Lab-created DBS samples from venous blood versus gold standard.

	A1c	TC	HDL	TG	CysC	tHb	CRP
Tightness of fit (R^2)	0.99	0.86	0.87	0.95	0.91	0.99	0.87

36.4 Blood-type effect

EDTA is known as a preservative for cholesterol and various haematological assays, but the implications of the blood-type effect for the assays have yet to be studied. The implications can only be measured in combination with the dry-liquefy effect (Figure 36.1). We dropped both capillary blood and EDTA-treated venous blood from the same donor onto filter paper under lab conditions and compared the obtained values. We also compared the lab-created DBS values (i.e. without treating them in other fieldwork and shipping conditions) with the gold standard SV. Table 36.2 shows tight correlations for all markers except for TC and tHb, after controlling for spot size, age, sex and BMI, which substantially improves the fit to the gold standard SV.

Table 36.2: Lab-created DBS samples from capillary blood versus gold standard.

	A1c	TC	HDL	TG	CysC	tHb	CRP
Tightness of fit (R^2)	0.96	0.60	0.85	0.98	0.92	0.36	0.997

36.5 Polish nurse experiment

The main challenge is now to set up a translation formula that takes into account donor and fieldwork conditions and converts the DBS values into gold standard SV values. The ideal way to conduct such a validation study is to obtain both DBS and venous blood samples in the field. We conducted such an experiment in a small sub-study in Poland in which nurses took both DBSS and venous blood samples that were then assayed for A1c, TC, HDL, TG and CRP. This process is described in detail in Chapter 38 in this volume. Although the distributions of the DBS laboratory results are different from the distributions of the results obtained from plasma values (wet blood values in case of A1c), conversion formulae that include fieldwork conditions produced a very good fit between plasma and DBSS values for all markers (Table 36.3).

Table 36.3: DBS versus SV under actual field conditions.

	A1c	TC	HDL	TG	CysC	tHb	CRP
Tightness of fit (R^2)	0.95	0.67	0.92	0.95	n.a.	n.a.	0.99

36.6 Simulating fieldwork conditions

Because the sample was very small, these results are only indicative. Therefore, we replicated this experiment on a much larger scale in the UW lab in which we simulated field conditions. We took venous blood from approximately 50 donors, used it to create approximately 3,700 DBS samples of three different sizes on filter paper and then exposed the DBS samples to a large number of combinations of different drying times, humidity protections, outside temperatures and shipment times that are typical of the conditions experienced by field-collected DBS during collection and shipment in SHARE. We then compared the treated DBS values with the gold standard values, thereby conditioning on the treatment variables, their interactions and the available donor characteristics.

Figure 36.3 shows the results for the four markers TC, HDL, CysC and tHb. The light orange bars show the significant variation in the raw laboratory values from DBSS and their distance from the dashed equality line. The grey values use a simple bivariate regression while the darker orange values are based on estimations accounting for the simulated fieldwork conditions and donor characteristics.

36.7 Combining the components

By combining all components (treatment effects, dry-liquefy effect and blood-type effect), we obtain a conversion formula that translates the DBS values obtained under simulated fieldwork conditions into gold standard values. The prediction accuracy of this conversion formula is high for A1c, HDL, CysC and CRP (Table 36.4). Prediction accuracy is lower for TG and tHb in one component but high in the other, whereas TC is weak in both components.

Table 36.4: Prediction accuracy.

	A1c	TC	HDL	TG	CysC	tHb	CRP
Blood-type and dry-liquefy effect (R^2)	0.97	0.76	0.82	0.97	0.89	0.79	0.99
Treatment effects (R^2)	0.87	0.79	0.94	0.75	0.95	0.98	0.97

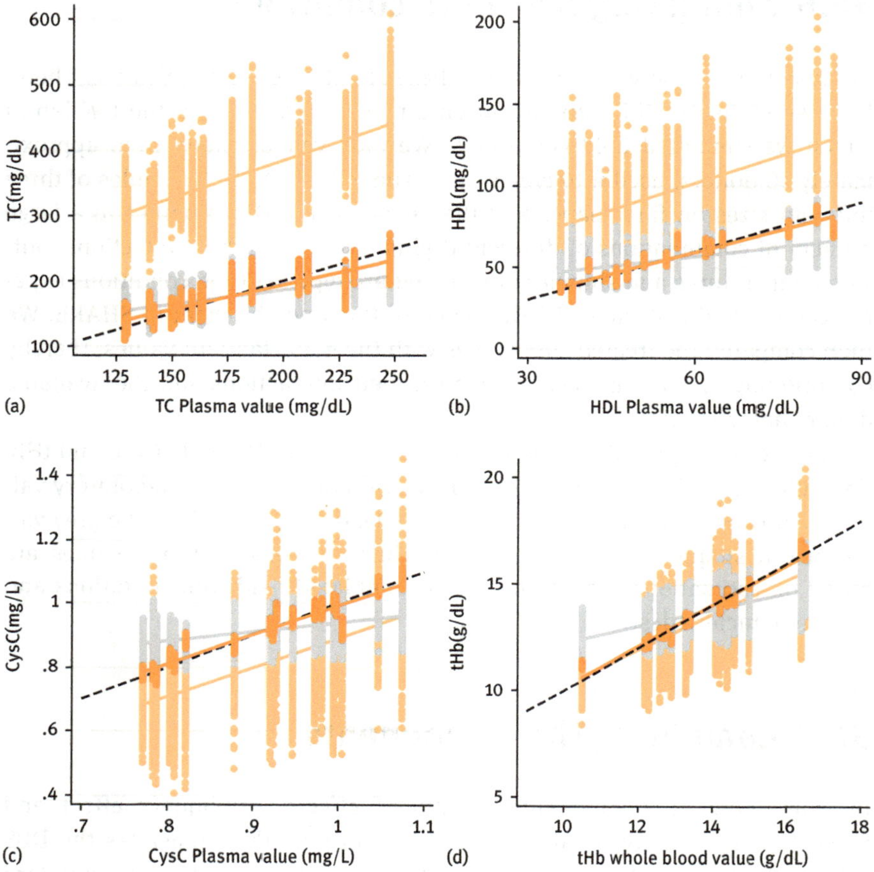

Figure 36.3: Adjusting for simulated fieldwork conditions (N ~ 3,700).
Note: For more details and legend of colours: see text.

We finally applied this conversion formula to the values obtained in the Polish nurse experiment to test its validity. Figure 36.4 shows the original DBS values (light orange) and the values obtained from the conversion formula (orange) on the vertical axis plotted against the actual gold standard values taken from plasma on the horizontal axis. The grey dots represent the predicted values if the blood-type effect is ignored. Note that the plasma values were obtained from a laboratory in Poland with different analysers from those used in our UW-based validation studies and that the circumstances of the transportation of the venous blood in Poland generated additional variation in the plasma values. Additionally, not all

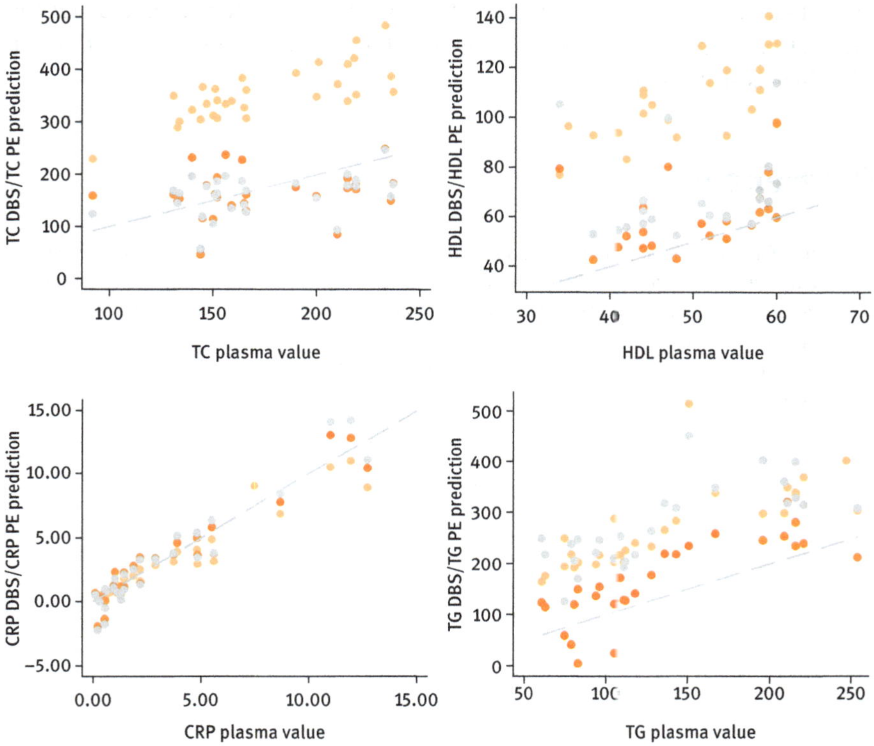

Figure 36.4: Raw and estimated gold standard values versus actual gold standard values.
Note: For more details and legend of colours: see text.

fieldwork conditions previously mentioned could be used to create the used formula because not all of them were observed in the Polish nurse experiment. Nevertheless, we observe a good convergence to the dashed equality line.

36.8 Conclusions

The overall conclusion from our structured validation experiments is that we can reliably measure A1c, HDL, CysC and CRP from DBS samples. We also learned that it is very important to take into account the blood type and the various treatment effects. The treatment effects are somewhat less accurately predicted for TG and the blood-type effect for tHb. As expected, TC is by far the weakest of the seven analytes, but the qualitative information contained in the TC values is still useful.

References

Crimmins, Eileen M., Kim, Jung Ki, McCreath, Heather, Seeman, Teresa (2013) *Results from the Health and Retirement Study Biomarker Validation Project* [Online]. Available at: hrsonline.isr.umich.edu/sitedocs/genetics/HRSBiomarkerValidation.pdf (Accessed: 1 September 2018)

Karvanen, Juha (2003) 'The statistical basis of laboratory data normalization', *Drug information journal*, 37(1),p101–107.

Luzia M. Weiss and Axel Börsch-Supan

37 Influence of fieldwork conditions and sample quality on DBS values

- Fieldwork conditions and sample quality during blood collection significantly influence DBS values
- Small spot size is the main challenge; in particular, TC, CysC and HbA1c are sensitive to small spot size
- In turn, tHb, TG and CRP are relatively robust regarding fieldwork conditions and sample quality
- Conversion formulae between DBS and the medical gold standard can be significantly improved when they include fieldwork conditions and sample quality

37.1 Introduction

The collection of dried blood spot (DBS) samples is an innovative method aimed at collecting objective health data. DBS samples are increasingly used in large-scale surveys. However, because the samples are collected during regular fieldwork, they are exposed to varying field conditions that might influence the obtained sample quality.

In SHARE Wave 6, we collected DBS samples from approximately 27,000 respondents during face-to-face interviews at respondents' homes. A randomly drawn first batch of approximately 8,000 samples was analysed for up to seven biomarkers. They include high density lipoprotein (HDL), total haemoglobin (tHb), glycated haemoglobin (HbA1c), total cholesterol (TC), triglycerides (TG), C-reactive protein (CRP) and Cystatin C (CysC). The number and types of analysed markers for each single DBS sample depend on the amount of available blood material. We call the obtained analysis results 'raw' DBS values and obviously do not know the corresponding 'gold standard' values taken from venous blood.

This chapter explores the systematic associations of raw DBS values with a set of fieldwork conditions and quality measures. Our main result is that some of these associations are statistically significant and substantially large. Moreover, these associations cannot be measured in isolation because they interact with each other, such as short drying time and the lack of humidity protection. Therefore, understanding DBS results requires understanding the fieldwork process.

https://doi.org/10.1515/9783110617245-037

37.2 Fieldwork conditions and sample quality

Five dimensions of fieldwork conditions and sample quality have been measured or estimated during or after the fieldwork. To break down the complexity of the possible influences, they are coded as dummy variables.

Outside temperature: High temperatures could affect the integrity of the biomarker molecules that might, as a consequence, deteriorate more rapidly. The deterioration products might not be detected by the laboratory assay, leading to a spuriously decreased blood level result.

Interviewers were asked to estimate the actual outside temperature during the interview. A temperature variable for 'high outside temperature' was created that took the value of 1 if the estimated outside temperature reached 30°C or hotter and 0 otherwise (as long as any estimation was given).

Spot size: The diameter of a regular dried blood spot is approximately 1 cm. Sometimes, smaller spots occur for a variety of reasons, which might lead to a deviant distribution of the marker molecules inside the analysed material, resulting in spuriously increased analysis values.

The size of the analysed blood spot is estimated on the basis of the following information. For HbA1c, we know whether it has been analysed from an otherwise unsuitable spot (which is usually 'unsuitable' because of its small size) or from a regular spot that, in general, should be larger. For TC, TG, CRP and CysC, we know whether from the entire sample only this set of markers (the so-called 'B-markers') has been analysed (indicating that only one punch was possible at all and, thus, the used spot must be very small) or whether further markers have been analysed (and the used spot was probably larger). This information was used to create a binary variable for 'small spot size' with a value of 1 for small spots and 0 for larger ones. No spot size information is available to date for tHb and HDL ('A-markers' other than HbA1c).

Drying time: The main threat of insufficient drying time is that the blood on the filter paper might still be wet during shipment. Humidity can lead to the deterioration of biomarker molecules.

At the end of the computer-assisted interview, the interviewer was asked via a programmed item to prepare the DBS sample for shipment. The time from the end of the DBSS specific module to the end of the interview was calculated using keystroke analysis, and the resulting time was used as estimated drying time (in minutes). This estimate was approximate because the interviewers might have ignored the request and might have packed the sample at an earlier or later point in time, leading to shorter or longer 'true' drying times. The dummy variable for 'short drying time' is 1 if the estimated drying time is shorter than 6 minutes. This value is very conservative; as far as we know, optimal drying times would be much longer.

Shipment time: Biomarker molecules might continue to deteriorate during shipment unless they are frozen (at delivery). Short shipment times, hence, are preferable.

The shipment time is the time between the date of the interview (which equals the date of the blood collection) and the date of the DBS sample arriving at the biobank. A variable for 'long shipment time' takes the value of 1 for a DBS sample arriving at the biobank more than six days after the blood collection and the value of 0 for shorter durations.

Humidity protection: As previously described, humidity might lead to biomarker molecule deterioration. Therefore, all DBS samples should be protected from ambient humidity during shipment.

Interviewers were trained on how to protect the DBS samples against humidity during shipment. Namely, each sample should be put into a polyethylene (PE) bag together with a desiccant. The PE bag had to be closed tightly (via a ziplock system). These humidity protection measures have been evaluated for each sample at its arrival at the biobank (bag available and closed; desiccant available inside the bag). A variable for 'insufficient humidity protection' takes the value of 0 only if all described measures were taken, and 1 otherwise.

We also hypothesize that these fieldwork conditions interact, that is, the presence of one condition affects the strength of another condition:

- *Drying time X humidity protection*: Insufficient humidity protection might have a stronger impact on an incompletely dried sample.
- *Humidity protection X shipment time*: Biomarker molecules might deteriorate faster at high humidity levels. Hence, longer shipment times have a stronger impact on badly protected samples.
- *Outside temperature X shipment time*: Biomarker molecules might deteriorate faster at a high temperature. Hence, longer shipment times have a stronger impact when the outside temperature is high.
- *Outside temperature X drying time*: Samples might dry faster when the outside temperature is high. Hence, shorter drying times might have a weaker impact in this case.

37.3 Respondent characteristics

Analysis results from DBS will depend on respondents' health and other characteristics. For example, respondents with a high body mass index are more likely to have high levels of HbA1c. To control for this variation and to better isolate the effects of field conditions and sample quality, all associations will be conditioned on age (standardized), body mass index score (BMI score; standardized), sex, smoking (yes or no), activity level (low, middle, high), education level (low, middle, high; according to ISCED 1997) and a set of self-reported conditions or diseases possibly related to the biomarkers: heart attack, high blood pressure, high cholesterol level, stroke, diabetes mellitus, rheumatoid arthritis, osteoarthritis and kidney disease.

37.4 Interviewer effects

Some field conditions and sample quality measures, such as drying time and humidity protection status, probably depend on the reliability and the care of our interviewers. Other conditions, such as shipment time and some biomarker levels themselves, are possibly clustered in regions. To account for unobserved heterogeneity at the interviewer level, we include interviewer fixed effects in all associations. Because respondents and interviewers are clustered on a regional basis, this also accounts for regional effects. As an example, regarding high density lipoprotein (HDL), the intraclass correlation for clustering in interviewers is only 0.14, but some coefficients and significance levels vary when calculating the same models with or without interviewer fixed effects.

37.5 Results

We express our results for the seven SHARE biomarkers as coefficient plots. A dot at the left of the dashed line means a lower than expected DBS raw value; a dot to the right means the opposite. Whiskers represent 95 per cent confidence intervals. The biomarkers are described in groups of markers with similar patterns regarding their associations with field conditions and/or their interactions.

Figure 37.1 shows that HbA1c and TC are sensitive to some field conditions, but no significant associations exist with their interactions – at least not at the 5 per cent level. HbA1c is sensitive to small blood spot sizes; TC is sensitive to long shipment times, high outside temperatures or small spot size.

Regarding respondent characteristics, the HbA1c level is high in diabetics, as was to be expected. Furthermore, this level increases with age and BMI, is lower with rheumatoid arthritis and slightly lower in people with a high education level.

The TC level is associated with age and sex, as expected. A lower TC level is observed with higher BMI (driven by lower HDL levels). TC is also lower in

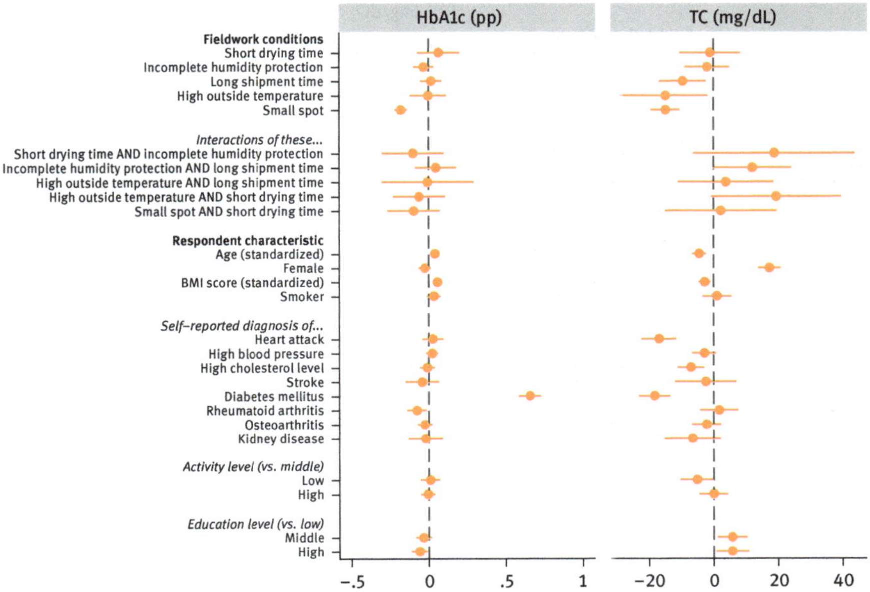

Figure 37.1: Assay results associated with field conditions.
Note: Mean (and median) levels: HbA1c 5.6 (5.5) %, TC 374 (370) mg/dL.

people who reported the diagnosis of a heart attack, diabetes mellitus or high cholesterol. Higher levels would have been expected in these patients. After the diagnosis, these people might be more likely to actively lower their cholesterol levels. Higher TC levels are observed in people with a middle and high level of education.

As illustrated in Figure 37.2, the analysis results of HDL and CysC not only show associations with single field conditions (incomplete humidity protection and long shipment times for HDL, short drying times and small spot sizes for CysC) – these biomarkers are also sensitive to interactions of these conditions: a short drying time, for example, seems to not be a problem for HDL as long as the samples are well protected against humidity during shipment. However, if this protection is insufficient, a short drying time increases the raw DBS value. Similarly, the measured level of CysC is lower after short dying times and in small blood spots. High outside temperatures do not show a significant effect as long as the used blood spot is large. However, for small spots, high outside temperatures have a significant effect on CysC (in the opposite direction as a small spot at lower temperatures). Note that no information is available on the size of the blood spots used for HDL analysis.

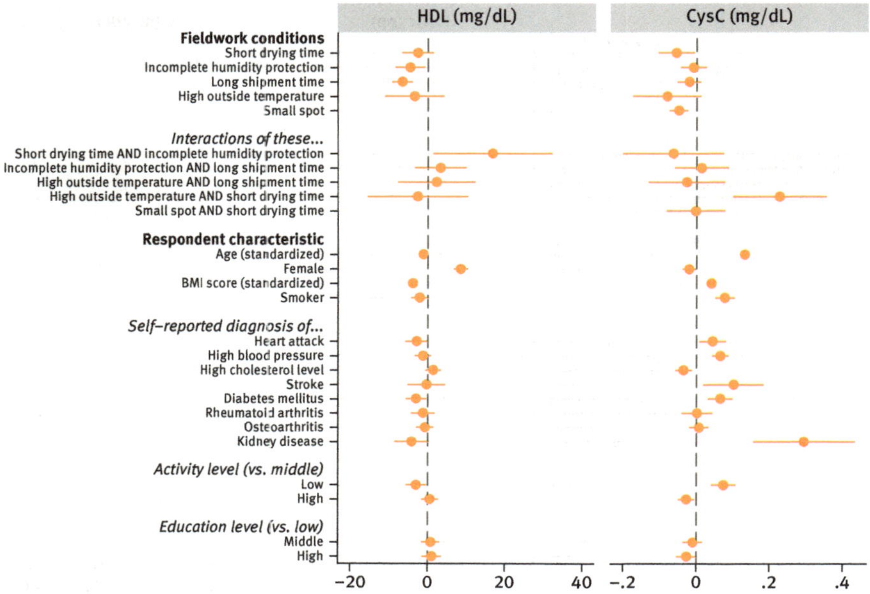

Figure 37.2: Assay results associated with interactions of field conditions.
Note: Mean (and median) levels: HDL 107 (105) mg/dL, CysC 1.17 (1.11) mg/L.

Regarding respondent characteristics, the plots show expected associations: high BMI scores, diabetes and low activity levels are accompanied by lower HDL levels. Females generally show higher HDL levels.

The CysC level increases with age, BMI and less physical activity. CysC is lower in women and higher in smokers, and is negatively associated with the reported diagnosis of high cholesterol and positively with the reported diagnosis of a heart attack, high blood pressure, stroke or diabetes mellitus. Not surprisingly, CysC is also highly associated with reports of kidney disease.

Some markers do not show any significant sensitivity to fieldwork conditions, namely, tHb, TG and CRP (see Figure 37.3). Note that information on spot size is not available for tHb.

Women show remarkably lower tHb levels than men. Higher levels are associated with higher BMI scores and smoking. The TG level is associated with age, sex, BMI score and a reported diagnosis of high cholesterol or diabetes mellitus. TG is lowered in highly active people. CRP increases with age and BMI, and is higher in women and smokers. CRP decreases with a higher activity level and is lower with a reported diagnosis of high cholesterol.

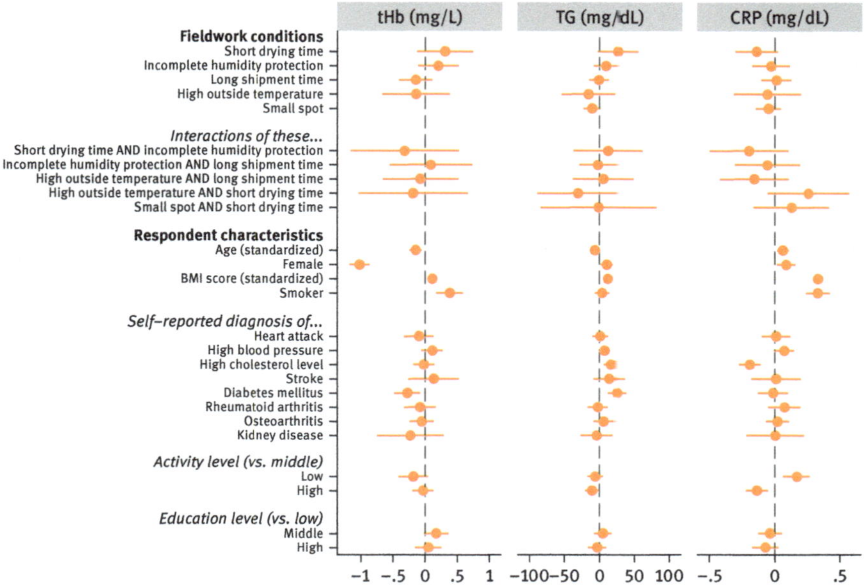

Figure 37.3: Assay results showing no significant interactions with field conditions.
Note: Mean (and median) levels: tHb 14.0 (13.9) mg/L, TG 263 (234) mg/dL, CRP 1.38 (1.0) mg/L.

37.6 Conclusions

Fieldwork conditions during blood collection and sample quality measures influence the raw DBS value obtained through laboratory analysis. Many of the effects are statistically significant, matter in terms of substance and interact with each other. Some biomarkers analysed for SHARE show sensitivity to a variety of fieldwork conditions, HDL and CysC additionally to interactions of these. Small spot size is the main challenge; TC, CysC and HbA1c are sensitive to small spots. Short drying times seem to affect CysC and HDL values, the latter only with high outside temperatures. Long shipment times are problematic for HDL and TC. High outside temperatures might affect the DBS values of TC and CysC, the latter only after a very short drying time. Some markers seem relatively robust regarding fieldwork conditions and sample quality, namely, tHb, TG and CP. Overall, the results presented in this chapter show that conversion formulae can be significantly improved when they include fieldwork conditions and sample quality.

Luzia M. Weiss, Martina Börsch-Supan, Michal Myck, Katarzyna Nocoń, Monika Oczkowska, Roman Topór-Mądry, Karen Andersen-Ranberg and Axel Börsch-Supan

38 Blood collection in the field – results and lessons from the polish test study

- This study was an unique opportunity to compare the assay results from both field-collected dried blood spot samples and respondent-matched venous-blood draws, the so-called gold standard values
- The collection of dried blood spot samples at respondents' homes can yield high-quality biomaterial, but the logistics for the handling of the verous samples poses major challenges
- Straightforward correction formulae accounting for fieldwork conditions were determined, but due to small sample size further, more extensive validation studies are needed

38.1 Introduction

Deriving blood-marker values from a venous draw is still the gold standard in medicine. The values obtained from dried blood spots (DBS) are, therefore, likely to be challenged: Collecting DBS is cheaper and easier to administer in a survey context (McDade et al., 2007) and the scope of assays available for the analysis of biomarkers in DBS is growing, though still much smaller relative to the analyses possible using venous blood. The obtained DBS results differ in absolute values from the venous results. For the blood markers that SHARE intended to analyse, the literature still provides scarce evidence on the relevance of the information acquired from DBS collected under fieldwork conditions and its comparability with results obtained from venous blood (Sugden et al., 2015).

The Polish test study to be introduced in this chapter takes this challenge head-on. Our aim was twofold. First, we collect venous blood samples in addition to DBS samples under sometimes difficult circumstances during the fieldwork of a population survey and compare the analyses results from both types of blood samples. Second, the study serves as the basis of a potential wider collection of biomaterials among a large and representative population.

Polish country-specific bioethical regulations require all studies that collect human blood or other biomaterials to involve professionally trained medical staff; they do not allow the appointment of trained lay interviewers. Yet, the

https://doi.org/10.1515/9783110617245-038

financial resources required for interviewers and nurses to jointly conduct the survey and collect DBS in the full sample were too high.

Hence, we implemented a small-scale test study in Poland in which nurses visited the respondents after the completed standard SHARE interview. The blood collection was conducted during a separate nurse visit with SHARE Wave 6 pretest respondents. To use the full potential of nurses' engagement, both DBS and venous blood were taken and the collection was supplemented with an additional short questionnaire and a health examination. Thus, the Polish test study provides important input into the future application of DBS in large, representative surveys.

In this chapter, we outline the concept and implementation of blood sample collection in the field through this small-scale experiment. We describe unanticipated obstacles that affected the data collection and, as a result, reduced the initially expected number of participating respondents. Nevertheless, as shown in Section 3, the collected samples allowed for a meaningful comparison of the DBS and venous blood results, and the exercise has provided a number of useful lessons for the conduct of similar studies in the future.

38.2 Wave 6 pretest in Poland: Follow-up nurse visits

The test study to collect DBS and venous blood was conducted as a follow-up of the SHARE Wave 6 pretest and required the engagement of several research centres and contractors. The study was led by the Collegium Medicum at the Jagiellonian University in Krakow (JUK) in cooperation with the Polish SHARE country team from the Centre for Economic Analysis (CenEA). The University of Southern Denmark in Odense (SDU) granted support with medical matters and surveyed the quality of the DBS samples sent to the SHARE biobank before intermediate storage. The venous blood samples were analysed at JUK. The University of Washington in Seattle (UW) conducted the analyses of the DBS. The Munich Center for the Economics of Ageing (MEA) coordinated the entire process and assisted with legal issues and overall study guidelines. Fieldwork was handled by the Polish survey agency Kantar TNS, who also conducted the entire SHARE Wave 6 fieldwork in Poland.

The pretest of SHARE Wave 6 in Poland took place in June and July 2014. During the interview, the respondents were asked whether they would be willing to participate in the additional blood collection. Of the 137 respondents, who were interviewed in the pretest, 63 agreed to a subsequent nurse visit.

Eventually, only 36 participated in the test study. The final drop-out number of those, who initially had agreed to participate, was higher than expected and the reasons are difficult to identify, possibly related to the significant delay between the pretest interview and the nurse visit which finally took place in early 2016 due to unanticipated administrative and procedural delays. Even though in the meantime the survey agency kept contact with the respondents by phone or personally to remind them about the study and to secure their participation, a timelier visit may have helped to improve the final participation rate.

During their visit, the nurses obtained informed written consent from the respondents. Then, they collected the DBS samples, followed by blood pressure and other anthropometrical measurements and a brief health-focused paper-and-pencil questionnaire. The visit finished with the collection of venous blood. The tubes with venous blood were put in a cooler and were supposed to be delivered immediately to local blood banks, all written materials and DBS samples were shipped to Kantar TNS. Later, the DBS samples were sent in two batches to SDU. Within three days following collection, the venous blood samples were transported by courier on dry ice to the main laboratory at the JUK.

The venous blood samples were analysed for the following biomarkers: Vitamin D, triglycerides (TG), total cholesterol TC, high density lipoprotein (HDL), low density lipoprotein (LDL), C-reactive protein (CRP), HbA1c (glycated haemoglobin), fasting glucose, BDNF and the cytokines TNF-α and IL-6. The DBS samples were sent to the laboratory at UW and have been analysed for TG, TC, HDL, CRP, HbA1c, and Cystatin C (CysC). Thus, the results from five markers are available for both types of blood samples.

38.3 Blood collection in the field: Challenges, obstacles and lessons learnt

As previously noted, one of the main shortfalls of the study was the unexpected delays related to a number of contractual and procedural demands. Therefore, the final nurse visits happened much later than was announced during the interview. This delay may have affected the high degree of withdrawal from the study among respondents, who initially had agreed to participate. Thirty-six respondents eventually participated in the study, among them one refused to participate in the DBS and venous blood collection and four others refused one or the other.

The geographic distribution of respondents' households with respect to the nearest local blood bank turned out to be a larger challenge than expected. 21

local blood banks had been selected all over the country because the venous blood samples collected by the nurses were expected to be delivered in portable coolers to those blood banks within one hour after collection. Though the nurses were instructed to deliver the samples as soon as possible, Figure 38.1 shows a relatively large difference between the expected time of delivery (based on Google Maps driving time) and the actual time recorded by the nurses. The additional time needed may be due to the quality of the roads and weather conditions during the study or other unanticipated delays. In addition, the extended delivery time may have influenced the quality of blood samples, a factor that should be accounted for in the analyses of further studies.

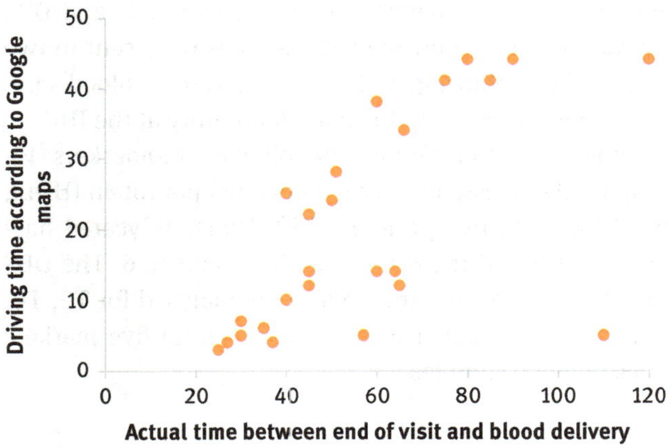

Figure 38.1: Expected and actual time of delivery of blood samples to local blood banks.
Source: Based on SHARE Wave 6, Polish pretest supplementary blood collection data.

38.4 Initial results: Comparing DBS and venous blood

Apart from testing the complex fieldwork procedures involved in venous blood collection in the field, a key issue of interest behind the exercise was the comparison of the collected DBS and venous blood samples (Crimmins et al., 2014). Although such comparisons have been previously made in laboratory settings, we know of no other field exercise which would allow for this. In Table 38.1, we present the initial results based on the data collected during the nurse visits.

Table 38.1: Comparison of laboratory results of DBS and plasma.

		Mean	Min	Max
HbA1c	DBS value	5.4	4.7	6.5
	Wet blood value	5.8	4.9	8.1
Total cholesterol	DBS value	356	230	486
	Plasma value	173	92	237
HDL	DBS value	106	77	141
	Plasma value	50	34	65
Triglycerides	DBS value	308	165	1301
	Plasma value	178	61	1523
CRP	DBS value	3.0	0.3	11.0
	Plasma value	4.1	0.1	26.5

Source: Based on SHARE Wave 6, Polish pretest supplementary blood collection data.

Apart from a few descriptive statistics, we present an approach to adapt the non-standard DBS results from the main SHARE DBS study to hypothetical gold standards.

Table 38.1 shows that the distributions of the DBS laboratory results for the analysed markers are different from the distributions of the results obtained from plasma values (or wet-blood values in the case of HbA1c), which are considered the gold standard. Therefore, direct DBS data requires a different interpretation than most SHARE users would expect; they need to be converted to avoid spurious data analyses and results.

Hence, for the DBS data to be easily usable, we seek to develop an equation resulting in (converted) values that are as close as possible to the values we would have obtained from our respondents' venous blood using gold standard methods. The Polish nurse experiment provides encouraging results, indicating that this goal indeed can be reached. Figure 38.2 shows how we obtained this goal using the HDL values as an example.

Figure 38.2 plots the actual DBS values against the respondent-matched HDL values measured in plasma. The dashed line corresponds to the line of equality. Clearly, the DBS values are overall higher than their corresponding plasma values (Figure 38.2a).

Plotting the results of $HDL_{plasma} = \beta_0 + \beta_1 \cdot HDL_{DBS}$ against the actual plasma values yields Figure 38.2b. The corrected results are much closer to the equality line and, hence, to the values obtained by gold standard laboratory methods.

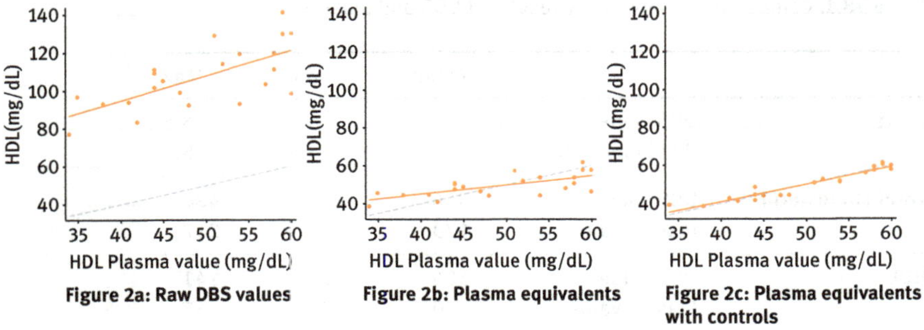

Figure 38.2: Comparing HDL values in DBS and venous blood samples.
Source: Based on SHARE Wave 6, Polish pretest supplementary blood collection data.

Extending the equation with variables for sampling conditions (namely, the estimated drying time of the DBS, shipment time to the biobank, availability of humidity protection and the interactions of all of these conditions) and controlling for the usual respondent characteristics (age, sex and body mass index), the estimated HDL values come even closer to the equality line (Figure 38.2c).

This extension indicates that the approach to converting the raw DBS values in estimated plasma equivalents can lead to values that are very close to the gold standard. However, because the Polish experiment only consists of a small number of observations, the equations to be finally applied should be obtained from further validation studies. Such a validation, aimed at converting the raw SHARE DBS values into plasma equivalents, was conducted at the University of Washington recently.

38.5 Conclusions and lessons learnt

A significant advantage of the DBS is the ease with which the biomarkers can be collected in different settings and conditions, either by the respondents/patients themselves or with the help of a trained lay assistant. However, although the extent of the analyses which can be conducted on DBS material continuously grows as technology develops, venous blood still allows for far more marker assays. The test study conducted in Poland on a sub-sample of SHARE respondents offered a unique opportunity to test the challenges of venous blood collection in respondents' homes together with the chance to compare the results based on venous blood collected in the field with those based on corresponding DBS samples. We know of no other field exercise that would allow for such comparisons.

The key result of the study shows that straightforward correction formulae can be gained for the results based on DBS such that they very closely reflect the gold standard values based on venous blood. Another important lesson is that, with sufficient care and careful logistics, high-quality biomaterial can be collected at respondents' homes. However, such an approach is a complex undertaking, and time for preparations and planning as well as sufficient resources should be allocated to ensure its success. As our experience demonstrates, taking for granted certain administrative and legal procedures can result in unnecessary delays and disruptions in the flow of the study. In addition, realistic delivery times need to be considered for transporting the blood samples to local blood banks.

Regarding the adaptation of the raw DBS laboratory results to gold standard equivalents, the results of the study are promising. With this in mind and with further, more extensive validation studies in due course, we are convinced to be able to release easy-to-use biomarker data in SHARE.

References

Crimmins, Eileen, Jung Ki Kim, Heather McCreath, Jessica Faul, David Weir & Teresa Seeman (2014) 'Validation of blood-based assays using dried blood spots for use in large population studies', *Biodemography and social biology*, 60(1), pp. 38–48.

McDade, Thomas W., Sharon Williams, & J. Josh Snodgras (2007) 'What a drop can do: dried blood spots as a minimally invasive method for integrating biomarkers into population-based research', *Demography*, 44(4), pp. 899–925.

Sugden, Karen, Andrea Danese, Idan Shalev, Benjamin S. Williams & Avshalom Caspi (2015) 'Blood substrate collection and handling procedures under pseudo-field conditions: evaluation of suitability for inflammatory biomarker measurement', *Biodemography and social biology*, 61(3), pp. 273–284.

Nis Borbye-Lorenzen and Martina Börsch-Supan

39 Identification of cytokine and lipoprotein markers for analyses in SHARE Wave 6 dried blood spots

- The identification of inflammation markers in the blood can help elucidate cardiovascular and Alzheimer's disease risk factors
- We identified ten promising blood-based protein and inflammation markers from SHARE Wave 6 DBS samples that could potentially predict the risk of cardiovascular and Alzheimer's diseases

39.1 Introduction

In 2015, SHARE introduced dried blood spot (DBS) sampling in its Wave 6 to complement self-reported health and to gain more detailed and objective information on common ageing-related health conditions, such as cardiovascular disease, diabetes, declines in kidney function and cognitive impairment. Blood collected by this minimally invasive method from survey respondents can be reliably analysed for several blood-based protein markers and blood fats.

SHARE attempts to understand the complex relationships among the biology, health behaviour and socioeconomic status in the ageing process. Among the underlying factors that cause ageing-related diseases, inflammatory pathways are considered to play an important role in, for example, atherosclerosis, cardiovascular disease, obesity, diabetes, mild cognitive decline and Alzheimer's disease. Cytokines are small blood-based proteins prominently involved in the inflammatory process. They are signalling molecules between cells and are important in other immune responses, which they modulate as pro- or anti-inflammatory molecules because sometimes inflammation is the body's response to fighting off infections. However, cytokines can become dysregulated and pathological in some forms of inflammation, autoimmune disease, trauma and sepsis.

Cytokines are not routinely analysed in a blood count, but in research they offer the opportunity to more closely investigate low-level chronic inflammation, such as in atherosclerosis, to fine-tune the search for the risk

https://doi.org/10.1515/9783110617245-039

of cardiovascular disease among the survey respondents beyond blood-fat (such as cholesterol) values and to biologically back up the results of objective cognitive testing in the survey questionnaire. Using multiplex immunoassay analysis, multiple markers (up to ten) can be analysed from very small amounts of blood, such as in DBS. By introducing cytokine analyses from the DBS collected in its Wave 6 survey, SHARE is testing an innovative method to gain a more detailed look at cardiovascular disease and cognitive decline in a population, not a patient sample. Here, we describe the selection of ten protein markers to be determined from SHARE Wave 6 DBS.

39.2 Identifying markers

After searching the literature for the involvement of cytokines and other blood-based analytes in cardiovascular (Mehra et al 2005) and neurodegenerative diseases (Brosseron et al 2014), 31 potentially interesting protein markers involved in ageing-related health conditions were identified for screening (Table 39.1). This list also includes the Apolipoproteins APOe4 and Clusterin (APOJ) which are involved in cholesterol transport to the brain and clearance of damaged cells, respectively. People carrying the *APOe4* gene variant are known to have a higher risk for cardiovascular disease and cognitive decline (Rasmussen et al. 2015).

It was unknown to us, which of the markers we would possibly detect in DBS samples collected under field work conditions during the SHARE survey and at which concentration levels. Our goal was to establish a multiplex immunoassay (see section 39.1) to test the SHARE DBS samples for the occurrence and levels of up to ten of the markers listed in Table 39.1 to use the full potential of our analysis platform (see below).

Therefore, we screened the 31 candidate markers to reveal the ones that could be measured simultaneously in the assay. We used excess DBS samples from the field collection from the youngest (60 years or younger) and the oldest (80 years or older) respondents in the SHARE Wave 6 cohort to check for the detectability of a marker and to cover the extremities of analyte concentration levels. Having chosen age as a condition that affects analyte levels, this procedure allowed us to understand the lowest and highest levels of the analytes, in particular, those that change with age to ensure that the method was sensitive to and independent of the age of participants.

Table 39.1: Short description of the 31 cytokine and lipoprotein markers chosen from the literature for screening.

	Marker/Analyte	Short description of marker type	Pass/Fail of marker in round		
			1	2	3
1	**IL-1β**	Pro-inflammatory cytokine; increases inflammation (e.g. to regulate defence against pathogens); excess production may contribute to atherosclerosis	–	–	**Out**
2	**IL-6**	Pro-inflammatory; also present in adipose and muscle tissue; capable of crossing blood-brain barrier	–	–	**Out**
3	**IL-8**	Signalling molecule; potent promotor for the formation of new blood vessels (angiogenesis)	✓	✓	***Selected**
4	**IL-10**	Anti-inflammatory; involved in down regulation of inflammation	–	–	**Out**
5	**IL-1α**	Pro-inflammatory; see IL-1β	–	**Out**	
6	**IL-13**	Pro-inflammatory; mediator of allergic reaction (e.g. asthma)	–	**Out**	
7	**IL-16**	Pro-inflammatory, chemokine; cerebral pathologies and vascular dementias	✓	***Selected**	
8	**IL-18**	Pro-inflammatory; see IL-1β; correlates positively with MMSE in patients with mild cognitive decline	✓	✓	***Selected**
9	**IL-12/23 p40**	Pro-inflammatory; see IL-1β	✓	***Selected**	
10	**TNF-α** tumour necrosis factor- alpha	Pro-inflammatory; see IL-1β	✓	–	**Out**

(continued)

Table 39.1 (continued)

	Marker/Analyte	Short description of marker type	Pass/Fail of marker in round		
			1	2	3
11	**IFN-γ** interferon-γ	Pro-inflammatory; see IL-1β; also involved in viral inhibition, indication of autoimmune/inflammatory disease	–	**Out**	
12	**MCP-1** monocyte chemo-attractant protein	Pro-inflammatory; induces chemical reactions in nearby cells; levels correlate positively with MMSE in patients with mild cognitive decline	✓	***Selected**	
13	**VEGF-A** vascular epithelial growth factor	Signalling molecule in vascular tissue; potent mediator in angiogenesis	✓	***Selected**	
14	**VCAM-1** vascular cell-adhesion molecule	Vascular injury marker; atherosclerosis, arthritis	✓	✓	**Selected**
15	**BNF (NT-pro BNP)** brain natriuretic peptide	Heart failure; cardiac insufficiency	–	**Out**	
16	**YKL;** also called chitinase 3 like 1 (CHI3L1)	Inflammatory processes in cardiovascular disease, coronary artery disease, arthritis, cancer, cerebrospinal pathologies	✓	**Selected**	

17	**BDNF** brain-derived neurotrophic factor	Neuronal growth factor; neuroprotective, involved in depression, dementia, mild cognitive decline, Alzheimer's disease; levels increase e.g., with mobility/exercise and social contacts	✓	***Selected**	
18	**NGF** nerve growth factor	Growth, survival, differentiation of neurons; survival of insulin-producing cells; immune-system regulation	–	**Out**	
19	**EGF** epidermal growth factor	Stimulates cell growth and differentiation	✓	✓	***Selected**
20	**Leptin**	Hormone involved in body weight regulation; inhibits hunger	–	–	**Out**
21	**Clusterin** ApoJ lipoprotein	Regulation of inflammation, oxidative stress, apoptosis (cell death), ageing, late onset Alzheimer's disease	✓	✓	***Selected**
22	**GSK 3β** glycogen synthase kinase 3 beta	High levels associated with memory loss; dysregulation observed in pathophysiological processes	(✓)	**Out**	
23 24 25	**Aβ38** **Aβ40** **Aβ42**	Amyloid β (Aβ); main component of amyloid plaques in Alzheimer's disease	–	**Out**	
26	**sAPP-α** soluble amyloid precursor protein α	Decreases the generation of Aβ	–	–	**Out**
27	**APOe4 lipoprotein**	Involved in fat metabolism of the body, principal carrier of cholesterol to the brain; involved in atherosclerosis, cognitive impairment, cerebrovascular and Alzheimer's disease	(✓)	✓	***Selected**

(continued)

Table 39.1 (continued)

	Marker/Analyte	Short description of marker type	Pass/Fail of marker in round		
			1	2	3
28 29	**Total Tau (τ)** **Tau (τ) 181**	Abundant in neurons and the central nervous system; misfolded forms appear in neurodegenerative disease (tangles in Alzheimer's disease); elevated in cerebrospinal fluid and plasma of dementia patients and mild cognitive decline	**Out**		
30	**S100b**	Calcium-binding protein; altered expression of gene implicated in neurological, neoplastic and other diseases	–	**Out**	
31	**A1M** Alpha-1-macroglobulin	Protective against oxidative stress, radical scavenger; degrades heme	**Out**		

Note: Source of test kits:
A) Antibodies and reagents for markers 1–21, 23–26 bought from MesoScale Diagnostics; **B**) Kits for cell culture analyses plus recombinant calibrator for markers 22, 28, 29 bought from Signalchem/MyBioSource; tests adjusted by Statens Serum Institut; **C**) Antibodies and recombinant calibrator for markers 27, 30, 31 bought from R&D Systems/Agilent/MyBioSource; tests developed by Statens Serum Institut.
✓: Marker well placed in the middle or higher than standard curve;
(✓): samples within detection limit; clear division between positive and negative samples (APOe4); -: in the low part or below standard curve;
*: selected as marker for the final 10-plex analysis platform. MMSE = Mini-mental state examination.

39.2.1 Multiplex immunoassay: The method of choice

For the qualitative and/or quantitative determination of very small amounts of physiologically relevant molecules (such as cytokines) in the limited amount of blood material available from the DBS samples, immunoassays are the method of choice. They take advantage of a matching antibodies' strong specificity for a particular protein. Immunological methods allowing for simultaneous measurements of multiple proteins in the same small sample volume are called multiplex immunoassays.

Current technological platforms – the chemistry and the detection instrument as a unit is called a platform – allow measuring up to ten specific proteins in one reaction in as little as 25 µL of protein extract (e.g. MesoScale Diagnostics). The protein extract of each sample is derived from two small punches, each 3.2 mm in diameter, cut out of the blood-containing filter paper of a DBS (Skogstrand et al. 2005).

To enable immunological multiplex analyses, it is essential to obtain antibodies with high specificity for the protein analytes that are to be measured. In addition, to allow for simultaneous measurements, it is important that the concentration levels of the analytes to be determined are within a similar range in the measured samples. The screening of each of the 31 marker candidates occurred in three rounds (Table 39.1). In the first round, analyses were performed according to the conditions recommended by the antibody manufacturer (e.g. MesoScale Diagnostics). If the analyte was measurable in the DBS samples, the analyses parameters were changed in rounds 2 and 3 to meet the preferred conditions for multiplex analyses. Three to six random samples of SHARE participants ≤ 60 years of age and ≥ 80 years of age were tested for each analyte in each round.

39.2.2 The selected markers

From the screening, 12 final candidates were identified and the ten markers subsequently listed were selected for cytokine testing of the SHARE DBS samples. The other 19 candidates did not meet the technical and methodological requirements. Typically, the marker in the sample material was not sufficiently abundant. To confirm the results the ten selected candidates were QC (quality)-tested at MesoScale Diagnostics before being combined to one final 10-plex analysis platform (Tables 39.1 and 39.2).

- Regarding the pro-inflammatory markers **IL-8, IL-16, IL-18, IL-12/23p40** and **MCP-1**, the elevated levels of one or several of these cytokines will better inform us about the type of inflammation, its degree and the inflamed

Table 39.2: 12 Markers measurable in DBS samples comparing Europeans ≤ 60 years old with those ≥ 80 years old.

Markers having passed selection criteria	General detection range of markers	Detection range in youngest respondents	Detection range in oldest respondents
		≤ 60 years old (n = 5) ± SD	≥ 80 years old (n = 5) ± SD
Concentration in	pg/ml	pg/ml	pg/ml
IL-8*	0.0587–165	3.57±0.99	7.59±5.02
IL-12/23 p40*	0.469–928	4.14±1.90	11.06±3.18
IL-16*	6.48–2,450	151.4±52.1	146.9±35.8
IL-18*	0.197–2,500	86.8±12.3	89.5±21.0
VEGF-A*	0.287–315	31.1±8.53	25.2±2.69
BDNF*	2.94–10,000	166±44.4	158±40.4
MCP-1*	1.62–448	49.8±10.5	61.1±5.75
VCAM-1	38.7–56,800	5,623±866	8,807±2,179
YKL	27.2–100,000	4,359±1,394	4,828±1,015
EGF*	0.317–465	13.3±8.46	6.50±1.90
Clusterin[a)]*	19.2–200,000	500,000–1,000,000	500,000–1,000,000
APOe4[b)]*			

*Markers selected for the final 10-plex.

a): The high level of Clusterin well above the standard curve was one of the challenges when creating this assay. During QC-testing at MesoScale Diagnostics, Clusterin was artificially lowered to allow the inclusion of this marker in the final 10-plex.

b): APOe4 does not vary with age. The protein is either present or not but its level may vary.

tissue type. The results from these markers may confirm a report of cardiovascular disease by a respondent or show undetected inflammation and/or (onset of) cognitive impairment.

- **VEGF** and **EGF** both signal cell growth, which can be important in healing (e.g. in blood vessels) but may also indicate cancer.
- **BDNF** is a neuronal growth factor. It is neuroprotective, and its level increases e.g., with movement/exercise and social embeddedness and is decreased during cognitive decline. The results from the assay can be connected to reports of SHARE respondents regarding their social networks and exercise behaviour (Salinas 2016).

- Last not least are **APOe4** and **Clusterin (APOJ)**; the e4-variant of the apolipoprotein indicates an elevated risk of cardiovascular disease and cognitive impairment (Rasmussen et al 2015). Clusterin has the general vital function in the organism to clear misfolded proteins or cell debris and seems to act neuroprotective in mild cognitive decline and Alzheimer's disease.

The preparation of the SHARE DBS samples, the screening of the 31 candidate markers and the establishment of the final 10-plex analysis platform was performed at Statens Serum Institut in Copenhagen.

39.3 The next steps

With this analysis tool in hand, ca. 16,000 SHARE samples were prepared for analyses of the selected markers. As previously mentioned, the analysis of cytokines and other markers involved in cardiovascular disease and mild cognitive decline gained from DBS collected in a population survey during fieldwork is new. To our knowledge, whether the DBS values of cytokines gained here can be converted to match values gained from venous blood samples in other studies is unknown. Therefore, a validation experiment that compares the analysis results for these markers from venous blood and matched DBS samples and that also controls for sample exposure during blood collection in a survey will have to follow. SHARE will initiate such a study.

A small control study comparing blood samples (venous and DBS) from patients diagnosed with mild cognitive decline and age-matched controls is ongoing. The results for both studies will be reported once available.

References

Brosseron, F. et al (2014), Body Fluid Cytokine Levels in Mild Cognitive Impairment and Alzheimer's Disease: A Comparative Overview, *Mol Neurobiol*, 50, pp. 534–544.

Mehra, V.C., Ramgolam, V.S. and Bender, J.R. (2005), Cytokines and cardiovascular disease, *J Leukoc Biol*, 78, pp. 805–818.

Rasmussen, K.L. et al (2015), Plasma levels of apolipoprotein E and risk of dementia in the general population, *Ann. Neurol*, 77, pp. 301–311.

Skogstrand, K. et al (2005), Simultanous Measurement of 25 Inflammatory Markers and Neurotrophins in Neonatal Dried Blood Spots by Immunoassay with xMAP Technology, *Clin Chem*, 51 (10), pp. 1854–1866.

Salinas, J. (2016), Social Relationships, Serum Brain-derived Neurotrophic Factor, and the risk for Stroke and Dementia: The Framingham Heart Study, *Neurology*, 86, 16 suppl. P1.098.

